MASTERING

Practical Grammar

Palgrave Master Series

Accounting
Accounting Skills
Advanced English Language
Advanced Pure Mathematics
Arabic
Basic Management
Biology
British Politics
Business Communication
Business Environment
C Programming
C++ Programming
Chemistry
COBOL Programming
Communication
Computing
Counselling Skills
Counselling Theory
Customer Relations
Database Design
Delphi Programming
Desktop Publishing
e-Business
Economic and Social History
Economics
Electrical Engineering
Electronics
Employee Development
English Grammar
English Language
English Literature
Fashion Buying and Merchandising
  Management
Fashion Marketing
Fashion Styling
Financial Management
Geography
Global Information Systems

Human Resource Management
International Trade
Internet
Java
Language of Literature
Management Skills
Marketing Management
Mathematics
Microsoft Office
Microsoft Windows, Novell
  NetWare and UNIX
Modern British History
Modern European History
Modern German History
Modern United States History
Modern World History
The Novels of Jane Austen
Organisational Behaviour
Pascal and Delphi Programming
Personal Finance
Philosophy
Physics
Poetry
Practical Criticism
Practical Grammar
Psychology
Public Relations
Shakespeare
Social Welfare
Sociology
Statistics
Strategic Management
Systems Analysis and Design
Team Leadership
Theology
Twentieth-Century Russian History
Visual Basic
World Religions

www.palgravemasterseries.com

Palgrave Master Series
Series Standing Order ISBN 0–333–69343–4
(outside North America only)

You can receive future titles in this series as they are published by placing a standing order. Please contact your bookseller or, in case of difficulty, write to us at the address below with your name and address, the title of the series and the ISBN quoted above.

Customer Services Department, Macmillan Distribution Ltd
Houndmills, Basingstoke, Hampshire RG21 6XS, England

MASTERING

Practical Grammar

Sara Thorne

First published 2012 by
PALGRAVE MACMILLAN

Palgrave Macmillan in the UK is an imprint of Macmillan Publishers Limited,
registered in England, company number 785998, of Houndmills, Basingstoke,
Hampshire RG21 6XS.

Palgrave Macmillan in the US is a division of St Martin's Press LLC,
175 Fifth Avenue, New York, NY 10010.

Palgrave Macmillan is the global academic imprint of the above companies
and has companies and representatives throughout the world.

Palgrave® and Macmillan® are registered trademarks in the United States,
the United Kingdom, Europe and other countries

ISBN: 978-0-230-54290-7

This book is printed on paper suitable for recycling and made from fully
managed and sustained forest sources. Logging, pulping and manufacturing
processes are expected to conform to the environmental regulations of the
country of origin.

A catalogue record for this book is available from the British Library.

A catalog record for this book is available from the Library of Congress.

10 9 8 7 6 5 4 3 2 1
21 20 19 18 17 16 15 14 13 12

Printed and bound in Great Britain by the MPG Books Group,
Bodmin and King's Lynn

Contents

Preface

In literature, we are taught about similes, metaphors and alliteration – techniques which allow writers to enhance the effect of their writing. Yet often we do not learn how to identify and talk about the words and grammatical structures of a text, the building blocks of all speech and writing. Once we learn to notice these, we begin to understand how language works.

Mastering Practical Grammar is not a return to the kind of learning by rote where definitions of nouns, adjectives, verbs and adverbs are used, then neatly filed away until the next grammar lesson. Instead, grammar is presented as something practical – an integral part of every reading, writing, listening and speaking experience. The aim is to establish a grammatical knowledge base that can be used in everyday situations: to understand the persuasive power of an advertisement or recognise how a comedian makes us laugh; to appreciate a poem or become a powerful and engaging speaker; to write an effective letter or enjoy the skill of a sports commentator.

The focus on grammar is explicit, beginning with definitions, explanations and examples. With the basic principles under your belt, reading tasks focus on your ability to recognise and interpret the linguistic and grammatical features of a text; writing tasks provide opportunities for you to experiment in your own writing. The aim is to develop your confidence so that you can use terminology and key concepts to explore and evaluate the effects created by the language and structure of real texts.

To help you work in an organised way, *Mastering Practical Grammar* is divided into five key areas, each focusing on an element of language. Beginning with words, readers will be taken logically through the levels of language, concluding with discourse, the study of written and spoken texts. The focus is on language in action, tying grammar immediately to usage and relevance. There are a wide range of examples, commentaries to suggest how linguistic analysis can be tackled, and lots of practical tasks. Many of the texts have been written specifically for this book – where they have been taken from an existing source, information about the writer, the context and the date of composition is included.

In any grammar book, a decision has to be made about the kind of terminology and approach to be adopted. There is no single school of thought and if you pick up a range of grammar books you will find different ways of describing grammar. This book uses the descriptive approach of functional analysis as its basis while trying to take on board some of the discrepancies which this will create for students of formal, analytic linguistics.

Whether you are following an examination course or want to undertake a more personal and random exploration of the ways in which language works, this book aims to make grammar interesting and relevant. Having worked through it, you will look at language in a new way.

SARA THORNE

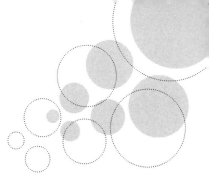

Symbols and conventions

Form labels

ACl	adverbial clause
Adj	adjective
AdjP	adjective phrase
Adv	adverb
AdvP	adverb phrase
Cl	clause
CompCl	comparative clause
CompP	comparative phrase
Conj	conjunction
Det	determiner
MCl	main clause
mod	modal auxiliary verb
N	noun
NCl	noun clause
neg	negative
NFCl	nonfinite clause
num	number
obj	object pronoun
poss	possessive noun or pronoun
pre-det	predeterminer
prep	preposition
PrepP	prepositional phrase
prim	primary auxiliary verb
pron	pronoun
RelCl	relative clause
SCl	subordinate clause
sconj	subordinating conjunction
subj	subject pronoun
V	verb
V*base*	base form verb
V*ed*	*-ed* participle (past)
V*inf*	infinitive verb

V*ing*	*-ing* participle (present)
V*less*Cl	verbless clause
VP	verb phrase
V*pass*	passive verb phrase
V*past*	past tense verb
V*perf*	perfective verb phrase
V*pres*	present tense verb
V*prog*	progressive verb phrase
wh-Cl	*wh-* clause

Function labels

A	adverbial
aux	auxiliary verb
C	complement
Co	object complement
Cs	subject complement
dumS	dummy subject
h	head
interj	interjection
m	pre-modifier
lex	lexical verb
O	object
Oi	indirect object
Od	direct object
P	predicator
part	particle
q	qualifier or post-modifier
S	subject
(S)	delayed subject
Ø	omitted word(s) or clause element (s)
voc	vocative

Other abbreviations

Fr	French
Ger	German
L	Latin
ME	Middle English
n-SE	non-Standard English
OE	Old English
ON	Old Norse
RP	Received Pronunciation
SE	Standard English

Brackets

‹ ›	main clauses
( )	phrases

]	subordinate clauses
‿	links separated constituents of a phrase

ymbols used in spoken language transcripts

(.)	timed pause
)	micro pause
ne	raised intonation
ne	falling intonation
pretty↑	raised pitch
see↓	lowered pitch
igh	stressed word
ō	lengthened syllable
.	incomplete word
ɔiano'	quiet
˙orte'	loud
ˋccel'	getting faster
:all'	getting slower
˪aughs]	non-verbal vocal effect
=	latching (a smooth transition between one speaker and the next)
	interrupted turn (participants speak at the same time)

Phonemic symbols

Consonants

/p/	pit, top	/ʃ/	shin, bush
/b/	ban, rub	/ʒ/	beige, treasure
/t/	ten, step	/h/	hit, behind
/d/	din, bad	/ʧ/	cheap, latch
/k/	cave, scar	/dʒ/	jeep, judge
/g/	gave, dig	/m/	mat, small
/f/	fan, rough	/n/	net, snow
/v/	van, love	/ŋ/	bring, singer
/θ/	thin, athlete	/l/	lot, pill
/ð/	this, either	/r/	rat, bran
/s/	sit, loss	/j/	yet, cure
/z/	zoo, easy	/w/	wit, one

Pure vowels

/æ/	cat, crash	/ɔː/	port, talk
/ɑː/	bar, heart	/ʊ/	put, wood
/iː/	beat, key	/uː/	boot, rude
/ɪ/	bit, busy	/ʌ/	but, blood
/e/	bet, many	/ɜː/	bird, word
/ɒ/	pot, want	/ə/	about

Diphthongs

/eɪ/	bay, late	/əʊ/	boat, know
/aɪ/	buy, die	/ɪə/	beer, here
/ɔɪ/	boy, noise	/eə/	bare, pear
/aʊ/	pout, cow	/ʊə/	jury

Acknowledgements

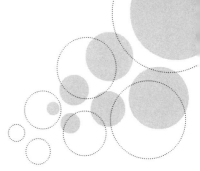

The author would like to thank all those who have taken the time to read, comment and make suggestions on this book; and to everyone who has so kindly contributed source material.

The author and publishers also wish to thank the following for permission to reproduce copyright material:

Alex Thorne for an extract from his 'SFML Coder' blog (20.04.2011).

Andrew Webster for an extract from his sermon (31.10.2004).

Carcanet Press Limited for p. 66 from Edwin Morgan, *Selected Poems*, Carcanet Press Limited (1985).

Ladybird Books Ltd for extract of text from *Little Yellow Digger* by Nicola Baxter (1995).

Ladybird Books Ltd for extract of text and illustrations from *Read With Me: Let's Play* by William Murray, Jill Corby and Chris Russell (1990).

Ladybird Books Ltd for extract of text from *Key Words: 1b Look at this* by William Murray (1964).

Lulu Press for pp.33–4 from Hilda Hobart, *Daisy: A Norfolk Childhood* (2007).

Rachel Thomas for an extract from her summary of *Twilight* (2010).

The National Archives for public sector information licensed under the Open Government Licence v1.0 (http://www.nationalarchives.gov.uk/doc/open-government-licence/): Hansard p. 355 (Oral Answers, 10.11.2010) and p. 396 (House of Commons Debate, 'Public Order (NUS Rally)' 11.11.2010).

Till Kleinert for an extract from the script of his film 'Boys Village', Schattenkante and the Festivals Company (2011).

Every effort has been made to trace rights holders, but if any have been inadvertently overlooked the publishers would be pleased to make the necessary arrangements at the first opportunity.

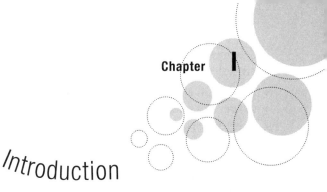

Chapter **1**

Introduction

Grammar. The word can provoke strong reactions: confusion, dread, boredom, frustration. This book aims to be different. Definitions and technical information are still part of the process, but because the emphasis is on **using** grammar rather than just 'learning' it, the experience should be more rewarding.

1.1 What is grammar?

Grammar is the systematic study of the ways in which language is put together to create meaning. It consists of rules that are integral to language use. It sounds complicated, but we assimilate our first language as children and our brains deal with these rules intuitively. We instinctively put words in the right order, with the right endings to communicate in speech and, later, writing; we realise when the 'rules' have been broken.

This innate understanding should give us confidence and yet, when we hear the word 'grammar', the alarm bells start ringing. Even though we use it every time we open our mouths, pick up a pen or type into a computer, every time we read a book or watch a film, the thought of studying grammar worries us. We can **use** it, but we don't necessarily **know** about it.

1.2 Why learn about grammar?

Learning about grammar helps us to be more aware of our instinctive language use. If we can recognise and understand the underlying patterns we use, we will be more able to appreciate the effects we create. To do this, we need to be able to **name** the language we use: terminology gives us a shorthand to describe patterns; a knowledge of structure enables us to see relationships between words. While learning about grammar will not automatically turn us into better readers, writers and speakers over night, it will alert us to the possibilities of our language. In informal conversation, we will continue to speak spontaneously with little conscious thought about grammar; when we write shopping lists or personal diaries, grammar will be of less importance than the content. It is in more formal situations that grammatical knowledge can affect the way in which we speak and write.

So why should we learn about grammar? Knowledge of grammatical terms an structures can help you:

> to write an application letter or a formal essay
> to speak in public or make a presentation
> to learn a second language
> to see how a political speech or an advertisement aims to influence you
> to understand how a novelist creates character or atmosphere
> to recognise how a comedian makes you laugh
> to appreciate the emotions underlying a poem or song.

The list is endless – understanding how language works will help you to see the pat terns and interpret the effects they create; it will make you a more effective languag user.

1.3 Approaches to learning grammar

Grammar used to be taught in terms of 'definitions' and 'recognition' – exercise tested your ability to identify a noun or verb, to 'parse' a sentence. There was littl consideration of grammar in meaningful texts and little discussion of the lin between grammatical patterns and the construction of meaning.

This book certainly starts with definitions, but it moves beyond these to focu on grammar in real texts and in your own writing. As you become more confident you will be able to consider the different ways in which meaning can be constructed by identifying grammatical features, exploring their effects and evaluating them The emphasis will be on:

> understanding the terms and frameworks
> identifying and describing key features
> interpreting and evaluating their effects.

Don't worry – learning about grammar does not have to be a negative experience. This book guides you through the terminology and structures so that you can develop an explicit understanding of the ways in which we manipulate language to communicate effectively in speech and writing.

1.4 Levels of language

To help us understand the structures that underpin all language use, language is often divided into levels. Within each of these levels, there are certain rules and pat terns that describe how language elements can be combined and how they relate to the elements of other levels.

Approaching language study level by level helps us to deal with a small unit of grammar at a time. It allows us to become familiar with one concept before moving on to its relationship with another concept.

Level 1: words

We can classify **words** according to their grammatical similarities and dissimilari ties, and the places in which they occur in written and spoken language. The **open class** includes nouns (*table, book*), verbs (*to jump, falling, borrowed, written*), adjectives (*brave, sunny*) and adverbs (*slowly, significantly*). The **closed class** includes grammatical or function words: determiners (*the, a, some*), pronouns (*he, they, ours, mine*), prepositions (*in, on, beside, through*), conjunctions (*and, but, because*).

Level 2: phrases

This level of language analysis considers the ways in which words can be combined in groups, or **phrases**. We can study the relationship between words, the patterns in which they occur and their function within a phrase.

> the gloomy forest   quite slowly   had been running

Level 3: clauses

Phrases combine to make **clauses** which either make sense on their own (**independent**) or need to occur alongside another clause (**dependent**). We can study the elements that make up a clause, the different types of clauses and the jobs they do.

> the class were noisy   when the doctor came
> INDEPENDENT   DEPENDENT

Level 4: sentences

Clauses combine to make **sentences**, the largest unit of grammatical structure. We can analyse the elements that make up a sentence, the information they contain, the order of the information and the ways in which the different elements are joined. A sentence must have at least one independent or **main clause** if it is grammatically complete. There may, however, be additional main or dependent (subordinate) clauses. In written language, a sentence will start with a capital letter and end with a full stop.

> The firemen jumped into the fire engine.
> MAIN CLAUSE

> The firemen jumped into the fire engine   because the station bell rang.
> MAIN CLAUSE   SUBORDINATE CLAUSE

Level 5: discourse

Sentences combine to make **discourse**, spoken and written texts of more than one sentence. In discourse analysis, we look at meaning and the ways in which it is communicated. We study how a speaker or writer can shape a text according to the subject matter, audience, purpose and context.

1.5 Getting started

Some of the terminology and concepts here may be unfamiliar, but the examples will not have caused you any problems – your innate understanding of English helped you to process the information contained in each one. This book aims to help you see more explicitly how we put words together and the effects we create. The focus is on words, phrases, clauses and sentences and the ways in which we combine them to create meaningful discourse. The table below summarises these levels of language. It should provide you with an overview and a checkpoint as you work through the book, developing your reading and writing skills and putting your knowledge about the levels of language to practical use.

Language level	What is analysed	Examples of terminology
Word	Types of words The form of words	Word classes Nouns, adjectives, verbs, adverbs Determiners, pronouns, prepositions, conjunctions Inflections
	The meaning of words	Denotations, connotations
Phrase	Types of phrases	Simple, complex Noun, adjective, verb, adverb, prepositional Function, form
	The elements of phrases	Head, modifier, qualifier
Clause	Types of clauses	Main, subordinate Non-finite, adverbial, relative, noun, comparative, verbless
	The elements of clauses	Subject, predicator, object, complement, adverbial, vocative
	The position of clauses	Sentence elements; embedded clauses
Sentence	Types of sentences	Simple, compound, complex, compound-complex, minor
	Linking sentences	Co-ordination, subordination, lexical cohesion, substitution, referencing, ellipsis
	Sentence organisation	Marked themes, initial position, foregrounding, end focus, dummy subject
	Grammatical mood	Declarative, interrogative, imperative, exclamatory, subjunctive
Discourse	Register Variations	Mode, field, tenor User-related, use-related Layout, organisation, function Chronological, non-chronological
	Text type	Instructive, informative, persuasive, creative, expressive, phatic
	Context	Situation, circumstances, audience, purpose Standard English, non-Standard English, language variation

1.6 How to use this book

Grammar is hierarchical so you may find it useful to read the book section by section: begin with words and work through the levels of language. By the time you finish, you should have a secure understanding of basic grammar. This will inform your study of written and spoken texts and help you make appropriate choices in your own language interactions.

Mastering Practical Grammar can also be used as a reference book – the contents list and index can help you to identify particular definitions, concepts or principles that interest you. For instance, you may wish:

- to develop your understanding of a particular key term
- to find out about a particular grammatical feature
- to look at some examples of textual analysis
- to explore ways in which you can develop your own speaking or writing.

The book works through practical reinforcement, encouraging you to be an active participant. The reading and writing tasks look at language in action: they require you to apply your knowledge in close reading of a range of spoken and written texts, or to produce your own texts. They shift the emphasis from recognition to understanding and evaluation. Although you need to be able to identify key language features, you also need to be able to comment on the effects they create, to recognise their influence on the audience, and to understand the way in which the context shapes a writer's or speaker's choices.

There is no guarantee that grammar books improve the quality of our speech and writing, but understanding how language works gives us choices. We can see how other writers and speakers try to influence us; we can choose appropriate structures and styles in formal contexts; and we can develop a sense of personal identity from the forms of language we choose to use.

As an introductory book, I hope that *Mastering Practical Grammar* will lead you comfortably through the complexities and introduce you to the fascination of studying language.

Part I

Words

Chapter 2

Words

WORDS are our starting point. We use them, hear them, understand them and evaluate them on a day-to-day basis, and yet we tend not to think about them as separate and distinctive units of language.

After working through this chapter, you should be able:

▸ to recognise and label different kinds of words
▸ to describe their position in a sentence
▸ to understand the jobs they do

2.1 Word classes

We can divide words into two basic groups:

▸ words that communicate the **main meaning** in a sentence (open class)
▸ words that have a grammatical **function** (closed class)

Open class words

Read the two sentences below and think about their **meaning**.

> The boy sat in the **chair**.   The boy sat in the **cinema**.

We can see immediately that the only difference is in the final word. Replacing *chair* with *cinema* creates a completely new meaning. Similarly, we can change the meaning by replacing *The boy* with *The eminent politician*, or *sat* with *slept*. These words are part of the open class which contains nouns, verbs, adjectives and adverbs.

The **OPEN CLASS** is a very large group of words that is constantly expanding to reflect changes in the world around us: social (*tweenagers, hoodies, chavs*); scientific (*smart materials, nanocide*); technological (*shareware, social networking, shoulder surfer*); cultural (*celebutante, supersize, vanity sizing, chick lit*); medical (*abdominoplasty, gastric bypass*); business (*glocalization, pharming*).

Closed class words

If we change *in* or *the* in the examples you have just read, the meaning does not change significantly, but the focus of the sentence does. These words have a grammatical **FUNCTION** – they change the relationships between the words in a sentence.

A boy sat on the chair.   The boy sat **beside** the chair.   The boy sat on **that** chair.

In the examples above, *beside* focuses on position while *A* and *that* focus on the difference between particular boys and chairs. They are part of the CLOSED CLASS which contains prepositions, pronouns, determiners and conjunctions.

The **closed class** is a smaller group of words that has remained unchanged for hundreds of years. They are sometimes called the 'building blocks' of a language because they help us to build a sentence by creating links between words.

Recognising word classes

You will quickly begin to recognise the class into which most words fit. Initially, your decision may be based on your understanding of the meaning, your instinctive knowledge of words and their position in a sentence, or on the FORM of the word.

It is unlikely that a word will belong to both an open and a closed class, but in some cases a word can belong to more than one group. In each of the pairs of examples below, the highlighted words look exactly the same, but the job each does is quite different.

CLOSED CLASS

That is **his**.   Why has he left **his** coat behind?
I would like to buy **these**.   **These** chocolates are the best I've tasted.

OPEN CLASS

I want to ask a **question**.   The police-officer must **question** the suspect today.
The **field** is full of horses.   I don't want to **field**; I want to bat.

Can you explain the differences here? A good starting point is to think about:

> the position of the highlighted words
> the words that come before and after the highlighted words
> their meaning

If you can, write an explanation of the job of each highlighted word in its context. You may be able to see how the words are functioning but don't yet feel able to explain – don't worry! Working through the rest of the chapter will help you to pinpoint and explain the differences in grammatical terms.

2.2 Nouns (N)

Traditionally, NOUNS are called 'naming words', but this is a very general definition. It works for nouns that refer to physical objects (*table, aeroplane, toys*), people (*Marco, Juliet, Emebet*) and places (*Ethiopia, Newcastle, Europe*), but is less clear for nouns such as *knowledge, solution, idealism*.

Language tests can help us to classify words more precisely: by asking key questions, or by looking for familiar patterns, we can see whether words conform to our expectations.

To check if a word is a noun, we can normally:

> put **the** or **some** in front of it

```
the + book              the + traveller
some + opportunities    some + experience
```

▸ add an –*s* inflection (or ending) to indicate 'more than one'

```
fact → facts            story → stories
```

▸ put an – *'s* inflection (singular) or –*s'* (plural) to mark possession

```
the boy's coat          the boys' coats
Mark's                  America's
```

These tests will help you to decide whether a word is a noun or not. They will not always provide you with conclusive proof, but they will support your instinctive knowledge about words.

Common and proper nouns

Nouns can be divided into two main groups. PROPER NOUNS are the names of specific people (*James, Megha, Martin*), companies (*Playmobil, Microsoft*), places (*France, Mount Fuji*), times (*Monday, June*) and occasions (*Easter, Eid*). Proper nouns

▸ do not usually have a plural form
▸ rarely occur with determiners (*a, the, some, any*)
▸ are written with an initial capital letter

There are, however, exceptions.

> **Mondays** are always very busy in our house.   (PLURAL)
> Do you know if a **Mr Dreyfuss** lives in this street?   (DETERMINER)

Because of their special features, the noun tests do not usually work for proper nouns.

All other nouns are COMMON. They usually have

▸ a plural form
  (*dog → dogs; potato → potatoes; story → stories; man → men;
  leaf → leaves; child → children*)
▸ a determiner
  (***the** school, **some** chocolate, **a** car*)

Common nouns represent a very large group and we can divide them into smaller groups: **concrete** and **abstract**; **count** and **non-count**; **collective**. These classifications are of particular use when you begin to explore the ways in which meaning is created in spoken and written texts.

Concrete and abstract nouns

CONCRETE NOUNS refer to physical things such as people, objects and places – things that can be observed and measured.

```
car    wall    dome    tower    computer
```

ABSTRACT NOUNS refer to ideas, processes, occasions, times and qualities, which cannot be observed.

| challenge | bravery | excitement | foolishness | meeting |

Using concrete nouns allows writers and speakers to create a strong physical sens of time and place; choosing abstract nouns tends to create texts that are reflectiv and discursive.

Count and non-count nouns

We can also classify nouns according to their number. Concrete nouns can usual be counted; many abstract nouns cannot.

COUNT NOUNS refer to individual items that can be counted. They can be use with

- the determiner *a* (*a grape*)
- a number (*five* grapes)
- an indefinite determiner (*some* grapes)

To indicate 'more than one', we need to add a PLURAL **ending** (or INFLECTION) to th noun. In most cases, this will be an –*s* inflection.

| a cupboard → three cupboard**s** | chocolate → some chocolate**s** |

IRREGULAR nouns, however, take a different ending. The plural inflection ma be

- –*es* for words ending in –*o, -s, -sh, -ss, -tch* or -*x* (*potato* → *potato**es***)
- –*ies* for words ending in –*y* (*story* → *stor**ies***)
- –*ves* for some words that end in –*f* or –*fe* (*life* → *li**ves***, *thief* → *thie**ves***)

Other nouns form their plural by

- changing a vowel (*tooth* → *t**ee**th*)
- using a different inflection (*child* → *child**ren***)

Some nouns are the same in both singular and plural form (*sheep, deer, offspring* so we have to rely on the context to know whether the reference is singular or plural Other nouns occur only in a plural form (*scissors, trousers, congratulations, cattle* We have to be careful with some nouns that end in –*s*: they may look like plura forms, but they are not (*news, physics*).

NON-COUNT NOUNS refer to substances and qualities that cannot be counted.

| music | knowledge | physics | bread |

They

- have no plural form
- cannot usually follow the determiner *a*
- can occur after determiners such as *some* or *much*.

We use *less/the least* with non-count nouns, but *fewer/fewest* with count nouns.

| **less** information | **fewer** girls |

Where there is a number giving the size of a quantity or where the noun *number* is included, we can also use *less* for count nouns.

| **less** than **eight** days | **fewer** days |
| the **number** of visitors was **less** than last year | **fewer** visitors than last year |

e can indicate 'number' for non-count nouns by using an expression or by putting em after *piece of* or *bit of*.

two pieces of **bread**   five blades of **grass**

Je use count nouns and non-count nouns occurring in an expression in recipes, struction texts, technical reports, scientific texts and shopping lists where we need define quantities. Non-count nouns occur more frequently in spoken and written xts that focus on abstract reflections or discussion.

ollective nouns

COLLECTIVE NOUNS refer to groups of people, animals and things.

government   herd   family   committee

ccording to the point of view a writer or speaker wishes to develop, collective ouns can be followed by

- singular verbs, pronouns and possessive determiners
- plural verbs, pronouns and possessive determiners

Jsing singular forms focuses on the unity of the group.

The government **is** committed to improving education. **It aims** to raise standards.
The class **has** reached an agreement about **its** favourite book.

Choosing plural forms draws attention to the individual members of a group.

The government **are** committed to improving education **They aim** to raise standards.
The class **have** reached an agreement about **their** favourite book.

n writing, it is important to be consistent: whether you choose singular or plural orms, you must continue using the same throughout.

Nouns and other word classes

Nouns very often appear in spoken and written texts with other words which are lirectly linked to them. These words usually precede the noun and provide us with additional information.

the **round** balloon   the **hot air** balloon   the **deflated** balloon   the **growing** balloon
     N   N   N   N

The underlined words are said to **modify** the noun because they direct our attention to a particular feature of the balloon. Modifying words change our perception: in each of the examples above, the modifiers create a different visual image.

Where we wish to refer to a group or class of people, an adjective following the determiner *the* can be used to act as a noun.

the **young**   the **old**   the **Welsh**   the **literate**

2.3 Adjectives (Adj)

In traditional grammar, ADJECTIVES are called 'describing words'. They give us extra information about nouns by modifying or changing our frame of reference.

A noun standing alone provides us with no specific descriptive detail. If a writ refers to *the dog*, for example, we are free to imagine any kind of dog. The additic of adjectives narrows our frame of reference by focusing our attention on particul details.

> the **black** dog   the **small** dog   the **friendly** dog   the **unpredictable** dog

Each of the highlighted adjectives draws attention to a particular featur colour, size, character, mood. The details encourage us to visualise a different dc in each case. Adjectives can convey physical detail (*grey, small, hairy, glossy*) c communicate a sense of character (*innocent, aloof, moody, cynical, polite*); the can create an atmosphere (*gloomy, bright, chaotic, romantic, noisy*) or stir our emc tions (*horrible, miraculous, ghastly, disgraceful, marvellous, sensational*). Equal. they can provide precise factual information (*educational, symmetric, financia political, electrical*).

We use adjectives in all kinds of contexts:

- creative writers use them to develop a sense of place, atmosphere or characte
- estate agents and advertisers use them to persuade us to purchase their proc ucts
- script writers use them in stage directions to indicate physical details of prop sets and sounds
- politicians use them to promote their policies or to attack their politic: opponents

When a writer uses too many adjectives, critics use the term 'purple prose' t describe the style. It is a term used to describe writing that is extravagant and ornate where the adjectives become so excessive that they can distract a reader from th meaning. In the most effective writing, each adjective will contribute to the ton and purpose of a text, guiding the reader and shaping their response without bein; overwhelming.

Since other word classes can also be used to add descriptive detail, we need t be aware of two distinctive features of adjectives: their **position** and the fact tha we can **grade** them.

To check if a word is an adjective, we can normally:
- put it in front of a noun

> the **glorious** weather   the **infinite** universe   the **hopeful** student

- put an intensifying word (*very, terribly, dreadfully, so*) in front of it

> **very** beautiful   **unbearably** beautiful
> **so** chaotic   **pleasantly** chaotic
> **quite** moody   **really** moody

- add an *–ly* inflection

> **beautiful**ly   **chaotic**ally   **mood**ily

These tests will help you to decide whether a word is an adjective or not. They will not always provide you with conclusive proof, but they will support your instinctive knowledge about words.

Form

Although many adjectives do not have a distinctive form, there are a number of SUFFIXES (word endings) which can help you to identify words as adjectives. The table below lists some of the most common endings with examples of the kinds of words to which they can be added.

Suffix	Base word	Word class	Adjective
-able	present	V	presentable
-al	magic	N	magical
-ful	wish	N	wishful
-ic	metre	N	metric
-ish	child	N	childish
-ive	express	V	expressive
-less	penny	N	penniless
-ous	mystery	N	mysterious
-y	snow	N	snowy

Tone

Adjectives play a significant role in creating the tone of a text: choosing noticeably positive (*sunny, spacious, friendly, gentle, virtuous, communicative*) or negative (*brutal, disastrous, cruel, careless, hostile, vicious*) adjectives allows writers and speakers to develop a particular mood. We can look words up in a dictionary to find their literal meaning (DENOTATION), but they also have wider cultural or personal associations (CONNOTATIONS). The denotation of the adjective *autumnal*, for example, is 'pertaining to autumn' – it is a literal reference to the season. If a writer were to use the adjective in a text, however, we would also be aware of its wider connotations. The effect could be negative (focusing on stormy weather and the shortening hours of daylight) or positive (focusing on the fruitfulness of the harvest and the warmth of an Indian summer).

By changing the kind of adjectives we choose, we can create a new mood – if you can recognise where the adjectives change, you will be able to mark the turning point in a text.

Grading adjectives

GRADABLE adjectives can vary on a continuous scale (for instance, size, weight, colour, age, temperature). We use intensifiers before an adjective to indicate degree.

quite cold   **really** cold   **very** cold   **exceptionally** cold

Some adjectives are **non-gradable** because they cannot vary on a continuous scale.

digital   automatic   still   dead   electrical

These adjectives are **absolute** – there cannot be degrees of 'deadness' or 'stillness'. Although technically superfluous because these are either 'all-or-none' qualities, we do use intensifiers with some of these adjectives in everyday usage (*very still, nearly dead, almost impossible*).

Comparing adjectives

As well as using intensifiers before adjectives, we can also **compare** the particular quality that an adjective expresses.

> The boy was **fast**. His brother was **faster**. The professional sprinter was **fastest**.

You will see from these examples that we can compare adjectives in two ways.

COMPARATIVE **adjectives** compare one person or thing with another. We form comparative adjectives by

 ▸ adding an *–er* inflection to adjectives of one syllable

> bright → bright**er**   cold → cold**er**

 ▸ adding an *–er* inflection or using *more* with adjectives of two syllables

> happy → happi**er**/**more** happy   clever → clever**er**/**more** clever

 ▸ using *more* with adjectives of three or more syllables

> serious → **more** serious   philosophical → **more** philosophical

SUPERLATIVE **adjectives** compare three or more people or things. We form superlative adjectives by

 ▸ adding an *-est* inflection to adjectives of one syllable

> bright → bright**est**   fine → fin**est**

 ▸ adding an *–est* inflection or using *most* with adjectives of two syllables

> happy → happi**est**/**most** happy   clever → clever**est**/**most** clever

 ▸ using *most* with adjectives of three or more syllables

> serious → **most** serious   unpredictable → **most** unpredictable

Some adjectives are **irregular**, but you will probably use these forms instinctively.

> good → better → best   bad → worse → worst
>
> far → farther → farthest

If we compare people or things that **express a quality to the same degree**, we can use the structure *as … as.*

> Jane is **as tall as** her mother.

Writers often use this structure to create a simile: a descriptive relationship between two apparently unrelated things.

> The man stared at her emotionlessly. He was **as cold as** the North wind, **as blank as** a snow-driven plain.

If we compare people or things that **express a quality to a lesser degree**, we can use *less/least or less … than.*

> Jack seems **less confident** this week, but Mary is **least confident** of all the students.
>
> You are **less busy than** Julie these days.

Some adjectives have no degrees of comparison. If a flower is *perfect,* for instance, another flower cannot be 'more perfect'. Similarly, a *wooden* box cannot be 'more wooden' than another box. Such adjectives do not take comparative and superlative forms because their quality is **absolute.**

the **wooden** box   the **golden** harp   the **complete** set   the **silent** class

Order

Adjectives often occur together in strings of two or three and they usually follow a recognisable pattern. In most cases, the order will be as follows:

	SIZE	AGE	COLOUR	
the	large	modern	silver	box
the	tiny	Victorian	metallic	box
	GRADABLE	**NON-GRADABLE**		

Your instinctive knowledge of language will help you to recognise the correct order and rearranging the adjective in a list will often feel strange.

the young brown small dog

the brown small young dog

the small young brown dog   ✓

Position of adjectives

Most adjectives can occur in two **positions** in a sentence. They can come

▸ **before a noun** (attributive adjectives)

the **overcast** sky   the **glorious** day   the **grateful** children

▸ **after a** COPULAR **verb** such as *be, become, appear, remain, feel, seem* or *grow* (predicative adjectives).

the sky became **overcast**   the day was **glorious**   the children appeared **grateful**

In each case, the meaning is the same, but the emphasis is slightly different.

Writers and speakers can create different effects by choosing to put adjectives before a noun or after a verb.

ATTRIBUTIVE **adjectives**:

▸ develop a particular attribute of the noun they precede
▸ place the main stress or focus on the noun.

PREDICATIVE **adjectives**:

▸ stand alone after the verb or in parenthesis
▸ assume a greater semantic significance because the focus is on the adjective.

Predicative adjectives can also appear in parenthesis, separated from the main body of a sentence by commas, dashes or brackets.

The lecturer stood, **tall and straight**, waiting for silence to spread among the talkative students.

In some cases, adjectives can follow a noun without a copular verb.

> The **responsible** man   is arriving early.
>
> The man **responsible** for booking the table   is arriving early.
>
> The **sad** girl   is sitting by herself.
>
> The girl **sad** to be leaving   is sitting by herself.

Moving the position of the adjective creates a slightly different meaning: it tends to be general if the adjective precedes the noun and more specific where the adjective follows the noun. In some cases, the adjective can stand alone after the noun, but in most we need an additional expression.

> The people **present**   were all very helpful.
>
> The man **responsible**   is arriving early.

2.4 Verbs (V)

In traditional grammar, VERBS are called 'doing words', but this definition is rather narrow since it does not take account of verbs that express 'states' and 'conditions'. In language study, we call the 'doing' verbs DYNAMIC **verbs** – they involve some kind of physical or mental action (*jump, see, write, sleep*); we call the verbs that express states and conditions STATIVE **verbs** (*grow, become, be, appear, seem*).

Verbs have a number of distinctive characteristics that help us to check whether a word is a verb or not. To check if a word is a verb, we can

▸ put 'to' in front of it

> to **bark**
>
> to **discover**
>
> to **finalise**

▸ put an –*ing* inflection on it

> bark**ing**
>
> discover**ing**
>
> finalis**ing**

▸ change the time at which an action takes place by adding an –*s* inflection (present), or an –*ed* inflection to regular verbs (past)

> bark**s**   bark**ed**
>
> discover**s**   discover**ed**
>
> finalise**s**   finalis**ed**

Verbs and meaning

Every grammatically complete sentence must have a verb. We use verbs to communicate actions, processes, and states. By changing the form we can alter the time at which an action takes place (*visit, visited*); by adding additional verbs we can ask a question (*Do you visit on Tuesdays?*), create a negative (*We did not visit*) or intro-

...uce semantic subtlety reflecting the likelihood of an action happening (*We may visit soon*) or our control over it (*I must visit today*).

Lexical verbs (lex)

LEXICAL VERBS make up a very large group, with a wide range of meanings. They function as the main verb in a sentence and are semantically important.

> We **calculate** percentages very quickly.
>
> We **dig** the vegetable beds very quickly.

In the examples above, the lexical verb *calculate* communicates something very different from the lexical verb *dig*. Both are dynamic verbs – they represent an action – but each denotes a very different process: where one is a mental process, the other is physical.

Auxiliary verbs (aux)

There are only 12 AUXILIARY VERBS. They have a grammatical function supporting the main verb in a sentence by indicating changes in time scale, MOOD, person or number. They are always followed by a lexical verb. There are two types:

- the **primary** auxiliaries *to be*, *to have* and *to do*
- the **modal** auxiliaries *can/could, shall/should, may/might, will/would, must*

The primary auxiliaries (prim)

The verb *to do* helps us to construct **questions** and **negatives** (using the **particle** *not*), and to create **emphasis**. It is followed by a BASE FORM verb.

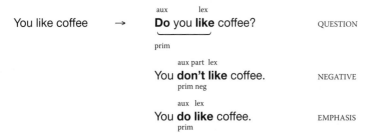

		aux	lex	
You like coffee	→	**Do** you **like** coffee?		QUESTION
		prim		

		aux	part	lex	
		You **don't like** coffee.			NEGATIVE
		prim	neg		

		aux	lex	
		You **do like** coffee.		EMPHASIS
		prim		

The verbs *to be* and *to have* help us to construct different **time scales**. They are followed by non-finite verb participles (*–ing* and *–ed/–en* participles).

I **am** running.	I **was** running.
We **have** finished.	We **had** finished.
It **has** broken.	It **had** broken.

The primary auxiliaries can also be used alone as lexical verbs.

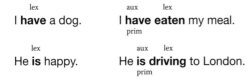

lex	aux	lex
I **have** a dog.	I **have eaten** my meal.
	prim	

lex	aux	lex
He **is** happy.	He **is driving** to London.
	prim	

The modal auxiliaries (mod)

The MODAL AUXILIARIES *may, might, can, could, shall, should, will, would* and *mus...* help us to convey shades of meaning. They are followed by a lexical verb in the bas... form. We label the auxiliary and lexical verbs above because this tells us what job th... verbs are doing, and the modal and base verb below because this tells us their form...

		aux	lex	
I work hard.	→	I **must work** hard.		NECESSITY
		mod	Vbase	

I **will work** hard. PREDICTION
mod Vbase

I **should work** hard. OBLIGATION
mod Vbase

I **may work** hard. POSSIBILITY
mod Vbase

I **can work** hard. ABILITY
mod Vbase

The modal auxiliary verbs have a range of meanings that colour the way we interpre... the lexical verb. The main meanings are summarised in the table below.

Modal verb	Meaning
can/could	possibility, ability, permission
may/might	possibility, permission
must	necessity, obligation
will/shall	prediction, intention
should	obligation
would	intention

Traditionally, the pairs of modal verbs were seen as present and past tense... forms. This distinction is relevant in some contexts (particularly in reported or indi-rect speech).

'I **can** visit on Friday.' DIRECT SPEECH present

He said that he **could** visit on Friday. INDIRECT SPEECH past

Modal verbs are also used to reflect shades of meaning linked to politeness, tenta-tiveness or certainty where there is no explicit indication of time scale.

Might I be able to visit on Friday? POLITENESS

Could I visit on Friday? TENTATIVENESS

I **should** visit on Friday. OBLIGATION

Agreement

When we describe verbs, we need to be able to talk about NUMBER (singular or plu-ral) and PERSON (first, second, third). We can classify this as follows.

Person	Number	
	Singular	Plural
1st	I	we
2nd	you	you
3rd	he, she, it	they

The person and number of a verb control its forms. In the present tense, for instance, we have to add an –s inflection in the third person singular. We call this relationship AGREEMENT or CONCORD.

I walk	1ST PERSON SINGULAR
you walk	2ND PERSON SINGULAR
Miriam walk**s**/ she walk**s**	3RD PERSON SINGULAR
we walk	1ST PERSON PLURAL
you walk	2ND PERSON PLURAL
they walk	3RD PERSON PLURAL

There are some irregular third person singular and plural verb forms.

		3RD PERSON SINGULAR	3RD PERSON PLURAL
to be	(present)	is	are
	(past)	was	were
to do		does	do
to have		has	have

In some dialects, the person and the verb form do not follow these patterns – there is no standard agreement.

I were	FIRST PERSON SINGULAR + PLURAL VERB FOM
we was	FIRST PERSON PLURAL + SINGULAR VERB FORM
they walks	THIRD PERSON PLURAL + SINGLAR VERB FORM

While seen as inappropriate in formal written language, these kinds of structures are common in spoken language.

Past and present

One of the distinctive features of verbs is our ability to create different **time scales**.

PRESENT TENSE (**V*pres***) verbs refer to physical processes and states that are happening now, and to recurring events. They can also be used for dramatic effect.

he **throws** the ball in and **runs** back

We **go** to town on Wednesdays.

In English, the **base form** of the verb is used for the present tense except with *she*, *he* and *it* where we need to add an –s inflection. There are some verbs which require an –es inflection.

go	→	go**es**
do	→	do**es**
pass	→	pass**es**

PAST TENSE (**V***past*) verbs refer to physical processes and states that have take~~~~ place in the past and are complete. In English, we add an *–ed* inflection to the bas~ form of regular verbs.

walk	→	walk**ed**
pick	→	pick**ed**

IRREGULAR verbs take forms that you will probably know instinctively.

have	→	had
write	→	wrote
think	→	thought
fly	→	flew
take	→	took
swim	→	swam
sell	→	sold

Participles

There are two participles forms in English:

–*ing* **participles (V***ing***)**   **–***ed* **participles (V***ed***)**

In some books, you may find these identified as present participles (*–ing*) and pas~ participles (*–ed*). This can be confusing, however, because these verb forms do no~ specifically indicate tense.

Participles usually occur with the primary auxiliaries *have* and *be*. We label the auxiliary and lexical verbs above because this tells us what job the verbs are doing, and the primary and base verb below because this tells us their form.

We **have climbed** the mountain.   They **are climbing** the mountain.

They help us to communicate different time scales. Usually, although not always, *–ING* PARTICIPLES refer to an event that is on-going, and *–ED* PARTICIPLES to an event that is complete.

We also use participles adjectivally: they can occur before a noun in the site where we would expect to see an adjective. In this context, they function as **modifiers**.

the **broken** wall   some **trapped** cavers   the **fleeing** soldiers
    Ved   N   *Ved*   N   *Ving*   N

In some cases, the modifying participle may occur after the noun.

the girl **hidden** in the woods   the tree **damaged** by the storm
    N   *Ved*   N   *Ved*

Future time

Linguists do not usually refer to a future 'tense' in English because there are no verb endings to indicate events that have not yet taken place. Instead, we can refer to UTURE TIME in three different ways:

1 the modal auxiliaries *will/shall* + *base form verb*

He **will visit** France in the summer.

2 the primary auxiliary *to be* + *going* + *infinitive* (the **particle** *to* + base form verb)

We **are going to buy** a new television.

3 the primary auxiliary *to be* + *–ing* participle

I **am seeing** Jack next week.

Finite and non-finite verbs

Verbs that are marked for person and number, and verbs that are marked for tense are FINITE. You can test whether a verb is finite or not by seeing if you can change the person or number, or the tense.

He carries the shopping.	**They carry** the shopping.
3RD PERSON SINGULAR	3RD PERSON PLURAL
The boys work hard.	**The boys worked** hard.
PRESENT	PAST
3RD PERSON PLURAL	3RD PERSON PLURAL

Participle forms are NON-FINITE verbs: they never change and are not marked for tense, person or number.

flying	fallen	wanted
V*ing*	V*ed*	V*ed*

INFINITIVES (**V***inf*) and base form verbs (**V***base*) used as commands or after a modal auxiliary verb are also non-finite.

to go	Go!	can go
V*inf*	V*base*	mod V*base*

Multi-word verbs

Multi-word verbs are verbs which are linked to one or two other words which we call PARTICLES (**part**).

to look at   to call on   to take up   to think about

We can often check whether a verb is a multi-word verb by substituting a single verb for the verb and particle(s).

to break up	→	to separate
to go in for	→	to compete
to cut down on	→	to reduce
to put up with	→	to tolerate

Many multi-word verbs are idiomatic – we cannot understand their meaning b
adding up the meaning of the individual words. They are common in spoken, infor
mal language – some people therefore believe that in formal writing they shoul
be avoided.

Different types of multi-word verbs

In some grammar books, multi-word verbs are divided into different categorie
according to the kind of particles that follow them. Verbs can be followed by prepo
sitions (see Section 2.8), by adverbs of place (see Section 2.5), or by both an adverl
and a preposition.

Prepositional verbs

We call a verb followed by a preposition a PREPOSITIONAL VERB. A noun can follow
the preposition.

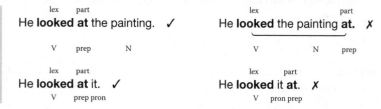

In some examples, there will be a clause after the preposition – a CLAUSE (Cl) is a
unit of language that contains a finite or tensed verb, or a non-finite participle. You
will cover clauses in more detail in Chapter 6, but at the moment you just need to
be able to recognise the kind of verb following the particle.

    lex   part   lex   part

I don't **approve of** [dropping litter].   We **talked about** [when we <u>were</u> lost in that storm].

  V + prep Cl (non-finite V–*ing*)   V + prep   Cl (finite – past tense)

The verb and particle in a prepositional verb cannot be separated.

    lex   part   lex   part

He **looked at** the painting. ✓   He **looked** the painting **at.** ✗

    V   prep   N   V   N   prep

    lex   part   lex   part

He **looked at** it. ✓   He **looked** it **at.** ✗

  V   prep pron   V   pron prep

Phrasal verbs

We call a verb followed by an adverb (Adv) a PHRASAL VERB. The particle can be followed by a noun, but phrasal verbs often stand alone.

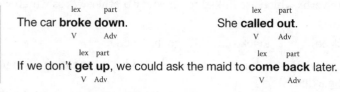

If a phrasal verb is followed by a noun, the verb and particle can be separated.

it is followed by a pronoun, the verb and particle must be separated.

lex part		lex part
He **put up** <u>it</u>. ✗		He **put** <u>it</u> **up**. ✓
V Adv pron		V pron Adv

hrasal-prepositional verbs

We call a verb followed by two particles (an adverb and a preposition) a PHRASAL-REPOSITIONAL VERB.

                lex   part   part
You'll never **get away with** that story.
                V   Adv   prep   N

dentifying multi-word verbs

1 some cases, although a verb may be followed by a preposition or an adverb, there no semantic connection between the words.

    The fireman kicked in the door.   The old man stayed in.

he word *in*, for instance, has an identical form in each of the examples above, but is functioning in a different way. In the first example, it is a **particle** directly linked) the verb: *to kick in* is a phrasal verb – we can move the particle and the sentence till makes sense, and it can also come after a pronoun.

    The fireman **kicked** the door **in**.   The fireman **kicked** it **in**.

1 the second example, *in* is linked to place: it is an adverb telling us **where** the old 1an stayed. We could change it for another adverb and the sentence would still 1ake sense.

    The fireman kicked **still** the door. ✗   The old man stayed **still**. ✓

luestions

f we wish to ask a QUESTION, we can do so in three ways. We can

1 use the primary auxiliary *do* at the beginning of a statement + *base form verb*

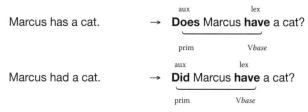

                             aux   lex
Marcus has a cat.   →   **Does** Marcus **have** a cat?
                                prim   V*base*

                             aux   lex
Marcus had a cat.   →   **Did** Marcus **have** a cat?
                                prim   V*base*

2 change the order of the auxiliary verb and the person (subject)

    We have finished the film.   →   **Have we** finished watching the film?

3 use a *wh-* **question word** and change the order of the auxiliary verb and the person

    You are visiting your aunt.   →   **Why are you** visiting your aunt?

We can also make a statement into a question by adding a TAG QUESTION on the end. If the statement is positive, the tag question will be negative.

> He's back in this country, **isn't he**? The children are playing in the sand, **aren't they**?

If the statement is negative, the tag will be positive.

> He isn't home yet, **is he**? The children aren't playing in the sand, **are they**?

In spoken language, instead of changing the order of the words, we often use RISING INTONATION to mark a statement as a question.

> You are visiting your áunt?

In linguistic analysis, we call question and answer structures ADJACENCY PAIRS. In cooperative situations, a question will have an answer and the adjacency pair is described as complete. If there is no answer, if the answer fails to provide the necessary information, or if a question is met by another question, we describe the adjacency pair as incomplete. Incomplete question–answer structures are often linguistic markers of uncooperative interaction. They can, however, also be used for comic effect.

Negatives (neg)

To make a statement **negative**, we usually add the negative particle *not* after a single lexical verb or after the first auxiliary verb.

     lex   lex part
The book is on the shelf. → The book is **not** on the shelf.
     V*pres*   V*pres* neg

     aux   lex   aux   part   lex
The book was stacked on the shelf. → The book was **not** stacked on the shelf.
     prim   V*ed*   prim   neg   V*ed*

     aux   aux   lex   aux   part aux   lex
The book should have been on the shelf. → The book should **not** have been on the shelf.
     mod   prim V*ed*   mod   neg   prim V*ed*

If there is a single lexical verb (other than *to be*), we need to add the primary auxiliary verb *do* + *not* before the verb.

                     aux   part   lex
I make cakes. → I **do not** make cakes.
                     prim neg V*base*

In spoken language, CONTRACTIONS in negative sentences are common.

is not	→	isn't
do not	→	don't
does not	→	doesn't
should not	→	shouldn't
will not	→	won't

.5 Adverbs (Adv)

ADVERBS provide us with extra information – they can usually be omitted from a sentence, but it will still make sense. They are very versatile words giving us information about:

▶ verbs	The boy ran **quickly**.
▶ adjectives	The children were **very** happy.
▶ adverbs	The mother waited **quite** anxiously to hear the news.
▶ whole sentences	**Unfortunately**, the match had been cancelled. The day, **however**, was not ruined.

To check if a word is an adverb, you can:

▶ ask yourself the key questions how? where? when?

the wind blew **lazily**	HOW?
the wind blew **outside**	WHERE?
the wind blew **often**	WHEN?

▶ see if it has an –*ly* ending

passionate**ly**   silent**ly**   particular**ly**   frequent**ly**

▶ check whether it is commenting on what is being said or written

obviously   ridiculously   probably   sadly   perhaps

▶ put an intensifying adverb such as *very*, *quite* or *so* in front of it

very soon   **so** slowly   **quite** probably

Form

The most easily recognisable adverbs are those with an –*ly* suffix. They are often formed by adding the inflection to an adjective.

sad + ly → sadly   effective + ly → effectively

Other suffixes, although less common, can be used:

–wards	skywards	forwards
–wise	likewise	clockwise
–ways	sideways	lengthways

Many adverbs are simple single word constructions (*now, often, then, here*), but others are described as compound words.

thereby   somehow   therefore

Meaning

By including adverbs in a sentence, we can subtly alter the way readers or listeners respond. Adverbs can modify the way we interpret a verb, qualify the degree of an adjective, or reflect on a whole sentence. The examples below show how adverbs can be added to a simple grammatical sentence in order to provide an extra layer of meaning.

The child told his story **cautiously**.	V + Adv → HOW
The child told his story **outside**.	V + Adv → WHERE
The child told his story **yesterday**.	V + Adv → WHEN
The child told his **rather** unusual story.	Adv + Adj → DEGREE
Luckily, the child told his story.	Adv + Sent → ATTITUDE
The car journeyed on. **Meanwhile**, the child told his story.	Sentence + Adv → RELATIONSHIP BETWEEN EVENTS

Each example would still make sense if the adverbs were omitted, but the additional information colours each sentence differently.

Function

Writers and speakers use adverbs:

- to give information about manner (*quickly, carelessly, foolishly*)
- to give information about place (*here, outside, right, left, there*)
- to give information about time (*tomorrow, before, now, often, soon*)
- to convey degree (*very, quite, rather, terribly*)
- to communicate attitudes (*sadly, luckily, doubtless, indeed, frankly*)
- to develop contrasts between sentences (*besides, moreover, meanwhile, so*).

ADJUNCTS give us information about 'how', 'where', 'when' and 'to what extent', and relate directly to the verb. They include adverbs of manner (*carefully, accidentally*) adverbs of place (*outside, downstairs*), adverbs of time (*later, often*) and adverbs of degree (*very, sufficiently*). We can ask ourselves the questions how? where? when? and how much? to decide which kind of adjunct is being used. **DISJUNCTS** comment on what is being said or written (*Unfortunately, literally*) and **CONJUNCTS** link one sentence, or part of a sentence, to another (*however, consequently*).

Position

Adverbs are the most flexible elements in a sentence – by changing their position, we can change the focus of a sentence.

Seriously, the artist should have finished the painting.	DISJUNCT (expression of attitude)
The artist should finish his painting seriously.	ADJUNCT (expression of manner)

Adverbs of degree linked to an adjective are less mobile since they are governed by the position of the adjective in a sentence.

He was (**very** serious).
      Adv   Adj

The girl was a (**quite** brilliant) musician.
      Adv   Adj

An adverb in the **medial** position carries less semantic significance than an adverb in the **initial** or **final** position.

We edged **carefully** along the cliff.	MEDIAL
Carefully, we edged along the cliff.	INITIAL
We edged along the cliff **carefully**.	FINAL

While adverbs can be moved quite freely around a sentence, some people object to them being put between *to* + *verb* (the infinitive). This is called a SPLIT INFINITIVE.

part   lex
I had to **carefully** check my work.

prep   Adv   V*inf*

Traditionalists argue that the adverb should be moved to another position in the sentence.

I had to check my work **carefully**.
                                 Adv

Others believe that splitting the infinitive can be used for dramatic effect.

part   lex
To **boldly** go where no man has gone before.

prep   Adv V*inf*

This example demonstrates the way in which an adverb can be given semantic significance by placing it between the preposition and the base form verb. The split infinitive is common in informal speech.

We want to **like** go to town.

He wants to **really** sort out his life.

Grading and comparing

We can **grade** and **compare** adverbs in the same way as adjectives.

▸ we can grade adverbs by pre-modifying them with another adverb

very late	**unacceptably** late	**so** late	**rather** nervously

▸ we can compare MONOSYLLABIC adverbs using an *–er* (comparative) or *–est* (superlative) inflection.

late	later	latest

▸ we can compare POLYSYLLABIC adverbs using *more* and *most*.

more significantly	**most** significantly

▸ we can compare adverbs to a lesser degree with *less/least*

less anxiously	**least** anxiously

▸ we can use adverbs with comparative structures *as . . . as* and *less . . than*

as seriously **as**	**less** seriously **than**

Irregular adverbs correspond to the irregular adjectives:

well → better → best   badly → worse → worst

little → less → least

2.6 Determiners (det)

DETERMINERS indicate the number and definiteness of nouns, and occur before the noun to which they refer. The table below categorises some of the determiners we can choose to create a different kind of semantic relationship between the noun and its determiner.

Articles	Possessives	Demonstratives	Quantity	Wh–	Numbers
the	my	this	some	whose	one
a	your	that	any	what	four
an	his	these	no	which	second
	her	those	each		fifth
	its		every		
	our		other		
	their		enough		
			another		

Determiners do not carry the main meaning in a sentence, but they can influence the way in which we interpret written and spoken language. They allow us to make very clear references to the nouns we use in speech and writing. We can differentiate between

▶ a general reference (***a** question*)
▶ a specific reference (***the** question*)
▶ a reference that directly relates to a given context (***this** question*)

We can

▶ express an attitude (***what** a question!*)
▶ describe a quantity (***two** questions; **enough** questions*)
▶ establish ownership (***her** question*)
▶ ask a question (***which** question shall I do?*)

There are three kinds of determiner.

1 **central** determiners, which are always followed by a noun and can never be used together
2 **predeterminers**, which are used before a central determiner
3 **postdeterminers**, which follow central determiners but precede adjectives

Central determiners

CENTRAL DETERMINERS are the most common. There are seven main types:

1 the **definite article**, which refers to a specific noun that has already been mentioned.

The teacher talked to the class today.   SPECIFIC REFERENCE

2 the **indefinite article**, which refers to a noun in a more general way or to a general state of affairs – it does not assume that the noun has been mentioned already.

A teacher talked to the class today.   NON-SPECIFIC REFERENCE

I'm training to be **a** teacher.   GENERAL REFERENCE

3 **possessive** determiners, which mark ownership of a noun – it is important to remember that if possessive words appear without a noun (for example, *mine, his, yours, theirs*) they are pronouns (see Section 2.7) rather than determiners.

His dog is the most friendly.   Let's hope **our** friends will find us.

4 **demonstrative determiners**, which express a contrast between things that are near and things that are distant

This book is the best I have read for ages.   I want **that** shirt.

We would normally expect demonstrative determiners to be accompanied by some kind of gesture (pointing, for instance) to link them directly to the context.

5 **quantity determiners**, which help us to define general amounts of a particular noun

every dog   **some** pictures   **no** pens   **any** child

Some quantity determiners can be used with count nouns and non-count nouns (*no, any*), others can only be used with either singular (*each, every, another*) or plural (*some, enough, other*) nouns.

6 **wh– determiners**, which are used to ask questions

Which colour do you like best?   **Whose** bag is this?

What colour did you choose?

7 **numbers (num)**, which help us to define exact amounts

I'll have **six** apples, please.   There are **ten** marks for each question.

Predeterminers (pre-det)

Many central determiners can be preceded by PREDETERMINERS like *what* or *such* to express strong feelings about something, or the quantity determiners *all of/both of/a third of.*

What a day!   **all of** the essays   **both** the children   **Such** an experience!

It is unusual for there to be two consecutive predeterminers, but there are some cases where this may occur.

All such questions must be put directly to the board.

There are a small group of **POSTDETERMINERS** which occur after a central determiner quantity determiners (*many, more, most, few, fewer, fewest*), cardinal numbers (*one two, three*) and ordinal numbers (*first, second, third*).

| the **many** visitors | the **first** visitors | some **more** cake |

2.7 Pronouns (pron)

PRONOUNS stand in place of nouns and any words linked to them, helping us to avoid unnecessary repetition (*the girl → she; the dog which had a brown patch over its eye → it*). They can also help us to make a general reference where specific information is unknown (*somebody*). They are not accompanied by other words and can occur at different positions in a sentence. They have different forms according to the person, number, and job they are doing. There are eight types of pronouns and each has a specific function.

Subject and object pronouns

We call subject and object pronouns **PERSONAL PRONOUNS**. They refer to participants in a written or spoken text, identifying who or what is responsible for performing the action or process of the verb (subject) and who is affected by it (object). We can define personal pronouns according to their number (singular or plural) and person (1st, 2nd or 3rd).

Person/number	Subject	Object
1st singular	I	me
2nd singular	you	you
3rd singular	he she it	him her it
1st plural	we	us
2nd plural	you	you
3rd plural	they	them

SUBJECT (**subj**) pronouns usually occur before the verb and **OBJECT** (**obj**) pronouns after the verb.

We visited the museum last week.	The boy gave **me** some books
pron V	V pron
subj	obj

Possessive pronouns (poss)

POSSESSIVE PRONOUNS express ownership.
They can occur before or after the verb.

| **Hers** is over there. | The dog is **ours**. |
| V | V |

Person/number	Possessive
1st singular	mine
2nd singular	yours
3rd singular	his hers its
1st plural	ours
2nd plural	yours
3rd plural	theirs

Reflexive pronouns

REFLEXIVE PRONOUNS create a link with the noun or pronoun that occurs in front of the verb.

Person/number	Possessive
1st singular	myself
2nd singular	yourself
3rd singular	himself herself itself
1st plural	ourselves
2nd plural	yourselves
3rd plural	themselves

They usually occur after the verb.

The dog shook **itself** vigorously.   They congratulated **themselves** for their hard work.
   N   V   pron   V

Reciprocal pronouns

RECIPROCAL PRONOUNS (*each other, one another, each other's, one another's*) like reflexive pronouns create a link with the noun or pronoun that occurs in front of the verb.

The two gangs hated **each other**.   The strangers looked at **one another** suspiciously.
   N   V   N   V

Demonstrative pronouns

DEMONSTRATIVE pronouns allow us to create a contrast between nouns that are near (*this/these*) and nouns that are distant (*that/those*) We call these pronouns **exophoric references** because they often refer to something in a particular situation – they have no clear frame of reference to anyone outside the context. We need to use a gesture that 'points' to the specific feature to which we are referring.

Look at **that**!   Why did you do **this**?   I want **those**.

Interrogative pronouns

INTERROGATIVE pronouns allow us to ask questions about nouns using *who, whose, to whom, which* and *what*.

> **Who** told you to sit down?   **Which** will you choose?   **What** did you see?

The answer to questions like these replaces the interrogative pronoun with a noun and any words related to it (a noun phrase).

> **The headteacher** told me to sit down.   I'll choose **the pizza and salad**.   I saw a **spider**.
>   N   N   N   N

Relative pronouns

RELATIVE PRONOUNS help us to link a relative clause (see Section 6.2) to the noun that it follows. The linking pronouns are *who, whom, whose, which* and *that*; the clause they introduce may be separated from the rest of the sentence by punctuation marks.

> The room, **which** was far too hot, was crowded and airless.
>   N

> The pianist – **who** was sitting silently – suddenly nodded to the conductor and began.
>   N

When part of a sentence is marked out in this way using commas, brackets or dashes, we say that the section marked out by the punctuation is in PARENTHESIS. The relative pronoun and its clause give us additional information, but the sentence would still make sense if we removed it.

It is important to be aware that interrogative and relative pronouns often have the same form. To work out what kind of pronoun is being used you therefore need to look at their **position** and **role** in a sentence. Relative pronouns always occur after the noun they refer to while interrogative pronouns will often occur in the INITIAL POSITION (the front of the sentence); relative pronouns provide additional information while interrogative pronouns request information.

Indefinite pronouns

INDEFINITE PRONOUNS (*some, any, one, none, all, enough, much, several, another*) are used to define quantities. Each pronoun usually replaces a more specific noun reference.

> Can I have **some**?   →   Can I have **some cake**?
>   pron   det N

> We've had **enough** for today.   →   We've had **enough giggling** for today.
>   pron   det   N

> Get me **another**, please.   →   Get me **another drink**, please.
>   pron   det   N

Numerals can also function in this way.

> The children took **seven**.   →   The children took **seven balloons**.

> There were **six** present in the   →   There were **six members** present in the
> meeting.   meeting.

The compound pronouns *every, some, no* and *any + thing, body, one* are also indefinite.

> **No-one** should tell the teacher **anything**.　**Nothing** is important to **anybody** these days.

Determiners and pronouns

You may have noticed that the words *some, enough, another, seven* and *six* in the examples above can be used by themselves and with a noun: they are included in the set of indefinite pronouns and the set of central determiners. In order to distinguish between determiners and pronouns, you must always remember:

▸ **pronouns** stand alone; they often replace a noun

> **Some** were early.　　　**Which** do you want?
> pron　　　　　　　　　　pron

▸ **determiners** always occur with a noun

> **Some guests** were early.　　**Which book** do you want?
> det　　N　　　　　　　　　det　　N

2.8 Prepositions (prep)

PREPOSITIONS are words which we place before a noun or a pronoun to express a relationship between elements in a sentence, providing information about time (when?), place (where?) and association. They can be a single word or can consist of two or three words, and are usually followed by a noun or a pronoun. The table below categorises some common prepositions.

Time	Place	Association: cause	Association: exception	Association: support/ opposition	Association: concession
after	above	because of	apart from	for	in spite of
before	across	on account of	except with	against	despite
at	behind		besides	with	
until/till	about		not withstanding		
about	up				
since	down				

> We will drive **around** the village **until** lunchtime.　　I will go **in spite of** the rain.
> (place)　　　　　　　(time)　　　　　　　　　　　(concession)

Some prepositions can fall into two categories of meaning, giving us different kinds of information according to their function in a sentence.

> I got off the bus **at** the bus stop.　　　　The boy arrived **at** 2 o'clock.
> (place)　　　　　　　　　　　　　　　　　(time)

> They live **in** the country.　　　　　　　The bus will arrive **in** one hour.
> (place)　　　　　　　　　　　　　　　　(time)

Prepositions and adverbs

Like determiners and pronouns, some prepositions and adverbs have the same **form**: for example, *down, about, up, off, by, in, on, over*. To decide whether a preposition or an adverb is being used, remember that a preposition will be followed by a noun where an adverb will stand alone.

> The old man walked **down** the road.   The old man sat **down**.
> prep   N   Adv

In formal grammar, this distinction is not drawn and *down* would be classed as a preposition in both the examples (see Section 4.6). In the first case, it is directly linked to additional information provided by the noun (*road*), and in the second it stands alone.

2.9 Conjunctions

CONJUNCTIONS are joining words. We can use them to link words, phrases (groups of words), clauses (units of language that usually contain a finite verb) or sentences.

Co-ordinating conjunctions (conj)

CO-ORDINATING CONJUNCTIONS link words, phrases and clauses of equal value using *and, or, but, either … or, neither … nor*.

WORDS	WORDS	PHRASES
sweetcorn **or** peas	pale **and** delicate	**neither** black trousers **nor** a red shirt
N conj N	Adj conj Adj	Adj + N conj det + Adj + N

CLAUSE	CLAUSE	CLAUSE	CLAUSE
(We went to town) **and**	(saw a film), **but**	(didn't eat out) **or**	(have a drink afterwards).
V conj	V conj	V conj	V

We use co-ordinators to add similar items together: *but* allows us to develop a contrast; *or, neither … nor, either … or* create alternatives; *and* can be used to intensify the meaning.

> The rain fell harder **and** harder (i.e. very hard)

We can also use *and* to imply an on-going action or to distinguish between apparently similar items.

> We drove **and** drove.   There are hard questions **and** hard questions.

When co-ordinating conjunctions are used, we call it SYNDETIC co-ordination; when there are no co-ordinators, we call it ASYNDETIC.

> The walls were lined with bookshelves **and** posters **and** more clocks than you can imagine.

> The walls were lined with books, posters, more clocks than you can imagine.

While the presence of co-ordinating conjunctions creates a sense of finality, their absence suggests that the listed items are just some of many more examples which could be included. We can therefore alter the semantic effect of a sentence by choosing to use syndetic or asyndetic co-ordination.

Subordinating conjunctions (sconj)

SUBORDINATING CONJUNCTIONS join clauses or sentences that do not have the same grammatical status: they link dependent grammatical units that do not make sense by themselves to independent units that can stand alone.

I like ebooks INDEPENDENT	**because** I can download them easily. DEPENDENT
If I love the sun, DEPENDENT	I should prefer summer to winter. INDEPENDENT
I went to town INDEPENDENT	**so that** I could sort out the Christmas shopping. DEPENDENT

The table below lists some of the more common subordinating conjunctions.

Subordinating Conj	Meaning	Examples
if, unless, supposing, in case	condition	I will take an umbrella **in case** it rains.
because, since, as	reason	The children cried **because** they were afraid.
so, so that	result	He got his work done **so that** he could see his friends.
while, whereas	contrast	**While** I like reading, I prefer to play computer games.
in order	purpose	She went swimming **in order** to get fit.
as if, as though	comparison	They looked at me **as though** I should know them.
although, if, whereas	concession	**Although** it snowed, the trains were still running.
where, wherever	place	We went to the park **where** we had a picnic.
after, as, before, since, when, while, until, till	time	**Before** the sun rose, I was up to prepare for the climb.

Subordinating conjunctions of time and prepositions

Because some subordinating conjunctions of time have exactly the same form as certain time prepositions (*after, before, since, until, till*), it is important to be able to recognise the function of these words in context. A subordinator will always be followed by a group of words with a finite or non-finite verb functioning as a verb; a preposition will be followed by a noun, a determiner + noun or a pronoun.

He always has a shower **after** the match.　　He always has a bath **after** he plays football.
　　　　　　　　　　prep + det + N　　　　　　　　　　　　　　　　　sconj　　Vpres

Before breakfast, I got dressed.　　**Before** having breakfast, I got dressed.
prep　+　N　　　　　　　　　　　　　sconj　　Ving

2.10 Conclusion

Words are the basic building blocks of the English language and understanding the information on word classes in this chapter gives you a starting point for your analysis of spoken and written texts. You will use the knowledge you have gained to underpin the work in the following chapters, considering how writers and speakers communicate meaning; how they entertain, inform, persuade, instruct their intended audience; how they manipulate ideas or reflect general attitudes. In your own writing, you will begin to see how to use language consciously to create particular effects.

Chapter **3**

Using your knowledge

In this chapter, you have the opportunity to apply the knowledge you have gained about word classes. The close reading activities require you to consider the effects created by the words writers or speakers choose. The writing tasks encourage you to think about word classes and appropriate lexical choices by focusing on different audiences, text types and purposes.

3.1 Nouns

Writers and speakers use nouns to establish a lexical field – the kinds of nouns chosen reflect the subject matter or focus of a text. The nouns may be concrete or abstract, or a mixture, depending upon the nature of the topic.

TASK 1   Concrete nouns in instruction texts

1 Read the recipe below carefully.

Tuna-Stuffed Courgettes
      4 courgettes
      4 tomatoes, halved
      2 tbsp olive oil
      1 garlic clove
      25g stale breadcrumbs
      185g can of tuna
      1 tbsp fresh basil, chopped

1. Preheat the oven to 200°/180° fan/Gas 6.
2. Using a sharp knife, halve the courgettes lengthways. Scrape out a little of the flesh from the middle and set aside.
3. Place the courgettes and the halved tomatoes cut side up in a roasting tin.
4. Drizzle with half the olive oil, season with salt and pepper and roast for 20 minutes.
5. Meanwhile, heat the rest of the oil in a pan. Crush the garlic and cook with the courgette flesh for 3–4 minutes until golden.

6. Put in a bowl and stir in the breadcrumbs, tuna and basil.
7. After 20 minutes, remove the tomatoes from the oven and set aside.
8. Pile the tuna mixture into the courgettes and return to the oven for 10–15 minutes to heat through.
9. Serve with the roasted tomatoes and rice or fresh new potatoes.

2 Underline the concrete nouns in the text.
3 Make notes on the relationship between the nouns you have identified, the subject matter and the text type.

NOTES

- instruction text: emphasis on concrete nouns
- sequence important – anyone who follows instructions must be able to produce the same end product each time
- layout distinctive: use of bold, listed ingredients, numbered stages
- lexical sets of concrete nouns typical of text type – direct link to content i.e. preparing food
  - food
  - equipment
- repetition of concrete nouns (ingredients in opening list) is typical – narrow range of reference

Concrete noun	Number of repetitions
courgettes	6
tomatoes	4
tuna	4
oil	3
basil	2
breadcrumbs	2

- noun references varied by words that precede them
  - numerical quantities: *4, 2 tbsp, 25g*
  - adjectives providing additional information: *stale, fresh, sharp*
  - non-finite verbs marking the completion of a particular instruction: *halved tomatoes* (Ved), *roasted tomatoes* (Ved)
- count nouns and expressions of quantity typical of text type
  - plural count nouns: *tomatoes, courgettes, breadcrumbs*
  - non-count noun with an expression to convey amount: *a little of the flesh*
- use of articles typical of text type
  - general references to equipment using singular count nouns + indefinite article: *a bowl*
  - more specific references use definite article: *the oven* (most kitchens will only have one), *the olive oil, the breadcrumbs* (reference to listed ingredients)
- precise references to time are important to the outcome: *for 3–4 minutes, After 20 minutes*

4 Collect examples of different instruction texts. Underline the concrete nouns and then think about the way in which they are used in each text. Is it different from or similar to the recipe here?

You may like to think about:

- the purpose of the text
- the subject matter
- the lexical sets of concrete nouns
- the form of the nouns
- the range of their reference
- any other linguistic features that interest you

ASK 2   Writing an instruction text ▬▬▬▬▬▬▬▬▬▬▬▬▬▬▬▬

1 Write an instruction text in which you provide a step-by-step sequence of instructions to produce or make something.

You need to pay particular attention to the concrete nouns that refer to the materials and equipment required.

When you have completed your text, evaluate the key linguistic features. You may like to use the suggested framework for analysis in Appendix A.

ASK 3   Considering the relationship between nouns and text type ▬▬▬▬▬▬

1 Read through the examples below and identify the nouns. Think about the kind of nouns used in each case and the way in which they relate to the content and purpose of the text.

TEXT 1   Travel guide

Staying in Felline, a small Apulian village on the western coast of Italy's heel, gives you the opportunity to visit some very special places. Whether you are with a tour guide or making your own way, there are some things that should not be missed. Apulia is an area still relatively untouched by tourists; it offers you silvery olive groves, dense forests and sun-kissed beaches. Within easy reach are Gallipoli, with its atmospheric Old Town of winding white-washed streets and Aragonese castle, and Lecce. Not yet a well-beaten track on the tourist trail, this town is famous for its extravagant baroque architecture – many call it the 'Florence of the South'. The history of Lecce can be traced back millennia with the dramatic ruins of the amphitheatre as a testament to its importance in Roman times.

TEXT 2   Blurb from a book club catalogue

This innovative book is just full of great ideas for the kitchen. Easy step-by-step instructions show you how to make perfect pastry and mouth-watering muffins, as well as cakes and puddings for all occasions. Combining the classic and the contemporary, there's something here for everyone. With full colour pictures and a stylish design, this wonderful book is unmissable.

TEXT 3   Anonymous poem from the 13th century (an extract) 'Sumer is icumen in'

> Sumer is icumen in,
> Loud sing cuckoo!
> Groweth seed and bloweth mead
> And springeth the wood now.
> Sing cuckoo!
>
> Ewe bleateth after lamb,
> Cow loweth after calf,
> Bullock starteth, buck farteth,
> Merry sing cuckoo!

2 What can we learn about texts by exploring the relationship between nouns, content and text type?

In answering this question, you should use appropriate terminology and linguistic frameworks to explain and evaluate the use of nouns in the three texts.
   You may like to think about:

- the text type
- the intended audience
- the subject matter and purpose
- the structure
- the type and form of the nouns, and the words linked to them
- the function of the nouns and their range of reference
- any other linguistic features that interest you.

COMMENTARY

These three texts are written for different purposes and for different intended audiences. As a contemporary text appearing in a book catalogue, the audience for Text 2 is defined by the circulation of the catalogue which can be accessed online, in a paper form as an insert in daily newspapers or as a direct mailing to customers. It aims to persuade readers or online browsers to purchase a particular book. Text 3 is a written version of an oral text; its purpose is to entertain. Its original circulation would have depended on social gatherings, but readers now have to access the text online or in anthologies of poetry – the modern audience is therefore specialised.

The purpose of Text 1 is more complex since it combines a number of purposes. Travel writing aims to inform the reader, but also to entertain: it must engage the audience through both its factual information and its descriptive detail. In some cases, it will also be persuasive since it may form the basis for an extended advertisement in a travel supplement in a newspaper. Equally, readers may decide to use the text as a guide, visiting the locations described and taking advice offered.

The use of nouns in each text reflects the purpose. While all three texts have examples of concrete and abstract nouns, the proportion of each varies. The concrete nouns in Text 1 can be classified into a number of lexical sets: natural (*coast,* roves, forests, beaches); historical (*castle, architecture, amphitheatre*); location (*village, places, area, streets, town*). These are all subject specific, relating directly to the topic – the western coast of Italy and its tourist attractions. They convey a physical sense of the area. Since the writer is introducing the reader to a specific region, here are a number of proper nouns which mark out particular areas of interest (*Felline, Italy's, Apulia, Gallipoli, Old Town, Lecce, 'Florence of the South'*). The use of proper nouns is a distinctive feature of travel writing – there are no proper nouns in Texts 2 and 3.

Text 3 is a celebration of the coming of spring and the lexical sets of concrete nouns are directly linked to the environment. One set consists of natural elements (*seed, mead, wood*). The verbs linked to these are dynamic and full of energy as the natural world returns to life after winter. The other set consists of animals (*Ewe, lamb, cow, calf, Bullock, buck*). The relationship between each pair of nouns (parent/offspring) is indicative of the theme of new life at the heart of the poem. The repetition of the concrete noun *cuckoo* is symbolic – its song is a sign that the new season has begun.

The language of the poem is straightforward, perhaps reminiscent of its oral beginnings. It is an ecstatic statement of joy at the start of new life. Although it uses no modifying words to create an atmosphere, the reader is aware of the euphoric tone in the direct simplicity of the nouns and the verbs related to them. The language of Text 2, on the other hand, modifies many of the nouns. The aim is to persuade and the tone is therefore subjective – it communicates a particular point of view. Here the concrete nouns are linked to the lexical set of cookery (*kitchen, pastry, muffins, cakes, puddings*) or to the product itself (*book, instructions, classic, contemporary, pictures, design*). They are chosen to give us a physical sense of the product in terms of its content and form. The modifiers, on the other hand, are persuasive; the copywriter markets the book by choosing words with explicitly positive connotations (*innovative, great, Easy, perfect, mouth-watering, stylish, wonderful*). These help to convince the reader to choose this cookery book rather than another at the point of sale.

Similarly in Text 1, modifying words with positive connotations are used to convince the reader of the advantages of visiting the western coast of Italy. The concrete nouns are preceded by words that communicate the richness of the natural landscape (*silvery, dense, sun-kissed*) and the unique qualities of what the region can offer tourists (*very special, relatively untouched, extravagant, dramatic*). Other modifying words are factual, establishing location (*western*), heritage (*Aragonese, baroque*) and size (*small*).

The use of abstract nouns in these examples is more limited. There are references to time in Text 3 and Text 1. The reference to *Sumer* in the poem sets the time scale in terms of the cyclical patterns of the seasons. Having established this framework of reference, the poet then focuses on the physical features of the natural world to mark the change of seasons. In the travel writing, the abstract nouns of time are on a much larger scale: *millennia* and *Roman times*. Where the poem focuses on a specific moment, the travel writing provides a historical context.

The nouns in Text 1 are more varied because travel writing deals with the conceptual experience of travel as well as the physical details. There are therefore abstract nouns referring to the experience as a whole (*opportunity*) and to the historical significance of Lecce (*testament, importance*). By contrast, the abstract nouns in Text 2 (*ideas, occasions*) are more general, telling the reader something about the appeal of the book.

The form of nouns is mostly as we would expect. We see singular count-nouns where the range of the reference is limited by number to something specific or unique (*village, castle* Text 1; *book* Text 2; *Ewe ... lamb* Text 3) and plural nouns where the references are more general (*tourists, beaches* Text 1; *cakes, pictures* Text 2). The absence of plural nouns in Text 3 reflects the power of the poem as a vision of a particular place at a particular time. More distinctive forms can be seen in the use of the possessive inflection on the proper noun *Italy's* (Text 1) and the use of the adjectives *classic* and *contemporary* (Text 2) as nouns.

We can see from the examples here that different kinds of texts use different kinds of nouns. Where the content focuses on physical detail (travel writing; a poem about the natural world; a product), the nouns are concrete; where there is a wider field of reference (the benefit of travel; historical perspectives), the nouns are often abstract. Concrete language tends to be more direct, and abstract more reflective.

TASK 4   Using concrete nouns in different text types

1 Choose one of the following writing exercises. When you have completed your text, evaluate the key linguistic features. You may like to use the suggested framework for analysis in Appendix A.

EITHER
Write the opening 4–5 paragraphs of a novel in which you aim to create a strong sense of place.

You need to pay particular attention to the physical background, using concrete nouns to build an appropriate visual image for your readers.

OR
Write an extract from a travel guide in which you create a strong sense of a particular real or imagined place.

You need to pay particular attention to the physical background, using concrete nouns to build an appropriate visual image for your readers, but you may also like to refer to the broader experience using abstract nouns.

OR
Write a blurb for a direct-mail or on-line catalogue in which you market a product.

You need to pay particular attention to the physical features of your product, using concrete nouns to highlight what you see as the key selling-points.

3.2 Adjectives

Writers and speakers use adjectives to create atmosphere, develop physical descriptions or express opinions. The choices they make reflect the mood or tone of the text. Where the connotations of the adjectives change, we should be aware of a change in the focus or purpose of the text, or a change in the relationship established with the intended audience.

TASK 1   Creating mood with adjectives

1 Read the following passage carefully.

> It was a dull airless evening. To the east, the grey majesty of the sea was disguised by the breathless calm that hung over it. The distant horizon melted into the monotonous misty sky as idle, shadowy ships dawdled on the indolent waves. To the south, the high ridge of the dyke reared above the desolate beach, spreading a hostile darkness over all that lay beyond the shore. Here the lonely and unprosperous port with its forlorn wharfs and silent warehouses loomed out of the darkness, seemingly a ghost-town.
>
> A lone shaft of wayward light from the melancholic sunset cast its weary gaze over the empty sands, turning rock-pools to blood. Nothing stirred. No delicate breeze, no resplendent gull. Only the sea sluggishly following its tidal path.

2 Underline the adjectives and think about the effects that are created. What kind of mood does the writer create?

3 Re-write the passage using predicative rather than attributive adjectives.

You will need to re-position the adjectives after copular verbs or in parenthesis. You may not be able to include all the adjectives and you may have to make some alterations, but aim to keep your version as close to the original as possible.

4 When you have finished, compare your version with the passage below.

You will probably find that you have made different choices about the way in which to reposition the adjectives. This does not matter – there is no single 'correct' way to tackle this task. Language is flexible and as writers and speakers, we have to learn to make the linguistic choices that best suit the effects we wish to create. Your goal is to understand the way in which your choices affect the meaning: consider how readers will react to your re-write.

> The evening was dull and airless. To the east, the sea lay grey and majestic, apparently breathless in the calm that hung over it. The horizon seemed distant, melting into a sky that was monotonous and misty, while ships, idle and shadowy, dawdled on waves that appeared equally idle. To the south, the ridge of the dyke was high, hostile, rearing above the beach, which grew desolate in the darkness it spread over all that lay beyond the shore. Here the port loomed out of the darkness, lonely and unprosperous, its wharfs and warehouses now forlorn and silent, seemingly a ghost-town.
>
> A shaft of light from the sunset, lone and melancholic, cast its gaze wearily over the sands, which were now empty of the summer crowds. Rock-pools turned to blood, but nothing stirred. No breeze; no gull. Only the sea sluggishly following its path.

5 Write a commentary exploring the effects created by the two versions above.

You should use appropriate terminology and linguistic frameworks to explain and evaluate the texts.

You may like to consider:

- the information communicated to the reader
- the semantic weight of the words
- the focus of each passage
- other linguistic features that interest you

COMMENTARY

Both passages contain exactly the same information, but the grammatical structure of each throws emphasis onto different kinds of words. The attributive adjectives of Passage 1 direct our attention to the nouns they describe; the predicative adjectives of Passage 2 focus on the adjectives themselves, which gain added weight after copular verbs.

In Passage 1, the emphasis is on the nouns which focus on a particular place at a particular moment in time – they create a backdrop for some sequence of events which is about to take place. It is typical of the opening of a story where a settled situation establishes a context which will soon be disrupted. Concrete nouns (*waves, ridge, beach, port, wharfs, warehouses, sands*) establish the physical context; others develop the atmosphere by focusing on the scene at a specific time of day (*evening, horizon, sky, sunset*). The adjectives function as 'attributes' of the nouns, providing detail about the evening (*dull, airless*), the sea (*grey, breathless, indolent*), the sky (*monotonous, misty*), the light from the sunset (*lone, wayward, melancholic, weary*), the shore (*desolate, empty*) and the port (*lonely, unprosperous, forlorn, silent*). The negative connotations of these adjectives set the tone, but we recognise that their position in the sentence is unstressed.

The predicative adjectives of Passage 2, on the other hand, are stressed. Their position after the copular verbs (*was, lay, seemed*) gives them added weight – we recognise their grammatical prominence and thus the semantic importance they have within the text. Similarly, the co-ordinated adjectives in parenthesis (*idle and shadowy, lonely and unprosperous, forlorn and silent, lone and melancholic*) attract our attention both through the patterning of their balanced structures and their isolation within the sentence as a whole. The emphatic position of the adjectives places the mood rather than the physical location at the heart of the extract. The emphasis is on description, on developing an atmosphere that will affect the events and the characters linked to this place.

These narrative passages have been written specifically to demonstrate the difference between predicative and attributive adjectives. The heavy weight of adjectives makes this very dense prose – an equally dramatic effect could have been achieved with fewer adjectives. In your own writing and in texts that you read, writers and speakers will usually be more selective and will combine approaches. You need to make conscious choices: use attributive adjectives where the nouns have a greater semantic significance and predicative adjectives where the adjectives themselves need to be prominent.

1 Write a descriptive passage in which you aim to develop a strong sense of atmosphere.

You need to pay particular attention to the mood you wish to create, using adjectives to build an appropriate atmosphere for your readers.

2 Repeat Task 1, rewriting your passage to develop a contrasting mood.

You need to pay particular attention to the way in which you will change the mood, using adjectives with the opposite connotations to those you initially chose.

When you have completed your texts, evaluate the key linguistic features. You may like to use the suggested framework for analysis in Appendix A.

TASK 3   Adjectives in different text types

1 Read through the examples below carefully and identify the adjectives. Think about the kind of adjectives used in each case and the way in which they relate to the content and purpose of the text.

TEXT 1   Estate agent's details
Cannon Estate Agents are pleased to offer this individually designed, versatile and spacious accommodation. The property is decorated to a very high standard and is set in a lovely rural location. It benefits from double glazing, central heating, en-suite facilities to all four bedrooms and a new fitted kitchen which overlooks a mature and well-stocked garden. With easy access to local shops, primary and secondary schools and good transport links, this is a much sought-after property.

TEXT 2   Extract from a classic novel: *Dracula,* by Bram Stoker (1897)
His face was a strong – a very strong – aquiline, with high bridge of the thin nose and peculiarly arched nostrils; with lofty domed forehead, and hair growing scantily round the temples, but profusely elsewhere. His eyebrows were very massive, almost meeting over the nose, and with bushy hair that seemed to curl in its own profusion.

The mouth, so far as I could see it under the heavy moustache, was fixed and rather cruel-looking, with peculiarly sharp white teeth; these protruded over the lips, whose remarkable ruddiness showed astonishing vitality in a man of his years. For the rest, his ears were pale and at the tops extremely pointed; the chin was broad and strong, and the cheeks firm though thin. The general effect was one of extraordinary pallor.

Hitherto I had noticed the backs of his hands as they lay on his knees in the firelight, and they had seemed rather white and fine; but seeing them now close to me, I could not but notice that they were rather coarse – broad, with squat fingers. Strange to say, there were hairs in the centre of the palm. The nails were long and fine, and cut to a sharp point. As the Count leaned over me and his hands touched me, I could not repress a shudder. (Chapter II)

TEXT 3   Introduction to a Yr 9 English lesson
okay (.) be quiet now please (.) let's get started (1) we've got a new book today (.) it's called Lord of [interruption] no not Lord of the Rings it's Lord of the Flies (2) it's about a group of young boys who crash on a desolate island (1) they are completely alone

so they have to learn to (.) to look after themselves (1) the island is hostile and life i
not easy the writer (.) William Golding (.) has anyone heard of him (3) no (.) well we'll d
some research (.) anyway he focuses on the small details of their lives and we kind c
get dragged into their dark world (.) we'll watch the old film as well (1) it's a black an
white film but still very dramatic (2) who wants to read the first paragraph

2 How have the adjectives contributed to the style and purpose of each text?
In answering this question you should use appropriate terminology and linguisti
frameworks to explain and evaluate the use of adjectives in the three texts.
   You may like to think about:

   • the content and purpose
   • the different types of adjectives (or participle modifiers)
   • the meaning and connotations
   • the position
   • any other linguistic features that interest you

COMMENTARY

Each of these texts has a different purpose. Text 1 is persuasive; it aims to encourage
the reader to buy a particular house. Text 2 is designed to entertain; it engages the
reader by creating a vivid portrait of the main character. Text 3 is informative; i
introduces some background detail as a context for the study of a novel.

   The intended audience in each case is also quite different. Text 1 is produced
for a very specific group: adults who wish to purchase a house. Text 2 aims to attract
an adult readership, but may also be read by others – popular interest in Dracula
films and the horror genre may encourage younger readers. Text 3 is a written
record of the introductory speech at the start of a school English lesson for 13–14
year olds. The adjectives chosen in each case will be appropriate for the intended
audience and purpose of the text, and will affect the style.

   The nouns in Text 1 tend to be concrete because the extract is describing the
physical properties of the house which is for sale. The style is therefore descriptive
and persuasive. There is a recognisable lexical set of concrete nouns common to the
variety: *glazing, heating, bedrooms, kitchen, garden, shops, schools*. Noun synonyms
(*accommodation, property*) prevent the text being repetitive. The adjectives linked
to these nouns are all attributive. Their unstressed position reflects their role in the
text – they are dependent on the concrete reference to which they are linked. As
we would expect, they have positive connotations since the purpose of the text is
persuasive and the modifiers are chosen to attract interest.

   Adjectives such as *versatile, spacious, rural, mature, well-stocked, local* are part
of a common set used by estate agents to make a house seem desirable. Alongside
these are the adjectives that explicitly reflect an attitude: *very high, lovely, easy, good,
sought-after*. While all the adjectives are open to interpretation, these examples in
particular suggest a personal and subjective viewpoint.

   Because the text also needs to be informative, some adjectives provide factual
detail. The numeral *four*, the adjectives in familiar collocations (***double** glazing, **central** heating, **en-suite** facilities, **primary** and **secondary** schools*) and the participle

modifier in the phrase *fitted* kitchen are not persuasive, but objective descriptions of key features of the property.

Text 2, the extract from *Dracula*, is written from the point of view of one of the characters – Jonathan Harker keeps a journal and this is a record of what he wrote on his first meeting with the Count. Stoker's purpose is to create a strong visual portrait of the man at the heart of the novel. While Dracula is now a familiar character to many readers, it is important to remember that this description, which occurs early on in the book, is designed to alert us to some of the key characteristics of the man.

Just as the estate agent's details have a common set of concrete nouns, so too here we see a lexical set of nouns related to the body (*hands, fingers, nails*) and the face (*nose, nostrils, forehead, eyebrows, hair, moustache, teeth, ears, chin, cheeks*). The style is again descriptive with a semantic emphasis placed upon the adjectives. Some do not hint at the nature of the Count, but merely represent his physical features in a neutral way. Adjectives such as *strong, aquiline, high, arched, lofty, bushy, heavy, broad, strong, firm* and *fine* help us to construct a visual sense of his physical features. We do not get the impression from these adjectives that the Count has an evil nature. Instead, he seems a rather distinguished man.

Other adjectives play a significant role in introducing another side to the character. Some hint at the Count's larger than life presence (*massive, pointed*); others characterise his physical strength (*broad, squat*). The critical information, however, comes in the adjectives that have negative connotations. The description of the moustache using the past participle *fixed* and the compound *cruel-looking* begin to hint at Dracula's underlying nature – something which he does not explicitly display in his behaviour at this early stage in the novel. There is an irony in Stoker's choice of the intensifier *rather* preceding the compound adjective since it underplays the negative connotations of *cruel-looking*. It reflects the limitations of the first person narrative, leaving the reader as ignorant as the diary writer. Similarly, the descriptive detail focusing on the Count's teeth (*sharp*) and nails (*long, fine*) has great dramatic significance. The repetition of *sharp* in particular draws attention to elements of his physique that are crucial to the development of the narrative.

Repeated references to Count Dracula's pallor in the adjectives *white* and *pale*, and the adjective *extraordinary* modifying the noun *pallor* set him apart from humanity. This is enhanced by the repetition of the adverb intensifier *peculiarly* and by the contrasts created in the juxtaposition of adjectives (*fine/coarse, strong/thin*). We are encouraged to see the Count as a character of contradictions and this distances him from other characters in the novel.

Stylistically, it is interesting to see that a significant proportion of the adjectives in Text 2 are predicative, throwing additional stress onto semantically important descriptive detail. The emphasis is on Dracula's physical presence (*massive, broad*), on his pallor (*pale, white*) and on his underlying potential for evil (*fixed, cruel-looking, long, fine*). Most of the predicative adjectives follow the copular verb 'to be' (*was/were*), but the description of Dracula's hands follows *seemed*. This hints at the deceptive nature of the man and underpins the conflict between appearance and reality at the heart of the novel.

In Text 3, the style is less formal than the other examples because it is a spoken variety. The focus is less precise: where Text 1 focuses on a particular house and Text 2 on a character description, the adjectives here function in a wider context.

The adjectives in the opening utterances are practical. The first (*quiet*) is predicative allowing the teacher to call the class to order at the start of the lesson. Its position after the verb stresses the adjective. The second (*new*) is attributive: it communicates a particular attribute of the book the teacher is introducing. She then proceeds to outline the framework of the novel, using emotive adjectives to introduce the context of the story: the main characters are represented by the attributive adjective *young*; the setting by the adjective *desolate*. Each is designed to affect the audience. Where the first emphasises the vulnerability of the boys, the negative connotations of the latter colour our view of the island and set the tone that will dominate the narrative. The teacher's choice of the attributive adjective *dark* and the stressed predicative adjectives *alone*, *hostile* and *not easy* reinforce this.

Other adjectives have a more practical function. The reference to the *small details* suggests something about the writer's technique; the description of the film uses adjectives that are factual (*old*, *black and white*); and the use of the ordinal *first* establishes the beginning of a sequence of activities. By contrast, the predicative adjective *dramatic* intensified by *very* reflects the teacher's attitude to the film – she encourages her students to respond positively.

The adjectives in these extracts play a fundamental role in engaging the intended audience and ensuring that the purpose is fulfilled in each case. Text 1 uses adjectives to persuade, to make a sale; Text 2 uses adjectives to characterise, to create a strong physical presence of the Count; and Text 3 uses adjectives to engage the audience, to stimulate interest in the book that is to be studied.

TASK 4   Using adjectives in different text types

1 Choose one of the following writing exercises. When you have completed your text, evaluate the key linguistic features. You may like to use the suggested framework for analysis in Appendix A.

EITHER

Write an estate agent's blurb for a house that you know well.

You need to pay particular attention to the physical details, using adjectives to modify the concrete nouns so that you can communicate the key selling features of the house to your readers. Be persuasive.

OR

Write an extract from an original story in which you develop a strong sense of character.

You need to pay particular attention to the physical details of appearance, using adjectives to modify the concrete nouns. Try to build an appropriate visual image for your readers and begin to develop a sense of the function your character will have in the wider story from which he or she is taken.

OR

Write the opening introduction to a lesson in which pupils are about to begin a new topic.

You need to pay particular attention to the subject you wish to introduce, using adjectives to engage the class and make the topic seem interesting.

.3 Verbs

Writers and speakers use verbs to communicate the action, state or process of a sentence. The choices they make reflect the content and purpose of a text: action texts (such as a sports commentary) are dominated by dynamic verbs; reflective or informative texts are dominated by stative verbs. The form of verbs allows us to communicate subtle differences in meaning. In order to understand exactly what is happening in a text, therefore, we must look closely at the form of verbs. As linguists, it is our job to identify and understand why a text uses a particular kind of verbs.

ASK 1   Audience, purpose and verb form

1 Look through the texts in the previous tasks and try to list four or five key points about the verbs in each text type. You will need to think about the form of the verbs, their meaning and the role they play.

You should look at the recipe, the travel writing, the book description, the poem, the descriptive passage, the estate agent's brochure, the narrative and the spoken text.

COMMENTARY

Each of the eight texts considered in the previous tasks represents a distinctive genre and has a different intended audience and purpose. We would therefore expect there to be differences in the kinds of verbs used, in their forms and in their roles. The following notes record the most noticeable features of the verbs in each text. Although they refer specifically to the examples cited in the tasks, the general principles can be applied to other texts of the same genre or variety.

Recipes

Recipes are instruction texts designed to produce the same outcome each time the process is carried out. Following the numbered sequence is important if the end product is to be successful.

- the verbs are **commands** in the base form telling the reader exactly what to do
  e.g. *Place, heat, cook, Pile*
- the majority of the verbs are **dynamic**, based on a sequence of actions
  e.g. *halve, Scrape out, stir in, Pile*
- many of the verbs are **subject specific** linked directly to cookery
  e.g. *Preheat, Drizzle, season, roast, Crush, cook, set aside, Serve*

- verb **participles** are used descriptively to indicate the changed state of ingredients and to specify a piece of equipment
  e.g. *the **halved** tomatoes*   *a **roasting** tin*
- the verbs are not usually marked for **tense** – they indicate an on-going action and explain the reason for a particular process
  e.g. *Using, to heat*

Travel writing

Travel writing is informative and persuasive. The style is descriptive because the language is designed to create a strong visual image and develop a distinctive point of view.

- **present tense** verbs highlight the potential of a particular location
  e.g. *gives, are, offers, call*
- **stative** verbs are common, describing the features of a place
  e.g. *are, is*
- **participles** are used descriptively focusing attention on details of the place
  e.g. *sun-**kissed**, **winding**, white-**washed**, well-**beaten***
- sentences are rearranged so that *–ed* participle lexical verbs occur after the verb 'to be' (**passive**, see Section 4.4) – the person responsible for the action has no significance
  e.g. *can be traced, be missed*
- **modal** verbs are used to communicate a particular point of view
  e.g. ***should** not be missed*

Sales blurb

This is a form of advertising and the main function of the text is therefore to persuade. It is also necessary, however, to provide some information for readers so that they know what the book contains.

- **present tense** verbs dominate – promotion of a book currently on sale
  e.g. *is, show*
- **stative** verbs are repeated to draw attention to key features
  e.g. *is, 's*
- **participles** are used descriptively to persuade the reader to purchase the book
  e.g. *mouth-**watering***
- the **semantic range** of the verbs is limited – the purpose of the text is to communicate a point of view

Poem

Although poetry varies significantly from text to text, we can comment on the features of this poem as an example of the verse oral tradition. It is composed to be spoken aloud and is therefore clearly patterned so that it is memorable.

- the verbs all have third person singular *–eth* **archaic** inflections
  e.g. *Groweth, bloweth*
- a **stative** verb is used to identify the focus of the poem's content, i.e. statement of fact – 'summer is coming'
  e.g. *is*

- **dynamic** verbs indicate natural activity (arrival of summer)

  e.g. *Springeth, starteth, farteth*
- **repetition** draws attention to the most important sign of summer

  e.g. *sing*

escriptive writing

his kind of writing aims to create a vivid sense of a particular place at a particular
1oment in time. The focus is on description and the purpose is to engage the reader
1 the physical and emotional nature of the location.

- typical of a narrative, verbs are **past tense**

  e.g. *hung, melted, cast*
- the **semantic range** is wide because the writer is using language creatively

  e.g. *dawdled, reared, loomed, stirred*
- a **stative** verb is used emphatically to establish an existing state of affairs

  e.g. *was*
- *-ing* **participles** describe on-going actions creating a sense of inevitability

  e.g. *spreading, turning, following*

state agent's brochure

The purpose of this text is to sell a particular house: the language is therefore per-
uasive. It must also provide general information to indicate some of the physical
haracteristics of the property.

- **stative** verbs are common describing particular features of the property

  e.g. *is*
- verbs are in the **present tense** – characteristics described do not change

  e.g. *benefits, overlooks*
- **participles** are used descriptively to provide detail (subject specific language
  typical of variety)

  e.g. *designed, fitted, well-stocked, sought-after*
- sentences are rearranged so that *–ed* participle lexical verbs occur after the verb
  'to be' (**passive**, see Section 4.4) – the person responsible for the action has no
  significance

  e.g. *is decorated*

Narrative

A narrative text is designed to engage the reader in a fictional world inhabited by
fictional characters. Although different writers each have a distinctive linguistic
approach, they all use language creatively to construct a sense of time, place and
character.

- most verbs are in the **past tense**

  e.g. *showed, protruded, leaned, touched*
- **stative** verbs draw attention to characteristic qualities

  e.g. *was, were, seemed*
- **participles** provide distinctive descriptive detail

  e.g. *arched, domed, fixed, cruel-looking, pointed*

- **primary auxiliary** verbs are used alongside lexical verbs to create a differen[t] time scale – some events are put further in the past
  e.g. *had noticed, had seemed*
- **modal auxiliaries** create shades of meaning

  e.g. *so far as I could see*   (suggests limited point of view)
  I could not but notice   (more emphatic than positive 'noticed')
  I could not repress   (response is instinctive – hints at sinister natur[e] of Dracula)

Spoken

The spoken text mixes formal and informal linguistic features because of its contex[t] and purpose. The purpose (education) and the relationship between teacher an[d] pupils (status/age) are formal, but there is also an element of familiarity – the par[-] ticipants work together regularly and therefore know each other within the contex[t] of the classroom.

- **present tense** verbs dominate – discussion about a text that still exists althoug[h] written in the past
  e.g. *crash, are, is, focuses, wants*
- **contractions** – informal
  e.g. *'ve, 's, 'll*
- **colloquial** multi-word verbs typical of speech
  e.g. *get started, look after, get dragged*
- **future time** is created using a modal verb
  e.g. *'ll do, 'll watch*
- verb **forms** are varied because the text is fulfilling a number of functions (engag[-] ing pupils, communicating information, establishing a plan of action)
  e.g. *be* (command); *'ve got, **has** heard* (prim verb + Ved); *to learn, to read* (Vinf[)] *let's get started* (*let's* + Vbase used to make a suggestion)

TASK 2   Verbs in different text types

1 Read the extracts below and underline the verbs. Label the different kinds of ver[b] forms using appropriate terminology.

TEXT 1   Newspaper sports report

The Greens booked their place in next summer's finals when Colin Jones hit a late goal, snatching qualification from the rivals.

The team began tentatively and their backline was soon uncovered allowing the Dragons' Steve Timms to break through in the fourth minute. He was beaten to the ball by the skilful Brian Kerr. The Greens' keeper smashed Kerr's attempted clearance against the legs of Timms, however, and was lucky that th[e] ball spun out of play rather than into th[e] open net.

In the second half, the Greens wer[e] more controlled at the back.

Gary Davies displayed his talent[s] when he ran at the Dragons' defenc[e] before being beaten to the ball by the vig[-] ilant Robert White.

And the game was finally up for th[e] visitors when they conceded from the free-kick awarded when Michael Dawkins picked up his second booking for using his arm to pull down Andy Moss.

Rick Walker started the move, shifting the ball left for Alec George to take a shot from long range which ricocheted in the area before falling to Jones, who brought the ball under control before coolly slotting it home.

TEXT 2   Extract from David Cameron's Party Conference speech (8 October 2009)

I want to get straight to the point.

We all know how bad things are, massive debt, social breakdown, political disenchantment. But what I want to talk about today is how good things could be.

Don't get me wrong, I have no illusions. If we win this election, it is going to be tough. There will have to be cutbacks in public spending, and that will be painful. We will need to confront Britain's culture of irresponsibility and that will be hard to take for many people. And we will have to tear down Labour's big government bureaucracy, ripping up its time-wasting, money-draining, responsibility-sapping nonsense.

None of this will be easy. We will be tested. I will be tested. I'm ready for that – and so, I believe, are the British people. So yes, there is a steep climb ahead.

But I tell you this. The view from the summit will be worth it.

TEXT 3   Science text book

The preparation of an insoluble salt

To make the insoluble salt AB, two solutions are required: one containing the cation of A and the other the anion of B. This is called a precipitation reaction.

$$AC + DB \rightarrow AB + DC$$

In the preparation of the insoluble salt silver chloride, for example, the solutions used are silver nitrate (soluble salt of silver) and a soluble chloride (sodium, potassium etc).

silver nitrate + sodium chloride $\rightarrow$ silver chloride + sodium nitrate

$$AgNO_3 + NaCl \rightarrow AgCl + NaNO_3$$

Experiment

1. Add the sodium chloride solution to the silver nitrate solution.
2. Allow the white precipitate of silver chloride that will form to settle.
3. Carefully add a few more drops of solution to the supernatant liquid to ensure that all the silver has been precipitated.
4. Use filter papers to filter the precipitate and then wash it with water to remove any contaminating liquids.
5. Dry the solid in an oven.

2 Write a commentary exploring the writers' and speakers' use of verbs and the effects they create in the extracts.

You should use appropriate terminology and linguistic frameworks to explain and evaluate the use of verbs in the three texts.

You may like to think about:

- the content and purpose
- stative and dynamic verbs

- auxiliary (primary/modal) and lexical verbs
- form (past/present tense; participles)
- any other linguistic features that interest you

COMMENTARY

Text 1 is a written account of a football match. We can recognise one of the distinc tive features of the genre in the number of dynamic verbs which describe the action taking place on the pitch: *hit, smashed, spun, ran, to pull down, ricocheted*. Because the focus is on action, there are only two simple past tense stative verbs. The singular primary verb *was* allows the reporter to foreground the predicative adjective *lucky* the plural primary verb *were* focuses attention on the comparative form of the *-ed* participle modifier *controlled*. In each case, the copular verb introduces a descrip tion of a particular state of affairs: the luck of the Greens' keeper; an improvement in the defence players.

In this kind of subject specific writing, it is important to avoid over-using certain verbs. To do this, the reporter replaces a common verb like 'kick' with synonyms: *hit, shifting* and *slotting* could all be replaced by an appropriate form of 'kick'. There are, however, subject specific verbs that can be seen as typical of the lexical field: *to break through, conceded* 'a goal', *awarded* 'a free-kick', *to take* 'a shot'.

In the report, there are examples of language being used creatively to engage the reader. Descriptive verbs (*ricocheted*) and the use of a familiar collocation (*booked their place*) in an unfamiliar context attract our attention. We tend to asso ciate booking a place with buying tickets for a concert, organising a holiday or reg istering for a course. The reporter uses the collocation here to communicate a sense of the anticipation and excitement that accompany the team's win. The dynamic verb *snatching* gives the abstract noun *qualification* a tangible quality; its connota tions reflect the last-minute drama of the match and enhance the excitement.

The verbs are in the simple past tense, reflecting that this is a retrospective report. While some are inflected with the regular past suffix *–ed* (*booked, displayed awarded, started*), others have irregular forms (*hit, began, spun, brought*). The past tense verbs describe actions that are complete, but the non-finite *–ing* participles communicate a sense of on-going action. Dynamic participles such as *snatching, being [beaten], shifting, falling* and *slotting* all mark a moment of dramatic intensity.

While most verbs are in the simple past tense, there are examples of *–ed* par ticiples. In three cases, the participles occur with the primary auxiliary 'to be' (*was … uncovered, was beaten, being … beaten*). These allow the reporter to refocus the sentence (see Section 4.4). In the first example, the emphasis falls on the noun *back- line*, bringing the winning Greens' team into prominence. In the other examples, stress is placed on the proper nouns (*Brian Kerr, Robert White*) following the prepo sition *by*, and the adjectives that precede them (*skilful, vigilant*).

Another noticeable feature of the report is the number of multi-word verbs (*to break through, was … up, picked up, to pull down*). These are often associated with casual conversation, marking the tone here as informal. Some people believe that multi-word verbs should be replaced with single word alternatives: for example, ifiltrate' for *break through*, 'finished' for *was ... up*, 'received' for *picked up* and *loor*' or 'topple' for *pull down*. They see the single word verbs as more formal alternatives that are preferable to the more colloquial verb forms.

The verbs in this report are chosen to communicate the drama and motion of a ootball match. The focus is, therefore, on dynamic verbs which aim to reflect the ctivity on the pitch. By contrast, the verbs in Text 2 tend to be stative rather than ynamic. The frequency with which the stative verb 'to be' recurs in this extract ndicates that David Cameron, at this point Leader of the Opposition, is describing state of affairs. The form of the primary verb varies. Present tense forms describe ie situation as he sees it under the Labour government of the time (*are*), refer to ie immediate context of the party conference speech (*is*), reflect Cameron's cer- ainty that both he (*I'm*) and the British electorate (*are*) are prepared for the diffi- ulties ahead, and introduce a metaphor for the political situation (*is*). Future forms ndicate events that have not yet happened – they emphasise the ways in which ameron believes the Conservative Party could change Britain's future and cata- ogue what a Conservative government will need to do should they win (*is going to e, will have to be, will be*).

Where dynamic verbs are used they have a dramatic impact. The negative con- otations of the dynamic non-finite verbs *to tear down* and *ripping up* are directly ssociated with the participles in the compound modifiers (*time-**wasting**, money- **raining**, responsibility-**sapping***). The effect is to juxtapose the supposed failures f the Labour Party with the severity of action required to restore good governance.

Because this speech is focusing on a hypothetical situation, the use of the base orm after a modal verb (*could be*) reflects 'possibility' – Cameron suggests this is transition point marking the potential for change The form of the verb draws ttention to the fact that what follows is theoretical rather than real, with the future orms marking both Cameron's prediction for the country and Conservative Party ntention.

Other present tense verb forms (*want, know*) allow Cameron to establish what ie sees as the current problems and to engage his audience in a shared vision. The inal lines return to the present tense in an emphatic personal statement (*I'm ready, believe, I tell you*) and an assertion of his belief in the support of the electorate so ... **are** the British people*).

The number of abstract nouns (*debt, breakdown, disenchantment, irresponsi- ility, bureaucracy, nonsense*) contributes to the theoretical and reflective tone of he extract. Their negative connotations clearly indicate the political point of view xpressed in the speech and mirror the traditional antipathy between the Labour nd Conservative Parties. To give the speech a concrete basis, however, Cameron ntroduces the metaphor of climbing a steep hill. The juxtaposition of the certainty f the present tense verb *is* (there **is** a steep climb ahead*) with the emphatic future orm *will be* (*The view from the summit **will be** worth it*) is designed to rouse party nembers to action however difficult the intervening route may seem. This provides climax at the end of the opening section

As is typical of a conference speech, the tone mixes formal and informal lin- juistic features. The abstract nouns and the lexical set of political words (*election, utbacks, public spending, government bureaucracy*) mark this text as formal – a tone that reflects the public and official nature of the occasion. There are, howeve some linguistic constructions associated with informal conversation:

- contractions (*Don't, I'm*)
- the colloquial use of the verbs 'to get' and 'to take' in informal expressions (*g straight to the point, Don't get me wrong, hard to take*)
- multi-word verbs (*to tear down, ripping up*)
- the use of conjunctions at the start of sentences rather than in the middle

All these linguistic features contribute to the informality of the speech, allowing th leader of the Conservative Party to speak to the conference delegates in a more per sonal way. They underpin the persuasive and rhetorical patterning of the repeate phrases and ensure that Cameron engages his audience.

Text 3 is taken from a subject specific science textbook. We see this immediate because of the subject specific language. Concrete nouns predominate in the name of chemicals (*silver nitrate, sodium chloride*), products (*solutions, precipitate, solid* equipment (*filter papers*) and technical terms (*cation, anion*). While a noun like *sa* is familiar, it is used here with a specific scientific meaning. On the other hand, th adjective *supernatant* is likely to be unfamiliar: it is a subject specific term denotir the liquid left on top of the precipitate. This kind of language marks the intende audience of the text as specialist.

Because the purpose of the text is to inform and to instruct, it begins with th general case for preparing a salt (information) and concludes with a step-by-ste experiment (instruction). The verb forms are therefore different in each section The title uses an abstract noun (*preparation*) which has its semantic root in the ver 'to prepare'. This description of the process is then communicated by the non-finit verb *To make*. Other verbs in the information section tend to be stative since the describe chemical properties (*are*). Non-finite participles (*containing, used*) give u additional information about the chemicals. The final verb in this opening sectio is typical of scientific texts. Because we are less interested in who is doing the exper iment than in the outcome, lexical *–ed* participles are often used after the verb 't be' (*are required*).

	aux	lex
… two solutions	are	required.
(thing affected)	prim	V*ed*

We call this the passive voice (see Section 4.4). It allows us to rearrange a sentenc by:

- eliminating who is responsible for the action of a verb
- bringing the thing that is affected by the verb to the front of the sentence,

We could rearrange the example here:

	lex	
Scientists	require	two solutions.
(person responsible)	V*pres*	(thing affected)

In the instruction section, the verbs are mostly command forms – they tell the per son carrying out the experiment what to do: *Add, Allow, wash* and *Dry*. Non-finit infinitive forms are common. They provide extra information about the reason for doing something (*to ensure, to remove*) or highlight a process that must be com-

leted before moving on (*to settle*). The text also uses the modal verb 'will' + base
ɔrm to indicate the predicted outcome of the process (*will form*) and a passive
tructure to bring the subject specific noun *silver* into a position of prominence.

<table>
<tr><td></td><td>aux   aux</td><td></td></tr>
<tr><td>all the silver</td><td>has been</td><td>precipitated</td></tr>
<tr><td>(thing affected)</td><td>prim prim</td><td>Ved</td></tr>
</table>

We could rearrange the sentence:

<table>
<tr><td></td><td>aux   lex</td><td></td></tr>
<tr><td>the solution</td><td>has precipitated</td><td>all the silver</td></tr>
<tr><td>(thing responsible)</td><td>prim   Ved</td><td>(thing affected)</td></tr>
</table>

While some verbs are commonplace (*Add, Dry*), others are subject specific (*pre-
ipitated, filter*). Verbs are particularly important in the instruction section because
he reader is being led through a sequence of actions in order to prove the theory
ɔf the informative section.

Verbs are central to written and spoken language – they shape texts according
ɔ their form and meaning. Each of these texts here has a different purpose and this
neans that the verbs take different forms. Stative verbs allow writers and speakers
ɔ focus on a particular state of being – a description of something or a state of
ɪffairs that exists. Dynamic verbs, on the other hand, focus on actions and processes.
Changes in time scale allow us to:

- reflect on completed actions (e.g. past tense verbs in a newspaper report)
- describe an existing state of affairs (e.g. present tense verbs in a political speech
  or information text)
- develop contrasts with a hypothetical future or indicate a potential outcome
  (e.g. 'future time' verb structures in political speeches or instruction texts)

We can also use command forms to direct readers or passive sentences (see Section
1.4) to rearrange key elements.

All of these choices control the semantic effect a verb has in a particular text.
We may be familiar with the everyday meaning of a verb, but we must also take
account of its form in each particular context and recognise how this modifies its
denotation. Equally, we may need to comment on a specialist meaning existing
alongside the general meaning; a verb being used in an unexpected context to surprise and engage us; or subject specific verbs occurring in a particular technical
field of reference that are new to us. In doing so, we can begin to understand the
relationship between form and meaning.

TASK 3   **Using verbs in different text types**

1 Choose one of the following writing exercises. When you have completed your
text, evaluate the key linguistic features. You may like to use the suggested framework for analysis in Appendix A.

EITHER

Write a newspaper report in which you summarise and evaluate a particular
event, informing your audience and communicating an opinion. You could write
about a football or rugby match, a fashion show, a film premiere, a book launch,
or some other occasion that interests you.

You need to pay particular attention to the tense, form and connotations of th verbs so that you can effectively describe and comment on what took place.

OR

Write the opening of a speech in which you explain how you will change thing for the better. You could write as a school council representative, as a politica party leader, as a club organiser or as a company rep.

You need to pay particular attention to the range of verb forms that you use in orde to create a contrast between what is happening now and what you will do to chang things. You must persuade your audience that they should support you.

OR

Write an extract from a subject specific text book in which you inform your read ers about a particular topic area. It will be important to establish the age of you readers before you start.

You need to pay particular attention to the use of subject specific verbs and a rang of verb forms. Think carefully about organising your content (structure and layout

3.4 Adverbs

We use adverbs to provide additional information and the kind of adverbs chose reflects the tone, function and meaning of a text. Adjuncts develop descriptive detai about time, place and manner. They can have positive or negative connotations an help writers and speakers to establish a tone. Disjuncts also affect the tone of a tex by communicating the attitudes or comments of speakers and writers. They are cho sen to influence the intended audience. Conjuncts, on the other hand, have a struc tural function. They enable us to create links by establishing a contrast o connection between sentences. These are often used in formal contexts since they help us to develop an argument or a particular point of view.

TASK 1   The function of adverbs

1 Read the three texts below carefully.

PASSAGE 1A

The mist hung eerily over the landscape, which stretched away tauntingly as far as the eye could see. The sun, meanwhile, hid sulkily behind low-lying clouds, adding to the atmosphere and the general air of the place. Everywhere water dripped into greedily expanding puddles, while the lush greenery grew relentlessly, twisting its way into the smallest crevices and splitting rocks ruthlessly. Unfortunately, the heat quickly reached such high temperatures that there were often sudden downpours. Perhaps the land-scape attracted those forms of life that yearned inexplicably for the damp, but for us it was alien, disagreeably clammy and unbearably hot.

PASSAGE 1B

The mist hung over the landscape, which stretched as far as the eye could see. The sun hid behind low-lying clouds, adding to the atmosphere and the general air of the place. Water dripped into expanding puddles, while the lush greenery grew, twisting its way into the smallest crevices and splitting rocks. The heat reached such high temperatures that there were sudden downpours. The landscape attracted those forms of life that yearned for the damp, but for us it was alien, clammy and hot.

PASSAGE 1C

The mist hung thinly over the landscape, which stretched away enticingly as far as the eye could see. The sun, sometimes, hid teasingly behind low-lying clouds, adding to the atmosphere and the general air of the place. Delicately, water dripped into gracefully expanding puddles, while the lush greenery grew elegantly, twisting its way into the smallest crevices and splitting rocks artistically. Fortunately, the heat occasionally reached such high temperatures that there were surprisingly sudden downpours. Understandably, the landscape attracted those forms of life that yearned consistently for the damp, but for us it was alien, pleasurably clammy and satisfyingly hot.

2 Underline the adverbs.
3 Make notes on the use of adverbs in each version of the text, commenting on the effects created.

You may like to think about:

- the nouns and adjectives
- the type of adverbs
- the connotations of the adverbs
- the position of the adverbs
- the semantic effect of each passage

COMMENTARY

The passages are all identical in form and language except for the presence or absence of adverbs. By starting with Passage 1B, it is possible to draw some conclusions about the language of the basic text:

▶ it is dominated by concrete nouns (*mist, sun, clouds, Water, puddles, greenery, crevices, rocks, downpours, landscape*) – this helps the writer to create a strong physical sense of place
▶ the connotations of some of the adjectives could be seen as negative (*low-lying, alien, clammy*)
▶ only one is explicitly positive (*lush*)
▶ most modifiers are neutral, providing factual information (*expanding, high, sudden, hot*)

This means that the reader is not influenced by the language the writer has chosen – the description of the landscape in Passage 1B allows us the opportunity to imagine the place in our own way.

The adverbs added to Passage 1A alter this by manipulating our response to the landscape. While some provide factual information, most are used to develop a negative tone. We can observe the following:

- factual adverbs provide details about place (*away, Everywhere*), time (*quickly* and frequency (*often*) – they do not create a particular mood
- most of the adjuncts give us information about 'how?'
  e.g. *eerily, relentlessly* (negative connotations)
- many reflect human characteristics, personifying the natural environment and creating a threatening sense of purpose
  e.g. *tauntingly, sulkily, greedily, ruthlessly*
- the degree adverbs have negative connotations – encouraging the reader to see the landscape in the same way
  e.g. **disagreeably** *clammy*, **unbearably** *hot*
- negative connotations are reinforced by disjuncts (*Unfortunately, inexplicably* – indicating narrator attitude
- the disjunct *Perhaps* draws attention to a conflict of attitudes: two different viewpoints are established (human inhabitants vs. natural life)
- reinforced by the opposition created between the positive connotations of the verbs *attracted/yearned* and the negative adjective *clammy*
- the disjuncts *Unfortunately* and *Perhaps* have semantic importance positioned at the front of the sentence

The adverbs in Passage 1A alter our response to the basic text by manipulating our experience of the landscape. The connotations of the adjuncts and the attitude communicated by the disjuncts distance us from the description by creating a negative atmosphere.

The adverbs added to Passage 1C also alter our response to the landscape. While some provide factual information, most are used to develop a positive tone. We can observe the following:

- factual adverbs provide details about place (*away*) and frequency (*sometimes, occasionally, consistently*) – they do not create a particular mood
- most of the adjuncts give us information about 'how?' and their connotations are positive – the landscape is portrayed as something of beauty and fragility
  e.g. *Delicately, gracefully, elegantly*
- the addition of adverbs can alter the semantic effect of certain words – *mist* often has negative connotations, but the addition of the adverb *thinly* modifying *hung* alters the balance
- a few adjuncts reflect human characteristics – personification (natural world as a playful and creative creature)
  e.g. *enticingly, teasingly, artistically*
- degree adverbs with positive connotations are used to modify adjectives
  e.g. **pleasurably** *clammy*, **satisfyingly** *hot*
- the positive connotations are underpinned by disjuncts in a stressed position at the front of the sentence
  e.g. *Fortunately, Understandably* (attitude of narrator)
- the disjunct *Understandably* draws attention to another point of view – the narrator appreciates a different way of seeing things

The adverbs in Passage 1C alter our response to the basic text by manipulating our experience of the landscape in a different way. The connotations of the adjuncts

nd disjuncts draw us into the landscape, encouraging us to see it in a positive
ght.

What these three versions of the same text show is that we can recreate a com-
letely different visual image by adding or changing the adverbs.

1 Write a descriptive passage in which you aim to develop a strong sense of atmosphere.

You need to pay particular attention to the mood you wish to create, using adjuncts
to give information about manner, time and place, and disjuncts to express attitude.
Aim to build an appropriate atmosphere for your readers through your choice of
adverbs.

2 Repeat Task 1, rewriting your passage to develop a contrasting mood.

You need to pay particular attention to the way in which you will change the mood,
using adjuncts and disjuncts with the opposite connotations to those you chose for
Task 1.

When you have completed your texts, evaluate the key linguistic features. You
may like to use the suggested framework for analysis in Appendix A.

ASK 3   Adverbs and meaning

1 Read the following extracts and identify the adverbs.

TEXT 1   Extract from a museum brochure

Here there is evidence of a restless earth and of forces capable of folding already
folded rocks. Earth-shaping events are taking place everywhere. Gradually, oceans
grow wider, tremors crack the ground and volcanoes erupt violently. We literally cannot
contain these forces: the cataclysmic events that have previously shaped the earth
will change it again. Perhaps we will not see these changes ourselves, but we know
that the shaping of our world is not yet finished.

    The natural cycle will indeed continue its progress steadily, changing the land slowly
over millions of years and sculpting new global landscapes. We have now begun to
understand this process, but, in the face of such titanic forces, there is little we can do
to alter the next stage in this epic story.

TEXT 2   Directions from a television script

The changing-room
*(Lit dimly, the room is bleak, with huddles of boys talking sporadically as they change.
The graffitied walls and dirty floor give the room a feeling of neglect. Carelessly bundled
clothes have slipped to the floor and the boys move spiritlessly.*

    *As the teacher passes casually through the room, the mood changes. The boys
shrink almost fearfully away from him as he passes. No-one catches his eye, instead
staring blankly into the middle distance. He stops suddenly in front of a lone boy and
glares threateningly.*

The bell rings brightly breaking the spell. The teacher moves away hurriedly and th *boys quickly grab clothes and bags. As we fade in, the face of the lone boy fills th* *screen: grey eyes, mousy hair and a look of terror fleetingly replaced by relief.*

TEXT 3   Extract from a debate

Two hundred years ago, the transatlantic slave trade was finally abolished. On the nigh that the Act of Parliament was passed, Reverend William Knibb declared, 'The monste is dead!' On the 27th March 2007, a commemoration service took place at Westminste Abbey to celebrate this momentous occasion. But was the 'monster' really dead c should we consider this as unfinished business? Should we perhaps ask ourselves 'is there a monster yet to slay?' Morally, have we done all that we can?

Around the world, children are still being trafficked. They are still being exploitec They are still being enslaved. They are still being forced to work in horrific conditions This new 'monster', however, doesn't require a hero, a William Wilberforce, to fight th good fight. Fortunately, what we need today are just ordinary people and small actions

2 Write a commentary exploring the effects created by the adverbs in each case.

You should use appropriate terminology and linguistic frameworks to explain anc evaluate the texts.

You may like to think about:

- the genre of each extract and its intended audience
- the kind of adverbs included (adjuncts, conjuncts, disjuncts)
- their contribution to the meaning
- any other linguistic features of interest

COMMENTARY

Each of the three extracts here communicates information, but for different reasons The first text aims to use information to educate museum visitors; the second to entertain viewers by creating an atmospheric context in which the drama can unfold; the third to persuade the audience to adopt the speaker's viewpoint. Because of these different functions, the type of adverbs used in each text is different.

Text 1 focuses on a description of the geological processes that have shaped the earth over millions of years. While there is one adjunct of manner expressing the power of these natural forces (*violently*), most refer to time and place. The adverbs of place are general references: *Here* (an exophoric reference relating to the wider context of the museum) and *everywhere* (broadening the reference to the whole earth). Time references, however, dominate the text. They communicate the scale of the processes involved: we get a sense of the past (*previously*), the present state of affairs (*yet, now*) and the changes still to come (*again*). Other references reflect the speed of the changes (*Gradually, steadily, slowly*) and their cyclical and inescapable nature – the modifier *already* reinforces our sense that the process is repeating itself.

Because Text 1 is a formal educational text, there are few disjuncts: an expression of attitude is secondary to the communication of factual information. The writer's use of *literally* is the closest we get to an expression of attitude. The adverbs therefore tend to have neutral connotations with the emphasis falling on description of the time scale. There is only one conjunct (*indeed*), which is emphatic and develops a sense of inevitability.

Where Text 1 is dominated by time adjuncts to draw attention to the time scale of the geological changes it describes, Text 2 uses manner adjuncts to develop the atmosphere. Most of the adverbs in the script directions give us additional information about the boys and their teacher, but *dimly* and *Carelessly* describe the physical scene. Their negative connotations immediately colour our response to the changing room and prepare us for the uneasy relationship which seems to exist between the boys and their teacher.

The adjunct of time (*sporadically*) establishes the mood of the boys and is reinforced by the negative connotations of *spiritlessly* and *almost fearfully*. These adverbs, which describe the way the boys move, are directly contrasted with the adverb *casually*: the nonchalance and self-assurance of the teacher reflect his dominance in the room. The opposition created between *blankly* and *threateningly* and the verbs to which they are grammatically linked (*staring/glaring*) develops this by drawing attention to the way in which the boys try to become invisible.

A turning point in the scene is marked by the use of the time adjunct *suddenly*. It is dramatic because it is the point at which the teacher identifies a particular boy as his victim. The tension, however, is relieved by the ringing of the school bell at the end of the lesson. The adjunct *brightly* changes the mood – it is the only explicitly positive adverb in Text 2 and saves the *lone boy* from something we suspect would have been unpleasant. The focus then returns to movement with the adjuncts *hurriedly* and *quickly* suggesting that both the teacher and the boys are aware of the tension in the room. As the camera zooms in on the face of the boy, the juxtaposition of the nouns *terror/relief* and the adjunct *fleetingly* characterise the boy as a victim. He may have been saved by the bell this time, but he knows that his respite is only temporary.

The adverbs in Text 2 are designed to be emotive. They contribute to setting the scene (adjuncts of place), characterisation (adjuncts of manner) and plot development (adjuncts of time). In Text 3, however, they fulfil a wider range of functions. Time adjuncts create a link between 200 years ago when slavery was abolished (*finally*) and now (*yet, still, today*). The function of the adverbs is to persuade the audience that there is still work to be done – that slavery continues to exist around the world if we open our eyes to see it. The adverbs challenge our complacency: the persistent repetition of *still* and the negative verbs it modifies (*trafficked, exploited, enslaved, forced*) drives home the point the speaker wishes to make.

The adverbs have an emotive effect on us and this is reinforced by the disjuncts. Each performs a slightly different function: *perhaps* gives us the opportunity to recognise for ourselves what ought to be done; *Morally* foregrounds the ethical choice – its position at the front of a direct question makes the only possible answer to the question 'no'; *Fortunately* brings the moral argument to its climax since we are forced to realise that this is now an issue for which we all have responsibility. Our accountability is reinforced by the degree adverb *just* which modifies the phrases *ordinary people* and *small actions*. The emphasis is on encouraging us to recognise how easy it is to make a difference.

By looking at these three texts, it is possible to see a direct link between the choice of adverbs and the function and tone of a text. The disjuncts, along with the conjunct *however*, are distinctive to Text 3 because its tone is formal and its function is to persuade. In Texts 2 and 3, on the other hand, adjuncts of time, place and manner have a greater semantic weight because the emphasis is on description.

TASK 4   Using adverbs in different text types

1 Choose one of the following writing exercises. When you have completed your text, evaluate the key linguistic features. You may like to use the suggested framework for analysis in Appendix A.

EITHER
Write a set of directions for the producer of a television or stage production. Introduce a context and characters using adverbs to create the atmosphere and to develop a sense of character relationships.

You need to pay particular attention to the way in which you create the mood and relationships, using adjuncts to provide additional information about time, place and manner, and disjuncts to communicate attitude.

OR
Write the opening of an opinion or argument essay in which you have to convince your readers of a particular point of view.

You need to pay particular attention to your choice of adverbs. Use adjuncts to establish any key details of time, place or manner, but disjuncts and conjuncts should be your main focus. These are critical to the effect of your argument on the reader since they help to communicate attitude and develop a logical structure.

OR
Write an extract from a tourist brochure in which you both inform readers of a particular place, exhibition or topic and persuade them to visit it.

You need to pay particular attention to your choice of adjuncts, but you may wish to use disjuncts to communicate your attitude and conjuncts to create connections between sentences.

3.5 Conjunctions

Conjunctions are very useful because they enable us to join words, phrases and clauses. This prevents unnecessary repetition and creates interesting structural connections between different elements of a text. By understanding the function of conjunctions, we can begin to see how texts influence us: additive and contrastive conjunctions have different semantic effects and we need to be able to evaluate the role they play in each context.

1 Read the passage below and identify the conjunctions.

The air had been warm and transparent through the whole of the bright day. Shining metal spires and church-roofs, distant and rarely seen, had sparkled in the view; and the snowy mountain-tops had been so clear that unaccustomed eyes, cancelling the intervening country, and slighting their rugged height for something fabulous, would have measured them as within a few hours' easy reach. Mountain-peaks of great celebrity in the valleys, whence no trace of their existence was visible sometimes for months together, had been since morning plain and near, in the blue sky. And now, when it was dark below, though they seemed solemnly to recede, like spectres who were going to vanish, as the red dye of the sunset faded out of them and left them coldly white, they were not yet distinctively defined in their loneliness, above the mists and shadows.

Little Dorrit, Charles Dickens (1855–7) 411

2 Decide whether the conjunctions are co-ordinating or subordinating and under-line the grammatical units they link.
3 Write a commentary which explores the effects created by the conjunctions and the ways in which they underpin the meaning.

You should use appropriate terminology and linguistic frameworks to explain and evaluate the texts.

You may like to think about the function and the effect they have on the meaning:

· are they joining words or phrases?
· are they joining clauses or sentences?
· are the grammatical units dependent (do not make sense by themselves) or inde-pendent (make sense by themselves)?

COMMENTARY

In this descriptive extract, Dickens uses mainly co-ordinating conjunctions. The focus is on a particular landscape on a particular day as light gives way to the dark-ness of night. The repetition of *and* allows him to mirror the beauty of the day in the balanced patterning of the style. To emphasise the unique nature of this occa-sion, Dickens draws attention to key elements of the landscape in the co-ordinated nouns *Shining metal **spires** and **church-roofs***. These become symbols of the day's brightness while co-ordinated adjectives communicate the mood: *warm and trans-parent* are tactile adjectives, creating a sense of the physical qualities of the air; *dis-tant and rarely seen* suggest the grand perspective of the scene and the uniqueness of this particular day.

The whole passage appeals to our senses and, having focused on the manmade landmarks, Dickens turns to the mountain-tops. The co-ordinating conjunction at the end of line 2 after the semi-colon links the sentence about the distant churches to the sentence about *the snowy mountain-tops*. By co-ordinating two independent grammatical units which make sense on their own, Dickens is able to create a semantic balance – we recognise the importance of both elements of the landscape.

The grandeur of the mountains is emphasised by the co-ordination of two clauses which draw attention to the insignificance of people (reduced to *unaccustomed eyes*) in this landscape: *cancelling the intervening country,* **and** *slighting their rugged height for something fabulous.* Even as dark falls, the shadowy presence of the mountain tops is felt: the simile of them as *spectres* and the personification of *their loneliness* give them added semantic weight in the narrative.

Dickens draws attention to the change from day to night by using a co-ordinating conjunction at the beginning of a sentence. Its emphatic position has semantic significance and is reinforced by the adjunct *now*. To underpin this grammatical marker, Dickens develops a contrast between the co-ordinated adjectives *plain and near*, describing the mountains in daylight, and the co-ordinated verbs *faded out ... and left.*

Subordinating conjunctions are used to provide additional information. Dickens uses *whence* ('from where') to emphasise the unique nature of the day since the mountains are often not visible *for months together*. It is a subordinating conjunction of place which reinforces the contrast between the valleys *below* and the mountains above. The following sentence uses three subordinating conjunctions to develop this contrast, building to a climax in the emphatic independent clause *they were not yet distinctly defined ....* The time conjunction *when* describes the darkness of the valley, while the subordinating conjunction of concession (*though*) marks the different kind of change that darkness brings to the mountains, which *recede* but do not disappear. The subordinating conjunction of time *as* also draws attention to the change, setting *the red dye of the sunset* against the *coldly white* mountain peaks.

In a practical sense, conjunctions enable us to create links between grammatical units, but they can also play an important part in communicating meaning: they control the way in which we receive and process information. We can see in this extract that Dickens has used them to develop a balanced pattern of descriptive details and to build a contrast between two key elements of the landscape.

Part **II**

Phrases

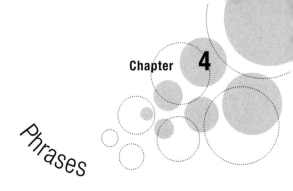

Chapter 4

Phrases

Phrases are our next step in this grammatical journey. They are part of every sentence we speak or write and yet many of us are not conscious of their presence. They are made up of groups of words that are dependent on each other and do a particular job in a sentence. The work you have just done on words will help you to see the underlying patterns which bind particular words together into strings.

After working through this chapter, you should be able:

▸ to understand the relationships between words in distinctive lexical strings
▸ to recognise and label different kinds of phrases
▸ to describe their position in a sentence
▸ to understand the jobs they do

4.1 What is a phrase?

A PHRASE is a grammatical structure made up of a head word and any modifying words, phrases or clauses. It may consist of a single word (which could be expanded), or a group of words that are linked grammatically.

Even without the grammatical terminology that helps us to label them, we can instinctively see the connections between groups of words. If we look at a sentence, for instance, we will see the links.

The little boy was running very excitedly around the garden.

Because we understand this sentence, we would probably all divide it into the same lexical units:

The little boy

was running

very excitedly

around the garden.

It seems logical to connect *The + little + boy* because we recognise their semantic relationship: the determiner and the adjective give us important information about the concrete noun. Similarly, we see the connection between *was* and *running* – we know they are both verbs and that the PRIMARY VERB 'to be' is being used as an auxiliary to construct a distinctive time scale with the *–ing* participle.

Having identified the various units or phrases, we could probably all recognise which word was most important in each phrase:

> The little **boy**
>
> was **running**
>
> very **excitedly**
>
> around the **garden**.

The highlighted words carry the semantic weight in each lexical unit – they communicate the meaning while the other words in the phrase support or develop them. From this we see that while phrases can be made up of a number of words, one carries more weight than the others.

In a single word phrase, only the most important lexical item is used:

> Clouds bring snow occasionally.

Here each word constitutes a different phrase and fulfils a different grammatical function. It would be possible, however, to expand each one with additional words that provide extra information.

> (Low dark **clouds**) (will **bring**) (light icy **snow**) (very **occasionally**).

The key lexical items of each phrase are preceded by words fulfilling different functions: the adverb *very* qualifies *occasionally*, suggesting the infrequency of the event; the adjectives *Low, dark, light* and *icy* provide descriptive detail; the modal auxiliary *will* implies a future or hypothetical time scale.

We can use the principle of expansion to test for a phrase. From your instinctive understanding of language and the work you have done in Part I, you already know the kind of words that occur alongside nouns, verb, adjectives and adverbs. This allows us to experiment with the ways in which a single word can be expanded into a longer unit by adding extra words before and after it. We know, for instance, that determiners and adjectives can come before a noun, but adverbs and present tense verbs cannot.

those nasty little boys ✓	the slowly is dog ✗
det Adj Adj N	det Adv V N

We know that auxiliary verbs in a statement come before a lexical verb, but not after it.

aux lex	lex aux
The girl (was sprinting). ✓	The girl (sprinted has). ✗
prim V*ing*	V*ed* prim
lex aux	aux lex
The girl (sprint will). ✗	The girl (can sprint). ✓
V*base* mod	mod V*base*

When we begin to look at different types of phrases, you will be able to use the knowledge you have to check whether a single word is functioning as a phrase. If you can expand the word with the addition of other grammatically linked words and it still makes sense, it is a phrase.

It is this capacity for expansion that makes phrases such an interesting grammatical structure – writers and speakers can influence their intended audience by:

- adding descriptive detail
- changing the time scale of verbs
- indicating the intensity or frequency of an event
- suggesting something about time and place

a formalist approach

When we considered the sentence about the clouds and the snow, we divided it into four distinct units, each with one word carrying more semantic weight than the others.

(Low dark **clouds**) (will **bring**) (light icy **snow**) (very **occasionally**).

A formal syntactic analysis would consider the relationship between phrases in a different way. It would use two additional tests to check whether a group of words is functioning as a discrete phrase:

- can we replace a group of words with a single word?
- can we move the group of words as a unit?

If we apply the replacement test to the sentence, we can see the underlying syntactic relationships between the words.

(Low dark **clouds**) (will bring) (light icy snow) (very occasionally), but (white clouds) (**do**) (too).

We can replace the verbs *will bring* and the phrases that follow them with the verb *do* and the sentence still makes sense. The verb 'do' allows us to avoid repeating the same words – the lexical unit *will bring light icy snow very occasionally* is implied. We can also replace *Low dark clouds* with the pronoun *They*.

(**They**) (will bring) (light icy snow) (very occasionally), but (white clouds) (**do**) (too).

In formal analysis, this would suggest that there are two constituent phrases.

(Low dark **clouds**) (will **bring** light icy snow very occasionally).

Formal grammar explores the general principles for generating grammatical sentences by considering idealised examples of language. It is interested in the underlying knowledge we have that enables us to use and understand language. Functional grammar, on the other hand, considers the ways in which our use of language is shaped by the choices we make. Focusing on concepts like audience, purpose, context and text type, it looks at how meaning is created and how we can communicate effectively. Because this book is focusing on the meaning and use of grammar in real situations and real texts, it will adopt the functional approach rather than the formal analytical one.

Why learn about phrases?

Phrases are at the heart of grammatical analysis. Derived from five of the key word classes in Chapter 2, they combine words in distinctive patterns. If you want to understand how language works, you need to be able to discuss their form, position and function.

While we instinctively recognise the connections between strings of words, w
will have a better understanding of the rules underlying language if we can explai
the patterns. This section therefore introduces the linguistic terminology that help
us to identify and label the five different types of phrase used in English, each c
which has a distinctive structure and function. You will learn to identify wher
phrases start and stop, to understand their structure, and to see the ways in whic
we can develop or move them.

Labelling phrases

In order to understand the structure of phrases, we need to be able to label thei
constituent parts in terms of their FORM (word class or type of phrase/clause) an
their FUNCTION (the job they do in a phrase). This allows us to focus specifically o
the words a writer or speaker chooses and the effects they create. We use the labe
as a form of shorthand to annotate examples. Function labels are used above, whil
form labels are used below. To mark the beginning and end of a phrase, we us
round brackets.

> (The day) (broke) (over the mountain) and (we) (began) (our descent).

To label the **form** of words we use WORD CLASS terminology (N, V, Adv, det, pror
prep, conj), as well as **phrase** (AdjP, PrepP) and **clause** (RelCl, NCl, NFCl, CompCl
ACl) terminology. While you will find out more about clauses in Part III, this chapte
shows you how to <u>recognise</u> the form of words used in a phrase. To mark a SUBOR
DINATE CLAUSE within a phrase we use square brackets – we call this an EMBEDDEI
CLAUSE because it is dependent on the head of the phrase in which it occurs.

> (The <u>day</u> [which was so important to us all]) (finally) (broke) (over the mountain).

There are three key terms to describe the **function**: the head, pre-modifiers
post-modifiers. As we have already seen, one word in a phrase carries more weigh
than the others. We call this the HEAD WORD (h) – it is the most important semanti
element. Any related words that come before the head are called PRE-MODIFIERS (m
– they modify the head word. Any words that come after the head are called POST-
MODIFIERS or QUALIFIERS (q) – they qualify the head word.

In the example below, the labels on the top tell us what job each word is doing
and the labels beneath identify the type of word or phrase.

> FUNCTION   m   m   m   m   h
>   the flowing cool freshwater **stream**
> FORM   det   *Ving*   AdjP   N   N

We can use the expansion test to decide whether to use a word class or a phrase
label. We know from our work on verbs that we can add the primary auxiliary verb
be before the –*ing* participle. If we try to do this in the example here, however, the
phrase would no longer make sense.

> the (is flowing) cool freshwater **stream** ✗

This tells us that the verb *flowing* has to be labelled V*ing* – it is not functioning as
part of a phrase. If we add an adverb before the adjective *cool*, however, the sentence
does still make sense.

the flowing (really cool) freshwater **stream**. ✓

his tells us that the adjective is functioning as part of a phrase – we therefore label
: AdjP rather than Adj.

It is useful to be able to distinguish between the function and the form because
ometimes a word which appears to be identical can be functioning in very different
vays.

the light blue shirt   the desk light

n each example here the word *light* looks identical, but it is in a different position
n the phrase and is doing a different job. In the first case, *light* is part of an adjective
ohrase (see Section 4.3) in which it modifies the adjective *blue*; in the second, it is
t noun, the head word of the phrase. If we were to annotate the examples, they
vould look like this:

m	m	h
the (light blue) shirt

det   AdjP   N
Adj Adj

m	m	h
the desk light

det   N   N

4.2 Noun phrases (NP)

NOUN PHRASES are phrases where the key word is a noun – we call this the **head
word**. They are, along with verb phrases (see Section 4.4), the most important grammatical elements of English. They occur frequently and can be long and complex.

Simple noun phrases

In a single word noun phrase, only the head word is used and the phrase is described
as a **simple noun phrase**.

tree   bookcase   politician   Jack

If a determiner precedes the head word, the phrase is still described grammatically as a simple noun phrase.

a tree   this bookcase   the politician

It is important to remember that **pronouns** can also be the head of a simple noun
phrase because they act as a substitute for a noun. They are described as the acting
head of a noun phrase.

the tree → it   the politician → he/she   the boys and I → we

In some instances, an **adjective** can function as the head of a noun phrase.

the old   the beautiful   the wise

In examples like these, a noun is understood although it is not actually part of the
phrase – the adjectives above are implicitly linked to the noun 'people' and the
phrases could be expanded to include it as the head word. Semantically, however,
the use of the adjectives places greater emphasis upon the qualities of 'age', 'beauty'
and 'wisdom' rather on the people themselves.

Where noun phrases are expanded by the addition of extra words, we describe them as **complex noun phrases**. These can contain words before the head word (pre-modification), after the head word (post-modification), or both before and after (pre- and post-modification).

> the <u>leafy</u> **tree**   the **bookcase** <u>with warped shelves</u>
>
> the <u>local</u> **politician** <u>who fights for human rights</u>

In these examples, the head word of each noun phrase is in bold and the additional information is underlined. Different kinds of words and phrases can be used to expand a noun phrase and it is important to be able to recognise and identify these.

Pre-modification

Pre-modifiers occur before the head word of a complex noun phrase and can be:

- ordinal or cardinal numbers (num)   the <u>fifteenth</u> **voter**; <u>ten</u> **dogs**
- adjective phrases (AdjP)   some <u>chilly</u> **nights**
- nouns (N)   the <u>cherry</u> **orchard**
- –*ing* and –*ed* participles (*Ving* and *Ved*)   an <u>escaping</u> **prisoner**
      a <u>broken</u> **computer**

We know from the expansion test, that if we can expand a single word without creating a meaningless sentence, we are dealing with a phrase. Adjective pre-modifiers can be expanded by adding adverbs or some adjectives – we therefore know that the adjectives pre-modifying a head noun are phrases. Where adjective phrases consist of more than the head word, we identify them with round brackets within the brackets marking the noun phrase.

m	m	h
(some	(bright red)	**balloons**)
det	AdjP	N
	Adj Adj	

m	m	h
(all of the	(slightly small)	**jumpers**)
pre-det det	AdjP	N
	Adv Adj	

Where there is a sequence of adjective phrase pre-modifiers, there is an accepted order:

- size, age, colour   a <u>large</u>, <u>second-hand</u>, <u>silver</u> **car**
- gradable before non-gradable   the <u>vulnerable</u> <u>absent</u> **child**

Common nouns (*the <u>garden</u> **wall***), proper nouns (*an <u>Indian</u> **statue***) and possessive nouns (*<u>John's</u> **coat***) can also be modifiers.

As non-finite verbs, –*ing* and –*ed* participles do not fulfil the function of a verb within the noun phrase. We know they are not functioning as part of an embedded phrase because we cannot expand them – if we do the noun phrase will no longer make sense.

m	m	m	h	
the	predatory	(is hovering)	kite	✗
det	AdjP	VP	N	

m	m	m	h	
the	predatory	hovering	kite	✓
det	AdjP	V*ing*	N	

Instead, their role is descriptive – they provide additional information helping us to create a more precise visual image. We call them verb modifiers and they are

seful because they can create a sense of movement. Where an *–ed* participle mod-
ïer suggests an action that has been completed (*the broken* **window**), an *–ing* par-
iciple implies an action that is still in process (*the breaking* **window**).

Adverbs of degree (*very, so, rather, absolutely, quite*) can modify verb pre-mod-
fiers as well as adjectives. It is important to remember that the semantic relation-
hip is between the modifier and the adverb, not the head noun and the adverb.

```
m              m              m         h
the (slightly disappointing) examination results
det   Adv        Ving           N        N
```

We also label determiners as modifiers because they affect the way we respond
o a noun. The definite article (*the*), for instance, specifies something particular; the
ndefinite article (*a/an*) refers to any one of a kind or group of something. A refer-
nce to *a dog* therefore is general, while *the dog* suggests an animal that is known
y both speaker and listener. Determiners can be preceded by predeterminers that
lso function as modifiers (*all* the, *some of* the, *each of* the).

Post-modification

Post-modifiers occur after the head word and are usually made up of a phrase or a
clause. The qualifier can be omitted without affecting the meaning of a sentence,
but the use of post-modifiers allows writers and speakers to add additional information or descriptive detail.

More information about clauses can be found in Part III, but the following intro-
luction will help you to recognise the different kinds of post-modification used in
noun phrases. It is important to remember that clauses always contain a verb.
The most common qualifiers are PREPOSITIONAL PHRASES (PrepP) and RELATIVE
CLAUSES (RelCl).

```
m      h    q                       m     h    q
some days in the middle of spring   the man who thought he knew best
det    N   PrepP                    det   N    RelCl
```

Each of these structures is easy to recognise once you have identified the head
word of a noun phrase and checked the kind of word which follows. In the examples
above, the preposition *in* follows *days* and the relative pronoun *who* follows *man*.
These two words tell us what kind of post-modification is being used: a preposition
indicates a prepositional phrase as a qualifier; a relative pronoun indicates a relative
clause as a qualifier.

In a **prepositional phrase**, the preposition is always followed by a noun phrase
that provides extra information.

```
a tree of immense proportions       the girl with grotty hair and a gorgeous smile
   prep    NP                             prep    NP         conj      NP
```

A **relative clause** begins with a relative pronoun (*who, whom, whose, which,
that*) that immediately follows the head noun. We label the noun phrase with round
brackets and the embedded SUBORDINATE CLAUSE with square brackets.

```
m      h    q
(The actor [whom I saw in town]) is on television tonight.
       NP
det    N   RelCl
```

In some cases, it is possible to omit the relative pronoun.

    m   h   q
(The **actor** [Ø <u>I saw in town</u>]) is on television tonight.

We use *who* (and sometimes *that*) for people and *which* or *that* for things. Post modifying relative clauses help us to link ideas.

      m   m   h   h
I saw (a vicious **dog**). (It) was snarling and Ø crouching down threateningly.
           NP   NP
    det   AdjP   N   pron

      m   m   h   q
I saw (a vicious **dog** [<u>which was snarling and crouching down threateningly</u>]).
                          NP
    det   AdjP   N   RelCl   conj   RelCl

Other clauses which can post-modify a noun phrase are NON-FINITE CLAUSES (*the* **boat** *bobbing on the waves*) and NOUN CLAUSES (*the* **news** *that he was retiring*) We can recognise post-modifying **non-finite clauses** (NFCl) because a non-finite verb (*–ing* or *–ed* participle) immediately follows the head word of the noun phrase

    m   h   q
(The **clouds** [<u>gathered above us</u>])   looked ominous.
               NP
    det   N   NFCl (V*ed*)

    det   h   q
(The **clouds** [<u>gathering above us</u>])   looked ominous.
               NP
    det   N   NFCl (V*ing*)

In each case here, the head word *clouds* is followed directly by a non-finite verb (*gathered/gathering*) which is semantically linked to the noun. Infinitives can also function as post-modifiers, following the head noun.

    m   m   h   q
(The best **time** [<u>to visit town</u>])   is early on Saturday morning.
               NP
    det   AdjP   N   NFCl (V*inf*)

Noun clauses (NCl) functioning as post-modifiers always begin with *that* and the subordinating conjunction will directly follow the head noun. Relative clauses can also begin with the pronoun *that* – to check whether the post-modifying clause is a relative or a noun clause, see if 'that' can be replaced with 'which'. If it can, the clause is a relative clause.

    m   h   q
(The **dog** [<u>that rolled in mud</u>]) is dirty.
           NP
    det   N   RelCl

    m   h   q
(The **belief** [<u>that healthy eating is important</u>]) is widespread.
           NP
    det   N   NCl

In the first example, the relative pronoun *that* could be replaced with 'which'; in the second, *that* is a subordinating conjunction and cannot be replaced with 'which'. Noun clauses often follow abstract nouns: 'the **fact** that ...', 'the **belief** that ...', 'the **news** that ...' In some cases, the conjunction can be omitted.

m	h	q
It's (a **shame** [that we can't visit]).
NP
det N NCl

m	h	q
It's (a **shame** [Ø we can't visit]).
NP
det N NCl

Identifying noun phrases in context

Noun phrases are very important in English – they can fill the **subject** and **object** sites of a sentence (see Section 6.4). This means that they dominate written and spoken texts. You can have more than one noun phrase in a sentence: one before the main verb (subject) and one after (object).

To understand the structure of noun phrases in context, the first stage is to identify the **head word**. The noun fulfilling this function has to agree with the main finite verb of the sentence (a verb marked for present or past tense).

```
        m           m              m          h      q
(The government's (much admired) belief [that we should promote children's rights]) is vital.
                                          NP
det        N            Adv      Ved      N    NCl
```

Here the singular noun *belief* agrees with the third person singular present tense verb *is*. If you can change the head noun and the verb into a plural form ('beliefs' → 'are'), then you know that you have identified the head correctly.

Sometimes it is difficult to know where a noun phrase begins and ends. Having identified the head, therefore, you need to look at the words on either side. We know that determiners, predeterminers, numerals, adjective phrases, *–ing* and *–ed* participles, and nouns can fill the pre-modification site. Check the words that immediately precede the head word and decide on the relationship they have with the noun. Those that are linked semantically will be part of the noun phrase.

```
   m       m        h               m       m      h          m      h
(This  beautiful  scene) is inspiring.  (Our  garden  wall) protects (the  plants).
       NP                                     NP                      NP
det    AdjP       N               det    N      N          det    N
```

```
   m       m        h                  m        m       h          h
(Some  broken  windows) are never repaired. (Those  drifting  clouds) are like (dragons).
       NP                                       NP                      NP
de     Ved     N                        det     Ving     N              N
```

The examples here demonstrate the five different kinds of word class that can directly **precede** the head word: determiners, adjective phrases, nouns, *–ing* participles and *–ed* participles. They also show how a noun phrase can be simple – made up of a single noun (*dragons*) or a determiner + noun (*the plants*); or complex – made up of a head word and a range of pre-modification.

Similarly, we need to look at the word that directly **follows** the head word. We know that prepositions, relative pronouns, *–ing* and *–ed* participles, infinitives and the conjunction *that* can fill the post-modification site. Check the word that immediately follows the head word and decide on the grammatical and semantic relationship it has with the noun. Having established a link between the head noun and the subsequent word, think about the kind of structure that you would expect to accompany it (prepositional phrase, relative clause, non-finite clause or noun clause) – this will help you to decide where the post-modification stops.

```
      m       h          q                                        m       h
(The producer of the long-running television show)  won  (a prize).
                        NP                                        NP
   det     N        PrepP                                      det   N


   m    m      h          q                                  m          h
(A house builder [who always does a bad job])  doesn't get  (many customers).
                        NP                                          NP
  det   N     N        RelCl                                    det       N


      m    h        q                         m    m      h
(The circus [visiting the town])  had  (a good reputation).
                  NP                       NP
   det    N      NFCl                   det  AdjP    N


   m    m    h        q                      m       h       q
(The oak tree [struck by lightning])  stood as (a reminder of the storm).
                 NP                               NP
   det   N    N   NFCl                         det   N     PrepP


   m    h     q                            h     m      h
(The film [to avoid])  is released on  (DVD) in (two weeks).
            NP                           NP      NP
   det   N   NFCl                         N     num    N


   m     h       q                         m     h       q
(The news [that he was safe])  lightened  (the mood of the gathered crowd).
              NP                               NP
   det   N    NCl                           det   N   PrepP
```

The examples here demonstrate the six different kinds of words that can directl
follow the head word: a preposition (*of*), a relative pronoun (*who*), an –*ing* participl
(*visiting*) or an –*ed* participle (*struck*), an infinitive (*to avoid*) or the conjunctio
that. They also show how a noun phrase can contain both pre- and post-modifica
tion (*the oak **tree** struck by lighting*) and can occur more than once in a sentenc
(*the **circus** visiting the town* and *a good **reputation***).

If you look carefully at the examples above you will also notice that there ar
noun phrases embedded within the post-modifying structures. These have not beer
labelled separately so that the different types of post-modification stand out clearly
However, prepositional phrases are always made up of a preposition + noun phras
(*of the gathered crowd*); and most clauses will also contain noun phrases (*who alway.
gives bad news; visiting the town; struck by lightning; that he was safe*).

4.3 Adjective phrases (AdjP)

ADJECTIVE PHRASES are phrases where the head word is an adjective. They occur
after a COPULAR VERB or in parenthesis, separated from the rest of the sentence by
commas, dashes or brackets. They can also be embedded in a noun phrase before
the head word. Adjective phrases are used by writers and speakers to communicate
descriptive detail.

Simple adjective phrases

In a single word adjective phrase, only the head word will be used and the phrase is
described as a **simple adjective phrase**.

blue   fast   glorious   valiant   happy

Complex adjective phrases

Where adjective phrases are expanded by the addition of extra words, we describe them as **complex adjective phrases**. These can contain words before the head word (pre-modification), after the head word (post-modification), or both before and after (pre- and post-modification).

<u>bright</u> **green**

valiant <u>of spirit</u>

<u>extremely</u> **happy** <u>to be here</u>

In these examples, the head word of each adjective phrase is in bold and the additional information is underlined. Different kinds of words and phrases can be used to expand an adjective phrase and it is important to be able to recognise and identify these.

Pre-modification

Pre-modifiers occur before the head word of an adjective phrase and will almost always be adverbs – usually adverbs of degree (*very, much, really, quite, too, so*) or frequency (*often, always, never, sometimes, generally, occasionally*).

m	h		m	h		m	m	h
very	**thin**		sometimes	**early**		too	often	**late**
Adv	Adj		Adv	Adj		Adv	Adv	Adj

Post-modification

Post-modifiers occur after the head word and are usually made up of a phrase or clause. More information about clauses can be found in Part III, but the following introduction will help you to recognise the different kinds of post-modification used in adjective phrases. It is important to remember that clauses always contain a verb.

The most common qualifiers are **prepositional phrases** (PrepP) and **non-finite clauses** (NFCl).

h	q		h	q
glad	of your company		**happy**	[to be here]
Adj	PrepP		Adj	NFCl

Each of these structures is easy to recognise once you have identified the head word and checked the kind of word which follows. In the examples above, the preposition *of* follows the adjective *glad* and the infinitive *to be* follows the adjective *happy*. These words tell us what kind of post-modification is being used: a preposition indicates a prepositional phrase as a qualifier; an infinitive indicates a non-finite clause as a qualifier.

In a **prepositional phrase**, the preposition is always followed by a noun phrase providing extra information.

careful with <u>the old lady's possession</u>	**ready** for <u>the day ahead and its challenges</u>
prep · · · NP	prep · · · NP · · · conj · · · NP

A **non-finite clause** begins with a non-finite verb (*to help, getting*) that immediately follows the adjective to which it relates.

```
                    m        h              q
When he got home, he seemed (very busy [getting his things ready for the next da)
                                              AdjP
                    Adv      Adj      NFCl   (Ving)
```

```
                  m       h      q
Watching the news, we felt (really happy [to see the families together again]).
                                   AdjP
                  Adv     Adj   NFCl (Vinf)
```

Other clauses which can post-modify an adjective phrase are:

noun clauses	(**useful** _that you came_)
_wh_– clauses	(**unsure** _what to expect_)
comparative clauses	(**happier** _than she had ever been befor_

We can recognise post-modifying **noun clauses** (NCl) because _that_ will imm diately follow the head word of the adjective phrase and cannot be replaced 'which'.

```
            m    m      h           q
The boy was (so very anxious [that he do well]).
                        AdjP
            Adv  Adv   Adj        NCl
```

The qualifier can be omitted without affecting the meaning of the senten but it allows writers and speakers to add additional information or descripti detail.

COMPARATIVE CLAUSES (CompCl) functioning as post-modifiers can expr comparison or equivalence. To express comparison, the adjective takes a comp ative form using an _–er_ inflection or the adverb _more_, or it can be pre-modified the adverb _less_. It is followed by the subordinating conjunction _than_ and a subor nate clause or prepositional phrase.

```
            h      q                                        h      q
The girls are (tidier [than the boys are]).    The pace was (faster than last year).
               AdjP                                         AdjP
            Adj    CompCl                                Adj    PrepP
```

```
            m        h          q
The boy was (less enthusiastic than usual).
                 AdjP
            Adv      Adj        PrepP
```

```
            m       h        q
Why were you (less confident [than you were yesterday])?
                   AdjP
            Adv    Adj      CompCl
```

To express equivalence, the preposition _as_ precedes the adjective and also f lows it, introducing an accompanying post-modifying clause.

```
        h    q                                     h      q
I'm not (as fast [as I had hoped]).    The conflict was (as brutal [as we feared]
         AdjP                                          AdjP
        Adj CompCl                               Adj    CompCl
```

_WH_– CLAUSES are less common. They can be identified by the '_wh_–' word f lowing the head adjective: the pronoun or determiner _what_ (NCl), the relati adverb _where_ (RelCl), and the pronoun or determiner _which_ (RelCl). The _wh_– clau may be finite (marked for tense) or non-finite.

We were not (**sure** [<u>what to do next</u>]).   He was (**confident** [<u>which he should choose</u>]).

      h   q

      AdjP   AdjP

   Adj   NCl   Adj   RelCl

The student was (**unsure** [<u>which subjects to take</u>]).   I was (**happy** [<u>where I was</u>]).

      h   q

      AdjP   AdjP

   Adj   RelCl   Adj   RelCl

Identifying adjective phrases in context

Writers and speakers can create different effects by changing the position of adjectives in a sentence.

ATTRIBUTIVE adjective phrases are pre-modifiers: they come before the head noun in a noun phrase and cannot be post-modified.

      m   h   m   h

the (easy [to break into]) **door** ✗   an (afraid of spiders) **boy** ✗

     AdjP   N   AdjP   N

Embedded adjective phrases define attributes of the noun they precede and are, therefore, subordinate to the noun.

PREDICATIVE adjectives, on the other hand, carry more weight in a sentence because they fill a separate clause site (the complement site – see Section 6.4). They are described as predicative because they come after the PREDICATOR (verb).

      h   q

The car was (**glossy** with fresh polish).

         AdjP

     Adj   PrepP

Predicative adjective phrases stand alone, usually following a copular verb (*appear, become, grow, seem, be, feel*). If we wish to place grammatical and semantic emphasis on the adjectives in a sentence, therefore, we should position them after a copular verb rather than before a head noun.

To understand the structure of adjective phrases in context, we must first identify the **head word** – an adjective.

      h

Police were **certain** [<u>that</u> they would find the missing youngster alive] as the search went on.

      Adj

Sometimes it is difficult to know where an adjective phrase begins and ends. Having identified the head, therefore, you need to look at the words on either side. We know that adverbs can fill the pre-modification site, so check the words that immediately precede the head word and decide on the relationship they have with the adjective. Those that are linked semantically will be part of the adjective phrase.

      m   m   h

This breathtaking scene is (<u>just</u> <u>so</u> **incredible**).

        AdjP

   Adv Adv   Adj

      h   m   m   h

The painting is (**bland**) and (really quite **unimpressive**).

   AdjP   AdjP

   Adj   Adv   Adv   Adj

The examples here demonstrate some of the different adverbs that can directl\
precede the head word. They also show how an adjective phrase can be simple: mad\
up of a single adjective (*bland*) or complex (*just so **incredible**, really quite **unim***\
pressive), made up of a head word and a range of pre-modification.

Similarly, look at the word that directly follows the head word. We know tha\
prepositions (*of, with*), infinitives (*to + verb*) and conjunctions (*that, than, as*) mos\
commonly fill the post-modification site, but we can also look out for determiner\
or pronouns (*which, what*) and *–ing* participles. Check the word that immediatel\
follows the head and decide on the grammatical and semantic relationship it ha\
with the adjective. Having established a link between the head of the adjective\
phrase and the subsequent word, think about the kind of structure that you woul\
expect to accompany it – (prepositional phrase, non-finite clause, noun clause, com\
parative clause, relative clause) – this will help you to decide where the post-mod\
ification stops.

m   h q
The student was (sometimes **happy** with the quality of his work).
AdjP
Adv   Adj   PrepP

h   q
The mountain appeared (**gloomier** [than it had been the previous day]).
AdjP
Adj   CompCl

m m   h   q
The news of our friends was (so very **good** [to hear]).
AdjP
Adv Adv   Adj   NFCl

h   q   h   q
The children are (**happy** [where they are]) so I was (**glad** [that you could come over]).
AdjP   AdjP
Adj   RelCl   Adj NCl

h   q   h   q
She was (**uncertain** [which route to take]), but (**sure** [travelling by night would be quicker]).
AdjP   AdjP
Adj   RelCl   Adj   NFCl

The examples here demonstrate the different kinds of words that can directl\
follow the head word: a preposition (*with*), a relative determiner/pronoun (*which*),\
a relative adverb (*where*), an *–ing* participle (*travelling*), an infinitive (*to hear*) or a\
subordinating conjunction (*than/that*). They also show how an adjective phrase can\
contain both pre- and post-modification (*so very **good** to hear*) and can occur more\
than once in a sentence (***uncertain** which route to take* and ***sure** travelling by night*\
would be quicker).

4.4 Verb phrases (VP)

VERB PHRASES are phrases where the key word is a LEXICAL VERB – we call this the\
head word. The head may be preceded by up to four auxiliaries, although it is more\
common to see fewer. A multi-word verb will be followed by its particles. In some\
books, the term **verbal group** is used to describe the head verb and any related\
verbs and particles.

Verb phrases are used by writers and speakers to communicate the action of a sentence, or to describe states and processes. They, along with noun phrases, are the most commonly used constructions in English – all grammatically complete sentences contain a verb phrase.

Simple verb phrases

In a single word verb phrase, only the head word will be used and the phrase is described as a **simple verb phrase**.

Go!   run   contemplated   steals   took

These are lexical verbs that carry the meaning. They are finite and can be present tense (*run, steals*), past tense (*contemplated, took*) or use a base form verb as a command (*Go!*).

Where a single non-finite verb is at the front of a group of words, we label it as a subordinate clause rather than a phrase and mark it with square brackets. You will find out more about clauses in Section 6.2.

[**To queue** for a ticket] is very frustrating.   The day was spoilt, [**ruined** by bad weather].
SCl   SCl
V*infin*   V*ed*

[**Enjoying** the company of friends] makes time pass quickly.
SCl
V*ing*

Complex verb phrases

Lexical verbs in verb phrases can be supported by **auxiliary** verbs that come before them and support the meaning. Where verb phrases are expanded by the addition of extra verbs, we describe them as **complex verb phrases**. In the examples below, the head word of each verb phrase is in bold and the additional verbs are underlined. Only specific kinds of verbs can be used to expand a verb phrase and it is important to be able to recognise and identify these.

had **arrived**

may be **visiting**

is **laughing**

would have **fallen**

will **buy**

If there are auxiliary verbs in a verb phrase, the first auxiliary will be marked for tense (*had, is*). Modal auxiliaries (*may, would, will*) have no contrasting forms for tense, but are only used in finite verb phrases and are, therefore, assumed to be marked for tense.

Verb phrases and modification

In this book, the term **verb phrase** is used as a form label to identify the main verbal group(s) in a sentence. Other phrases linked semantically to the verb phrase are labelled separately.

(The fat **horse**) (**jumped**) (the **fence**) (**in** the field)
     NP   VP   NP   PrepP

In formal grammar, the verb phrase includes the finite verb and any phrases dependent on it. For instance, in the example above, the verb *jumped* is followed by phrases which only make sense in the presence of the verb and which could be replaced by a single word.

(The thin horse) (**did**) (too). i.e. 'jumped the fence in the field'
     NP   VP

The verb phrase is therefore seen to consist of the verb and the two phrases that follow it. This could be represented on a diagram.

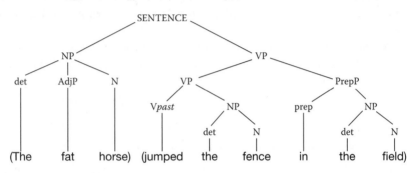

What this diagram shows is that there is one constituent made up of a noun phrase (*The fat horse*) and another made up of a past tense verb (*jumped*) with a complement (*the fence*) and an optional modifying prepositional phrase (*in the field*). We can see the connection because all the words in the two phrases can be traced back to a single point.

Tree diagrams show the grammatical relationships between words, but the approach in this book is functional rather than formal – the analysis will therefore focus on function and form labels, and the semantic effect of phrases rather than on the syntactic rules that describe the connections between sentence components.

The structure of verb phrases

The **structure** of a verb phrase (or verbal group) is much less flexible than a noun phrase: the lexical verb can be supported by up to four auxiliary verbs (modals and the primary verbs *be, have, do*). The longer verb phrases with four auxiliaries are less common in ordinary usage than the shorter ones. The primary auxiliaries *be* and *have* are used to construct different **aspects** and **voices**; the primary auxiliary *do* helps us to construct **questions** and **negatives**, and create **emphasis**; the modal auxiliaries are used to communicate **shades of meaning** such as possibility (*may*), prediction (*will*), obligation (*must*) and ability (*can*).

aux	lex	aux	lex	aux	lex	aux	lex
was	**running**	had	**contemplated**	may	**steal**	did	**leave**
prim	V*ing*	prim	V*ed*	mod	V*base*	prim	V*base*

aux	aux	lex		aux	aux	aux	lex		aux	aux	aux	aux	lex
should	have	**taken**		should	have	been	**sitting**		must	have	been	being	**checked**
mod	prim	V*ed*		mod	prim	prim	V*ing*		mod	prim	prim	prim	V*ed*

:rb phrases and aspect

ASPECT describes the timescale of a verb phrase, giving us more information about
hether the lexical verb is in progress or complete.

1e progressive aspect

he PROGRESSIVE ASPECT is constructed using the primary auxiliary *be + –ing par-
ciple*. It implies that an activity is on-going and is probably not complete. The verb
hrases in the examples below are in brackets with the head word of each phrase in
old.

	aux	lex			aux	lex
The children (are	**swimming**) every day this week.		The trees (were	**blowing**) in the wind.
	prim	V*ing*			prim	V*ing*

In the **present progressive**, we use *is/are*; in the **past progressive** we use
as/were. It is also possible to use other auxiliaries with this structure:

The children (might be **swimming**) later.   The trees (had been **blowing**) in the wind.

1 the first example, the modal auxiliary *might* is used to reflect a possible rather
1an a definite on-going action. It is followed by the base form *be + –ing participle*.
1 the second, the time scale has been altered by the addition of the primary auxil-
1ry *have* which suggests an on-going action in the past. It is followed by the *–ed*
articiple of *be + –ing participle*. We call this the **perfect progressive**: it can be in
1e present using *has/have been + –ing participle* (present perfect progressive); or
1e past using *had been + –ing participle* (past perfect progressive).

he perfective aspect

he **PERFECTIVE ASPECT** is constructed using the primary auxiliary *have + –ed par-
ciple*. It describes an activity that is complete. The verb phrases in the examples
elow are in brackets with the head word of each phrase in bold.

	aux	lex			aux	lex
The children (have	**swum**) every day this week.		The trees (had	**blown**) in the wind.
	prim	V*ed*			prim	V*ed*

In the **present perfective**, we use *has/have*; in the **past perfective** we use *had*.
The present perfective is used for a past action that has continuing relevance in the
resent. The past perfective describes an action that was completed at a previous
ime in the past.

It is also possible to use modal auxiliaries with this structure:

The children (could have **swum**) later.   The trees (must have **blown**) in the wind.

In the first example, the modal auxiliary *could* is used to reflect a possible action
n the past. In the second, the modal auxiliary *must* indicates a certain, complete
iction in the past. When using a modal auxiliary in the perfective aspect, it is always
ollowed by the base form *have + –ed participle*.

It is useful to be able to recognise these structures because it helps us to appreciate the subtle shades of meaning that can be conveyed by different time scales and by modality (the possibility or impossibility, the necessity, certainty or probability of something happening).

Verb phrases and voice

The action of a verb and the person(s) or thing(s) responsible for it can be conveyed in two ways using VOICE.

The active voice

The ACTIVE VOICE is the most common. It directly links the action of a verb to the person or thing carrying it out.

> The wind **slams** the door.　　The builder **broke** the glass.

The passive voice

The PASSIVE VOICE changes the focus of a sentence by reordering the elements and changing the form of the verb phrase using *to be* + *−ed participle*. To make an active sentence passive you should follow the stages below:

1 move the person or thing 'doing' the verb (the subject or actor of the sentence. See Section 6.4) to the end where it becomes the agent after the preposition *by* (or omit it)
2 bring the person or thing 'receiving' the action of the verb (the object of the active sentence, see Section 6.4) to the front of the passive sentence where it becomes the acting subject
3 identify the tense of the active verb phrase and use *is/are* for a present tense passive verb phrase, *was/were* for a past tense passive verb phrase or *has/have been* for a perfective passive verb phrase
4 change the lexical verb of the active sentence into a *−ed* participle.

> The wind <u>slams</u> the door.　　　　The door <u>is slammed</u> (by the wind).
>
> The iceberg <u>hit</u> the boat.　　　　The boat <u>was hit</u> (by the iceberg).
>
> The builder <u>has broken</u> the glass.　　The glass <u>has been broken</u> (by the builder)

The passive can be used to create suspense since the subject of the active sentence is delayed until the end of the sentence, or is omitted. In reports and scientific documents, where the process is more important than the people who carry it out, the passive voice without an agent is common.

> The metal **was placed** in a test tube and the acid Ø **added**. The reaction **was observed** and any visible effects Ø **recorded**. A hydrogen test **was carried out** to identify the gas produced in the reaction. The process **was** then **repeated** with different metals.

Identifying verb phrases in context

Verb phrases are very important in English – all grammatically complete sentences have one. It is the only element that cannot be omitted. Because the structure of verb phrase is quite restrictive, it is possible to identify one if you know the different kinds of auxiliaries and can recognise a verb in its various forms.

The first stage is always to identify the **head word** of the phrase – the lexical verb. Then look at the words before this in order to decide if any auxiliaries have been used. The particular kinds of auxiliaries help you to understand the shades of meaning communicated: **aspect** varies the time scale; **modals** affect the modality; **voice** changes the focus; **primary auxiliaries** create questions, negatives and emphasis.

Finite verb phrases are usually preceded by a noun phrase (subject). They are often also followed by a noun phrase (object) or an adjective phrase (complement, see Section 6.4). Non-finite clauses may be found in the initial position of a sentence, the middle position, or towards the end. We will consider this in more detail in later chapters when we explore the structure and function of clauses and sentences.

4.5 Adverb phrases (AdvP)

ADVERB PHRASES are phrases where the key word is an adverb - we call this the **head word**. They are used by writers and speakers to add details of time, place and manner.

Simple adverb phrases

In a single word adverb phrase, only the head word will be used and the phrase is described as a **simple adverb phrase**.

always	rather	gloriously	indeed	here

Complex adverb phrases

Where adverb phrases are expanded by the addition of extra words, we describe them as **complex adverb phrases**. These can contain words before the head word (pre-modification), after the head word (post-modification), or both before and after (pre- and post-modification).

very **happily**

unfortunately for Karen

so **unexpectedly** that it was dangerous

In these examples, the head word of each adverb phrase is in bold and the additional information is underlined. Different kinds of words and phrases can be used to expand an adverb phrase and it is important to be able to recognise and identify these.

Pre-modification

Pre-modifiers occur before the head word of an adverb phrase and will almost always be adverbs – usually adverbs of degree (*very, much, really, quite, too, so, slightly, somewhat*) or frequency (*often, always, never, sometimes, generally, occasionally, usually, rarely*).

m	h		m	h		m	m	h
<u>very</u> **sadly**			<u>sometimes</u> **unexpectedly**			<u>too</u> <u>often</u> **confidently**		
Adv	Adv		Adv	Adv		Adv	Adv	Adv

Post-modification

Post-modifiers occur after the head word when there is also a pre-modifying adverb intensifier (*more, so, too*). The most common qualifiers are **prepositional phrases** beginning with *for* (PrepP) and either **noun** or **comparative clauses**.

m	h	q		m	h	q
too **quickly** for comfort				more **quickly** [than I had expected]		
Adv	Adv	PrepP		Adv	Adv	CompCl

m	h	q
so **quickly** [that I didn't see anything]		
Adv	Adv	NCl

Each of these structures is easy to recognise once you have identified the head word and checked what precedes and follows it. In the examples above, the degree adverbs *too, more, so* precede the head word *quickly*; the preposition *for* and the conjunctions *than/that* follow it. These words tell us what kind of post-modification is being used: a preposition indicates a prepositional phrase as a qualifier; a subordinating conjunction indicates a comparative or noun clause as a qualifier.

It is important to recognise when a prepositional phrase following the head word is not part of the adverb phrase.

He visited (too **frequently** for my liking).   He came (**here**) from the mountains.

	AdvP			AdvP
Adv	Adv	PrepP		Adv

While the **prepositional phrase** *for my liking* only makes sense when it is part of the adverb phrase, the prepositional phrase in the second example (*from the mountains*) is not linked to the adverb.

Comparative clauses (CompCl) can express comparison or equivalence. To express comparison, the adverb will either take the comparative form (*more/ −er*) or will be pre-modified by the adverb *less*. In both cases, the adverb will be followed by the subordinating conjunction *than* and a subordinate clause.

m	h	q
The trees tossed (more **violently** [than they had before]).		

	AdvP	
Adv	Adv	CompCl

m	h	q
We read (less **expressively** [than we usually do]).		

	AdvP	
Adv	Adv	CompCl

Where *than* is used without a verb, the post-modification is in the form of a prepositional phrase rather than a comparative clause.

m	h	q		m	h	q
The trees tossed (more **violently** than before).				We read (less **expressively** than usual).		

	AdvP				AdvP	
Adv	Adv	PrepP		Adv	Adv	PrepP

To make a comparison in which equivalence is expressed, the preposition *as* precedes and follows the adverb, introducing a post-modifying clause.

The doctor came (<u>as</u> **quickly** [<u>as he could</u>]).

      h   q

      AdvP

     Adv   CompCl

The orchestra played (<u>as</u> **brilliantly** [<u>as it had the night before</u>]).

      h   q

      AdvP

     Adv   CompCl

Qualifiers can usually be omitted without affecting the meaning of the sentence, ~~b~~ut their use allows writers and speakers to add additional information or descrip~~ti~~ve detail.

The position of adverb phrases

~~A~~dverb phrases fill the adverbial site of a clause (see Section 6.4). They have three ~~m~~ain positions:

- the front position before the subject

  Quietly, Jack read his book.

- the middle position after the first auxiliary verb, after the copular verb *be*, or before the finite verb:

  Jack must **quietly** read his book.   Jack is **quietly** reading his book.

  Jack **quietly** read his book.

- the end position as the last word in the clause.

  Jack read his book **quietly**.

Each different type of adverb, however, is most commonly found in one partic~~u~~lar position. Manner (how?), place (where?) and time (when?) adverbs are usually ~~lo~~cated at the end of a sentence. Degree (how much?), frequency (how often?) and ~~le~~ngth of time (how long?) adverbs are usually located in the middle position. Link~~in~~g and comment adverbs are usually located in the front position. Adverbs as mod~~if~~iers come before the word they modify. By moving adverbs around, writers can ~~a~~lter the semantic importance placed upon them – they are the most flexible gram~~m~~atical element in English.

Identifying adverb phrases in context

~~A~~dverb phrases are restrictive in the kinds of pre- and post-modification they can ~~c~~ontain and it is unusual for them to have more than one pre-modifier and one post-~~m~~odifier. The process of identifying them within a sentence is the same as with noun ~~a~~nd adjective phrases: identify the **head**, then look at the words on either side. We ~~k~~now that adverbs fill the pre-modification site, so check the words that immedi~~a~~tely precede the head word and decide on the relationship they have with it. Those ~~t~~hat are linked semantically will be part of the adverb phrase.

The children ran home (<u>rather</u> **furtively**).

       m   h

       AdvP

      Adv   Adv

```
              h          m        h            m      h
The mountain rose (steeply) – (so impressively) and (very gracefully).
              AdvP              AdvP                  AdvP
              Adv       Adv     Adv                  Adv    Adv
```

The examples here demonstrate some of the different adverbs that can directly pre
cede the head word. They also show how an adverb phrase can be simple: made u
of a single adverb (*steeply*) or complex (*rather furtively, so impressively, very grac
fully*), made up of a head word and pre-modification.

Similarly, look at the word that directly follows the head word. We know th
prepositions (*for*), and the conjunctions *that* or *than* can fill the post-modificatic
site. Check the word that immediately follows the head and decide on the gram
matical and semantic relationship it has with the adverb. Having established a li
between the head adverb and the subsequent word, think about the kind of stru
ture that you would expect to accompany it – (prepositional phrase, noun clau
or comparative clause) – this will help you to decide where the post-modificatic
stops.

```
       h                      h            m     m      h       q
(Inevitably), the sharks (sometimes) came (too dangerously close for comfort).
   AdvP                      AdvP                       AdvP
   Adv                       Adv           Adv   Adv    Adv     PrepP
```

```
               m      h        q
This group came in (more quietly [than the earlier one did]).
                    AdvP
               Adv     Adv      CompCl
```

```
            h     m      h       q
The cliff dived (away) (so steeply [that it was breath-taking]).
                AdvP        AdvP
                Adv   Adv   Adv   NCl
```

The examples here demonstrate the different kinds of words that can directly follo
the head word: a preposition (*for*) or a subordinating conjunction (*than/that*). The
also show how an adverb phrase can contain both pre- and post-modification (*s
steeply that it was breathtaking*) and can occur more than once in a sentenc
(*Inevitably, sometimes* and *too dangerously close for comfort*).

4.6 Prepositional phrases (PrepP)

PREPOSITIONAL PHRASES are phrases where the key word is a preposition. They ar
optional elements of a sentence, but are used by writers and speakers to add extr
information about time, place, manner and reason.

Structure

Although the preposition is the key word of a prepositional phrase, it will usuall
be followed by a noun phrase.

```
under the car      in the Christmas holidays      around the outskirts of the town
prep  NP           prep      NP                    prep      NP
```

The noun phrase following the preposition may be simple, containing only
head word, or a determiner + head word.

in <u>town</u>   **over** <u>him</u>   **under** <u>the bed</u>

  NP   NP   NP

It may also contain pre- or post-modification (which may itself contain a prepositional phrase).

for <u>my next birthday</u>   **over** <u>the wall surrounding the factory</u>

without <u>regular water</u>   **between** <u>the books on the shelf</u>

In some cases, prepositions can be followed by a non-finite –*ing* participle, a *wh*–clause or an adverb.

You have achieved a great deal (**in** [<u>winning the race</u>]).

(**With** [<u>what we have found out</u>]), I am sure we will solve the case.

(**Over** <u>there</u>) the flowers have been completely eaten.

Prepositional phrases and adverb phrases

In traditional grammar, prepositions cannot stand alone as the head word of a phrase. If there is no post-modification, the word is functioning as a simple adverb phrase.

Jack crawled (**under** <u>the fallen branch</u>).   Jack crawled (**under**).

         PrepP   AdvP

      prep + NP   Adv

In formal linguistics, however, the word *under* would be analysed as a preposition, head of a prepositional phrase, in both these examples. The underlying rules of phrase structure would label the preposition in the second example as the head word in a simple prepositional phrase, which could be expanded to include a noun phrase.

In some grammar books, the terms TRANSITIVE and INTRANSITIVE are used. Transitive prepositions are followed by a noun phrase; intransitive prepositions are not. The preposition *with*, for instance, is transitive.

The boy came (with). ✗   The boy came (with his friend). ✓

Some prepositions are both transitive and intransitive.

We looked (around). ✓   We looked (around the room). ✓

Where traditional grammar would describe *around* in the first example as an adverb, the formal approach would label it as an intransitive preposition.

The function of prepositional phrases

As we have already seen, prepositional phrases commonly occur as **post-modifiers** in noun, adjective and adverb phrases. In these cases, they will respectively follow a head word that is a noun (*a <u>text</u> from my friend*), an adjective (*<u>afraid</u> of losing my glasses*) or an adverb (*<u>unexpectedly</u> for him*). Prepositional phrases, however, can also stand alone within a sentence – they are not preceded by a noun, adjective or adverb and do not therefore fulfil the function of post-modifier.

(**Beside** <u>the lake</u>), I found a comfortable spot and settled down to read.

The prepositional phrase in this example is not related to any other phrase in the sentence. It gives us information about where something is taking place and fills the adverbial site of the clause (see Section 6.4).

In order to check whether a prepositional phrase functions as a post-modifier or an adverbial, see if it can be moved to another part of the sentence. In the sentence above, for instance, the prepositional phrase could occur in a number of positions in the sentence.

> I found a comfortable spot (**beside** the lake), and settled down to read.   (middle)
>
> I found a comfortable spot and settled down to read (**beside** the lake).   (end)

In sentences where the prepositional phrase functions as a post-modifier, however, the position cannot change – the prepositional phrase must follow the head word.

> The man gave the girl (a box **of** books).   ✓
>
> (**Of** books) the man gave the girl a box.   ✗
>
> The man gave (**of** books) the girl (a box).   ✗

4.7 Phrases in sentences

Now that you have studied the five different types of phrase, you need to be able to recognise them in the context of a SENTENCE. This will help you to understand how a sentence is made up – you will begin to recognise the distinctive pattern of phrases in the English language. When we label the phrases in a sentence, we are analysing the **form**; we will consider the **function** of each phrase in Part III.

In order to work out where each phrase stops and starts, you will have to remember what you have learnt about the structure of phrases. If we look at the sentence below, we can begin by identifying the head words of each phrase.

> Alex played happily in the pool.

The sentence begins with a proper noun which stands by itself – we can therefore see that *Alex* is the head word. The next word, *played*, is a finite past tense verb and because there are no auxiliaries, we know that this too stands alone. The adverb *happily* has no pre- or post-modification; and the preposition *in* is followed by a noun phrase *the pool* and functions as a free-standing prepositional phrase telling us where the event takes place. We can therefore annotate the sentence as follows with the phrase labels indicating the form of each part of the sentence:

> (Alex) (played) (happily) (in the pool).
>   NP   VP   AdvP   PrepP

It is also possible to label the phrases in a diagrammatic way to show the relationships between them more explicitly. This is the approach adopted in formal grammar.

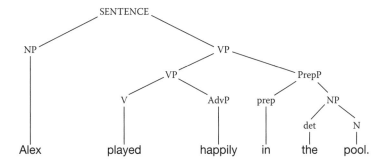

4.8 Conclusion

The information on phrases in this section helps us to see how words can be linked together into meaningful groups, enabling writers and speakers to provide descriptive detail, create shades of meaning and convey attitudes and opinions. Each linguistic choice affects the way we engage with a piece of writing or speech so it is important to recognise where words can be added in a phrase. Look for additions and omissions, and be prepared to discuss the effects created.

Understanding the form and function of phrases, and knowing how to combine phrases forms the basis for clause analysis. Before moving on to Part III, therefore, it is important to be confident in the recognition and labelling of phrases.

Chapter 5

Using your knowledge

In this chapter, you have the opportunity to apply the knowledge you have gained about phrases. The close reading activities require you to consider the effects created by the phrases the writer or speaker has chosen. The writing tasks encourage you to think about particular types of phrases by focusing on how language works in different contexts and for different purposes.

5.1 Noun phrases

Writers and speakers use noun phrases to establish a lexical field – they usually occur before and after the verb phrase. The kinds of words the noun phrases contain reflect the subject matter or focus of a text.

TASK 1   Noun phrases in greetings cards

1 Read the text below which is taken from a greetings card celebrating the birth of a baby boy.

What is a boy?
A powerhouse of energy,
A bouncing ball of fun,
A never-stopping whirlwind
That's always on the run!
Tunnel-digger,
Castle-builder,
Climber in the trees,
Frog-collector,
Puddle-jumper,
Crawler on his knees!
A heartful of adventure
That will fill you up with love,
An angel (sleeping peacefully!),
That's your baby boy!

2 Identify the noun phrases and underline the head word in each one. Then label the pre-and post-modification and make a list of the different types used.

3 Write a commentary exploring the use of noun phrases in the text and the effects they create.

You should use appropriate terminology and linguistic frameworks to explain and evaluate the texts.
You may like to think about:

- the content and purpose
- the different types of noun phrase
- the lexical choice
- the images
- the patterned structure

OMMENTARY

he noun phrases in this verse clearly celebrate the concept of 'boyhood' in a very sual way: the emphasis is on images of physical activity and creativity. While some f the head words create literal images (*digger, builder, Climber, collector, jumper, rawler*), others are figurative. Metaphors of the *powerhouse*, the *ball* and the *whirl-ind* are used to portray something of the child's inner nature. The connotations re dynamic – boys are represented as energetic, active and chaotic. The final image f the *angel* provides a contrast.

```
     m      h            q
An angel [sleeping peacefully!]
det    N         NFCl
```

The post-modified noun phrase suggests a passivity and purity that is quite dif-?rent to the fervour of the earlier images. The wry humour of the parenthesis is einforced by the exclamatory tone: sleep is the only time the epithet 'angel' is fitting.

The patterned structure of the listed noun phrases contributes to the energy of he verse. The reader is drawn into a world of activity: the pace increases as the pre-nd post-modified noun phrases of the first four lines are replaced with compound oun phrases in the middle section.

```
   m       h          m       h          m       h          m       h
Tunnel-digger     Castle-builder      Frog-collector      Puddle-jumper
  N       N          N       N          N       N          N       N
```

he rhythm of the four-syllable phrases with their strong initial position stress nderpins the meaning, communicating the essential vitality and resourcefulness f boys.

In the final lines, however, the use of a phrase post-modified by a prepositional hrase and a relative clause slows the pace as the verse builds to its emphatic cli-1ax.

```
   m      h         q
A heartful of adventure/[That will fill you up with love]
det   N      PrepP              RelCl
```

The last line is the only complete grammatical sentence other than the title – :s use of the demonstrative pronoun *That* as a reference backwards (**ANAPHORIC**) ɔ all the preceding noun phrases is conclusive. It provides an answer to the question

raised in the title, replacing the opening interrogative (*What is a Boy?*) with the ce‌
tainty of a statement (declarative, see Section 8.6).

The language is positive and vibrant, creating a dynamic tone that is indicati‌
of the subject matter. Even though there are no verb phrases to communicate dire
action, the non-finite verb modifiers develop movement within the descriptive nou‌
phrase structure. The *–ing* participle pre-modifiers *bouncing* and *never-stoppin‌*
for instance, build a sense of energy and perpetual motion. In addition, many of th‌
head words are nouns created from verbs: 'dig' – *digger*; 'build' – *builder*; 'climb'
climber; 'collect' – *collector*; 'jump' – *jumper*; 'crawl' – *crawler*. The pre-modifyin‌
nouns (*Tunnel, Castle, Frog, Puddle*) then specify the range of the reference, enhanc‌
ing the imaginative and creative life of the child. This is a world of active particip‌
tion and the language is energetic.

By using a sequence of noun phrases, this greeting card verse creates a vivi‌
portrait of a stereotypical boy. The images are immediately recognisable and this ‌
what engages the reader. The strong patterning, the concrete visual noun phras‌
and the poignant climax make this an effective celebration of the birth of a bab‌
boy.

TASK 2   Using noun phrases in a greeting card verse ═══════════════════

Compose a verse for a card to celebrate a special occasion: the birth of a baby gir‌
becoming a teenager, starting work, passing an exam or driving test, reaching adul‌
hood, middle age or old age.

Use a variety of noun phrases and think carefully about the stereotypical features of th‌
kind of person or occasion you are writing about. Think about the effects of rhythm an‌
pace, and build towards the climax of a grammatical sentence in the final line.

When you have completed your text, evaluate the key linguistic features. You ma‌
like to use the suggested framework for analysis in Appendix A.

TASK 3   Noun phrases in poems ═══════════════════════════════════════

1 Read the poem below carefully.

Spacepoem 3: Off Course
the golden flood   the weightless seat
the cabin song   the pitch black
the growing beard   the floating crumb
the shining rendezvous   the orbit wisecrack
the hot spacesuit   the smuggled mouth-organ
the imaginary somersault   the visionary sunrise
the turning continents   the space debris
the golden lifeline   the space walk
the crawling deltas   the camera moon
the pitch velvet   the rough sleep
the crackling headphone   the space silence
the turning earth   the lifeline continents
the cabin sunrise   the hot flood
the shining spacesuit   the growing moon

the crackling somersault   the smuggled orbit
the rough moon   the visionary rendezvous
the weightless headphone   the cabin debris
the floating lifeline   the pitch sleep
the crawling camera   the turning silence
the space crumb   the crackling beard
the orbit mouth-organ   the floating song
Edwin Morgan

2 Identify the noun phrases and underline the head word in each one. Then label the pre-modification and make a list of the different types of modifier used.

3 Write a commentary exploring the use of noun phrases in the poem and the effects they create.

You should use appropriate terminology and linguistic frameworks to explain and evaluate the text.
   You may like to think about:

• the content (character, time, place and events)
• the different types of noun phrase
• the lexical choice
• the images
• the patterned structure

COMMENTARY

In this poem about a space mission that goes wrong, the noun phrases are visual, tactile and aural, contributing to the strong narrative thread running through the text. Although there are no verb phrases (and therefore no direct action), this poem is clearly telling a story in which we engage with character, place and time.

Noun phrases are used to construct a concrete sense of space – a perspective in which we are aware of the astronaut's distance from home.

m	m	h		m	m	h
the	turning	continents		the	turning	earth
det	V*ing*	N		det	V*ing*	N

Repeated references to the lack of gravity (*weightless, floating*) and to physical details such as *the space debris* set the piece in context, while more metaphorical references to *the golden flood* and *the visionary sunrise* suggest the astronaut's awe. Other noun phrases linked to the spaceship and the astronaut's spacesuit reflect his physical experience. The pre-modifiers *hot* and *rough*, for instance, describing the spacesuit and the astronaut's disturbed sleep patterns, communicate the physical hardships of the journey.

To enhance the tension, the poet uses noun phrases to convey the passage of time. The pre-modifier *growing* describes the astronaut's beard and this becomes a symbol for the passage of time – the *–ing* participle indicates an action that is on-going rather than complete. Other references are more subtle: they juxtapose the astronaut's hopes with the reality of the journey. To dramatise this opposition, the poet repeats certain head words with different pre-modifiers.

m	m	h		m	m	h
the	shining	rendezvous		the	visionary	rendezvous
det	V*ing*	N		det	AdjP	N

The –*ing* participle modifier *shining* has positive connotations as the astronaut looks forward to his return journey. By the second half of the poem, however, the pre-modifier has been replaced with the adjective *visionary* – the *rendezvous* has become an illusory event that can be imagined but never realised.

Noun phrases describing the spaceship's course also create tension. During the space walk, the astronaut is conscious of *the camera moon*. This sets the ultimate destination at a distance – looking at the moon is like a picture book experience. In the next linked noun phrase, the pre-modifier *camera* has been replaced by the –*ing* participle *growing* with its suggestion of on-going movement. At this point in the poem, the journey is still on course, but the next noun phrase with *moon* as its head word changes the tone. The use of the adjective *rough* suggests that the spaceship is travelling at speed and that the surface of the moon is becoming frighteningly close – distant observation is now replaced by unavoidable detail.

An unexpectedly strong sense of character emerges from the poem despite the lack of direct references. The poet indicates implicitly what the astronaut is doing and what he feels through the noun phrases, developing our sense of him as a distinctive individual who sings, eats, tells jokes, imagines playing in zero gravity and marvels at the things he sees.

m	m	h		m	m	h		m	m	h
the	cabin	song		the	floating	crumb		the	orbit	wisecrack
det	N	N		det	V*ing*	N		det	N	N

m	m	h		m	m	h
the	imaginary	somersault		the	visionary	sunrise
det	AdjP	N		det	AdjP	N

The –*ed* participle pre-modifier *smuggled* with its connotations of something illicit develops our sense of the humanity of the unnamed character – he has brought something aboard which is unofficial, something that is of personal significance. The *mouth-organ* thus becomes a symbol of the astronaut's identity as a man rather than as an astronaut.

The noun phrase of the title, *Off Course*, prepares the reader for the final seven lines of the poem, but it is the structural marker (the indentation) that draws attention to the poem's turning point. Although the grammatical structure does not alter, the combination of head words and modifiers becomes more unexpected. The mundane is replaced by the potentially disastrous: the everyday relationship of words in the first 14 lines becomes more dramatic and shocking. The symbolic *golden lifeline* that protects the astronaut during his space walk, for instance, is now functionless. The positive connotations of the adjective modifier *golden* are replaced by the –*ing* participle *floating* with its suggestion of uncontrolled and undirected movement.

Similarly, head words from the first section of the poem appear in a different context: the astronaut's equipment (*headphone, camera*) is set adrift by the collision.

The re-cycled pre-modifiers (the adjective *weightless* and the *–ing* participle *crawling*) draw attention to its sudden uselessness. This change is underpinned by other references – *the cabin debris* joins *the space debris* and the *imaginary somersault* has become *the crackling somersault* of an astronaut no longer protected by his rocket.

Perhaps most emotive are the final lines where references used to characterise the astronaut as a distinctive individual earlier in the poem become dehumanised. The head words *crumb, beard, mouth-organ* and *song* are now detached from their human context.

m	m	h	m	m	h	m	m	h	m	m	h
the	space	crumb	the	crackling	beard	the	orbit	mouth-organ	the	floating	song
det	N	N	det	V*ing*	N	det	N	N	det	V*ing*	N

The noun modifiers *space* and *orbit* suggest that the crumb and the mouth-organ have joined the orbiting space debris; the *–ing* participles *crackling* and *floating* with their connotations of on-going activity place the astronaut in a metaphorical limbo. These noun phrases are a poignant reminder of human vulnerability in this vast, unknown domain

The recycling of language is an effective means of communicating both the monotony of space and its disturbing unfamiliarity. The poet intensifies the effect of the words on the reader by disrupting COLLOCATIONS (a recognisable combination of words). In breaking language patterns which we all recognise, the poet makes familiar things seem strange and threatening.

The noun phrase *the pitch black*, for instance, is a familiar description of darkness. Its original metaphorical links to 'pitch' (a black shining residue produced during the distillation of tar) have been lost and we now understand this as a 'set phrase'. The noun phrase *the pitch velvet*, however, develops an unexpected connection between 'pitch' and 'velvet', giving the darkness of space a viscous, tactile quality. By linking the two nouns, Morgan forces his reader to make connections that develop a new and startling image. In the final section of the poem, the noun phrase *the pitch sleep* pushes the connection one step further: the astronaut, catapulted from the safety of his spacecraft, becomes part of the blackness. The noun modifier *pitch* conveys the intensity of the darkness, while the head word is perhaps a euphemism for the astronaut's death.

Grammatical structure is integral to the effectiveness of this poem. Words are recycled: head words recur; pre-modifiers change places; meanings subtly shift. To understand the significance of these changes, we need to look at the context, understanding the semantic relationship between the head words and the pre-modifiers.

The poem may initially seem simplistic and disjointed, but on closer reading it communicates an intense vision of a particular individual experience. It draws the reader into another world and communicates a dramatic story with a strong sense of character and place. Although there are no verb phrases, we experience a sequence of events through the noun phrases. Initially, they create a sense of monotony as the astronaut awaits the conclusion of his journey, building to an emotive climax in the dramatisation of the collision.

1 Choose one of the following writing exercises. When you have completed your text, evaluate the key linguistic features. You may like to use the suggested framework for analysis in Appendix A.

EITHER
Create your own series of book or film titles using a range of noun phrase structures.

You may like to begin by collecting a range of book, film and CD titles that are made up of noun phrases and analysing the grammatical structure of the phrases. Experiment with different kinds of pre- and post-modification.

OR
Look at the examples below advertising different kinds of bags.

m	m	m	h		m	h	q
Blue	denim	messenger	bag		Leather	rucksack	with adjustable straps
AdjP	N	N	N		N	N	PrepP

m	m	h	q			m	m	h
Elegant	evening	bag	embroidered by hand			Printed	eco-cotton	bag
AdjP	N	N	NFCl			Ved	AdjP	N N

Choose a product you would like to advertise and write noun phrases to describe different versions of your chosen product.

You need to pay particular attention to the features that make each item different, using a range of modified noun phrases to build appropriate visual images.

OR
Write a noun phrase poem about a place, an event, a person or an experience. Each line should be made up of two pre-modified noun phrases with a variety of pre-modifiers.

Aim to dramatise your topic by freezing a moment in time and focusing on particular visual details. You will need to think about the focus of the head nouns and the effects created by the different kinds of pre-modifiers – remember that you can create a sense of movement by using verb modifiers.

If you wish, you can use the noun phrase poem below as a model.

The Season's Rage
the darkening day   the rising wind
the black clouds   the falling rain
the crashing thunder   the flashing light
the bleak landscape   the illuminated moment
the rearing horse   the fleeing fox
the winter night   the fallen tree
the twisted boughs   the blackened stump
the lifting darkness   the rising sun
the delicate dawn   the blue sky
the peaceful morning   the day's hope.

5.2 Adjective Phrases

Adjective phrases are used by writers and speakers to provide descriptive detail. They occur after the verb phrase in an emphatic position or before a head noun in a noun phrase. Their connotations affect the way the intended audience responds to the text.

TASK 1   Adjective phrases in different texts

1 Read through the texts below and think about their audience, purpose and context.

TEXT 1   An advertisement
Deliciously fruity and dangerously addictive. Try our new fruit bar before it's too late. It's tasty, it's wholesome and it's healthy!

TEXT 2   Extract from a classic novel, *Vanity Fair* by W. M. Thackeray (1847–8)
… A long engagement is a partnership which one party is free to keep or break, but which involves all the capital of the other.
    Be cautious, then young ladies; be wary how you engage. Be shy of loving frankly; never tell all you feel, or (a better way) feel very little. See the consequences of being prematurely honest and confiding, and mistrust yourselves and everybody.

(Ch.18)

2 Identify the adjective phrases in each text. Underline the head word, label any pre- and post-modification and make a list of the different types used.
3 Write notes on the use of adjective phrases in these texts and the effects they create.

You should use appropriate terminology and linguistic frameworks to explain and evaluate the texts.
    You may like to think about:

* the content and purpose
* the different types of adjective phrase
* the lexical choice
* the images
* the patterned structure

COMMENTARY

Each text has a different purpose and intended audience: the advert is persuasive, aiming to encourage us to buy a new product; and the narrative is instructive, giving young ladies advice about the way to avoid a broken heart. The adjective phrases therefore have a different function in each text.
    The images in the advertisement are designed specifically to persuade us to buy the fruit bar. The adjective phrases are either simple or pre-modified. The unmodified simple phrases *tasty, wholesome* and *healthy* appeal to our better nature: this

product is both good to eat and good for us. The pre-modifying adverbs fulfil the same function: the head word *fruity* is intensified by the adverb *deliciously*, combining the healthy connotations of 'fruit' with the sensuous quality of 'delicious'. Similarly, the head word *addictive* is made more exciting by the adverb *dangerously* – this product offers us a challenge. The pre-modified adjective *too late* also adds drama because it suggests that there is a time limit and that consumers could miss out. The adjective phrases allow the advertisers to make the fruit bar seem more than just a sensible nutritional choice: choosing this product could be life-changing.

The adjective phrases in the second text are far more complicated because many of them are post-modified with a phrase (*shy of loving frankly*) or clause (*free to keep*; *wary how you engage*). This complexity of style is appropriate for its intended audience, the reading Victorian public. The tone is instructive and Thackeray uses the IMPERATIVE MOOD (commands) to communicate his advice directly to his female readers. The head words are adjectives expressing emotional qualities (*cautious, shy, wary, honest*); they are used predicatively because the emphasis is on the importance of each particular quality.

Predicative adjective phrases place grammatical and semantic stress on the head word. In the examples here, additional patterning can be seen in the structure of each text as a whole. The advertisement uses patterning: co-ordinated pre-modified adjectives draw attention to the product in the first line, and tripling emphasises its positive qualities at the end. The patterning in the extract from *Vanity Fair* is perhaps less visual, but we are aware of the purposeful voice of the narrator in the co ordinated adjective phrase *free to keep or to break* and the tripling of *Be cautious ... be wary ... Be shy*. This gives a logical and rational tone to the advice, suggesting the underlying sense of what we are being told.

The language of each text is also distinctive because of the different purposes and intended audiences. In the advertisement, the adjectives are wide ranging: they deal with concrete sensual qualities (*fruity, tasty*) and time (*late*); they place adjectives with positive connotations (*wholesome, healthy*) in opposition with an apparently negative quality (*addictive*) as part of the appeal to consumers. In the novel the adjectives are explicitly emotional as befits the context: engagement, broken love and betrayal.

TASK 2   **Using adjective phrases in different text types**

1 Choose one of the following writing exercises. When you have completed your text, evaluate the key linguistic features. You may like to use the suggested framework for analysis in Appendix A.

EITHER
Write a review of a film, theatre production or concert that you have recently attended.

You will need to think about your intended audience, the content and where the review will be printed. Experiment with the position of the adjective phrases and aim to make your overall viewpoint clear by choosing adjectives with appropriate connotations.

OR

Write a paragraph describing some kind of image – a painting, a poster, or a photograph. The piece you write will be included in an auction catalogue so that potential buyers can get a vivid sense of the picture before they see it. You need to pay close attention to visual detail and technique, and to appeal to the senses.

You will need to think about the best way to recreate visual details in words and the different effects created by choosing predicative or attributive adjective phrases. Your lexical choices must communicate something of the composition, content and mood of the image to the reader.

OR

Write a direct mail letter which will be sent to a wide range of households persuading people to join the club you are representing. It could be a health club, a gym, a sports club or some other specialist group. Use adjective phrases to describe the club facilities and to show how membership could change the lives of its members. Be persuasive.

You will need to think about the genre, the intended audience and the club you are promoting. The connotations of the adjectives and the structure of the adjective phrases will play an important part in persuading your target audience.

5.3 Verb phrases

Verb phrases are the most important linguistic element – every grammatically complete sentence must contain one. Writers and speakers use verb phrases to communicate states, processes and actions – they usually occur after a noun phrase. The kind of words the verb phrase contains reflects the tense (past, present), aspect (progressive, perfective), modality (shades of meaning), and voice (active, passive) of a text.

TASK 1   Verb phrases in different text types

1 Read through the texts below thinking about their audience, purpose and context.

TEXT 1   Extract from a critical study of William Wordsworth
Wordsworth began to change direction as a poet at this time. We see him move away from simple, objective narrative towards a more personal kind of poetry. It was to be a period of subjective and introspective work. In the *Lucy* poems, for instance, we see a new tone of tenderness, which is quite different from the sense of social concern underpinning earlier poems.

TEXT 2   Extract from a newspaper article
I have witnessed more disasters first-hand, both natural and man-made than most people. I have seen the chaos left behind by freak storms in rural areas, the destruction wreaked by hurricanes and the horror of floods that have stolen homes and lives …

TEXT 3   Extract from a classic novel, *Persuasion,* by Jane Austen (1816)

While Sir Walter and Elizabeth were assiduously pushing their good fortune in Laura-place, Anne was renewing an acquaintance of a very different description.

　　She had called on her former governess, and had heard from her of there being an old school-fellow in Bath, who had the two strong claims on her attention, of past kindness and present suffering.

(Chapter 17)

TEXT 4   Spontaneous radio commentary

… and here beneath the lofty columns of this exquisite stone vaulted roof (1) they will soon be married (2) near the high altar are the seats (.) empty now (.) where in a short while he and his wife-to-be will take their places (1) looking across to the line of colourful banners with their bold heraldic designs and down the length of the chapel to the organ, the choir stalls and beyond to the nave (1) the air of expectancy is tangible …

2 Identify the verbs, label any auxiliary verbs and underline the lexical verb.
3 Decide whether the verbs are part of a noun phrase or stand alone as an independent verb phrase. Make a list of the different types of verb phrase used.
4 Write a commentary exploring the use of verb phrases in the texts above.

You should use appropriate terminology and linguistic frameworks to explain and evaluate the texts.
　　You may like to think about:

• the content and purpose
• the different types of verb phrase
• the lexical choice
• the link between the text type and the different kinds of verb phrases

COMMENTARY

The verb phrases in each text are quite different because each has a different audience, purpose and context. The formality of Text 1 (literary criticism) is in direct contrast to the spontaneity of Text 4 (commentary); and the personal tone of Text 2 (newspaper feature) can be set against the narrative approach of Text 3 (novel).

Text 1 is educative in its purpose. The writer's relationship with the intended audience is formal and the context is subject specific – it is written for people with a specific interest in literature. The language is directly linked to the subject matter: it draws on a literary lexical field (*poet, narrative, poetry, poems, tone*) and uses modifiers to establish the specific nature of Wordsworth's work (*simple, objective, personal, subjective, introspective*).

The extract uses the active voice in a direct explanation of the change in Wordsworth's style. Verb phrases linked to Wordsworth are in the simple past (*began, was*), while those linked to his poetry use the simple present (*see, is*). This is a standard distinction drawn in critical writing – since the poet is dead, we use the past tense to discuss his life; since his poems are still in existence and continue to be read and interpreted, we discuss them using the present tense.

Text 2 and Text 4 are intended to inform and entertain. The newspaper extract represents a personal perspective on living in a time when emergencies are *man-made* as well as *natural* – the repetition of the first person pronoun *I* signals this subjective point of view. The commentary, on the other hand, represents a more objective account of a ceremonial occasion – the formality is marked by the commentator's detached description. Concrete nouns re-create the physical setting for a radio audience (*columns, roof, altar, seats, banners, choir stalls, chapel, organ* and *nave*), with long complex noun phrases used to communicate the visual detail.

m	m	h	q

the lofty columns of this exquisite stone vaulted roof

det	AdjP	N	PrepP

The verb phrases of Text 2 prepare us for the argument that follows. The use of perfective verb phrases (*have witnessed, have seen*) demonstrates that these particular events have a present relevance. Had the journalist used simple past tense verbs 'witnessed'/'saw'), the effect would have been very different. While the simple past tense would have recorded events that are complete and at a distance from us, the present perfective emphasises their current significance. The perfective verb phrases, therefore, allow the writer to use past personal experience as evidence for case that he argues in the present. Other verbs (*left, wreaked*) are *–ed* participle modifiers – they post-modify noun phrases in which the head words (*chaos, destruction*) are central to the main argument of the text.

A commentary is spontaneous and is delivered as a sequence of events unfolds. The first verb phrase *will ... be married* immediately establishes the nature of this specific occasion. The modal verb phrases indicate a future time, reminding the listener that the commentary is taking place prior to the service, but simple present tense verb phrases (*are, is*) allow the commentator to set the scene. We are aware of his presence only through the non-finite verb phrase *Looking*, which draws attention to the fact that this commentary is delivered from a particular physical viewpoint in the chapel (the adverbs *beneath, across, down* and *beyond* reinforce this).

The final text here is literary. Its purpose is to entertain, but its context is formal – nineteenth-century novels are now more likely to be read by a specific rather than a general audience. Typical of its genre, Text 3 introduces character (*Sir Walter, Elizabeth, Anne, her former governess, an old school-fellow*) and place (*Laura-place, Bath*). The language is formal and many of the words are polysyllabic (*assiduously, acquaintance, governess*). The structure is directly linked to the development of a narrative and is therefore chronological.

Text 3 uses two different kinds of aspect (progressive and perfective), each with a different semantic function in the extract. Most novels are written in the past tense, but by using a progressive form, Austen suggests a process that has taken place over time and is not yet complete. The neat patterning of the past progressive verb phrases (*were ... pushing, was renewing*) sets the characters in opposition. Austen distinguishes between Sir Walter and Elizabeth, and Anne in the semantic associations of the two lexical verbs: while *renewing* has positive connotations, *pushing* suggests something of the insincere social aspirations of father and daughter.

The use of the adverb *assiduously* underpins this division, mirroring Austen's satiri
attack on the misplaced values of Sir Walter and Elizabeth.

The second paragraph changes the aspect: we move from progressive to pe
fective. Where the previous verb phrases described actions that were started in th
past but are still in progress, the perfective verb phrases (*had called, had hear*
represent actions that are complete. They form the basis for the renewal of frienc
ship described in the first paragraph. The fact that this friendship will be based o
past kindness and present suffering further distances it from the social climbing o
Sir Walter and Elizabeth.

In each of the examples here, the writers and speakers choose verb phrases tha
are directly linked to their audience, purpose and context. By choosing differer
voices, aspects and tenses, each writer manipulates our response to the text. It
therefore important to recognise the distinctive features of the verb phrases becaus
they are an integral part of the semantics and as such lead us towards a greate
understanding of a text.

TASK 2   Using verb phrases in different text types

1 Choose one of the following writing exercises. When you have completed you
text, evaluate the key linguistic features. You may like to use the suggested fram
work for analysis in Appendix A.

EITHER
Record a spontaneous commentary which could accompany a live event. Whe
you have finished, transcribe your commentary.

You need to pay particular attention to the tense of the verbs, their form and mear
ing so that you describe what is happening effectively and engage your audienc
Try to be as varied as possible.

OR
Write a report using the passive voice so that the person responsible for th
action of the verb assumes less importance than the process itself.

You could write about a scientific experiment, cooking a certain kind of food or eve
an everyday event. Remember that the focus is on the process rather than on th
person carrying out the actions.

When you have finished, rewrite the passage replacing the passive verb phrase
with active ones.

Think about the way the active and passive verb phrases change the reader's rela
tionship with the text.

OR
Write an extract from an opinion essay using a variety of verb phrases to put you
case. You could write about the facilities for young people in your area, the prob
lems of social unrest during a recession, or about the potential hazards of mobil
phone use.

You will need to use the present tense to discuss the current state of affairs, bu past tense verb phrases to make comparisons and to discuss events that have already taken place. Verb phrases referring to the future will enable you to suggest possible changes. Experimenting with the aspect will allow you to make wider references to things or events with an on-going relevance.

.4 Adverb phrases

.dverb phrases provide us with additional information about time, place, manner nd degree. They can also link sentences or communicate an attitude or comment. heir position tells us something about the importance of the information they pro-ide: they can occur at the beginning, in the middle or at the end of a sentence. If n adverb phrase is removed, a sentence will still make sense.

ASK 1   The effect of adverb phrases

1 Read through the texts below and think about their audience, purpose and con-text.

TEXT 1

New horizons came finally into view as the ship approached unknown waters. We had travelled far, endlessly voyaging into that long forgotten land of dreams. Sadly, we had lost some of our comrades, men who had signed up willingly, indeed innocently. Their contributions, so zealously remembered, had become part of the ship's history, its ornate tapestry of legendary tales. Usually guarded, the remaining sailors, like their famous ill-fated antecedent, told their tales to anyone who would listen, quite shame-lessly delaying ordinary passers-by in each port we visited.

This unfamiliar coastline now offered new challenges, more horribly ominous than any we had seen before. Brightly shining, the sun above us should have made every-thing bearable. Instead, it seemed to make the mist that cloaked the sheer cliff more sinister. Visibly distorted by the rising ghost-grey murk, the fortified pinnacles stood as sentries, guarding their land sternly, inflexibly, tyrannically. Hesitantly, silence fell on deck, tentatively broken now and again by cautiously muttered curses as we sailed closer uneasily. Frankly, we felt as if our end were unavoidably waiting for us.

TEXT 2

New horizons came into view as the ship approached unknown waters. We had trav-elled a long way, voyaging into that long forgotten land of dreams. We had lost some of our comrades, men who had signed up. Their contributions had become part of the ship's history, its ornate tapestry of legendary tales. The remaining sailors, like their famous ill-fated antecedent, told their tales to anyone who would listen.

This unfamiliar coastline offered new challenges. The sun should have made every-thing bearable, but it seemed to make the mist that cloaked the sheer cliff sinister. The fortified pinnacles stood as sentries, guarding their land. Silence fell on deck, broken by muttered curses as we sailed. We felt as if our end was waiting for us.

2 Identify which text uses adverb phrases and then underline the head words. Label any pre- and post-modification and make a list of the different types used.

3 Write notes on the use of adverb phrases in narrative by comparing the two versions of the texts.

You may like to think about:

- the content and purpose
- the position of the adverb phrases
- the kind of additional information provided
- the effect this has on the reader

NOTES

- both texts aim to **entertain** readers
- **sequence of events** remains the same
- in both, **noun phrases** provide clear visual picture of physical scene
- Text 1 – **adverb phrases** add depth to style by intensifying descriptive detail, draw attention to key elements of narrative
- Text 2 (**simplified** version) – absence of adverb phrases makes text:
  - more straightforward
  - significantly shorter (Text 1 has 178 words; Text 2 has 124 words)

Text 2 – simplified version

- adverb phrases guide responses and without them second version is without tonal shades
- no atmospheric detail
- with no time/place references, journey cannot be put into context
- no time adverb phrases:
  - text lacks dramatic intensity
  - no wider sense of past/present to underpin development of narrative
- no sense of development re. characters
  - remain remote
  - little sense of their experience
  - don't know how they feel
- lacks any concrete touchstones for the reader – no indication of narrator's tone of voice or opinions

Text 1

1 Time adverbs

- time adverb phrases help to:
  - establish long-term scale of events
  - focus attention on the importance of this particular moment
- use of *finally* immediately suggests ship's arrival in landscape has been long-awaited event → marks out extract as **narrative climax** or turning point
- other **time adverbs** establish direct contrast between past/present
  - *now* moves from recognition of past hardships to demands of the present

- *before* heightens tension → emphatic end position gives semantic importance, suggesting that horrors sailors are about to face will be worse than anything they have yet experienced in journey

2 Description of journey

- drama of moment reinforced
- adverb of place *far* communicates scale
- connotations of *endlessly* suggest monotony and inexorable movement forwards
- comparative *closer* draws attention to present moment and potential for disaster as ship approaches unknown and apparently hostile environment

3 'Manner' adverbs

- commenting on '**how**' something is done helps us:
  - engage with text
  - begin to understand underlying state of mind/mood of characters
- before voyage has begun, positive adverb phrases *willingly* and *innocently* establish **mood** of hope:
  - simple adverb phrases made up of adverb standing alone
  - effect is intensified by stark, unqualified nature of meaning

4 Effect of journey on sailors

- developed in use of adverb phrases describing **response to lost colleagues**
- fore-grounded time adverb *Usually* implies experiences have significantly changed sailors
- creates contrast between:
  - past → sailors characterised by verb *guarded*
  - present → pre-modified adverb phrases *so zealously* and *quite shamelessly* indicate intensity of desire to talk about lost companions
- pre-modified phrases are in direct contrast to artlessness of **simple adverb phrases** *willingly, innocently*
- suggest something of madness that appears to have descended upon survivors as result of their experiences

5 Adverb phrases describing landscape

- second paragraph → change of focus:
  - narrative moves away from crew and towards scene
  - adverbs describing landscape have negative connotations
- pre-modifying adverbs in comparative adjective phrase *more horribly ominous than any we had seen before* establish mood
- reinforced by simple adverb phrases personifying rocks (*sternly, inflexibly, tyrannically*)
- tripling of asyndetically listed phrases and position at end of sentence gives them semantic significance
- negative connotations dominate tone at end of paragraph

- only positive adverb phrase (***Brightly*** *shining*) is undermined by modality of verb phrase (*should have made*) → suggestion of expected action that remains unfulfilled
- description of silence falling on deck is symbolic of negative mood
- simple phrase *hesitantly* (front position) reinforced and developed by semantically similar adverbs (*tentatively ... cautiously ... uneasily*) → reflect nervousness of men
- framing sentence with initial and final position adverb increases tension of situation
- men's entrapment made more explicit in final sentence with simple adverb phrase *unavoidably*

5 Tone of narrator

- two **sentence adverbs/disjuncts** *Sadly* and *Frankly*:
  - convey his attitude to what is being described
  - help us to identify with characters and explicitly recognise mood

The adverb phrases in Text 1 add a range of information about time, place and manner. This detail colours an otherwise blank canvas: characterisation becomes more complex; the mood is developed; and the voice of the narrator emerges. Features like these add depth to the narrative, allowing the writer to explore a story as more than just a sequence of events. The semantic range of the adverb phrases, their position and connotations intensify the effect of the narrative, encouraging the reader to engage with the text at a number of levels.

TASK 2 Using adverb phrases

1 Choose one of the following writing exercises. When you have completed your text, evaluate the key linguistic features. You may like to use the suggested framework for analysis in Appendix A.

EITHER
Write an extract from a narrative in which you use adverb phrases to convey a sense of time, place and mood, and to develop a sense of the characters and narrator.

You need to pay particular attention to your choice of adverbs and the kind of information they give to the reader.

Re-write your extract as a simplified version for younger readers.

You will need to make your extract shorter and more direct by removing adverb phrases and by simplifying other phrases where appropriate.

OR
Write a newspaper report in which you describe an event which has taken place at a specific time and place.

Think about the kind of newspaper you are writing for and remember to use adverb phrases to give a clear sense of when and where things happened. You may also wish to include direct speech or statements by the people involved with disjuncts to indicate their attitude to what has happened.

OR
Script a formal or informal conversation between two people who have very different viewpoints on a particular issue.

Use sentence adverbs to convey the distinctive views of each person and conjuncts to develop each argument logically and coherently.

5.5 Phrases in different text types

Understanding the function of each kind of phrase and how they work together helps us to appreciate the ways in which writers and speakers create meaning. It is important to be able to recognise where they start and stop, and where we expect to find them in a sentence. This knowledge forms the basis for our study of different kinds of text; the terminology gives us a shorthand with which to describe how meaning is communicated.

TASK 1   The effect of phrases in different texts

1 Read through the texts below carefully.

TEXT 1   A car advertisement printed in a daily newspaper
The City Star (from £7190) also comes with body coloured bumpers, electric front windows, a sliding rear seat and remote control locking … And finally … there's always the option of the 1.4-litre.

TEXT 2   Extract from a diary
22 July
Too many unfinished conversations. Miles of uneasy pacing from room to room. An eternity of wakefulness more desolate than the Artic wastes. Mountains of words unspoken – lethal as the Black Widow's bite. So many years of things we didn't do. So many years of places we didn't go.
    The waste. The bitterness. Acrid as the chlorine clouding a pool.
    Yet now, looking back, I know it was sweet.

TEXT 3   Extract from a story for young readers developing confidence
One sunny spring day, Tinteeno and his friends were playing games near the forest, the darkest forest in all the land. Suddenly, they heard a … CRASH. Louder and louder it grew. Until from the dark burst out a horrible monster. A hundred sharpened teeth lined its roaring mouth.

2 Identify the different kinds of phrases used in each text and label their form.
3 Write a commentary exploring the effect of the phrases you have identified in each text type.

You should use appropriate terminology and linguistic frameworks to explain an
evaluate the texts.

You may like to think about:

- the audience, purpose and context of each text
- the type of phrases used
- their structure and position
- the semantic effect

COMMENTARY

Inevitably the intended audience, purpose and context of each text will affect th
kind of language structures chosen. While Texts 1 and 2 are clearly written for a
adult audience, Text 3 is designed for younger children who are only just beginnin
to read independently; while the diary extract is reflective and the story aims t
entertain, the advertisement is designed to inform and persuade; while the adver
tisement appears in a general publication that has a wide distribution and the stor
is published by a well-known children's publisher using a format suitable for younge
readers with large print and accompanying illustrations, the diary extract is mor
personal, written primarily for the writer alone. These factors will dictate the kin
of vocabulary and grammatical structures used in each case.

Text 1 uses finite verb phrases in the present tense (*comes with, 's*) because it i
promoting a particular product that is available at the time of publication. A prepo
sitional phrase in parenthesis (*from £7190*) establishes the price and adverb phrase
emphasise additional features available on the City Star model (*also*), indicate th
conclusion of the list (*finally*), and draw attention to the permanent availability o
a bigger engine (*always*). The extract, however, is dominated by pre-modified nou
phrases that represent the physical features of the car: *body coloured bumpers, elec
tric front windows, a sliding rear seat, remote control locking, the option of the 1.4
litre*. These are the means by which the advertisers hope to persuade their potentia
customers.

The phrases follow the grammatical order we would expect with a NP + VP +
NP structure. The prepositional phrase occurs near the front of the sentence since
price is an important element of the advertisers' approach. The adverb phrases occu
in the middle position before the finite verb (*also comes*) and after the copular verb
'be' (*'s always*), and in the front position before the subject and verb (*finally there's*)
Since these phrases are all in the first half of the sentence, they allow the advertiser
to develop their persuasive appeal to readers.

Text 2 uses phrases in a more distinctive way since it does not follow the
expected sentence pattern of NP + VP + NP. Although the writer uses capitalisation
and full stops, the extract is made up of pre- and post-modified phrases rather than
complete grammatical sentences. Only the final grammatical unit can be described
as a 'sentence' because it contains finite verb phrases (*know, was*).

The main body of the extract is made up of noun phrases. They create a
sequence of images describing the writer's relationship and developing our sense
of the ways in which it has failed. The head words suggest the ordinary (*conversa-*

ions, words) and the infinite (*eternity*). They set the diary entry firmly within the context of both the real and the potential ideal of a relationship: pre-modified noun phrases (*Too many unfinished conversations*), post-modified noun phrases (*Mountains of words unspoken*), and pre-and post-modified noun phrases (*So many years of places we didn't go*) suggest the failure of real love to live up to its romantic ideal. The language is marked by a lack of fulfilment – the connotations are negative and the mood is one of disappointment. The extract builds towards the simple noun phrases *The waste* and *The bitterness* that stand alone as symbolic images of a love that foundered.

The adjective phrases enhance the negative mood – the connotations of their head words reinforce the feeling of disillusion and disappointment. The comparative adjective phrase *more desolate than the Artic wastes* and the phrase expressing equivalence (*lethal as the Black Widow's bite*) underpin the futility of the noun phrases which precede them: the emptiness of the *wakefulness* and the meaninglessness of the *Mountains of words* that have been squandered. The climax of the extract is reached in an ambiguous expression of discontent where the post-modified phrase *Acrid as the chlorine clouding a pool* juxtaposes the positive connotations of a cleansing agent with the destructive potential of the chemical. The image seems to recognise the human potential for ruining things, bringing together all the previous images and expressing the complexity of any relationship.

The diary entry has been marked by a mood of regret, of disappointment, and yet the final sentence undermines the apparent climax that has been reached in the adjective phrase. Rather than reinforcing the mood, the grammatical sentence challenges our interpretation: this diary entry is a celebration rather than an expression of disillusion. The relationship may not have lasted, but the time the writer has spent with his lover is *sweet*. In the simple emphatic adjective phrase that concludes the extract, we are left with an uplifting tone that casts a new light over everything that we have read.

The phrases in this extract stand alone without the framework of a grammatical sentence around them. This allows the writer to stress the importance of each phrase as an expression of what his relationship has meant. The starkness of the style mirrors the tone. Only with the complete grammatical sentence does a sense of fulfilment emerge – the sentiments of the writer and his moment of realisation are reinforced by the contrastive conjunction *Yet* marking a turning point and the emphatic adverb of time (*now*). The diary entry thus becomes a personal declaration of the power of experience, both positive and negative, to enhance life.

Because Text 3 is written for a younger audience and uses a different genre, we would expect the structure and organisation of the phrases to be different. The noun phrases are descriptive, providing readers with detail that helps to establish a suitable narrative mood and to introduce time, place and character. Some are simple noun phrases (*Tinteeno and his friends, games, they, a ... CRASH*), but many are pre-modified:

m	m	m	h		m	m	h
One	bright	spring	day		a	horrible	monster
num	AdjP	N	N		det	AdjP	N

m	m	m	h		m	m	h
A	hundred	sharpened	teeth		his	roaring	mouth
det	num	V*ed*	N		det	V*ing*	N

Post-modification is used only once (*the darkest forest in all the land*) and the qualifier is a prepositional phrase – the most straightforward of the post-modifiers.

As may be expected in a narrative, verb phrases are in the simple past (*heard, grew, burst out, lined*), except for the past progressive *were playing*, which is used to indicate an on-going action. The co-ordinated comparative adjective phrase *Louder and louder* and the adverb phrase *Suddenly* add drama, while the prepositional phrases (*near the forest; from the dark*) develop a sense of movement.

The range of phrase types is broader here than in the other extracts and the author has moved certain phrases to unexpected positions in order to enhance the dramatic effect of the narrative. The adverb phrase *Suddenly* commonly appears in the initial position before the subject, but the comparative adjective phrase has been moved from the end of the sentence where it would usually occur after the copula verb *grew*. This adds to the suspense created by the capitalisation of the noun *CRASH* as the unknown creature moves towards the children. Similarly in the following sentence, a prepositional phrase has been brought to the front and the noun phrase *a horrible monster* (the subject of the verb *burst out*) has been delayed until the end. This creates suspense because we have to wait to discover exactly what is coming.

Four of the five sentences in this extract contain the NP + VP + NP pattern, which is common in English (the other uses AdjP + NP + VP). The movement of some phrases to the front allows the writer to create variety and to dramatise the events of his story. It is a flexibility that makes English a particularly rich language – we can change the emphasis of a sentence by moving phrases to unexpected positions.

Each of these texts demonstrates a different approach to the use of phrases. While they all conform to standard grammatical patterns, the variety, structure and position of the phrases depends upon the type of text, its audience and its purpose. We can conclude, therefore, that changes in phrase type, structure and position have an effect on the meaning of a text: semantic possibilities are linked not only to the kind of words we choose, but to the way in which we combine them in phrases.

Part III

Clauses

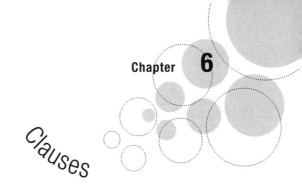

Chapter 6

Clauses

Grammar may seem more threatening as we begin to consider larger grammatical units, and clauses may seem particularly bewildering. We have been using terms such as 'word' and 'sentence' for years in a general way so they seem familiar – the concept of clauses, on the other hand, may be quite new. Despite this, there's no need to worry. Just as phrases represent combinations of words, clauses are just grammatical units built up from combinations of phrases. It will not take you long to learn about their distinctive patterns.

After reading this chapter, you should be able:

- to see how we link phrases together in distinctive patterns
- to recognise and label different kinds of clauses
- to describe their position in a sentence
- to understand the jobs they do

6.1 What is a clause?

A CLAUSE is a group of related phrases which must contain one finite verb phrase. Always begin by identifying any verb phrases (a head verb and any supporting auxiliaries) since this will help you to see how many clauses there are. We mark the beginning and end of a main clause with angled brackets, a subordinate clause with square brackets, and the phrases which make up the clause with round brackets.

A clause can contain:

- a single verb phrase

⟨ **(Sit)** ⟩!   ⟨ **(Go)** ⟩!
  VP   VP

- a verb phrase and a noun phrase

⟨ (The boy) **(laughed)** ⟩.   ⟨ (The mobile) **(is ringing)** ⟩.
  NP   VP   NP   VP

- a sequence of phrases before and after the verb phrase

⟨ (The sky) **(grew)** (black) ⟩.   ⟨ (The teacher) **(strode)** (around the class) (angrily) ⟩.
  NP   VP   AdjP   NP   VP   PrepP   AdvP

⟨ (Then), (in the heat of the afternoon), (a startling shout) **(broke)** (the day's lazy silence) ⟩.
  AdvP   PrepP   NP   VP   NP

6.2 Main and subordinate clauses

There are two types of clause: main and subordinate clauses.

Main clauses (MCl)

MAIN or INDEPENDENT CLAUSES must contain a finite or tensed verb phrase. They may consist of a single verb or a number of phrases, and make sense by themselves.

MCl
⟨ (**Run**) ⟩!
  VP

MCl
⟨ (The girl) (**runs**) (fast) ⟩.
  NP   VP   AdvP

MCl
⟨ (I) (**am running**) (up the road) ⟩.
 NP   VP   PrepP

MCl
⟨ (The children) (**ran**) (races) (on sports day) ⟩.
   NP   VP   NP   PrepP

Subordinate clauses (SCl)

SUBORDINATE or DEPENDENT CLAUSES do not make sense by themselves – they are usually linked to a main clause that completes their meaning. Subordinate clauses begin with a subordinating conjunction, a relative pronoun or a non-finite verb. We mark the beginning and the end with square brackets. If the clause is embedded in a phrase, it will have round brackets marking the beginning and end of the phrase.

MCl
⟨ (The board, [**which** was full of information]), stood in the corner of the room ⟩.
           SCl (relative pron)

MCl
⟨ [**Catching** a train] can be difficult at rush-hour ⟩.
   SCl (V*ing*)

MCl
⟨ We arrived early [**because** we wanted to get good seats] ⟩.
             SCl (sconj)

6.3 The six types of subordinate clause

We can divide subordinate clauses into six distinct types according to the word class of the first word in the clause.

Non-finite clauses (NFCl)

NON-FINITE CLAUSES start with a **non-finite verb**:

MCl
to + verb   (V*infin*)   ⟨ I helped [**to decorate** the bedroom] ⟩.
                      SCl – NFCl

MCl
verb + ing (V*ing*)   ⟨ We love [**taking** the dog for a walk] ⟩.
                     SCl – NFCl

MCl
verb + ed   (V*ed*)   ⟨ [**Varnished** regularly], wooden window frames last for ever ⟩.
                SCl – NFCl

Adverbial clauses (ACl)

ADVERBIAL CLAUSES are often introduced by a **subordinating conjunction** (see Section 2.9) and need a finite main clause to complete their meaning. They usually come at the end of a sentence, but can often be moved to the front. Adverbial clauses give us information about time (*when, after, as*), place (*where*), manner (*as, as though*), result (*so, so that*), reason (*because, as*), purpose (*so that*), concession (*although*), comparison (*as if, as though*), or condition (*if, unless*).

          MCl   MCl

⟨ [**While** I'm in town], I'll visit the library ⟩. ⟨ I often travel abroad [**because** I like the sun] ⟩.
 SCl – ACl (time)   SCl – ACl (reason)

Adverbial clauses can also begin with a ***wh–* word**. This kind of adverbial clause tends to comment on the sentence as a whole, expressing an attitude or making a connection. A *wh–* adverbial clause usually establishes some kind of condition that applies to the main clause.

    MCl

⟨ No-one will give you anything [**whatever** you say] ⟩.
                          SCl – ACl

              MCl

⟨ [**However** warm it is] you are not going out without a coat ⟩.
 SCl – ACl

In informal speech and writing, the preposition *like* is sometimes used to introduce adverbial clauses instead of the conjunctions *as* and *as if*.

I ran to the end of the road **like** she told me to.   She sounded **like** she might cry.
                   (as)   (as if)

In situations requiring formal language, it is more acceptable to choose *as* as a conjunction followed by a clause, and *like* as a preposition followed by a noun phrase.

Relative clauses (RelCl)

RELATIVE CLAUSES begin with the **relative pronouns** *who, which, what, that* (see Section 2.7). They do not make sense by themselves and need to be embedded in a noun phrase in a finite main clause.

    MCl

⟨ (The cat [**that** lives next door]) spends a lot of time in our garden ⟩.
             NP
  det N   SCl – RelCl

Traditionally, we use *whom* where the pronoun is referring to the object of a clause. In contemporary usage, however, *whom* is often replaced by *who*.

Some relative clauses begin with **relative adverbs** (*when, where, why*).

    MCl

⟨ (The place [**where** the family settled down for a picnic]) was beautiful ⟩.
                NP
  det   N   SCl – RelCl

    MCl

⟨ (The reason [**why** I revised so hard]) was to pass my exams ⟩.
             NP
  det   N   SCl – RelCl

In some cases, we can omit the pronoun or adverb (marked by Ø in clause analysis).

> MCl
> ⟨ (The place [**Ø the family settled down for a picnic**]) was beautiful ⟩.
>   det   N   NP SCl – RelCl

> MCl
> ⟨ (The reason [**Ø I revised so hard**]) was to pass my exams ⟩.
>   det   N   NP SCl – RelCl

Sometimes a preposition precedes the relative pronoun.

> MCl
> ⟨ (The software [**with which I work**]) can be unreliable ⟩.
>   det   N   NP SCl – RelCl

In informal writing and in speech, the preposition may occur at the end of a clause and the pronoun may be replaced by *that*.

> ⟨ (The software [**that I work with**]) can be unreliable ⟩.

Relative clauses give us more information about the noun or pronoun to which they are linked. They sometimes appear in parenthesis, separated from the noun with commas or dashes.

> MCl
> ⟨ (The lecturer, [**who is** running for the bus]), works in the Maths department ⟩.
>   SCl – RelCl

This kind of clause is known as a **NON-RESTRICTIVE** or non-defining relative clause because the information contained in the clause is additional. The clause could be omitted and the identity of the noun to which it is linked would still be clear since there is only one lecturer.

If the relative clause is not separated from the noun to which it refers, we call it a **RESTRICTIVE** or defining relative clause.

> MCl
> ⟨ (The lecturer [**who is** running for the bus]) (works) (in the Maths department) ⟩.
>   SCl – RelCl

Here the relative clause provides information that helps us to identify the noun's reference – it limits or restricts the range of the reference. If we omitted the clause, the reference would not be clear since there are a number of lecturers, but only one is running for the bus.

The choice of a restrictive or a non-restrictive relative clause can change the meaning of a sentence, so it is important to decide which one is appropriate.

> Food **which is unhealthy** should not be eaten regularly.

> Food, **which is unhealthy**, should not be eaten regularly.

In the first example, the restrictive relative clause implies that some food is unhealthy and should therefore be eaten in moderation. The use of a non-restrictive clause in the second example, however, suggests that all food is unhealthy. Where the restrictive clause offers useful advice, the non-restrictive clause is actually giving false information.

Noun clauses (NCl)

NOUN CLAUSES begin with a *wh–* word (*what, where, who, which, whoever, whatever, how*) or *that*. They are part of the main clause; they can stand alone or can be embedded in an adjective phrase as post-modification (see Section 4.3).

MCl
We can be (sure [**that** the news will be good]).
      AdjP
   Adj   SCl – NCl

MCl
[**Whatever** news you have] will be welcome.
SCl – NCl

Noun clauses standing alone function as a noun, coming before or after the verb of the main clause. We can test if the clause is a noun clause by replacing it with a more simple grammatical structure (a noun, a pronoun, or a noun phrase).

MCl
‹ [**Whoever** wants a ticket for the concert] should line up over there ›.
SCl – NCl
        (i.e. people interested in tickets for the concert)

MCl
‹ You know [**where** I live] ›. (i.e. my address)
    SCl – NCl

Comparative clauses (CompCl)

COMPARATIVE CLAUSES can either express comparison using *than* (with *less* or *more*) or equivalence using *as ... as*. They can be used with nouns, adjectives or adverbs and need to be embedded in a main clause.

MCl
‹ The old Severn Bridge took [**less** traffic **than** the new bridge does] ›.
         SCl – CompCl
              (with a noun)

MCl
‹ The snow fell [**more** relentlessly **than** I had expected] today ›.
     SCl – CompCl
             (with an adverb)

MCl
‹ I was [**as** certain **as** I could be] ›.
   SCl – CompCl
          (with an adjective)

Comparative clauses tend to come after the verb in a main clause and give us more information about the noun or pronoun that precedes the main verb.

Verbless clauses (VlessCl)

VERBLESS CLAUSES begin with a subordinating conjunction (see Section 2.9), but contain no verb. They need a main clause to complete their meaning.

MCl
‹ [**While** in town], I saw my French teacher ›.
SCl – VlessCl

It is important to be able to recognise the difference between phrases and verbless clauses.

‹ (With no revision), you can't pass your exams ›.
PrepP

‹ (Grateful for everything), the stranger went on his way ›.
AdjP

We could expand the underlined phrases by adding a verb and making them into clauses (*Without doing any revision*; *Feeling grateful for everything*), but it is not necessary because they already have a recognisable grammatical phrase structure.

	m	h		h	q
With no revision			Grateful for everything		
PrepP				AdjP	
prep	NP			Adj	PrepP

We would expect clauses beginning with a subordinating conjunction, on the other hand, to have a subject and a finite verb phrase – we call such clauses 'verbless' because they would normally contain a verb.

                              MCl
‹ [**Although** silly at times], the young boy had great potential ›.
SCl – VlessCl

                              MCl
‹ [**Although** he was silly at times], the young boy had great potential ›.
SCl – ACl

6.4 Clause elements

Recognising the phrase structure of a clause helps us to see how phrases can be combined, but we also need to know what job these phrases are doing. There are seven elements of clause structure which each contain particular types of phrases and fulfil a different function.

1 Subject (S)

The **SUBJECT** indicates who is performing the action or process of the verb phrase. To decide which part of a sentence is the subject, we can ask the question *who?* or *what?* is doing the verb.

The cat drank a saucer of milk.

> **what** drank the milk? = **the cat**

The old woman breathed a sigh of relief.

> **who** breathed a sigh of relief? = **the old woman**

The subject has a direct relationship with the verb phrase because it must agree with the verb.

‹ (**The girls**) love Bratz ›.   ‹ (**The girl**) loves Bratz ›.
3rd person plural present tense   3rd person singular present tense

The subject usually comes first in the clause, but writers and speakers can move it to give other grammatical elements semantic importance.

           S   S
‹ (**The thief**) stole the jewels (silently) ›.   ‹ (**Silently**), (the thief) stole the jewels ›.
   NP   VP   NP   AdvP   AdvP   NP   VP   NP

S
⟨ (**The jewels**) were stolen (silently) by the thief ⟩.
  NP   VP   AdvP   PrepP

In the first example, the clause elements are in a standard order with the subject in the initial position. The second version moves the adverb phrase *Silently* to the front of the sentence, giving it more emphasis by placing it in the site where we would expect to find the subject. The final version uses the passive voice (see Section 4.4) to delay the subject of the active sentence until the end of the clause in a prepositional phrase. This gives greater semantic significance to the noun phrase *the jewels*.

The subject can take the form of a noun phrase or a subordinate clause beginning with *that, what, whoever*.

    S   S   S
⟨ (**The work**) is minimal ⟩. ⟨ (**They**) ran for the bus ⟩. ⟨ [**What I can do**] is to try harder ⟩.
   NP   NP   SCl
 det   N   pron   NCl

2 Predicator (P)

The **predicate** is a traditional term referring to the verb and any other clause elements that follow it.

SUBJECT	PREDICATE
(The tortoise-shell cat)	**was prowling** through the bushes.
[Living in town]	**has** many advantages.

We call the verb element of the clause the PREDICATOR so that we can distinguish it from the form labels we use for verb phrases (VP) and verbs (V). The label 'predicator' indicates the role or function of the verb phrase in the predicate (everything in a sentence that follows the subject). It may be made up of one or more verbs and is the one obligatory clause element. The predicator communicates the action, process or state of being of the subject and is marked for tense, aspect and voice.

Jack (**ran**) to school.   The story (**is written**) by Jack.   Jack (**was becoming**) tired.
  ACTION   PROCESS   STATE
  Vpast   *Vpass*   *Vprog*

Some clauses have only a subject and a predicator.

    S   P
⟨ (The dog) (**barked**) ⟩.
          VP

Because *to bark* is an **intransitive** verb, it does not need anything to follow it. Other verbs need another element to complete their meaning.

  S   P   S   P
⟨ (I) (**need**) <u>a book</u> ⟩.   ⟨ (The next-door-neighbour) (**keeps**) <u>snakes</u> ⟩.
    VP   VP

Verbs that need another clause element to complete the meaning are called **transitive**. Some verbs can be both transitive and intransitive.

    S   P   S   P
⟨ (The vase) (**broke**) ⟩.   ⟨ (The sprinter) (**broke**) <u>her leg</u> ⟩.
          VP   VP

The predicator usually follows the subject at the beginning of the clause, but it can be used without a subject in commands.

> ⟨ (The rain) **(fell)** <u>suddenly</u> ⟩.   ⟨ **(Sit)** <u>down</u> ⟩!   ⟨ **(Give)** <u>it to me</u> ⟩.

The form of the predicator can be either a simple single-word lexical verb (*fell, Sit, Give*) or a lexical verb with one or more auxiliary verbs (see Section 4.4).

> (was singing)   (had been singing)   (should have been singing)
> VP   VP   VP

---

3 Direct Object (Od)

The DIRECT OBJECT is part of the predicate: it is directly affected by the action or process of the verb and usually follows the verb phrase. To decide which part of a sentence is the object, we can ask the question *who?* or *what?* is receiving the action of the verb.

> ⟨ The dog chased (<u>the cat</u>) ⟩.
>
> the dog chased **what?** = **the cat**

> ⟨ The footballer tackled (<u>his opponent</u>) ⟩.
>
> the footballer tackled **whom?** = **his opponent**

In a passive clause, the object of the active sentence precedes the passive verb phrase and functions as a subject.

> ⟨ **(The cat)** (was chased) by the dog ⟩.   ⟨ **(The opponent)** (was tackled) by the footballer ⟩.
>   NP   VP   PrepP   NP   VP   PrepP

Moving the object to the front of the clause gives it added weight. The *by + agent* (person or thing responsible for the action of the verb) at the end of the clause is often omitted:

- it may be obvious who is responsible
- it may be irrelevant
- it may not be clear who has carried out the action or process of the verb
- a writer or speaker may wish to withhold the information

Like the subject, the object can take the form of a noun phrase or a subordinate clause beginning with *that, what, whoever.*

> ⟨ The lecturer cleaned (**the board**) ⟩.   ⟨ Everyone agreed [**that the snow was deep**] ⟩.
>   NP   SCl
>   det   N   NCl

---

4 Indirect object (Oi)

The INDIRECT OBJECT receives the action or process of the verb and rarely occurs without a direct object. We call a verb that takes two objects **ditransitive**. The indi-

ꞏect object occurs before the direct object or after it in the form of a prepositional ꞏhrase beginning with *to* or *for*.

	Oi	Od						Od		Oi		

⟨ I gave (**him**) (a present) ⟩.   ⟨ I gave (a present) (**to him**) ⟩.

	Oi	Od					Od		Oi	

⟨ He bought (**Susan**) (a gift) ⟩.   ⟨ He bought (a gift) (**for Susan**) ⟩.

In form, it is usually a noun phrase, but it can be a prepositional phrase:

Oi   Od

⟨ We awarded (**him**) (a prize) ⟩.
NP

Od   Oi

⟨ Each year, we award (a prize [recognising exceptional achievement]) (**to the student**
SCl – NFCl   PrepP

[who attains the best examination marks]) ⟩.
SCl – RelCl

5 Complement (C)

The COMPLEMENT is part of the predicate and gives us more information about the subject or the direct object. Complements can take the form of a noun phrase, a predicative adjective phrase, a prepositional phrase or a subordinate clause.

Cs   Cs

⟨ The girl became (**a proficient dancer**) ⟩.   ⟨ The girl seemed (**very sensible**) ⟩.
NP   AdjP

Cs   Cs

⟨ The girl was (**in danger**) ⟩.   ⟨ The girl appeared [**to be sad**] ⟩.
PrepP   SCl – NFCl

The SUBJECT COMPLEMENT (**Cs**) occurs after copular verbs (*to be, to become, to appear, to grow, to seem, to remain, to feel*).

S   Cs   S   Cs

⟨ (The day) grew (**cold**) ⟩.   ⟨ (The boy) seemed (**happier than usual**) ⟩.

Although subject complements and direct objects both follow the predicator, each has a different function: the subject complement and the subject are linked semantically (their field of reference is the same); the direct object and the subject are two distinct entities.

S   Cs   S   Od

⟨ (The dog) was (**an Alsatian**) ⟩.   ⟨ (The dog) ate (**the bone**) ⟩.

In the first example above, the noun phrase *an Alsatian* gives us more information about the subject: it specifies the breed of the dog. We know it is a subject complement because there is a direct relationship between the noun phrases that precede and follow the predicator. In the second example, the two noun phrases have separate fields of reference – one performs the action of the verb (*the dog*), the other receives the action of the verb (*the bone*). In this case, the noun phrase that follows the predicator is a direct object.

The **OBJECT COMPLEMENT** (**Co**) occurs after the direct object. It gives us more information about the object.

$\qquad$ Od $\qquad$ Co
‹ The film made (the man) (**sad**) ›.

Where there are two clause elements following the predicator, you will need to decide whether they are two objects (direct and indirect) or a direct object and a complement.

$\qquad$ Oi $\qquad$ Od
‹ The student gave (her friend) (a present) ›.

$\qquad$ Od $\qquad$ C
‹ The student thought (her friend) (**a good runner**) ›.

In the first example above, we could re-write the clause, putting the noun phrase *her friend* at the end after the preposition *to*.

$\qquad$ Od $\qquad$ Oi
‹ The student gave (a present) (to her friend) ›.

If we can change the order of the grammatical units, we know that the clause elements are direct and indirect objects.

In the second example, we could take the two phrases that occur after the predicator (*her friend, a good runner*) and rewrite them as a clause using the verb *to be*

$\qquad$ S $\qquad$ Cs
‹ (Her friend) is (**a good runner**) ›.

If we can rearrange the elements following the predicator as a subject and subject complement, we know that the clause is made up of an object and an object complement.

6 Adverbial (A)

The **ADVERBIAL** is the part of the predicate that gives us additional information about time, place, manner and reason. It is the most flexible element and can occur at the beginning, the end or in the middle of a clause. By changing the position, writers and speakers can change the relative importance of the information it contains.

$\qquad$ A $\qquad$ MEDIAL POSITION
‹ The caged animal snarled (**viciously**) at the waiting crowd ›.

$\qquad$ A $\qquad$ FINAL POSITION
‹ The caged animal snarled at the waiting crowd (**viciously**) ›.

$\qquad$ A $\qquad$ INITIAL POSITION
‹ (**Viciously**), the caged animal snarled at the waiting crowd ›.

The initial and final positions tend to place more emphasis on the adverbial because the beginning and end of a clause have greater prominence.

Adverbials can usually be omitted without affecting the grammatical structure of a sentence.

$\qquad$ A
‹ The children laughed (**excitedly**) ›. $\qquad$ ‹ The children laughed ›.

To decide which part of a clause is an adverbial, we can ask the questions *when? where? how? how often? how long?* or *why?*

	A	(where?)

‹ The wind blew **(over the moors)** ›.

	A	(how long?)

‹ We are staying **(for two days)** ›.

	A	(how often?)

‹ The boys attended school **(regularly)** ›.

	A	(how?)

‹ The kitten mewed **(so pitifully)** ›.

	A	(why?)

‹ Babies cry [**because they are hungry**] ›.

	A	(when?)

‹ Are you coming **(this morning)** ›?

The adverbial can take the form of a noun phrase (*this morning*), an adverb phrase (*regularly, so pitifully*), a prepositional phrase (*over the moors, for two days*), or a subordinate clause (*because they are hungry*).

Using a range of adverbials helps writers and speakers to develop the atmosphere of a narrative.

A	(why?)	A	(how often?)	A	(how?)	A	(where?)

‹[**As if for vengeance**], the wind (**frequently**) blew (**like an enraged beast**) (**over the moors**) ›.
SCl – VlessCl · · · · · · · AdvP · · · · · · · · PrepP · · · · · · · · · · PrepP

Similes (*like a...; as a ...*) create a semantic link between apparently unrelated things (*the wind/an enraged beast*), often developing a visual analogy and helping the intended audience to appreciate the mood or physical quality of something in the text. Similarly, descriptive language (*As if for vengeance*) adds depth and variety.

Linking words (*therefore, meanwhile, besides, despite*) and phrases (*according to, on behalf of, on the other hand, like a ..., instead of*) also function as adverbials. These conjuncts allow us to make links with preceding clauses, sentences and paragraphs. They help us to develop arguments or express points of view:

	A

‹ (**In conclusion**), [recognising [that we are fighting for decent working conditions]]
PrepP

	A

is central to our case ›. ‹ We must, (**however**), be aware of opposition › and,
AdvP

A	A	A

‹ (**as a result**), plan our action (**accordingly**) ›. ‹ (**Otherwise**), we stand [to lose
PrepP · · · · · · · · · · · · · · · · · · AdvP · · · · · · · · · · · · · · · · AdvP

more support [than we gain]] ›.

7 Vocative (voc)

The VOCATIVE is an additional element that stands apart from the other clause elements – it is always separated from the rest of the clause by commas and is not counted as part of the clause structure. The vocative refers to the person(s) to whom a clause is addressed. It may be used as a means of attracting attention, to address a person according to their title or to convey a personal opinion about the person addressed. It can occur at the beginning, the end or in the middle.

	voc		voc

Can I come in, **Rob**? **Professor**, I can't work out how to do this question.

	voc		voc

Are you okay, **love**?   Get out, **idiot**, while I clear up the mess!

A vocative can be a name (*Parth, Tamara, Alex*), a family label (*Mum, Grandad, Aunt*), a status marker (*Sir, my Lord, my Learned Friend*), an occupational label (*waiter, nurse, councillor*), an evaluative term (*fool, pig, darling*) or a group label (*lads and lasses, ladies and gentlemen*).

Vocatives help us to adopt the appropriate tone in a formal situation and to create an appropriate relationship in an informal context. The social rules governing such usage are complicated – by choosing the wrong term of address, we can offend or anger. In parliament, for instance, if an MP fails to address a colleague in an appropriately formal manner (*My Honourable Friend*), she or he may be asked to leave the debate.

6.5 Clause structure

We can combine the clause elements to create seven distinctive **clause structures**.

				S P
S	**P**			⟨ (The boy) (ran) ⟩.

			S P O
S	**P**	**Od**	⟨ (The boy) (kicked) (the ball) ⟩.

				S P Oi Od
S	**P**	**Oi**	**Od**	⟨ (The boy) (gave) (the girl) (a rose) ⟩.

			S P Cs
S	**P**	**Cs**	⟨ (The boy) (was) (jubilant) ⟩.

				S P Od Co
S	**P**	**Od**	**Co**	⟨ (The boy) (put) (the girl) (in a good mood) ⟩.

			S P A
S	**P**	**A**	⟨ (The boy) (sat) (in the park) ⟩.

				S P Od A
S	**P**	**O**	**A**	⟨ (The boy) (put) (his bike) (in the shed) ⟩.

These structures will form the basis for our analysis – they are not the only possible clause patterns, but they help us to recognise the most common structures in English.

6.6 The position and function of clauses

The **position** of a clause is directly linked to its function: clauses may stand alone; they may fill the site of a clause element (subject, object, complement or adverbial); they may be embedded in a phrase. If a clause stands alone, it must be a main or independent clause. All other clauses will be subordinate or dependent clauses.

Clauses embedded in phrases

As we saw in Chapter 4, phrases can be post-modified by clauses. We describe these as EMBEDDED CLAUSES because they are linked to the head word of the phrase. Post-modifying clauses are all subordinate.

Noun phrases

Noun phrases, which fill the subject, object or complement site, can be post-modified by clauses (relative, non-finite, noun).

〈 (Everybody) (likes) (the post-grad [**who** is studying Modelling]) 〉.

  S   P   O

          SCl – RelCl

O = post-modified NP

〈 (Saturday) (is) (the best day [**to go** to town]) 〉.

  S   P   Cs

        SCl – NFCl

Cs = post-modified NP

〈 (The belief [**that** Father Christmas is real]) (excites) (little children) 〉.

     S   P   Od

      SCl – NCl

S = post-modified NP

If a head noun is followed by a non-finite –*ing* participle, we need to check whether it is:

- a post-modifying non-finite clause
- functioning as an adverbial in the sentence as a whole

         S   P   Od   A

〈 (The ambulance [**rushing** to the accident]) (lost) (its way) (in the city centre) 〉.

       SCl – NFCl [embedded in a NP]

      S   A   P   Od   A

〈 (The ambulance) [**rushing to the accident**] (lost) (its way) (in the city centre) 〉.

       SCl –NFCl [stands alone]

In the first example, the non-finite clause helps us to distinguish which ambulance is being referred to – it gives us additional information about the specific vehicle. In the second, the non-finite clause answers the question when? – it provides additional information about the point at which the ambulance got lost.

   In most cases, punctuation helps us to recognise the function of the non-finite clause: where it functions as an adverbial, it often appears in parenthesis, separated from the rest of the clause by commas, dashes or brackets.

    S   A   P   Cs

〈 (The tiger), [**tearing at the abandoned carcass**], (seemed) (content) 〉.

In addition, an adverbial non-finite clause can be moved to different positions in a sentence while a post-modifying non-finite clause must follow the head noun it qualifies.

        S   P   Od

〈 (The footballer [**taking the penalty**]) (equalised) (the score) 〉. [identifying

       SCl – NFCl [embedded in NP]   specific footballer]

     A   S   P   Od

〈 [**Taking the penalty**], (the footballer) (equalised) (the score) 〉. [initial position]

     S   P   Od   A

〈 (The footballer) (equalised) (the score) [**taking the penalty**] 〉. [final position]

     S   A   P   Od

〈 (The footballer), [**taking the penalty**] , (equalised) (the score) 〉. [medial position]

Adjective phrases

ADJECTIVE PHRASES can be post-modified by subordinate clauses (non-finite, noun and comparative) and they occur in the **complement** site. Because they follow the verb phrase, we call them **PREDICATIVE**.

      S   P   Cs
〈 (I) (was) (unsure [**what** I should do next]) 〉.
                   SCl – NCl

     S   P   Cs
〈 (The factory worker) (seemed) (glad [**to leave** at the end of the shift]) 〉.
                           SCl – NFCl

   S   P   Od   Co
〈 (I) (thought) (the situation) (**more** dangerous [**than** it had been before]) 〉.
                            SCl – CompCl

Adverb phrases

Adverb phrases can also be post-modified by noun and comparative clauses. They occur in the adverbial site.

     S   P   Od   A
〈 (The boy) (completed) (his homework) (**more** carefully [**than** he had on previous nights]) 〉.
                            SCl – CompCl

   S   P   A
〈 (I) (ran) (so fast [**that** I was soon out of breath]) 〉.
             SCl – NCl

Subordinate clauses as clause elements

Some subordinate clauses stand alone in a clause site – they are not directly linked to a noun, adjective or adverb. Subordinate clauses can occur in the subject, object, complement and adverbial sites.

      S   P   Cs
〈 [**Trying** hard] (is) (always important) 〉.
 SCl – NFCl

     S   P   Od
〈 (Our group) (believed) [**that** the presentation was effective] 〉.
               SCl – NCl

    S   P   Cs
〈 (Our plan) (was) [**to visit** the castle before dark] 〉.
           SCl – NFCl

       A   S   P   A
〈 [**When** darkness fell] (the lights) (shone) (brightly) 〉.
 SCl –ACl

We can check whether a subordinate clause **fills a whole clause site** or is **part of a clause element**:

- ▸ if the subordinate clause can be removed and some element of the clause is still left, we know that it is an embedded subordinate clause

- if we remove it and the clause site is empty, we know that the subordinate clause is functioning as a clause element

```
    MCl                 S                        P          Cs              A
< (The ducks [which were walking on ice] ) (looked) (very uncertain) [because they
              SCl – RelCl                                              SCl –ACl

kept slipping] >.
```

```
    MCl   S          P          Cs         A
< (The ducks Ø) (looked) (very uncertain) (Ø) >.
```

which were walking on ice = embedded subordinate clause (noun phrase left)

because they kept slipping = clause element (nothing left)

6.7 Identifying clauses in sentences

It is useful to understand how clauses interact because it helps us to see how writers and speakers control their material and guide audience response. In order to identify the different clauses, you can work through the following process.

Stage 1 How many clauses are there?

1 Find the verbs, or groups of linked verbs, and underline them.

We need to look for single present and past tense verbs (*goes, went*), participles in non-finite clauses (*going, gone*), verbs with auxiliaries (*has gone, is going, might go, should have gone*), and verbs with the preposition 'to' (*to go*).

In the sentence below, for instance, we have five verbs:

> We <u>like</u> <u>going</u> to town on Saturdays, but the main shopping precinct <u>was</u> too busy <u>to</u> <u>enjoy</u> when it <u>got</u> close to Christmas.

- three finite verbs
  like   →   first person plural present tense
  was/got   →   third person singular past tense
- two non-finite
  going   →   *–ing* participle
  to enjoy →   infinitive

From this, we know that there are five clauses.

Stage 2 Are the clauses main or subordinate?

1 Look at the finite verbs.

We know that a main clause must have a finite verb phrase.

> We (**like**) going to town on Saturdays, but the main shopping precinct (**was**) too busy to enjoy when it (**got**) close to Christmas.

We can see that the first person plural present tense verb *like* is preceded by a subject and followed by an object.

<pre>
       S   P   Od
  ‹ (We) (like) (going to town...) ...›
</pre>

It makes sense by itself and follows the pattern **S P O** (one of the seven distinctive clause structures in English listed in Section 6.5). This would suggest that it is a main clause.

We know that *but* is a co-ordinating conjunction linking two main clauses (see Section 2.9). It is followed here by another recognisable clause structure **S P C**.

<pre>
                     S   P   C
  but ‹ (the main shopping precinct) (was) (too busy ...) ›
  conj
</pre>

The third finite verb (*got*), however, is not part of a main clause because it is preceded by *when*, a subordinating conjunction of time. It is therefore part of a subordinate clause.

2 Look at the non-finite verbs.

Having identified the two main clauses, we know that the other underlined verbs must be part of subordinate clauses which do not make sense by themselves. We can identify their type by looking at:

- the **form** of the verb
- the **key word(s)** that precede the verb

> We like **going** to town on Saturdays, but the main shopping precinct was too busy **to enjoy** when it got close to Christmas.

Both *going* and *to enjoy* are non-finite. We therefore know that there are two non-finite subordinate clauses.

STAGE 3   Are the subordinate clauses embedded in phrases or filling a clause site?

We need to decide what job each subordinate clause is doing in the sentence by looking at its **position** and the **words that precede it**.

1 Look at the first subordinate clause

We can see that it is preceded by a finite verb phrase (*like*): the subordinate clause, therefore, is functioning as a clause element. We can ask the question 'what?' to get the answer *going to town*, which suggests that the clause is filling the object site (see Section 6.4).

<pre>
       S   P   Od
  ‹ (We) (like) [going to town] ...
                  SCl – NFCl
</pre>

2 Look at the second subordinate clause

It follows the adjective *busy* and we know that adjectives can be post-modified by non-finite clauses (see Section 4.3). The clause is therefore embedded in a predicative adjective phrase which follows the verb *to be* in the complement site.

<pre>
                        S   P   Cs
  ‹ ... (the main shopping precinct) (was) (too busy [to enjoy]) ... ›
                                             SCl – NFCl
</pre>

▌ Look at the third subordinate clause

t functions as a distinct clause element: it fills the adverbial site and answers the
question 'when?'

<table>
<tr><td></td><td>S</td><td>P</td><td>Cs</td><td>A</td></tr>
</table>

‹ ... (the main shopping precinct) (was) (<u>too busy **[to enjoy]**</u>) [<u>when it **got** close to</u>

                  SCl – ACl

<u>Christmas</u>...] ›

Stage 4 Which clause elements are used?

This is the point at which you put together all the information you have gathered
so far. We already know the following:

MCl S P   Od   MCl   S   P

‹ (We) (like) [going to town] on Saturdays ›, but ‹ (the main shopping precinct) (was)

     SCl – NFCl   conj

       Cs   A

(too busy [to enjoy]) [when it got close to Christmas] ›.

   SCl – NFCl SCl – ACl

As you can see, we label the main clauses above, with subordinate clauses and conjunctions below.

The only section not yet labelled is the prepositional phrase *on Saturdays* and
we now need to consider the function of this phrase. It provides the answer to the
question 'when?', but it is not filling the adverbial site of the sentence – it is dependent on the non-finite clause in the object site. We know there is a direct link
between these two grammatical units because if the object were removed, the
phrase *on Saturdays* would no longer make sense.

     S P

  ‹ (We) (like) Ø (on Saturdays) ... ›

This is because *like* is a transitive verb: it requires an object to complete its meaning.
The prepositional phrase, therefore, is part of the object site.

We can now complete our clause analysis of this sentence:

MCl S P   Od   MCl   S   P

‹ (We) (like) [going to town on Saturdays] ›, but ‹ (the main shopping precinct) (was)

     SCl – NFCl   conj

       Cs   A

(too busy [to enjoy]) [when it got close to Christmas] ›.

   SCl – NFCl SCl – ACl

Sometimes writers and speakers do not conform to clause patterns that we can
easily recognise, but the more practice you do, the quicker you will become at this
kind of analysis. Look at the **position of phrases** and ask yourself the **appropriate
questions** and you should be able to identify the clause elements in most sentences.

6.8 Grammatical ambiguity

Sometimes we can label the grammatical structure of a clause in more than one
way. We refer to this as **grammatical** AMBIGUITY. Changing the grammatical struc-

ture can change the meaning and grammatical ambiguity may therefore create semantic ambiguity. The context will usually help us to decide which meaning is intended, but writers and speakers can intentionally create grammatical ambiguity for comic effect.

We are familiar with the kind of joke that puns on the meanings or spellings of particular words.

> Q. What did the grape do when someone stepped on it?
>
> A. It let out a little wine.

The humour here lies in the semantic ambiguity created by the use of a HOMOPHONE: a word that has the same pronunciation, but a different spelling and meaning (e.g. *threw*, *through*). The joke requires us to understand the semantic connection between *wine* (the drink produced by fermenting the juice pressed from grapes) and *whine* (a high-pitched plaintive cry or moan).

Similarly, jokes can use a HOMONYM: two words that are spelt the same, but have different meanings (e.g. *wind* – a noun, a current of air; *wind* – a verb, to tighten the spring of a clockwork mechanism). Many, however, rely on POLYSEMY – a term used to refer to a word that has a range of different meanings.

> Q. Why should you take a pencil to bed?
>
> A. To draw the curtains.

In this case, the verb *draw* can mean 'to pull together or away' and 'to depict or sketch a picture in lines'. Linguists find it difficult to distinguish between polysemia (one form but lots of meanings) and homonymy (two words which happen to have the same form).

Sometimes, grammatical ambiguity can create unintentional humour. In the following example taken from a news report, there is a non-deliberate ambiguity:

> Too many policemen can't shoot straight or take bribes.

We know there are two clauses here joined by a co-ordinating conjunction (*or*).

> S P A P O
> ⟨ (Too many policemen) (can't shoot) (straight) ⟩ or ⟨ (take) (bribes) ⟩.
> conj

In grammatical terms, we expect the negative modal auxiliary *can't* to be repeated in the second verb phrase. Humour is therefore created in the suggestion that policemen are inefficient because they do not take bribes. This kind of accidental grammatical ambiguity will often be spotted by readers who send examples in to programmes like *The News Quiz* (Radio 4) and *Have I Got News for You* (BBC 1).

In advertising, slogans sometimes use grammatical ambiguity for dramatic effect.

> No ticket.
>
> Fine.

This example from the back of a city bus allows public transport systems to warn their users of the risks of travelling without buying a ticket. It is eye-catching because of its ambiguity. On one level, we can read *Fine* as an adjective phrase tanding alone: it could be a colloquial justification for having no ticket. Since this clearly not a message that a transport system would be promoting, we look again. As a noun, *Fine* represents the penalty which must be paid for failing to buy a ticket - it is an emphatic reminder of the consequences.

5.9 Conclusion

The information on clauses in this section helps us to see how phrases can be linked together into larger semantic units. We need to understand the ways in which main and subordinate clauses can be used, the effects created when clause elements are included or omitted, and the significance of the position of clauses and clause elements. This is the starting point for a consideration of style: in their choice of clause structure, writers and speakers can control the complexity of their text, guide the response of their audience, and reflect the form and tone of a particular genre.

An understanding of the form and function of clause structure and a knowledge of the ways in which we combine clauses forms the basis for sentence analysis. Before moving on to Part IV, therefore, it is important to be confident in the recognition and labelling of clauses.

Chapter 7

Using your knowledge

In this chapter, you have the opportunity to apply the knowledge you have gained about clauses. The close reading activities require you to consider the effects created by the clauses the writer or speaker has chosen. The writing tasks encourage you to experiment with different clause types, structures and positions.

7.1 Using main and subordinate clauses

Writers and speakers use main and subordinate clauses in a variety of ways. By making distinctive choices, they can vary the complexity of a text, change the pace, appeal to different kinds of audiences or attract attention to certain pieces of information.

TASK 1   The effect of main and subordinate clauses in different text types

1 Read through the texts below.

TEXT 1   Extract from a fairytale for younger readers

Once upon a time there was a little girl called Little Red Riding Hood. She lived in a pretty little cottage near the forest with her mummy and daddy. The forest was big and dark and scary. It was not a nice place for a little girl.

Little Red Riding Hood's grandmother lived in the forest. Sometimes Little Red Riding Hood visited her grandmother, but she was very careful in the forest. She never left the path.

TEXT 2   Extract from an adult education course brochure

All full and concessionary course fees are shown in the prospectus and online. You should refer to the Financial Assistance section below to see whether or not you qualify for financial assistance or the concessionary fee.

Payment can be made by cheque, postal order, cash, Switch/Maestro or Visa/Master Card. Fill in relevant card details on the form or attach a cheque/postal order.

Do not send cash through the post. Cheques should be made payable to CLE.

Where an employer is to pay the course fees and wishes to be invoiced, a Purchase Order should be provided to this effect, which should be attached to the enrolment form.

2 Identify the main and subordinate clauses used in each text and label their form.
3 Write a commentary exploring the use of main and subordinate clauses in each text.

You should use appropriate terminology and linguistic frameworks to explain and evaluate the texts.
You may like to think about:

- the content and purpose
- the structure of the verb phrases
- the number and type of clauses
- the position of clauses
- the effect on the reader

COMMENTARY

Text 1 is a simple narrative designed for younger children. It retells a well-known fairytale and uses straightforward language and short sentences. Text 2, on the other hand, is subject specific and formal. It uses subject specific language and longer, more complex sentences. The intended audience can be narrowly defined since the text is aimed at people wishing to enrol on a course at a particular institution. Where Text 1 aims to entertain, Text 2 aims to inform.

The structure of the verb phrases mirrors the different intended audiences and purposes of the two texts. Text 1 uses mainly simple past tense verb phrases: some are regular in form (*lived, visited*), but others are common irregular verbs (*was, left*). Every one of the nine verb phrases is a single word phrase and there is little variety in the lexical verbs with *lived* occurring twice and *was* occurring four times. This passage is taken from a narrative that would probably be read aloud and this, as well as the age of the intended audience, dictates the form of the verb phrases. They are short and familiar and could therefore be processed quickly.

Some of the verb phrases in Text 2 are also simple single word phrases: simple present tense (*qualify, is*) and command forms (*Fill in, attach, Do not send*). There is, however, far more variety than in Text 1 and the verb phrases tend to be more complex. There are six passive verb phrases (*are shown, can be made, should be made, to be invoiced, should be provided, should be attached*); many are made up of auxiliary and lexical verbs.

aux	aux	lex		aux	aux	lex	
can	be	made	(possibility)	should	be	provided	(obligation)
mod	prim	*Ved*		mod	prim	*Ved*	

There are also three non-finite verb phrases (*to see, to pay, to be invoiced*). This wider range of verb phrases reflects the formality of the text, its technical content (enrolment and fees) and its adult audience.

Although both extracts are made up of seven sentences, the balance of main and subordinate clauses in each text is quite different. As we would expect, Text 1 is dominated by main clauses, with only one subordinate clause.

       A   dumS   P   (S)   (See Section 8.5 for dumS)
⟨ (Once upon a time) (there) (was) (a little girl [called Little Red Riding Hood]) ⟩.
                                                     SCl – NFCl

The subordinate clause is an embedded post-modifying non-finite clause which gives us more information about the noun phrase *a little girl*. This is a familiar construction and does not complicate the narrative.

Text 2 is significantly more complex. The seven sentences here are made up of 15 clauses: eight are main clauses, seven are subordinate. Six clauses have a passive verb phrase. The opening sentence is straightforward, containing only one clause with the clause elements in a standard order:

                       S   P   A
⟨ (All full and concessionary course fees) (are shown) (in the prospectus and online) ⟩.

Other sentences, however, contain a number of clauses – often in the adverbial element of the sentence.

                     A   A
⟨ [Where an employer is [to pay the course fees]] and [Ø wishes [to be invoiced]],
  SCl – ACl   SCl – NFCl   conj   SCl – ACl   SCl – NFCl

MCl   S   P   A   S
(a purchase order) (should be provided) (to this effect), [which should be attached

                                                            SCl – RelCl

to the enrolment form] ⟩.

In this sentence, there are six clauses – three are in the passive voice. The adverbial site of the clause contains two free standing co-ordinated adverbial clauses.

Where an employer **is** … and … Ø … **wishes.**
    sconj   VP   conj   sconj   VP

Within this structure there are two further non-finite subordinate clauses (*to pay, to be invoiced*) which function as direct objects in the adverbial clause.

The complexity of the sentence (five of the seven subordinate clauses occur in it) and the fact that the co-ordinated adverbials appear in the initial position place a heavy load on the reader: we have to wait for the verb that functions as the verb phrase of the main clause (*should be provided*). An additional complication occurs in the apparently free standing relative clause (*which should be attached …*) at the end of the sentence. Although this is at the end of the main clause, it is post-modifying the noun phrase in the subject site (*a purchase order*). The style and the use of passive verb phrases are indicative of the formality of the text, which is legalistic in its need to establish appropriate procedures.

The texts here demonstrate clearly how main and subordinate clauses can be used in different ways for different purpose and audiences. By choosing simple verb phrases and main clauses rather than subordinate clauses, we can ensure that a spoken or written text is straightforward. Where the content and purpose are themselves more complicated, however, it is unlikely that short main clauses will enable he writer or speaker to communicate effectively with their intended audience. The key to effective communication lies in recognising what is grammatically appropriate for the audience and purpose of the text, and in controlling and balancing clauses.

TASK 2   Experimenting with main and subordinate clauses

1 Write a simple descriptive paragraph using only main clauses.

You need to think carefully about the topic you choose – for instance, standing in a queue, being at a party, visiting a favourite place, describing a particular object, or walking through a busy town centre. Remember that you need to use verb phrases with simple past or present tense verbs.

2 Add subordinate clauses to your paragraph.

You need to think about the type and position of subordinate clauses you can include as post-modifiers in phrases, or as clause elements.

When you have completed your text, compare and contrast it with your earlier text, evaluating the key linguistic features and commenting on the semantic differences. You may like to use the suggested framework for analysis in Appendix A.

TASK 3   Using main and subordinate clauses to create different styles and tones

1 Read through the two newspaper reports below. They both have the same content, but each adopts a different style and tone.

TEXT 1   Compact newspaper

Baby Tearful safe for children, makers insist

THE MANUFACTURERS of the number one Christmas toy, Baby Tearful, strongly defended her safety yesterday after reports that her tears might contain toxic chemicals.

The company said the doll was "totally harmless" and had passed "meticulous testing" for health and safety in an industry that was renown for its safety standards.

The company issued a statement assuring anyone who had already purchased Baby Tearful or was about to purchase one that the toy is 100 per cent safe and complies with all US and European toy safety standards.

The statement was released after a consumer research group said tests had revealed traces of a strong chemical, which can cause headaches, nausea and dizziness, at unacceptable levels in her tears.

Baby Tearful, sold worldwide, is tipped to be the biggest-selling toy with stocks already running low across Britain.

TEXT 2   Tabloid newspaper

Boo Hoo Hoo for Baby Tearful
'TOXIC' TOY TOO HOT TO HANDLE

BABY TEARFUL cries toxic tears. The shocking claim by a consumer watchdog has angered the firm behind this year's Christmas top-seller.

Traces of a chemical that exceeded permitted levels were found and the furious manufacturers have threatened to SUE the organisation over its 'flawed' tests.

A spokesman for the toy company said: 'The publication of unfounded claims at this time of year is unfair. We have stringent safety and quality standards. We work very hard to produce safe toys.'

Parents have stripped shelves in the Christmas scramble. But the consumer guide's big **NO NO** to the number one must-have gift may affect sales.

British stores stand behind the toy and have no plans to withdraw it so the weepy wonder continues to top Santa's list for many three to nines.

2 Identify the main and subordinate clauses in each report and label the clause elements.

3 Complete the table below, recording the number of sentences, main and subordinate clauses, and the different types of subordinate clause.

Text	Sentences	Main	Sub	NCI	NFCI	RelCl	ACI
Compact							
Tabloid							

4 Write a short commentary comparing and contrasting the two reports.

You may like to think about:

- the intended audience
- the tone and language
- the clause structure

COMMENTARY

The style of each report aims to appeal to a distinctive readership: tabloids are often read by people who prefer a newspaper to be entertaining, compacts by readers who choose a more formal approach to journalism. The tone of each report here, therefore, is quite different. The tabloid headlines treat the story in a more light-hearted way, using alliteration (*TOXIC TOY*) and the colloquial expressions *Boo Hoo Hoo* and *TOO HOT TO HANDLE*. The compact headline, by contrast, chooses neutral language – it uses a more subtle approach to draw attention to the product, foregrounding the object (the manufacturers' counter claim) in a marked position at the front of the sentence.

          Od   S   P

⟨ [Ø Baby Tearful Ø safe for children] (makers) (insist) ⟩.
  SCl – NCl

While both the articles cover the same kind of material, the order in which the information is presented is quite different. The focus of the compact report is on the manufacturers' defence of the toy with three out of five paragraphs addressing their argument. The language is therefore formal with verbs reflecting the company position (*defended, assuring*), direct quotations (*'totally harmless', 'meticulous testing'*) and references to their report challenging the consumer group research (*issued a statement*). Details of the consumer report and of sales occur only in the final two paragraphs.

The language of the tabloid is more emotive (*shocking, angered, furious*) and informal with compound words (*top-seller, must-have*), conversational expressions (*stripped, scramble, big NO NO*) and colloquial terms of address (*weepy wonder, Santa*). Here there is a greater emphasis on the apparent problem with the toy: the sensational alliterative noun phrase **toxic tears** appears in bold print in the first sentence of the report. Where the compact uses the tentative modal verb phrase *might contain* and focuses initially on the manufacturers' defence of their product underpinned by the adverb *strongly*, the tabloid aims for shock tactics. In using the more assertive present tense verb **cries**, the report does not immediately record the challenge to the consumer group claim.

The clause structure reflects the audience of each newspaper. The compact uses many more subordinate clauses which make a greater demand upon the reader. The use of noun clauses in particular reflects the number of reported clauses.

	S	P	Od		Od
⟨(The company) (said) [that the doll was ...] ⟩ and ⟨[∅ had passed "meticulous testing"]... ⟩					

⟨(The company) (said) [that the doll was …] ⟩ and ⟨[Ø had passed "meticulous testing"]… ⟩
             SCl – NCl   conj   SCl – NCl

In all but two cases, the noun clauses fill the object site of the sentence. Other subordinate clauses, however, are embedded in noun phrases: the relative clauses and several of the non-finite clauses are directly linked to nouns.

    m   h   q   h   q
… an industry [that was renown for …]   anyone [who had already purchased …]
   det   N   RelCl   pron   RelCl

    m   h   q   m   h   q
… a statement [assuring ….]   … Baby Tearful, [sold worldwide …]
   det   N   NFCl   N   N   NFCl

Because the tabloid article has more sentences and fewer subordinate clauses it is easier to read. Two non-finite clauses fill the object site (*to SUE …, to top*), but the others are embedded in phrases, as is the one relative clause.

  c   m   h   q   m   h   q
… very hard [to produce …]   … no plans [to withdraw …]
          AdvP   NP
  Adv   Adv   NFCl   neg   N   NFCl

    m   h   q
… a chemical [that exceeded …]
           NP
   det   N   RelCl

The main clauses tend to be short and the use of direct rather than indirect speech reduces the complexity. If the actual words spoken are quoted, the clauses

can be written separately, avoiding the need for subordinate clauses in the objec
site.

```
      MCl              S              P
< (A spokesman for the toy company) (said) >:

      MCl              S                      A         P    Cs
'< (The publication of unfounded claims) (at this time of year) (is) (unfair) >.'
```

Similarly, the use of the contrastive conjunction *But* in the initial positio
divides two main clauses into separate sentences.

```
     S          P             Od                  A
< (Parents) (have stripped) (shelves) (in the Christmas scramble) >.

                                        S
But < (the consumer guide's big NO NO to the number one must-have gift)
conj

     P         Od
(may affect) (sales) >.
```

This co-ordinating conjunction would usually occur in the middle of two mai
clauses, but because the subject site in the second clause is filled with a particularl
long noun phrase, the repositioning of the conjunction reduces the demand on th
reader.

```
     m        m          m       m      h        q
The consumer guide's big (NO NO) to the number one must-have gift
     det      N          N     AdjP     N      PrepP
```

These two reports cover the same story in different ways: they present the reade
with the information in a different order and they use different grammatical struc
tures to engage their readers. The conversational style, short sentences (average o
13 words) and main clauses make the tabloid report a more informal text; the for
mality of the compact report is marked by the use of standard lexis, subordinatio
and longer sentences (average of 27 words).

**TASK 4   Creating different styles and tones with subordinate and main
clauses**

1 Choose one of the following writing exercises. When you have completed you
  text, evaluate the key linguistic features. You may like to use the suggested framework for analysis in Appendix A.

  EITHER
  Write three age-appropriate texts focusing on a common theme but each using a
  different genre.

  For example, you could write the **script** for a magazine programme like *Blue Peter*
  focusing on looking after or training a pet dog, the first chapter of a **story** describing
  a pet dog and its relationship with one of the characters, and a **short information
  passage and comprehension questions** for primary school pupils
  You need to pay particular attention to choosing a topic suitable for your intended
  audience and to using appropriate clause structures.

OR
Choose a topical story and write two reports of about 100–150 words each: one for a tabloid newspaper and the other for a compact.

Think about the intended audience, the tone, the language, the style and the clause structure. Vary the type of clauses you use to keep the interest of your readers. Remember that subordinate clauses can stand alone or can be embedded in phrases as post-modifiers.

OR
Produce an information leaflet for a particular resort or attraction.

Use an appropriate layout, address your audience directly, choose language with positive connotations and think carefully about the clause structure. You need to avoid very long clauses so that you do not alienate your readers.

7.2 Text type and clause structure

Writers and speakers use clauses in different ways to create different kinds of texts. The choices they make reflect their intended audience, the kind of material they are writing or speaking about, the format or genre they are using, and the effect they wish to create.

TASK 1   Exploring the relationship between text type and clause structure

1 Read through the texts below carefully.

TEXT 1   Extract from a fashion feature printed in a daily tabloid newspaper

Christmas is approaching and you should be busy sprucing up your party outfit. This season sparkle is in so look out for sophisticated sequins and glitzy jewellery. With cropped and tailored jackets, girlie dresses and killer shoes, you can be the star of any occasion.

TEXT 2   Extract from a classic text, *The Sketch-Book of Geoffrey Crayon, Gent.* by Washington Irving (1819)

'The Broken Heart'
It is a common practice with those who have outlived the susceptibility of early feeling, or have been brought up in the gay heartlessness of dissipated life, to laugh at all love stories, and to treat the tales of romantic passion as mere fictions of novelists and poets. My observations on human nature have induced me to think otherwise. They have convinced me that, however the surface of the character may be chilled and frozen by the cares of the world, or cultivated into mere smiles by the arts of society, still there are dormant fires lurking in the depths of the coldest bosom, which, when once kindled, become impetuous, and are sometimes desolating in their effects.

TEXT 3   Text messages

- Hey u! How r u? Wuu2? Aint seen or spoken 2 u 4 ages! How is everyone? Tb :) x

- Im ok thx. U? im watchin simpsons, but got loads of hw. R there any films u wan ♦ c this hol? U cld come over nd we cld go 2 cinema. Wuu2?

- Im at ice hockey. We drew 2-2 nd it was reli gd. Lol. Not sure abou nxt sat coz w♦ might be going 2 c my auntie.

TEXT 4   An extract from a picture-book

The sun was shining and Sophie was happy.

She was going to the farm.

Sophie liked the farm.

There were lots of animals. Cows and horses and pigs and dogs and chickens an cats and lambs.

Sophie wanted to feed the lambs.

2 Label the clause elements, identifying the main and subordinate clauses.
3 Make notes identifying the main linguistic features of each text type, paying par ticular attention to the language, the structure of the phrases and the use o♦ clauses.

NOTES

TEXT 1   Fashion feature

Audience/purpose

- ▸ adult
- ▸ inform/entertain
- ▸ style straightforward

Lexical choice

- ▸ lexical sets e.g. clothing: *outfit, jackets, dresses, shoes*;
- ▸ current fashionable look: *sparkle, sequins, glitzy, jewellery*
- ▸ seasonal theme: *Christmas, party*
- ▸ subject specific verbs: *sprucing up, is in*
- ▸ direct address repeated: *you*

Phrases

- ▸ **noun phrases** are descriptive: pre-modifiction provides detail

m	h	m	h		m	m	h
sophisticated	sequins	and	glitzy	jewellery	cropped	and tailored	jackets
V-*ed*	N	conj	AdjP	N	V-*ed*	conj V-*ed*	N

- use of compound phrases – focuses reader on theme of article
  e.g. ... *sequins and ... jewellery, ... dresses and ... shoes ..., cropped and tailored*
- only post-modified noun phrase is used in climax, i.e., what you can become if
  you follow journalist's advice

m   h   q
the star of any occasion
det   N   PrepP

- only **adjective phrase** is post-modified: focus of article, i.e., ways to look good
  without spending money

h   q
busy [sprucing up your party outfit]
Adj   NFCl

- **verb phrases** are quite varied
  e.g. progressive: *is approaching* (on-going time scale, i.e., countdown to Christmas); modals: *should be* (obligation), *can be* (possibility); simple present tense:
  is (latest trends); command: *look out for* (suggests necessary action)

Clauses

- dominated by main clauses
- follow traditional patterns: S P conj S P C, A S P A conj P Od, A S P C
- co-ordinated main clauses (*and, so*), but only one subordinate clause – non-
  finite post-modifier in complement site (*busy* sprucing up ...)
- two adverbials brought to front of clause giving added semantic weight i.e. focus
  of article (seasonal fashion advice)

A   S   P   A
⟨ (This season) (sparkle) (is) (in) ⟩.

A   S   P
⟨ (With cropped and tailored jackets, girlie dresses and killer shoes), (you) (can be)
PrepP   NP   VP

C
(the star of any occasion) ⟩.
NP

EXT 2   Sketch

Audience/purpose

- adult reader
- entertain – explore thoughts on particular topic i.e broken hearts
- style complex

Lexical choice

- lexical sets e.g. love/emotions: *feeling, heartlessness, romantic, passion;* linked
  to metaphor of fire: *fires, kindled;* developing contrast: *chilled, frozen, coldest*
- juxtaposition: *dormant fires lurking* (internal); *the surface of the character ...
  chilled ... frozen ... cultivated* (external)
- negative potential of love: *impetuous, desolating*
- repetition of first person pronouns (*I, me*) i.e. personal observations

- sentence adverbials mark expression of attitude i.e. writer presenting case, e.g. *otherwise* (showing alternatives); *however* (contrasting ideas)

Phrases

- **noun phrases** tend to be long and complicated with post-modification as well as pre-modification – linked to reflective tone and date of composition

m   m   h   q
a common practice with those [who have outlived the susceptibility of early feeling]
det   AdjP   N   PrepP   RelCl

m   h   q   q
dormant fires [lurking in the depths of the coldest bosom], [which, [when once kindled]
AdjP   N   NFCl   RelCl   ACl

become impetuous], and [Ø are sometimes desolating in their effects].
                   conj   RelCl

- only one simple **adjective phrase**: *impetuous* – meaning is set against stasis implied by –*ed* participles (*chilled, frozen*)
- **verb phrases** are very varied, e.g.:
  present
    is, are (indicate main argument)
    become (potential of hidden passions to be awakened)
  present perfect (suggests events that have lead writer to his present opinions
    have induced, have convinced
  modals (possibility)
    may be chilled … frozen … cultivated
  passive (moves object to front, refocusing clause)
    may be chilled …
  multiword verb (ongoing event)
    have been brought up

Clauses

- four main clauses with 14 subordinate clauses – indicative of period and discursive tone
- follow traditional patterns:
    dumS P (S) conj (S) C conj Ø C   (see Section 8.5 for dummy subject)
    S P Oi Od A
    S P Oi Od A Od

- shortest main clause is in emphatic position – introduces writer's viewpoint and explicitly sets it against other viewpoints , i.e., between the two longer sentences

S   P   Oi   Od   A
< (My observations on human nature) (have induced) (me) [to think] (otherwise) >.
                                               SCl – NFCl

- co-ordinated main clauses: *and*, (*to laugh* … **and** *to treat* …)
- nine subordinate clauses as independent clause elements
  e.g. *to laugh … and to treat* (complements), *to think …*(object), *that … are …*

(object), *however ... may be chilled and frozen ..., or cultivated, when ... kindled* (adverbials), *desolating ...* (complement)

- five dependent post-modifiers in noun phrases to add detail
  e.g. *those who have outlived ... have been brought up, fires lurking ... which ... become ... are ...*)
- three passive clauses draw attention to writer's counter argument (*romantic passion* can still stir heart)
  e.g. *may be chilled and frozen ...or cultivated ...*
  - bring object of active sentence (*the surface of the character*) to front of clause to add semantic weight
  - delay subjects of active sentence (*the cares of the world ... the arts of society*) i.e. these affect only 'surface'

EXT 3   Text messages

Audience/purpose

- two teenage friends
- informal, social communication; interactive
- style telegraphic; marked by distinctive abbreviations; colloquial tone

Lexical choice

- everyday language
- phatic communication (language used to establish atmosphere or to maintain social relationship) – focuses on greetings/questions re. family, meeting up
- age related topics (*simpsons, films, ice-hockey*)
- abbreviations (shorter texts often cheaper to send) – spellings focus on:
  - traditional abbreviations: *ok, hol, coz, hw* (homework)
  - sound relationship: *u* (you), *r* (are), *4* (for), *2* (to), *c* (see), *reli* (really)
  - removing vowels: *cld* (could), *gd* (good), *nd* (and), *nxt* (next)
  - dropping final consonant: *wan* (want), *watchin* (watching)
  - acronyms: *wuu2?* (what you up to?), *Tb* (text back), *lol* (laugh out loud)
  - simplification of consonant clusters: *thx* (thanks)
  - informal colloquialisms: *aint* (haven't)

Phrases

- **noun phrases** are mostly simple, often with a pronoun as the head word : *i, u, everyone, we*)
- pre-modifying determiners omitted: *simpsons, cinema* (emphasis on being succinct)
- some pre- and post-modification – straightforward rather than descriptive

h q	m h q
loads of hw	any films [Ø u wan [2 c] this hol]
N PrepP	det N RelCl NFCl

- **adjective phrases** – communicate opinions

m h	h q
reli gd	Not sure about nxt sat
Adv Adj	neg Adj PrepP

- **verb phrases** quite varied:
  mostly simple present tense (reflects immediacy of communication)
    e.g. *r, is, m, wan*
  progressives (on-going events)
    e.g. *m watchin, be going*
  simple past (recently completed events)
    e.g. *drew, was*
  present perfect (past event with current relevance)
    e.g. *aint seen ... spoken, Ø got*
  modals (possibility)
    e.g. ***cld*** *come over ...* ***cld*** *go,* **might** *be going*
- some verb phrases/auxiliary verbs are omitted (telegraphic style)
  e.g. *w Ø uu2, Ø got, Ø Not sure*

Clauses

- dominated by main clauses
- mostly short; many use question form with inverted subject and verb
- follow traditional patterns:

A P S	S P C	S P A
‹ (How) (r) (u) ›?	‹ (I) (m) (ok) (thx) ›.	‹ (I) (m) (at ice-hockey) ›.

- co-ordinated main clauses (*or,* **but,** *nd*)
- four verbless clauses (*wuu2?, u?, Not sure ...*)
- two dependent subordinate clause post-modifiers

```
    m       h      q
  any    films   [Ø  u    wan    [2 c] ]
  det     N            RelCl          NFCl
```

- adverbial subordinate clause

```
         S        P            A
  [coz (we) (might be going) [2 c my auntie] ]
  sconj                      SCl – NFCl
```

TEXT 4   Picture book

Audience/purpose
- child listening to adult reading/young reader
- entertain
- style simple
- can be interactive – young readers can predict next word after listening

Lexical choice
- lexical sets
  e.g. farm: *animals, Cows, horses, pigs, dogs, chickens, cats, lambs*
  e.g. words with positive connotations: *shining, happy, liked*
- subject specific verbs: *to feed*
- repetition of name establishes character: *Sophie*

Phrases

▶ **noun phrases** are simple: either head noun standing alone (*Sophie, Cows*), or with a determiner (*the farm, the lambs*)
▶ only one post-modified noun phrase – reflects intended audience

h   q
lots of animals
N   PrepP

▶ the only **adjective phrase** is simple and familiar: *happy*
▶ **verb phrases** are simple past tense: *was, liked, were, wanted* (typical of narrative)
▶ **past progressive** verb phrases (actions not yet complete)
e.g. *was shining*, i.e., the sun is continuing to shine
e.g. *was going*, i.e., planned but not yet carried out

Clauses

▶ dominated by main clauses – appropriate for intended audience
▶ follow traditional patterns: S P conj S P C, S P A, S P Od
▶ 1 co-ordinated main clause (*and*)
▶ 1 subordinate clause as independent clause element – short so does not affect readability of text

S   P   Od
‹ (She) (wanted) [to feed the lambs] ›.
               SCl – NFCl

▶ one verbless clause made up of a syndetic list of simple noun phrases – mirrors spoken style of young children
e.g. *Cows and horses and pigs ...*

TASK 2   Using different clause structures ━━━━━━━━━━━━

1 Choose one of the following writing exercises. When you have completed your text, evaluate the key linguistic features. You may like to use the suggested framework for analysis in Appendix A.

EITHER
Gather some examples of abbreviated text messages sent in a range of different contexts and rewrite them in a grammatically complete form.

Label the clause elements and identify the main and subordinate clauses in both versions.

Then take a short extract from a play, print advertisement, newspaper or novel and rewrite it in abbreviated text-message form.

You need to think about the kind of grammatical elements that must be omitted from the texts.

OR
Look at some examples of graphic novels in which the pictures are accompanied

by speech and thought bubbles, onomatopoeic words and narrative markers.

Write your own extract for a graphic novel. If you wish, you could adapt an extract from a novel which you have already read.

You need to pay particular attention to the ways in which language and different kinds of clauses are used to create atmosphere and setting, and to develop characters.

OR

Watch a range of television and radio advertisements and transcribe the voice-overs.

Read through the material you have collected and make notes on the key linguistic features, including the type, structure and position of the clauses. Using the notes you have made, create voice-overs for the following spoken advertisements:

- a product targeted at 15-18 year olds advertised during a post-watershed film premiere
- a toy for 5-7 year olds advertised early on Saturday mornings
- a service targeted at the 50+ age group advertised early on week-day afternoons

You need to think carefully about the target audience, the content and the language. Remember that subordinate clauses can stand alone or can be embedded, but keep the clause length appropriate for the age group and the genre (spoken advertisement).

7.3 Grammatical ambiguity

Writers and speakers can use grammatical ambiguity to play with meaning for comic or dramatic effect. Being able to recognise the different ways in which a clause can be analysed helps us to appreciate the effects that can be created and enables us to manipulate language in our own writing.

TASK 1

1 Read through the jokes below carefully.

A woman walked into a pet shop and said, 'I'd like a frog for my son.'
'Sorry, Madam, ' said the shopkeeper, 'we don't do part exchanges.'

Q. Why did the tomato turn red?
A. It saw the salad dressing.

TEACHER   Write I must not forget my gym kit 100 times.
PUPIL   But, Sir, I only forgot it once.

Q. What did the light say when it was turned off?
A. I'm delighted.

2 Label the clause structures.
3 Explain the different ways in which the grammatical structure can be analysed for comic effect.

COMMENTARY

The answer to the first joke relies on the function of the prepositional phrase *for my son*. We can analyse this as an independent element of the clause – an indirect object following the noun phrase *a frog*.

```
        S       P         Od           Oi
    〈 (I) ('d like) (a frog) (for my son) 〉.
                                 PrepP
```

The comic effect is created by the shopkeeper's interpretation of the phrase as a contracted post-modifier following the noun phrase *a frog*.

```
        S       P              Od
    〈 (I) ('d like) (a frog in exchange for my son) 〉.
                           NP
```

In the second joke, humour is created by the structure of the noun phrase in the object site of the clause. There are two ways in which we can label the function of the words:

```
    m    m    h           m    h    q
  the salad dressing     the salad dressing
  det   N    N           det   N    NFCl
```

We recognise the pre-modified phrase with the head word *dressing* as typical of the lexical field of food suggested by the question. The comic effect, however, is developed in relation to the emotional connotations of 'turning red' to show embarrassment. Classifying *dressing* as the *–ing* participle of a dynamic verb rather than as a noun builds on this meaning of the colour adjective.

As well as grammatical ambiguity, Joke 3 depends upon the lack of punctuation in spoken language to underpin the dual meaning. With no inverted commas to identify exactly what the pupil needs to write out, the noun phrase *100 times* can be analysed in two distinctive ways.

```
        P                        Od
    〈 (Write) 〈 I must not forget my gym kit 100 times 〉 〉.
```

```
        P                   Od                    A
    〈 (Write) 〈 I must not forget my gym kit 〉 (100 times) 〉.
```

While the teacher intends the noun phrase to be an adverbial indicating how many times the sentence should be written out, the child interprets it as part of the object element. Humour is therefore created in the juxtaposition of the two frequency phrases *100 times* and *once*.

The final joke uses a more complex grammatical ambiguity focusing on the word *delighted*.

```
    S    P     C              S       P
  〈 (I) ('m) (delighted) 〉.    〈 (I) ('m delighted) 〉.
```

As a complement, *delighted* is an adjective phrase conveying pleasure; as a predi cator, it is part of a passive verb phrase in which the meaning of the verb 'to light' has been changed by the addition of the prefix *de–* to indicate the removal of some thing. The comic effect is created by the juxtaposition of a recognisable emotiona response with a made-up verb. While following a standard grammatical patter (the addition of a prefix), the verb 'de-lighted' is not one that we will find in a dic tionary.

Part IV

Sentences

Chapter **8**

Sentences

We can feel that we are on familiar ground with sentences. We know that they begin with a capital letter and end with a full stop; we use them every time we speak or write; we see them when we read. There is no new or challenging terminology to learn, but we will continue to use the clause analysis techniques introduced in Chapter 6. The key is practice – the more sentences you look at the easier it will be to see how they have been put together.

After working through this chapter, you should be able:

▸ to see how we link clauses together in distinctive patterns
▸ to recognise and label different kinds of sentences
▸ to describe the ways in which we link sentences together
▸ to understand the effects created by rearranging a sentence

8.1 What is a sentence?

A SENTENCE is the largest unit of syntax. A grammatically complete sentence consists of at least one main clause, but it can have additional main clauses or subordinate clauses. We mark each main clause with angled brackets, each subordinate clause with square brackets, and phrases making up the clause elements with round brackets. We could identify each phrase with a form label underneath, but we only label conjunctions and subordinate clauses since these help us to understand the clause structure.

```
MCl    S        P          A
⟨ (The rain) (fell) (relentlessly) ⟩.


MCl    S        P          A          MCl        S          P      Cs
⟨ (The rain) (fell) (relentlessly) ⟩ and ⟨ (the streets) (were) (empty) ⟩.
                                       conj


MCl              S                     P      A        MCl        S          P      Cs
⟨ (The rain [which was unexpected] ) (fell) (relentlessly) ⟩ and ⟨ (the streets) (were) (empty)
          SCl – RelCl                                          conj


                 A
[because everyone had stayed indoors] ⟩.
      SCl – ACl
```

When we 'see' and 'hear' sentences in real contexts, they do not always conform to expected patterns. In speech, boundaries between sentences can be blurred, and writers can choose to punctuate sentences in a non-standard way to reflect thought patterns or mood, or to create an informal tone.

8.2 Sentence types

There are five main types of sentence.

Simple sentences

A SIMPLE SENTENCE consists of a single clause with one finite verb phrase. It is independent and makes sense on its own.

> MCl S   P   Od   A
> ⟨ (We) (**should have visited**) (the park) (yesterday) ⟩.

Compound sentences

A COMPOUND SENTENCE contains two or more main clauses each with a finite verb phrase. It is linked by a co-ordinating conjunction (*and, or, but*). Each main clause is independent and makes sense on its own.

It can be helpful to see a sentence visually where the relationship between the different linguistic levels is represented on a diagram. In the example below, the different clauses are all represented on the same level because each main clause carries the same semantic weight in a compound sentence.

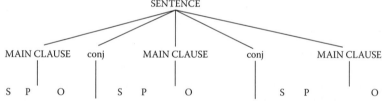

⟨He **eats** cakes⟩ and ⟨he **eats** plain chocolate⟩ but ⟨he **hates** all kinds of biscuits⟩.

It is, of course, also possible to represent grammatical information in a more compact way using function and form labels.

> MCl S   P   Od   MCl S   P   Od
> ⟨ (I) (wanted) (an Indian take-away) ⟩ but ⟨ (I) (didn't have) (enough money) ⟩.
>   conj

Complex sentences

A COMPLEX SENTENCE contains a main clause with a finite verb phrase and at least one subordinating clause. The main clause is independent and makes sense on its own, but the subordinate clause is dependent.

It can be particularly helpful to represent subordination on a diagram because we can clearly see the relationship between the different grammatical levels. In the example below, the clauses are on different visual levels because they do not carry the same semantic weight: the main clause is independent, but has dependent sub-ordinate clauses in the object site.

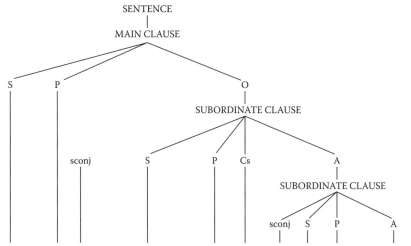

⟨Many people **said** [that (the journey to work) **was** difficult [when they **set off** this morning]]⟩.

With function and form labels, we can still record details about main and subordinate clauses, the clause elements and the types of subordinate clause used. The diagrammatic system is more effective if you wish to show the relationship between the different levels and the embedding of clauses.

The brackets can look quite confusing, but if you sort out where each pair starts and stops it is not too complicated.

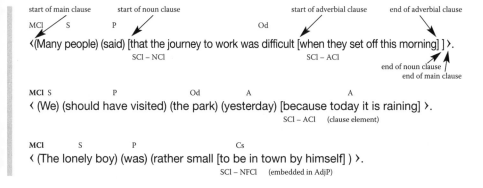

Compound-complex sentences

A **COMPOUND-COMPLEX** sentence contains two or more main clauses linked by a co-ordinating conjunction and at least one subordinating clause. The main clauses are independent and the subordinate clause(s) dependent.

In a diagram of a compound-complex sentence, some clauses are level because they are of equal semantic weight, others are subordinate and therefore represented on lower branches of the tree.

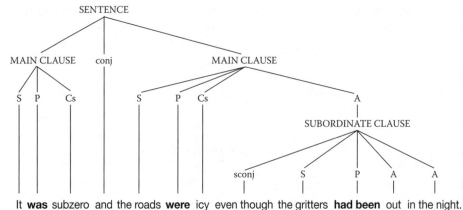

It **was** subzero and the roads **were** icy even though the gritters **had been** out in the night.

Using function and form labels, a compound-complex sentence could be annotated like this:

MCl S P   Cs   MCl S   P   Cs   A
〈(It) (was) (subzero)〉 and 〈(the roads) (were) (icy) [even though the gritters had been out …]〉.
                conj   SCl – ACl   (clause element)

MCl S   P   Od   A   A
〈 (We) (should have visited) (the park) (yesterday) [because today it is raining] 〉 and
                                                        SCl – ACl   (clause element)   conj

MCl A   S   P   Od
〈 (now) (I) (can't feed) (the ducks) 〉.

MCl   S   P   Cs   MCl   S
〈 (The lonely boy) (was) (rather small [to be in town by himself]) 〉 and 〈 (the policeman)
                                  SCl – NFCl   (embedded in AdjP)   conj

    P   Oi   Od
(asked) (him) [whether he was lost] 〉.
        SCl – NCl   (clause element)

This book uses the more compact version of labelling function and form in sentences for practical reasons, but you should choose the method which best helps you to see the grammatical patterns. The diagrammatic method is a useful way of recognising the relationship between subordinate and main clauses, but can get complicated with longer sentences.

Minor sentences

A **MINOR SENTENCE** does not follow standard grammatical patterns: it lacks some of the essential clause elements, but will often follow the rules of basic phrase structure. There are several common types.

Social expressions	*Hello.*	*Thanks.*	*Pleased to meet you.*	
Interjections	*Hey!*	*Ouch!*	*Ugh.*	
Exclamations/commands	*If only!*	*No Smoking*	*As if!*	*For Sale*
Expressions	*One day to go!*	*Wish you were here!*		
Sayings	*Out of sight, out of mind.*	*Red sky at night shepherd's delight.*		

Minor sentences may sometimes look like simple present tense sentences. They cannot, however, be changed into past tense and this tells us that they are minor sentences.

> God save the Queen! God **saved** the Queen! ✗
>
> A stitch in time saves nine. A stitch in time **saved** nine. ✗

Minor sentences are often used in advertising, in newspaper headlines, and on labels and signs. They are also common in conversation.

8.3 Analysing sentences

To understand how a sentence is constructed, we need to be able to analyse clause structure. This allows us to come to some conclusions about the type of sentences being used so that we can begin to think about the effects they will have. You can work through a very similar process to the one introduced in Section 6.7: ask yourself the same four questions and work through the same procedure. We then need to add one final question.

STAGE 1 **How many clauses are there?**
STAGE 2 **Are the clauses main or subordinate?**
STAGE 3 **Are the subordinate clauses embedded in phrases or filling a clause site?**
STAGE 4 **Which clause elements are used?**
STAGE 5 **What type of sentence is it?**

We need to consider the different types of clauses that make up a sentence in order to decide what kind of sentence it is.

Clauses	Sentence type
1 main clause	simple
2 or more main clauses linked with a co-ordinating conjunction	compound
1 main clause + 1 or more subordinate clauses	complex
2 or more main clauses linked with a co-ordinating conjunction + 1 or more subordinate clauses	compound-complex

Look at the example below to see the process in action.

MCl   S   P   A   MCl S
‹ (The news of financial chaos) (**was featured**) (in every bulletin) › **and** ‹ (people)
                                                                                            conj

         P   Od   A
(**were beginning**) [**to queue** outside banks] [**because** they **feared** [**that** their savings
                SCl – NFCl (clause element)   SCl – ACl (clause element)   SCl – NCl (clause element)
were under threat]] ›.

Stages 1–4

five clauses: *was featured, were beginning, to queue, feared, were*
finite verbs: *was* (+ *-ed* participle), *were* (+ *-ing* participle), *feared, were*

non-finite:	*featured* (*-ed* participle), *beginning* (*-ing* participle), *to queue*
main clauses:	*The news ... was featured ... people were beginning ...* (linked by co-ordinating conjunction *and*)
subordinate clauses:	*to queue* ... (non-finite verb – non-finite clause)
	because they feared ... (subordinating conjunction – adverbial clause)
	that their savings were ... (subordinating conjunction – noun clause)
clause elements	S P A conj S P Od A

Stage 5

We can see that this is a **compound-complex clause** because it has:

▸ 2 main clauses linked with *and*
▸ 3 subordinate clauses functioning as clause elements in the object and adverbial sites, marked by a non-finite verb (*to queue*) and two subordinating conjunctions (*because, that*).

8.4 Linking sentences

We have already seen how we can link different parts of a sentence by using co-ordinating or subordinating conjunctions (see Section 2.9), but we now need to consider the ways in which we can create links between sentences. We call this COHESION and it helps us to understand how writers and speakers develop texts that are longer than a single sentence or utterance.

Lexical cohesion

We can create links in a text by choosing words which belong to the same SEMANTIC FIELD (a theme or topic developed through the use of words with associated meanings). These may be SUBJECT SPECIFIC (linked to a particular field or register), words with similar connotations, or repeated words and their derivatives.

The extract below is taken from a spontaneous commentary. It has no traditional punctuation because full stops, commas, semi-colons and colons are written sentence markers. Spoken transcripts mark pauses in seconds and record their length in brackets. These help us to see the grammatical units. This passage demonstrates all three kind of lexical cohesion.

> the home team (1) take the lead (1) Phillips put it in at the near post Wilson could do nothing about it (2) after six minutes (1) there's a really good finish by Phillips (2) and Thompson provides the cross (.) he picks it up from Clarke look at Phillips going in front of Davies (.) lovely flick (.) with the left foot and (.) Wilson's left hand couldn't keep it out (6) and (1) after six minutes (1) Phillips (2) a sweet finish on the near post

The audience would immediately recognise the proper nouns (*Phillips, Wilson, Thompson, Clarke, Davies*) as the names of players in a particular team. These form a cohesive LEXICAL SET along with the subject specific noun phrases (*near post, the ross, left foot, left hand)*, which have distinctive meaning in the semantic field of *football*. The connotations of the modifiers (*good, lovely, sweet*) are cohesive in that they mirror the mood of the moment, while repetition of prepositional phrases draws attention to the important elements of the occasion: the time (*after six minutes*) and the position of the ball (*at the near post/on the near post*).

Substitution

Links can be made both within a sentence and between sentences by **replacing** one linguistic item with another shorter one where the identity of the person or thing is clear.

We can replace noun phrases with pronouns in the subject or object sites.

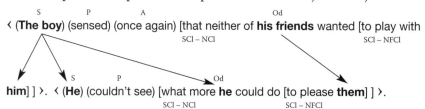

```
         S        P        A                       Od
⟨ (The boy) (sensed) (once again) [that neither of his friends wanted [to play with
                                   SCl – NCl                          SCl – NFCl

                    S     P              Od
him] ] ⟩. ⟨ (He) (couldn't see) [what more he could do [to please them] ] ⟩.
              SCl – NCl                    SCl – NFCl
```

The pronoun *He* in the subject site of the second sentence is a substitute for the noun phrase *The boy* in the first. The object pronoun *him* also refers directly back to this noun phrase. Similarly, the object pronoun *them* is a substitute for the noun phrase *his friends*. It is important that the substitution agrees with the noun phrase it replaces in number and person.

We can also use indefinite pronouns (*one, some, the same*) as a substitute for the head or the whole of a noun phrase.

Can I have **a hot chocolate**, please?   Sure, I'll have **one** too.

I'm working on **the Applied Mechanics problems** this weekend. I'm doing **the same**.

We call this kind of substitution **referencing** because the pronouns point to something else in the sentence or discourse (spoken or written text). There are three kinds of reference.

Anaphoric references

ANAPHORIC references point backwards in a text: the reader or listener must look back to a previous noun to make sense of the pronoun.

```
         S        P         Od          A              S       P     Cs
⟨ (The actors) (shook) (their heads) (in surprise) ⟩, but ⟨ (they) (were) (amused) ⟩.
  NP ◄———————————————————————————————————————————— pron
```

Cataphoric references

CATAPHORIC references point forwards: the reader or listener must look ahead to a noun phrase to understand the pronoun's field of reference.

```
     S     P      Cs              S     P              Od
⟨ (That) (is) (beautiful) ⟩.   ⟨ (I) (love) (the last light of a summer's day) ⟩.
  pron ———————————————————————————————————————————————► NP
```

Exophoric references

EXOPHORIC references point outside: the reader or listener must make a connection with something that exists beyond the discourse. A gesture or clearly defined context is often needed to make sense of the exophoric reference.

```
        P        Od        A
  〈(Make) (the beds) (like this) 〉.  ───▶ Accompanying actions will define the exact nature of 'this'
                          pron
```

Superordinates

SUPERORDINATES (general words) and HYPONYMS (subdivisions of general words) can also be used as substitutes in the subject and object sites.

SUPERORDINATES	HYPONYMS
dog	husky, Alsatian, collie
flower	rose, daisy, dahlia, daffodil
food	potatoes, lettuce, chicken

Auxiliary verb 'do'

As we have seen with the phrase replacement test, verb phrases and the lexical items that follow them can be replaced by the **auxiliary verb** *do*.

```
     S     P              Od              A              S    P    A
  〈 (We) (love) [going to the cinema] (in the evening) 〉.   〈 (We) (do) (too) 〉.
                  SCl – NFCl
```

'So' and 'not'

Similarly, a clause can be replaced by *so* (positive) or ***not*** (negative).

```
          A              S      P        Cs
  〈 (In the city centre) (a flat) (is) (harder [to find] ) 〉.
                                          SCl – NFCl
```

```
   Od    S     P
〈 (So) (they) (say) 〉.   i.e., they say that a flat is harder to find in the city centre
```

```
  S     P
〈 (I) (think) (not) 〉.   i.e., I don't think a flat is harder to find in the city centre
```

Ellipsis

Sometimes we leave out part of a sentence to avoid repetition – often after the co-ordinating conjunction *and*. We call this ELLIPSIS.

We can elide noun phrases, lexical or auxiliary verbs, or whole clauses, but only where it is clear what the omitted words are. It is important to avoid any ambiguity.

```
      S         P          A                              P          Od
〈 (The dog) (dashed) (across the road) 〉 and 〈 Ø (barked at) (the postman) 〉.
    NP                                      conj  NP omitted
```

```
      S          P        Od         A                    S         Od
〈 (The boys) (played) (football) (on Tuesdays) 〉 and 〈 (the girls) Ø (basketball) 〉.
                VP                                  conj      lex verb omitted
```

```
        S              P                    Od                        P        A         A
⟨(Jo) (had been preparing for) (his next exam)⟩ and ⟨(Ø revising) (seriously) (all day)⟩.
              VP                                       conj     aux verbs omitted
```

```
   Od     P    S      P       A            A
⟨ (What) (do) (we) (need) (for the party) (tonight) ⟩?
           ‿‿‿‿‿‿‿‿‿‿
   Cl
```

```
   P      Od       S      P
⟨ (Ask) (Susan) ⟩.  ⟨ (She) (knows) Ø ⟩.
                              noun clause omitted
```

Linking adverbs (conjuncts) and conjunctions

The following examples show how **linking adverbs** (conjuncts) and **conjunctions** can be used to produce a coherent piece of writing. They can help us to develop an argument, to create contrasts, to explore cause and effect, and to establish a time-scale. They can link clauses within a sentence or separate sentences. There are four different types.

Additive adverbs

Additive adverbs (*moreover, likewise, finally, as well*) and the co-ordinating conjunction *and* add information to a sentence, as a list or sometimes as an after-thought.

```
            S         P                        Cs
⟨ (Many people) (are) (pleased [that the government banned smoking in public places] ) ⟩.
                                   SCl – NCl
```

```
                  S       P                  Od
⟨ Furthermore, (they) (believe) [that the price of cigarettes should be increased] ⟩.
conjunct                              SCl – NCl
```

Adversative adverbs

Adversative adverbs (*nevertheless, alternatively, yet, on the other hand*) and the co-ordinating conjunction *but* create a contrast between two clauses or two sentences.

```
  S   P                   Cs                      S   P                    P
⟨ (I) (am) (disappointed by the quality of the candidates) ⟩  ⟨(I) (will), however, (make)
                                                                            ‿‿‿‿‿‿
                                                                            conjunct
```

```
      Od
(an effort [to vote] ) ⟩.
     SCl – NFCl
```

Causal adverbs

Causal adverbs (*as a result of, therefore, consequently*) and certain subordinating conjunctions (*because, since, as*) link two clauses or sentences by suggesting that one has been the result of the other.

$$\text{S} \qquad\qquad \text{P} \qquad\qquad\qquad \text{S} \qquad \text{P} \qquad\qquad \text{A} \qquad\qquad\qquad\qquad \text{P}$$
⟨(The storm clouds) (blew in)⟩ and ⟨(the rain) (lashed) (at the windows)⟩. ⟨**Thus** (ended)
                                conj   conjunct

$$\text{S}$$
[what had been a dark and miserable day] ⟩.
SCl – NCl

Adverbs that change the emphasis

Adverbs that change the **emphasis** (*incidentally, by the way*) move attention from one topic to another.

$$\text{S} \qquad\qquad \text{P} \qquad\qquad\qquad\qquad \text{P} \qquad\qquad \text{Od} \qquad\qquad \text{S}$$
⟨(The passengers) (unpacked)⟩ and ⟨(settled into) (their room)⟩. ⟨(The crew) **meanwhile**
                           conj   conjunct

$$\text{P} \qquad\qquad\qquad \text{Od}$$
(were preparing for) (an imminent departure) ⟩.

Distinguishing between a subordinating conjunction and a linking adverb

A subordinating conjunction and the clause that accompanies it often fills the adverbial clause site, but linking adverbs are not part of the clause structure as a whole.

$$\text{S} \quad \text{P} \qquad\quad \text{A} \qquad\quad \text{A} \qquad\qquad\qquad\qquad \text{S} \quad \text{P} \qquad \text{A} \quad \text{A}$$
⟨ (I) (could go) (into town) (at 1 o'clock) ⟩ . ⟨ **Otherwise**, (I) ('ll go) (in) (later) ⟩.
                                             conjunct

$$\text{S} \quad \text{P} \qquad\quad \text{A} \qquad\quad \text{A} \qquad\qquad\qquad \text{A}$$
⟨ (I) (could go) (into town) (at 1 o'clock) [**because** it's my dinner break] ⟩.
                                               SCl – ACl

To check this, we can see if the adverbial provides an answer to a question. In the example above, for instance, the subordinate clause beginning with *because* provides an answer to the question '**why** can you go to town at 1 o'clock?' The conjunct *Otherwise*, however, does not perform the same function: we cannot ask '**why** can you go to town ...?, '**how** can you go to town . . .' or '**when** can you go to town . . .?' and get the answer *Otherwise*. This tells us that although the conjunct is linking the two sentences semantically, it is not directly involved in the clause structure.

While adverbials can be given additional prominence after *it* + *be* + relative pronoun, conjuncts cannot.

$$\text{S} \quad \text{P} \qquad \text{Od}$$
Instead, (I) (got) (a pizza).
conjunct

$$\text{Od} \qquad\qquad\qquad\qquad\qquad\qquad\qquad\qquad\qquad \text{S}$$
It was (a pizza) that I got instead ✓   It was (me) who got a pizza instead. ✓
rel pron   rel pron

It was (instead) I got a pizza. ✗
conjunct

8.5 Sentence organisation

We can rearrange sentences in order to emphasise particular features or to attract the reader's attention. The rearrangements linked to asking a question, using a negative or ordering someone to do something are functional. In the cases below, however, the rearrangement is directly linked to meaning: sentence elements are moved in order to change the emphasis.

Marked themes

In a standard grammatical sentence, the subject occurs first. We call it the GRAMMATICAL THEME because it establishes information that is general knowledge, has already been mentioned or is known from the context.

> S   P   A   A
> ⟨ **(The sun)** (shines) (every year) (on my birthday) ⟩.
> Theme

The order of this sentence is therefore described as being **unmarked** because it follows a traditional pattern with the subject of the sentence first, followed by the main verb in the predicator site.

Some clause elements other than the subject can be moved to the front of a sentence, the initial position, to give them greater prominence. THEMATIC ADVERBIALS are most common.

> A   S   P   A
> ⟨ **(Every year)** (the sun) (shines) (on my birthday) ⟩.

In speech and in literary texts, **thematic verbs, objects** and **complements** are sometimes used.

> S   P   A   P   S   P
> ⟨ (The boy's behaviour) (will not improve) (immediately) ⟩, but ⟨ **(improve)** (it) (will) ⟩.
>
> conj   V*base*   mod

> Cs   P   S
> ⟨ **(Most impressive of all)** (is) (the painting in the new gallery) ⟩.

> Od   S   P   Oi
> ⟨ **(Another assignment)** (they) (gave) (us) ⟩.

More than one clause element can be moved to the initial position, changing the order of the information and the relative semantic significance of each element.

> S   P   A   A
> ⟨ (The disused summerhouse) (stands) (over the field), (beyond the lake) ⟩.

> A   A   P   S
> ⟨ **(Over the field)**, **(beyond the lake)** (stands) (the disused summerhouse) ⟩.

Altering the order of clause elements in the sentence above changes the emphasis. Where the first version is unmarked, the second draws attention to the location of the summerhouse by bringing the adverbial elements to the initial position and delaying the subject until the end.

Moving any clause element (other than the subject) to the initial position is called FRONTING or FOREGROUNDING – it creates a MARKED THEME which carries more semantic weight. This linguistic flexibility allows us as writers and speakers to control the effects we wish to create.

End focus

Information at the end of the sentence is also in a prominent position – often it contains something new and requires the audience to focus attention on it. Delaying new information until the end of a sentence or repositioning a particular clause element at the end draws attention to the information it contains. We call this END FOCUS.

>   S   P   Od   A
> ‹ (Ben) (had) (more than three helpings) **(at Hassan's party)** ›.

>   S   P   A   Od
> ‹ (Ben) (had) (at Hassan's party) **(more than three helpings)** ›.

Where clause elements are particularly long, it is often better to keep these until the end of a sentence: it is easier to understand a sentence where the weight falls at the end rather than at the beginning.

>   S
> ‹ [Whether we should immediately raise the issue of the new cafeteria rule
>
> SCl – NCl
>
> [which forbids us [to sit down] and [eat our sandwiches] [unless we have bought them
> SCl – RelCl   SCl – NFCl   conj SCl – NFCl   SCl – ACl
>
>   S   P
> on the premises]]] or [whether we should wait until the staff-student meeting] (is)
>   conj SCl – NCl
>
>   A   A
> (at the top of the list) (today) ›.

The subject of the sentence above has six clauses and this creates a very heavy weight of information at the beginning. By rearranging the sentence and moving the subject to the end site, we can make it seem less dense.

>   A   A   P   S
> ‹ (At the top of the list) (today) (is) [whether we should immediately raise the issue of the
>   SCl – NCl
>
> new cafeteria rule [which forbids us [to sit down] and [eat our sandwiches] [unless we have
>   SCl – RelCl   SCl – NFCl   conj SCl – NFCl   SCl – ACl
>
>   S
> bought them on the premises]]] or [whether we should wait until the staff-student meeting].
>   conj SCl – NCl

Dummy subjects

We can reorganise a sentence by filling the subject site with a lexical item that has no semantic significance and moving the subject to another position. There are three ways in which the elements of a sentence can be rearranged.

Existential sentences

EXISTENTIAL sentences point to the general existence of some state of affairs. They use *there* as a dummy subject followed by the simple present or past tense of the verb *to be*. This delays introducing the real subject of the sentence and thus gives it greater semantic weight.

                    S   P   A

⟨ (Lots of computer books) (are) (upstairs) ⟩.   UNMARKED

    dum S   P   (S)   A

⟨ (There) (are) (**lots of computer books**) (upstairs) ⟩.   MARKED

In the second version of the sentence above, *there* has no meaning: its function is to move the real subject into a more prominent position. The existential *there* structure enables us to change the FOCUS, or centre of interest, of the sentence. It draws attention to new information.

The dummy subject *there* may be followed by a verb other than *to be* – although this tends to be more common in literary texts than in everyday usage. Verbs such as *occur, arise, exist* may be used after a dummy subject.

Cleft sentences

We can also use *it* as a dummy subject, splitting a sentence into two and creating two clauses each with their own finite verb. We call the sentences formed in this way CLEFT SENTENCES. The basic pattern is: *It + be* + (S/O/A) + *that* + clause.

            S   P   Od   A   A

⟨ (Jo) (put) (his hot water bottle) (in the kitchen) (last night) ⟩.   UNMARKED

    dum S   P   A   S   P   Od   A

⟨ (It) (was) (**last night**) [that (Jo) (put) (his hot water bottle) (in the kitchen)] ⟩.   MARKED
                         focus

The clause element that follows the first verb is given added semantic weight – it is the **focus** of the sentence.

Extraposition

Where an element of a sentence (usually the subject) is made up of a noun clause or a non-finite clause, we can move it from its usual position to the end of the sentence. The subject site is then filled with the dummy subject *It*. We call this EXTRAPOSITION. The basic pattern is: *It + be* + (C/O) + clause.

            S   P   Cs

⟨ [What I was told] (is) (very important) ⟩.   UNMARKED
    SCl – NCl

    dum S   P   Cs   (S)

⟨ (It) (is) (very important) [**what I was told**] ⟩.   MARKED
                          SCl – NCl

                   S   P   Cs

⟨ [Taunting crocodiles] (is) (always dangerous) ⟩.   UNMARKED
    SCl –NFCl

    dum S   P   Cs   (S)

⟨ (It) (is) (always dangerous) [**taunting crocodiles**] ⟩.   MARKED
                          SCl – NFCl

If the subject contains a long subordinate clause, altering the order of sentence elements and delaying the clause makes it easier for the audience. It removes the heavy weight of information from the front of the sentence and makes it seem more balanced.

⟨ [That the modelling assignment is due in after Easter] (is) (clear) (on the sheet) ⟩.
S — P — C — A

⟨ (It) (is) (clear) (on the sheet) [that the modelling assignment is due in after Easter] ⟩.
dum S — P — Cs — A — (S)

⟨ (I) (think) [spending hours in the gym every day] (a joke) ⟩.
S — P — Od — Co

⟨ (I) (think) (it's) (a joke), [spending hours in the gym every day] ⟩.
S — P — dum O — Co — (Od)

8.6 Grammatical mood

Grammatical mood describes the function of a sentence. We can make a statement, ask a question, command someone to do something or express our feelings or emotions in an exclamation.

The declarative

The most common mood is the **declarative mood**. We use this to make statements. Most declarative sentences have a subject and a predicator.

⟨ (The dog) (barked) ⟩.   ⟨ (We) (read) ⟩.
S — P   S — P

Other clause elements are optional.

⟨ (The dog) (barked) (ferociously) (outside the door) (at midnight) (again) ⟩.
S — P — A — A — A — A

⟨ (We) (read) (the newspaper article) (to the class) [because it was relevant] ⟩.
S — P — Od — Oi — A
SCl – ACl

Declarative sentences usually follow the traditional order of clause elements (S P O/C/A), but we can vary this basic order by bringing a clause element other than the subject to the initial position (see Section 8.5).

⟨ (Outside the door), (the dog) (barked) (ferociously) (at midnight) (again) ⟩.
A — S — P — A — A — A

⟨ (Ferociously), (the dog) (barked) (outside the door), (at midnight) (again) ⟩.
A — S — P — A — A — A

⟨ (At midnight), (the dog) (barked) (ferociously) (outside the door) (again) ⟩.
A — S — P — A — A — A

⟨ (Again), (the dog) (barked) (ferociously) (outside the door) (at midnight) ⟩.
A — S — P — A — A — A

In each case here, the fronted adverbial emphasises a different kind of information: *Outside the door* draws attention to location; *Ferociously* to the manner; *At midnight* to the time; and *Again* to an event that has taken place before. This kind of semantic rearrangement allows writers and speakers to guide audience response by controlling the order in which they receive information and its relative importance. It is important to recognise, however, that in a declarative sentence, the order of the subject and predicator should not change.

The interrogative

To ask a question, we use the INTERROGATIVE mood. In the interrogative, the subject and predicator change places and in written language we replace the final full stop with a question mark. If there is an auxiliary in the verb phrase, the subject and auxiliary swap places.

DECLARATIVE			INTERROGATIVE			
S	P	A	P	S	P	A
⟨ (You)	(can go)	(to the cinema) ⟩.	→ ⟨ (Can)	(you)	(go)	(to the cinema) ⟩?
	mod *Vbase*			mod	*Vbase*	

Where there is more than one auxiliary, the subject changes place with the first one.

DECLARATIVE			INTERROGATIVE			
S	P	Od	P	S	P	Od
⟨ (We)	(should have finished)	(our work) ⟩.	→ ⟨ (Should)	(we)	(have finished)	(our work) ⟩?
	mod prim *Ved*			mod	prim *Ved*	

If there is no auxiliary in the verb phrase, we use the primary auxiliary *do* as a dummy operator – it has no meaning, but allows us to invert the subject and verb.

DECLARATIVE			INTERROGATIVE			
S	P	Od	P	S	P	Od
⟨ (He)	(understands)	(Calculus) ⟩.	→ ⟨ (Does)	(he)	(understand)	(Calculus) ⟩?
	Vpres			prim	*Vbase*	

The questions above are called CLOSED QUESTIONS because they require a *yes* or *no* answer. Other questions are described as OPEN QUESTIONS because they require an answer that provides more specific information. This kind of question usually begins with a *wh–* word. The subject and verb also change places in *wh–* questions except where the *wh–* question word fills the subject site.

The table overleaf summarises the form and function of the most common *wh–* words.

In spoken language, we can use rising intonation to mark a question rather than an inversion of the subject and object. Because there is no inversion, however, the grammatical mood is declarative rather than interrogative.

We can also use a **tag question** at the end of a declarative sentence. The tag question is made up of an auxiliary verb and a pronoun.

DECLARATIVE	S	P	Od	
	⟨ (I)	(should do)	(my work),	shouldn't I ⟩?
				tag question

Where there is no auxiliary in the main clause, the tag question will include *do*.

DECLARATIVE	S	P	Od	
	⟨ (I)	(like)	(dark chocolate),	don't I ⟩?
				tag question

Wh- Word	Form	Clause site	Example
who	pronoun	S (person)	**Who** sits in this chair? (no inversion of subject and verb)
whose	determiner pronoun	O/C (possession)	**Whose** coat is this? **Whose** is this?
what	determiner pronoun	O/C (something)	**What** book shall I read? **What** is the result of the match?
which	determiner pronoun	O (limited possibility)	**Which** team do you support? **Which** shall I buy?
when	adverb	A (time)	**When** can I visit?
where	adverb	A (place)	**Where** do you live?
how	adverb	A (manner)	**How** can you see anything in this light?
how long	adverb	A (time)	**How long** have you been reading this book?
how often	adverb	A (frequency)	**How often** do you go to the theatre?
why	adverb	A (reason/cause)	**Why** are you wearing fancy dress?

After a positive main clause, the tag question is negative and usually expects a positive *yes* answer; where the main clause is negative, the tag question is positive and expects a negative answer *no*.

DECLARATIVE   S   P   A   A
⟨ (He) (had been) (to France) (before), hadn't he ⟩?
positive MCl   neg tag question

DECLARATIVE   S   P   A
⟨ (They) (couldn't come) (tonight), could they ⟩?
negative MCl   positive tag question

The imperative

To direct someone to do something, we use the **IMPERATIVE** mood. The use of an exclamation mark does not necessarily indicate that a sentence is in the imperative – grammatically, there should be no subject and the verb should be in the base form with no endings.

P   Od   P   Od
⟨ (Close) (the window) ⟩.   ⟨ (Stop) (fighting) ⟩.

Imperatives can be preceded by a vocative, which is stressed, to attract the attention of the person or people to whom the command is directed.

voc   P   Od   A   voc   P   A
⟨ (**You**) (stop) (that) (now) ⟩!   ⟨ (**Everyone**) (get) (out of the way) ⟩.

```
                          voc                    P          Od              A
⟨ (The man with the brown jacket) (put) (your hands) (above your head) ⟩.
```

We can use imperatives to make an offer (*Have a seat*), an invitation (*Come in*), a suggestion (*Have fun*) or to give instructions (*Take the next left*). To make a command negative we add *don't* before the base form verb; to make it more polite we add the adverb *please* at the beginning or end; to add emphasis we can put *do* before the verb.

```
        P                             P      Oi    Od                    P          Od
⟨ Don't stare ⟩.          ⟨ (Please) (get) (me) (a ticket) ⟩.       ⟨ (Do take) (care) ⟩
  prim neg  Vbase                Adv    Vbase                         prim   Vbase
```

We can also use tag questions after imperatives. Adding *won't you* after a positive imperative and *will you* after a negative imperative makes the command sound more like advice.

```
     P         Od        Co                            P          C
⟨ (Buy) (something) (sensible), won't you ⟩?      ⟨ (Don't get) (lost), will you ⟩?
                            neg tag                   prim neg  Vbase            tag
```

Exclamatory sentences

EXCLAMATORY SENTENCES express our feelings and emotions about something. They often have no verb phrase and are usually punctuated with an exclamation mark to indicate the strength of feeling. Many exclamations are minor sentences (see Section 8.2).

    Great!   Blast!   Hey you!   Well I never!   Fancy bumping into you!

We can also use expressions beginning with *What* (+ noun phrase) or *How* (+ adjective phrase).

    What a surprise!   What unexpected fun!   How very sad!   How ridiculous!

These are EXCLAMATIVE **sentences**. Some exclamatives contain a subject and finite verb phrase after a foregrounded object or a complement.

```
DECLARATIVE                              EXCLAMATIVE
S        P       Od        A             (Od)            S       P       A
⟨ (You) ('ve had) (bad luck) (recently) ⟩.    ⟨ (What bad luck) (you) ('ve had) (recently) ⟩!

DECLARATIVE                              EXCLAMATIVE
S      P       Cs                        (Cs)            S       P
⟨ (That) (was) (terrifying) ⟩!      ⟨ (How terrifying) (that) (was) ⟩!
```

Bringing the object or complement to the front of the sentence after a *wh*– word gives the object or complement added semantic significance – it is another form of marked theme.

The subjunctive

The SUBJUNCTIVE is used in some formal idioms, to express an intention or proposal about the future, or to communicate something hypothetical. In the subjunctive, the verb is in the base form or the plural form where we would normally expect a third person singular *–s* form.

If it **were** to rain, the picnic would have to be cancelled   (was)

I propose that she **be** appointed Treasurer.   (is)

We insist that he **sell** the house immediately.   (sells)

The subjunctive is quite rare in English and is more likely to be found in formal or written registers. Increasingly in contemporary usage, the –s form is more common than the subjunctive, except in idioms (*God save the Queen! Come what may ...*).

8.7 Conclusion

The information in this section helps us to see how clauses can be linked together to create different kinds of sentences. Being able to recognise the different types and understanding the ways in which they underpin meaning is central to textual analysis. We can become more effective as readers and listeners if we can appreciate how a writer or speaker uses sentence structure to organise the content, engage the audience, and communicate meaning in an appropriate way; we can be more effective as writers and speakers if we can ourselves manipulate sentence structure consciously.

An understanding of the form, function and position of clause elements within a sentence, a knowledge of the ways in which we combine clauses, and an appreciation of the different kinds of grammatical mood form the basis for discourse analysis. Before moving on to the next chapter, therefore, it is important to be confident in the recognition and labelling of different kinds of sentence types.

Chapter 9

Using your knowledge

In this chapter, you have the opportunity to apply the knowledge you have gained about sentences. The close reading activities require you to consider the effects created by the sentences the writer or speaker has chosen. The writing tasks encourage you to put the knowledge you have gained to practical use in your own texts.

9.1 Sentence type and structure

Analysing sentence structure in a text allows us to understand how a writer is organising and developing his or her material; it allows us to see how the writer wishes to affect the intended audience. In identifying changes to the standard pattern or in recognising the way in which a writer moves between different types of sentence structures, we can begin to appreciate the ways in which grammatical structure underpins meaning.

TASK 1 Sentence structure in texts for younger readers

1 Read the following extracts and think about the sentence structure in each case.

TEXT A

This extract is taken from the first book of a traditional Ladybird Reading Scheme for 4–5 year olds, Key Words 1b *Look at this* by William Murray. Each section would appear on a separate page in large sans serif print with an accompanying full-page picture on the right. The text would be read aloud to a teacher, parent, guardian or reading partner.

> A shop.
> I like shops.
>
> Jane is in a shop and Peter is in a shop.
> Here is a ball in a shop.
> Jane likes the ball.
> ...
> Jane has a shop.
> Here is Jane's shop.
>
> The shop has toys.
> Jane's shop is a toy shop.

© Ladybird Books Ltd, 1964. Reproduced by permission of Ladybird Books Ltd

TEXT B

This is an extract from *Litte Yellow Digger*, a story book for young children written b
Nicola Baxter published by Ladybird in the *Little Stories* series. Colour pictures suppor
the text and extend the story. The text is designed to be read aloud to a child.

Bright and early one morning, the Little Yellow Digger went to a big green field.

'I've a Very Important Job for you,' said a man, looking at a huge piece of paper.
'We need to dig a hole right here.'

'When there's digging to be done, I'm the digger to do it!' said the Little Yellow
Digger. 'But can you tell me what ...'

'Sorry,' said the Man with the Plan. 'I'll have a word later. I'm just nipping off for
some breakfast.'

So with a *clank clankety clank* the Little Yellow Digger started to dig. Soon he had
made a neat round hole and a little pile of earth and grass.

2 Use the table below to record the clause elements so that you can compare the
sentence type and structure for each extract. The first sentence in each text has
been done for you.

TEXT A   *Peter and Jane*

Conjunction Coord Sub	Subject	Predicator	Object/ complement	Adverbial	Interjection/ vocative
	A shop				
	I	like	shops		

TEXT B   *The Little Yellow Digger*

Conjunction Coord Sub	Subject	Predicator	Object/ complement	Adverbial	Interjection/ vocative
				Bright	
and				early	
				one morning	
	the L YD	went		to a big green field.	

3 Write a commentary exploring the language and structure of each extract.

You should use appropriate terminology and linguistic frameworks to explain and
evaluate the texts.
    You may like to think about:

•   the intended audience and purpose
•   the vocabulary

- the phrase structure
- the clause structure and sentence type
- the effect of the writers' choices.

COMMENTARY

While both extracts have the same intended audience (pre-school children and those in their first years of school), their purpose is different: Text A aims to develop first reading skills – it would be read aloud by a child to an adult or reading partner; Text B aims to engage young children with a narrative – it would be read aloud to a younger child by a more experienced reader. The visual difference in the layout immediately suggests a difference in approach. The short and concise linguistic units of Text A are quite unlike the longer more complicated structures of Text B.

The vocabulary in Text A is repetitive. The proper nouns *Peter* and *Jane*, the possessive noun *Jane's*, the concrete nouns *shop, shops, toy* and *ball* and the verbs *like, likes, is* and *has* recur frequently. All the words, except for *Peter*, are monosyllabic. The vocabulary is limited to lexical items that will be familiar to the target audience and the repetition is designed to give young readers confidence as they learn to recognise key words. Each page contains only one or two short sentences in a large print size.

Text B, on the other hand, is far more varied since it draws from a range of word classes: concrete nouns (*field, grass, paper*), adverbs (*later, soon*), adjectives (*Bright, early, huge*), past tense verbs (*went, said, started*), present tense verbs (*have, 's, 'm*), modal verbs (*can, 'll*), co-ordinating conjunctions (*and, But*), subordinating conjunctions (*When*) and onomatopoeic sound words (*clank clankety clank*). Longer units of text on each page reflect the fact that the book will be read aloud by a more experienced reader.

The only repeated words in Text B are the names of characters (*Little Yellow Digger, the Man*) and nouns (*hole*) and verbs (*dig, digging*) linked directly to the narrative. The vocabulary of Text B engages the target audience through a narrative context and recognises that young children understand more words than they are actually able to read themselves. The variety of words in this extract, therefore, more closely resembles the language we use on a day-to-day basis.

The phrase structures in Texts A and B mirror the division in their vocabulary. Text A is dominated by simple noun phrases (*Peter, a shop, Jane's shop*) and verb phrases (*likes, is, has*); it uses one adverb phrase (*Here*) and one repeated prepositional phrase (*in a shop*). The only pre-modified complex noun phrase (*a toy shop*) is made up of words that will be familiar since readers will already have encountered them earlier in the book.

Text B is more challenging since it uses a wide range of phrase structures. There are some simple phrases:

m h	m h	h	lex
a man	**a word**	**soon**	**need**
NP	NP	AdvP	VP
det N	det N	Adv	Vpres

The majority, however, are longer and complex. Noun phrases contain both pre
and post-modification, giving the reader details that help to develop the narrative.

m	m	m	h

a big green field
det AdjP AdjP N

m	h	q

the digger [to do it]
det N NFCl

m	m	h	q

a (Very Important) Job for you
det AdjP N PrepP

All the verb phrases in Text A use the simple present, but Text B uses both auxiliaries and lexical verbs to develop different time scales or to indicate shades c
meaning.

aux	lex

can . . . tell
mod Vbase

'll have
aux lex
mod Vbase

had made
aux lex
prim Ved

Simple present is used in the direct speech (*I've*; *I'm*); simple past for the narrativ
(*went*); and past perfective to indicate that an event is complete (*had made*). Mod
auxiliaries suggest ability (*can*) and certainty (*will*).

Although still using language in a straightforward way, Text B conforms to th
expectations of any narrative: it establishes mood with the opening compoun
adverb phrase *Bright and early*; it introduces time (*one morning*), place (*a big gree
field*), character (*the Little Yellow Digger*) and a problem or mystery (*the hole*). Th
variety of phrase structures therefore directly engages the target audience with th
plot and introduces them to real language in use.

The clause and sentence structure of Text A is, as we would expect, basic an
repetitive. It uses only simple and compound sentences and has no examples of sub
ordination. The most basic clauses contain a subject, a predicator and an object.

S   P   Od
〈 (I) (like) (shops) 〉.

S   P   O
〈 (The shop) (has) (toys) 〉.

Of the nine sentences, however, five follow a different pattern. The final sentenc
contains a complement.

S   P   Cs
〈 (Jane's shop) (is) (a toy shop) 〉.

In one of the compound sentences, there is a repeated adverbial of place.

S   P   A   S   P   A
〈 (Jane) (is) (in a shop) 〉 and 〈 (Peter) (is) (in a shop) 〉.
                         conj

There is a minor sentence (*A shop*) consisting of a noun phrase standing alone. Th
marks the introduction of a new word which will be accompanied by an image t
reinforce the meaning. The most complicated grammatical structure can be see
in the two sentences which invert the order of the clause elements by using th
adverb *Here* in the initial position. It functions as an exophoric reference to th
accompanying picture.

A   P   S   A
〈 (Here) (is) (a ball) (in a shop) 〉.

A   P   S
〈 (Here) (is) (Jane's shop) 〉.

Despite this, no sentence is very long and most have no more than three clause ele
ments. In the compound sentences, all elements are repeated so that the conter
remains at the most simple level, avoiding new verb forms and vocabulary.

‹ (Jane) (is) (in a shop) › and ‹ (Peter) (is) (in a shop) ›.   Peter and Jane <u>are</u> in a shop.
conj

Text B has a very different linguistic profile – there is little repetition; clauses and sentences are varied.

```
 S        P         Od        A                                                    [SIMPLE]
‹ (I)  ('ll have)  (a word)  (later) ›.
```

```
 A       S      P           Od                       S     P          Od
‹ (Soon) (he) (had made) (a neat round hole) › and ‹ (Ø) (Ø) (a little pile of earth and grass) ›.
                                               conj                            [COMPOUND]
```

```
            A                        S    P        Cs
‹ [When there's digging [to be done] ] (I) ('m) (the digger [to do it] ) ›.
  SCl – ACl (clause element)   SCl – NFCl (embedded)      SCl – NFCl (embedded)   [COMPLEX]
```

As can be seen in the example above, clause elements are often made up of subordinate clauses and clause elements do not always appear in the standard order. By bringing particular elements to the front of a sentence, the writer can put additional emphasis on the information. The foregrounding in Text B, for instance, draws attention to the adverbials of time (*Bright and early*; *Soon*) and manner (*With a clank clankety clank*). Other foregrounding contributes to the narrative in different ways: the initial position conjunction *But* imitates the style of informal conversation; the fronted *So* is a traditional oral narrative technique to drive the story forward.

Where Text A uses only limited clause types, Text B uses a wide range. As well as the S P O and S P A patterns, the narrative includes:

A S P A   l. 1
A S P C   l. 4
S P O A   l. 6
conj A S P O   l. 8
A S P O conj Ø O   ll. 8–9

The number and position of adverbials is typical of narrative: they provide descriptive detail and can be moved around the sentence for creative effect.

The linguistic and grammatical choices in each extract are directly linked to the audience and purpose. The simplicity of Text A aims to make reading more approachable so that young children can begin to recognise basic monosyllabic, high frequency words. While encouraging recognition, however, there is little sense of a developing narrative to engage young readers.

In Text B, on the other hand, the narrative itself plays a central role: the mystery of the *hole* keeps both characters and readers guessing. This unanswered question underpins the narrative and we need to read on to reach a resolution. While this approach clearly encourages young children to engage with the story – it is likely to foster a love of reading – it does not necessarily help them to tackle the complexities of the reading process. The text does not limit the range of lexis and grammatical structure in the way that Text A does and it may alienate a beginner reader. In order to make effective readers, therefore, we can balance the intentional limitations of reading scheme books with the variety and interest of a story which combines a strong sense of character, time and place with an engaging plot.

1 Choose a text that might be read in the early years of secondary school: for instance, *Vajak Paw*, *The Didakoi*, *The Machine Gunners*, *The Wolves of Willoughby Chase*, *Mrs Frisby and the Rats of NIMH*.

2 Select a key passage and analyse the sentences, paying particular attention to the clause elements and sentence types.

3 Re-write the passage for a younger audience using only short simple and compound sentences. Decide which information is important for a younger reader and which can be omitted.

You need to think about the type, structure and length of the sentences you are creating and the effect these will have on a younger, less experienced reader.

When you have completed your text, compare and contrast it with the original text, evaluating the key linguistic features and commenting on the semantic differences. You may like to use the suggested framework for analysis in Appendix A.

1 Read the extracts below carefully.

They are taken from William Golding's novel *The Inheritors*, which describes the prehistoric struggle for survival between two early human groups: the more advanced homo sapiens and the more primitive Neanderthal man.

TEXT A
Lok, a Neanderthal, is watching a stranger – an individual from the homo sapiens group who tries to shoot Lok from across the river with a bow and arrow.

The bushes twitched again. Lok steadied by the tree and gazed. A head and chest faced him half-hidden. There were white bone things behind the leaves and hair. The man had white things above his eyes and under his mouth so that his face was longer than a face should be. The man turned sideways in the bushes and looked at Lok along his shoulder. A stick rose upright and there was a lump of bone in the middle. Lok peered at the stick and the lump of bone and the small eyes in the bone things over the face.

TEXT B
Taken from near the end of the novel, Tuami, a member of the homo sapiens group, sails away.

Tuami sat in the stern of the dug-out, the steering paddle under his left arm. There was plenty of light and the patches of salt no longer looked like holes in the skin sails. He thought bitterly of the great squares they had left bundled up in the last mad hour among the mountains; for with that and the breeze through the gap he need not have endured these hours of strain. He need not have sat all night wondering whether the current would beat the wind and bear them back to the fall while the people or as many as were left of them slept their collapsed sleep.

2 Use a table to record the clause elements so that you can compare the sentence type and structure for each extract.

The first sentence in each text has been done for you.

TEXT A

Conjunction Coord Sub		Subject	Predicator	Object/ complement	Adverbial	Sentence type
		The bushes	twitched		again.	SIMPLE

TEXT B

Conjunction Coord Sub		Subject	Predicator	Object/ complement	Adverbial	Sentence type
		Tuami	sat		in the stern of the dug-out	SIMPLE
					the steering paddle under his left arm.	

3 Write a commentary exploring the style Golding uses in each extract and explaining the effect this has on the characterisation in each case.

You should use appropriate terminology and linguistic frameworks to explain and evaluate the texts.
You may like to think about:

- the lexical choice
- the phrase structure
- the clause and sentence type
- anything else you find interesting.

COMMENTARY

There is a conscious difference in the styles of these two extracts, linked this time to the demands of the narrative rather than to its intended audience and purpose. While Extract B is clearly more complicated than Extract A, the latter does not mirror the simplicity of linguistic and grammatical style demonstrated in the reading scheme text above. Because Golding is creating a sense of character, time and place, because he is developing a plot, he needs to draw on a variety of language structures to engage his readers. Real language in use is rarely as straightforward as a reading scheme book and Extract A, while less sophisticated than Extract B, still demonstrates a range of features.

The lexis of Extract A is dominated by concrete nouns linked to the human form (*head, chest, face, hair*) and to the environment (*bushes, trees, leaves*). These are known and familiar items, but the non-specific noun *things* suggests that Lok is describing something unfamiliar to him, something that exists outside his own cultural experience: the face of the homo sapiens is quite different to his own; references to *A stick/the stick* seem to indicate that the observer does not understand the nature of a bow and arrow.

There are also concrete nouns in Extract B: linked to boats (*paddle, sails*), the environment (*mountains, current, fall*) and the weather (*breeze, wind*). Where most nouns in Extract A are monosyllabic, however, at least half here are polysyllabic. In addition, abstract concepts of time are now referenced (*hour, night*). This is indicative of a more sophisticated community, which can not only build a boat and name it according to its construction (*dug-out*), but can also name its parts (*stern*).

A similar difference can be seen in the verbs. Where Extract A is dominated by simple past tense dynamic verbs that mark out physical processes integral to the Neanderthal way of life (*twitched, steadied, turned, looked*), Extract B also includes mental process verbs (*thought, endured, wondering*).

The phrase structure reflects a similar division. Extract A uses simple noun phrases: most are modified by a determiner.

m	h		m	h		m	h
The	bushes		his	face		A	stick
det	N		det	N		det	N

Other modifiers used are monosyllabic, relating to basic qualities of colour, size or physical make-up. Post-modification is used in very few phrases:

m	m	h		m	m	h		m	h	q		h	q
white	bone	things		the	small	eyes		a	lump	of bone		longer	[than a face should be]
	NP				NP				NP				AdjP
AdjP	N	N		det	AdjP	N		det	N	PrepP		Adj	CompCl

Golding's style helps us to engage with Lok. We recognise the relative simplicity of his viewpoint and this helps us to understand his experience of the world. In Extract B, however, the phrases are quite different. Many are longer with more varied pre- and post-modification and a greater range of phrase types.

m	m	h	q		h		m	m	h
the	great	squares	[Ø they had left bundled up]		bitterly		the	steering	paddle
	NP				AdvP			NP	
det	AdjP	N	RelCl		Adv		det	V*ing*	N

aux	lex		aux	aux	lex		aux	lex
would	beat		need	not	have endured		had	left
	VP			VP			VP	
mod	V*base*		mod	neg	prim	V*ed*	prim	V*ed*

The phrase structures here distinguish between the two viewpoints of the novel, drawing attention to the more sophisticated life style of the homo sapiens community.

The clause analysis table allows us see at a glance the same kind of differences emerging in the clause and sentence structure. Extract A is clearly more repetitive in its structure: the similarity of the phrases in each clause site reinforces our sense of the relative simplicity of Lok's viewpoint. The subject column is dominated by simple noun phrases, the predicator column by simple past tense verbs and the adverbial column by prepositional phrases. Sentences are either simple or compound (the co-ordinator *and* is repeated eight times), except for Sentence 5 where the subordinating conjunction *so that* introduces an adverbial clause of reason which also contains a comparative clause.

The clauses and sentences of Extract B are, as we would expect, more varied with the longest complex and compound-complex sentences carrying the greatest weight of information. The clause analysis table is therefore less patterned, with longer phrases in each of the clause sites. The subordinating conjunctions mark the growing sophistication of Tuami's language use.

Where the conjunctions of Extract A tend to be repetitive, those in extract B perform a range of functions. Although the simple co-ordinating conjunctions *and/or* are used in four places, there are also a wide range of subordinate clauses introduced by *whether* (indirect question), *as . . . as* (comparison), *for* (adverbial clause of reason), *while* (adverbial clause of time), *bundled up/wondering* (non-finite clauses functioning as adverbials of manner) and an unmarked relative clause (*the great square Ø they had left*). These subordinate clauses add depth to the narrative by providing additional detail, demonstrating the sophistication of Tuami's thought processes and developing a complexity of style that is in direct contrast to the straightforward prose of Lok's narrative.

Although both extracts are approximately the same length, the sentences are quite different in each case: where there are eight sentences with an average of 13 words in Extract A, Extract B has only four with an average of 28 words per sentence. This difference is not coincidental. Golding is using sentence patterning as well as differences in the vocabulary to characterise his two distinctive narrative viewpoints. Extract A is dominated by simple and compound sentences suggesting something about the essential nature of Lok; the reflective compound-complex sentences of Extract B mark the emergence of a new consciousness. The style of the text, therefore, as well as the content, can be used to develop a sense of character and to engage the reader.

ASK 4

1 Choose one of the following writing exercises. When you have completed your text, evaluate the key linguistic features. You may like to use the suggested framework for analysis in Appendix A.

EITHER

Look at extracts from some novels that use a distinctive style in order to create character: for example, *The Knife of Never Letting Go*, Patrick Ness; *Riddley Walker*, Russell Hoban; *Foxy-T*, Tony White; *The Color Purple*, Alice Walker; *Bimbo*, Keith Waterhouse, *The Kin*, Peter Dickinson; *ella minnow pea: A novel in letters*, Mark Dunn.

Write an extract from a first person narrative in which the central character has a distinctive point of view, limited by his or her age, cultural experiences or understanding.

You need to think carefully about the kind of sentence types and vocabulary that would be associated with the character you create.

OR

Write two versions of a reply to a problem page question. The first should adopt a very formal tone like the extract from the nineteenth century novel on page 103; the second should use a more personal and familiar tone as you might find in a twenty-first century newspaper. You can offer advice about relationships, financial worries, self-esteem issues or some other topic.

You need to make sure that the type, length and structure of the sentences you choose are appropriate for the tone – the formal piece will have longer sentences with more embedding.

OR

Write two emails, one informal (to a friend or relative) and one formal (perhaps to a prospective employer, university department or service provider). Use the same content, but change the focus and style to suit the intended audience.

You need to pay particular attention to the content, vocabulary, and the type and structure of the sentences. The informal email will have minor sentences rather than lots of subordination.

9.2 Linking sentences and sentence organisation

Writers and speakers use linking devices and sentence organisation to provide clear overall structure, to develop the content logically, to mirror a particular genre and to guide the response of their intended audience.

TASK 1   Cohesion and sentence organisation in different text types

1 Read each text carefully.

TEXT A   Formal speech in a school debate

The argument over MPs' expenses, however, rumbles on. Politicians may apologise for letting us, the electorate, down. They may repay nominal sums of money for moats, swimming pools, phantom mortgages and the like, but it doesn't easily put things right. Furthermore, at a time when many families are feeling the impact of the recession, this scandal has disillusioned voters. Promises of parliamentary reform seem hollow – consequently, we need to see action not words if they want us to support any of them at the General Election. In other words, politicians of all colours must reach out to the electorate and convince them that things can be different.

TEXT B   Formal letter from a service provider

Mr T. HOUSE
15, HIGH STREET
NEWTOWN
NN27 6PP

Contact us online at:
homeservices.co.uk/contracts
Call us on: 0800 800 8000
Write to: Home Services, PO Box 001
London SW1 6WS
29 March 2012

Information about your Direct Debit

Dear Mr House

We wrote to you in February confirming details of your Direct Debit payment and the date on which we would be collecting the payment from your bank/building society. Please ignore this earlier communication because unfortunately the date stated was incorrect. This error has now been resolved and I would like to confirm that your payment of £115 is now due.

What happens next

You do not need to do anything. The outstanding payment will be taken on 12 April 2012.

All future payments will be collected on the 12th of the month. If, however, you have any other questions not dealt with in this letter, please call one of our customer service advisors on 0800 800 8000. They will be happy to help you.

Please accept our apologies for any inconvenience that may have been caused.

Yours sincerely,

S. Smith

Sam Smith
Head of Billing and Payments

2 List the different forms of cohesion and sentence organisation each writer uses.
3 Write a commentary exploring the effects created by the linguistic features you identify.

You should use appropriate terminology and linguistic frameworks to explain and evaluate the texts.
    You may like to think about:

- lexical patterning
- subject specific words
- linking adverbs and conjunctions
- substitution
- marked themes
- any other distinctive language features

COMMENTARY

Each of the texts here has a distinctive function: Text A is a persuasive spoken text designed to encourage others to see a particular political situation in the same way as the speaker; and Text B is an information text, providing the reader with important facts about their method of payment for a particular service.

Lexical cohesion

The subject specific lexis in Text A focuses on two main lexical sets: politics (*MPs, Politicians, electorate, voters, parliamentary reforms, General Election*); a particular political issue (*expenses, repay, nominal sums of money, moats, swimming pools, phantom mortgages*). Perhaps most significant, however, are the words which express the opinion of the speaker. This lexical set communicates attitude and also creates a form of cohesion since the same tone runs throughout the extract. The connotations of adjectives like *nominal* and *hollow*, the verb *disillusioned* and the use of a negative verb phrase (*doesn't ... put things right*) directly communicate the attitude of the speaker.

Text B also has a subject specific lexical set, this time focusing on finance: *Direct Debit, bank/building society, Billing and Payments*. Repetition of the noun *payment(s)* with a variety of pre-modifiers (*Direct Debit, outstanding, future*) and semantically linked words (*incorrect, error*) draw the reader's attention to the main purpose of the letter. Cohesion is also developed in the date references which establish a framework for the information provided: the letter is formally dated (*29 March 2012*); there is a reference to the earlier letter (*February*) and the incorrect date for collection of a payment (*the date stated*); a new date is established for the outstanding payment (*12 April 2012*) and future payments (*the 12th of the month*).

Substitution

Anaphoric referencing is most common with pronouns replacing nouns: the subject pronouns *They* (politicians), *it* (repayment of expenses), *we* (*the electorate*) in Text A and *you* (Mr House) in Text B; the object pronoun *them* (politicians l.7, electorate l.8) in Text A. Cataphoric referencing is less common, but we see examples in both Texts A and B. In the persuasive text, the object pronoun *us* points forward to the parenthesis (*the electorate*) and in the letter the subject pronoun *I* points forward to the signature and printed name at the end. In this text, the plural first person subject pronoun *we* has no direct reference point – the reader understands that it is a general reference to the company providing the service, which is represented by the named advisor. We recognise this as a conscious semantic choice – it removes responsibility for the error in the previous letter from one individual by referring to the company as a whole. A similar approach is used in the passive verb phrase *has been resolved*, which removes the subject from the sentence.

Exophoric references in Text B extend beyond the immediate written context to the previous letter (*this earlier communication*) and in Text A to the wider circumstances reported in the newspapers (*this scandal*).

Conjuncts

Only Text A uses conjuncts. Since it is a persuasive text, it uses these linking words to develop a coherent argument. Adversative conjuncts create a contrast, moving the argument in a new direction (*however*); additive conjuncts develop the argument by accumulating evidence in support of the points being made (*Furthermore, In other words*); causal conjuncts reinforce the argument by recognising the result of particular course of action (*consequently*). These words enable the speaker to link all her points persuasively, creating a text that may influence the audience.

Structure

We can recognise that each text has a form that is representative of a particular genre: formal speeches and letters. The structure associated with each text type provides a form of cohesion.

In Text B, the recognised layout for a letter (address of sender and recipient; date; formal opening and closing) provides an overall framework. In addition, the use of headings (*Information about your Direct Debit*; *What happens next*) helps to divide the content up into manageable sections.

Sentence organisation

The conjuncts in Text A are also foregrounded for emphasis. The additive conjuncts *Furthermore* and *In other words* develop the argument, while the causal conjunct *Consequently* identifies a result or effect of the 'hollow promises'. Since the speech is designed to persuade the audience of a particular point of view, these fronted adverbials mark the development of the argument. The use of two marked themes in the fourth sentence is designed to throw weight onto the semantically important main clause.

> A   A
> ⟨ (Furthermore) (at a time [when many families are feeling the impact of the recession]])
> SCl – RelCl (relative adverb of time i.e. 'at which')

> S   P   Od
> (this scandal) (has disillusioned) (voters) ⟩.

After the adverbials, one of which is a long post-modified prepositional phrase, the delayed main clause with its simple phrases is emphatic. This is the key to the speaker's argument.

Most of the sentences in Text B use standard grammatical patterns in which a subject is followed by a predicator. There are, however, three sentences in which marked themes are used. The politeness marker *Please* followed by an imperative verb occurs at the beginning of three main clauses.

> P   P   P
> Please (ignore) …   please (call)   Please (accept)
> Adv   V*base*   Adv   V*base*   Adv   V*base*

This structure softens the semantic force of the imperative verb by making the command into a polite request.

In addition, a foregrounded conditional clause *If...*, with a parenthetical adversative conjunct *however*, addresses a potential situation: it establishes a course of action should the recipient of the letter require additional information. Conditional clauses are usually foregrounded because the subordinate clause establishes the particular circumstances in which the predicator of the main clause will be relevant.

Summary

Linguistic markers and structural patterns create links in a text which guide the reader or listener through the logical development of the content. In each text here, the cohesion and sentence organisation ensure that the argument (Text A) and the information (Text B) are communicated efficiently: the techniques used contribute to the overall structure and logical development of the material in each case.

TASK 2   Linking devices and sentence organisation in different text types

1 Choose one of the following writing exercises. When you have completed your text, evaluate the key linguistic features. You may like to use the suggested framework for analysis in Appendix A.

EITHER

Write a short speech in which you argue for or against an issue about which you feel strongly. Develop your argument clearly using appropriate linguistic devices.

You need to pay particular attention to sentence type, sentence linking and organisation and the kind of language you choose to convince your audience. Use conjuncts and conjunctions to develop your case logically, and disjuncts to communicate your opinions.

OR

Choose a topical issue and write an editorial for a compact newspaper expressing your opinion. You may find it useful to look at some examples of editorials before you start.

You need to pay particular attention to the content, the intended audience and the kinds of linguistic and grammatical features that would both inform and persuade the reader to see things as you do. Since space is limited, think carefully about the ways in which you link and organise your sentences.

OR

Write some posts for a social networking or microblogging site using no more than 140 characters for each text. You may choose to talk about yourself or about a particular issue, to promote a help group or business, or to report on a news event.

You need to pay particular attention to the word limit and the grammatical features appropriate for the genre. Think carefully about the ways in which you can use sentence linking and organisation to create an effective text – you need to convince readers that your posts are more interesting than other people's so that they keep returning to your site.

When you have completed your 140 characters, evaluate the key linguistic features and the techniques you have used to engage your audience.

9.3 Grammatical mood

The genre and purpose of some texts dictates the grammatical mood a writer or speaker needs to use: instruction texts are dominated by imperatives; narratives are dominated by declaratives; questionnaires are dominated by interrogatives; informal electronic texts are dominated by exclamations. In other cases, writers and speakers can move between different grammatical moods to change the pace, create a new atmosphere, or to establish a different relationship with their intended audience.

1 Read the texts below carefully.

TEXT 1 Product review

When it comes to style, you'll be hard-pressed to beat this classic cleaner without calling in the professionals. The rotating brush tackles dirt and stains with a heated wash solution to enhance performance. This machine makes tough work effortless. Above all, it is quiet and efficient – perfect for large and small jobs. A sleek performer at an acceptable price.

TEXT 2 Instructions on a work sheet

Calculus of Variations
Please hand in your solutions at the lecture on Thursday **25 February 2011**. The number of marks for each question is given in brackets after each question. The **questions marked with an asterisk** will count towards the coursework part of the assessment.

TEXT 3 Extract from a graphic novel

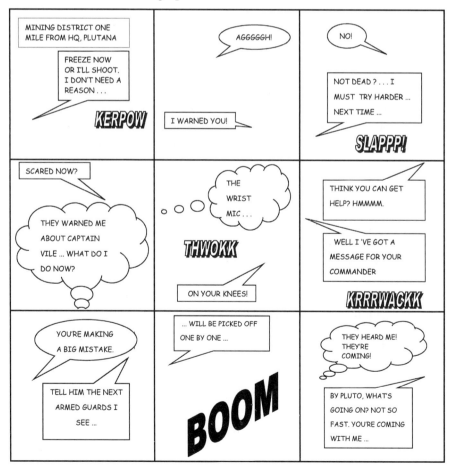

TEXT 4   Email

Hi! Thought I'd better say hello after so long! What have you been doing? Any news? We're all OK, but Andrew has had a cold. Boys are busy as ever. And your lot? Let us know how you're all doing. Have you heard about the burst pipe?

TEXT 5   News in brief

Tens of thousands of students will miss out on university places this year after record numbers apply. With the recession leaving one in five out of work and around 45,000 people reapplying after missing out last year, applications are currently up 100,000. But university budget cuts mean that there will be even more pressure on places.

2 Analyse the sentence structure of each text. You may like to use a clause analysis table like the one on page 181.

3 Make notes on the extracts, paying particular attention to:

- the relationship between the mood and the audience, purpose and genre
- the phrases
- the type and organisation of the sentences,
- the cohesion

TEXT 1   Product review

This kind of writing aims to provide information and supposedly objective comment. The focus is on assessing and evaluating a particular product. It is aimed at adults with domestic responsibilities who are potential purchasers. The grammatical mood is declarative because the focus is on making statements about a particular product.

Phrases

▶ mostly complex with pre-/post-modification to add detail

m	m	m	h	q		m	m	h	q
with	a	heated	wash	solution to enhance performance		A	sleek	performer	at an acceptable price

PrepP   NP
prep   det AdjP   N   PrepP
   det *Ved*   N   N   NFCl

▶ significant number of AdjPs because text is informative/persuasive

SIMPLE
   effortless   quiet and efficient
COMPLEX

h	q		h	q
hard-pressed	[to beat this classic cleaner]		**perfect**	for large and small jobs
Adj	*Ved* NFCl		Adj	PrepP

▶ verb phrases simple with present tense verbs (*comes, tackles*), i.e., current model
▶ modal verb phrase implies certainty (*'ll be*), i.e., emphatic claim about product

Sentences

‣ clause sites full
‣ mix of simple and complex sentences, but none very long (approachable style)

SIMPLE

       S   P   Od   Co

⟨ (This machine) (makes) (tough work) (effortless) ⟩.

COMPLEX

             S   P   Od   A

⟨ (The rotating brush) (tackles) (dirt and stains) (with a heated wash solution

[to enhance performance]) ⟩.

SCl – NFCl

‣ one minor sentence to end i.e. summative comment with emphasis on evaluation

ORGANISATION

‣ aims to draw attention to key features (design)
‣ two marked themes with foregrounded adverbials summarising best features (*When it comes to style ..., Above all ...*)

Cohesion

‣ tight because of the narrow range of the text, i.e., focus on one particular product
‣ lexical sets relating to: product (*brush, machine, cleaner, wash solution*), function (*dirt, stains, jobs*), evaluation (*performance, performer*)
‣ direct address engages reader (*you*)
‣ references: anaphoric (*machine* → *it*); exophoric references to accompanying picture (***this*** *classic cleaner,* ***This*** *machine*)

TEXT 2   Worksheet instructions

This kind of writing aims to inform and instruct. The focus is on providing specific details and directions. It is aimed at university maths students following a module in Calculus. The grammatical mood is typical of the genre: sentences are mainly declarative because the focus is on providing information, but there is one imperative (*hand in*) establishing what the students have to do.

Phrases

‣ often complex, because they need to contain a lot of information
‣ some simple **noun** phrases (*your solutions*), but most complex with post-modification (precise detail)

m	h	q		m	m	h	q
The	questions	[marked with an asterisk]		the	coursework	part	of the assessment
det	N	NFCl		det	N	N	PrepP

‣ prepositional phrases recur: references to place (*at the lecture*) and time (*on Thursday*)

- passive verb phrase (*is given*)
- future time draws attention to important element of course (*will count*)

Sentences

- clause sites full for clarity of instructions
- two simple sentences, one complex

SIMPLE

               S   P   A   A
‹ (The number of marks for each question) (is given) (in brackets) (after each question) ›.

COMPLEX

              S   P   A
‹ (The questions [marked with an asterisk]) (will count) (towards the coursework part
                       SCl – NFCl

of the assessment) ›.

- noun phrases in subject and adverbial sites long but not linguistically complicated
- focus on adverbials (information)

Organisation

- foregrounded politeness marker (*Please*).
- passive voice brings object (*The number of marks ...*) to front of active sentence for emphasis, i.e., person responsible for 'action' of verb not important

Cohesion

- subject specific lexical sets linked to: assessment (*number of marks, questions, coursework, assessment*), education (*lecture*), subject (*solutions*)
- lexical repetition focuses on topic (*question/questions*)
- bold print highlights key information

TEXT 3   Graphic novel

This kind of writing aims to entertain. The focus is on developing a narrative. It is aimed at young readers who enjoy the genre, or who may find reading longer texts less appealing. The wide-ranging grammatical moods are typical of the genre: declaratives (*I warned you*), imperatives (*Freeze now ...*), interrogatives (*What do I do now?*), exclamatory (*AGGGGGGH!, They heard me!*).

Phrases

- mostly short and undeveloped providing skeleton story to support pictures
- wide range of phrase types typical of flexibility of narrative
- many simple phrases – genre dominated by images
  - Noun phrases: *help, him, a reason*   Prepositional phrase: *By Pluto*
  - Adjective phrase: *dead*   Adverb phrases: *now, harder*
- some complex noun phrases:

m	m	h	m	h	q		m	m	m	h	q
The	wrist	mic	a	message	for your commander		The	next	armed	guards	[Ø I see]
det	N	N	det	N	PrepP		det	AdjP	Ved	N	RelCl

- wide range of verb phrases typical of narrative: present (*don't need, see*); future time (*'ll be picked off*); present perfective (*'ve got*); present progressive (*'re making, 're coming*); simple past (*warned, heard*)
- modal verb phrase implying certainty (*'ll shoot, must try*) – develops sense of character
- contractions indicative of informal tone – graphic novels use direct speech with very little narrative description

Sentences

- straightforward, short sentences – most clause sites contain only 1–2 words
- many clause sites empty, i.e., elliptical style – reflecting informal conversation (colloquial)

P	S	Cs			P	S	Cs	A
⟨ Ø	Ø (Not)	(dead) ⟩?			⟨ Ø	Ø	(Scared)	(now) ⟩?
	neg							

- minor sentences (*No!*), many onomatopoeic (*SLAPP!, KRRRWACKK, BOOM*)
- mainly simple sentences and one compound, i.e., approachable style

S	P	Od		P	A	S	P
⟨ (You)	('re making)	(a big mistake) ⟩.		⟨ (Freeze)	(now) ⟩ or ⟨ (I)	('ll shoot) ⟩	
					conj		

- complex sentence divided across 2 frames to make it more manageable

P	Oi		Od	
⟨ (Tell)	(him)	[Ø the next armed guards	[Ø I see] / will be picked off one by one] ⟩.	
	SCl – NCl		SCl – RelCl	

Organisation

- two marked themes: interjection develops theme of conflict (*Well ...*); exclamation links to context i.e. set on Plutana (*By Pluto ...*)

Cohesion

- lexical sets relating to conflict: nouns (*Captain, commander, armed guards*); verbs (*shoot, picked off*)
- number of interjections typical of comic book genre (*KERPOW, THWOKK*)
- anaphoric references (*commander → him; armed guard → one by one*)
- exophoric references link directly to pictures (*you, I, They*)

TEXT 4   Informal email

This kind of writing aims to exchange family news in an informal way. The focus is on a narrow range of personal events and people, and on establishing a relationship. It is written for a specific known reader. The grammatical mood is typical of informal electronic English. It has a wide range: declaratives (*We're all OK ...*), interjections (*Hi!*), interrogatives which engage with the reader in a delayed two-way communication (*What...?, Have...?*) and exclamations (*Thought I'd better ...!*).

Phrases

- mostly short and simple noun phrases (*We, Boys, your lot, Any news*)
- only occasional use of modification – phatic rather than descriptive function dominant

m	m	h		m	h		h	q
the	burst	pipe		so	long		busy	as ever
	NP			AdvP			AdjP	
det	V*ed*	N		Adv	Adv		Adj	PrepP

- verb phrases use a range of time scales: simple present (*are, know*), simple past (*Thought*), perfective (*has had, Have … heard*), progressive (*have … been doing 're … doing*)
- contractions typical of conversational tone

Sentences

- lots of short sentences
- clause sites not always full (elliptical – reminiscent of colloquial conversation)

P dumS	(S)		A	P	S		S	P		Od		A
⟨ Ø	Ø Any news? ⟩	⟨ And	Ø	Ø	your lot? ⟩	⟨	Ø	(Thought)	[Ø	I'd better say hello]	(after
			conj							SCl – NCl		

so long) ⟩.

- minor sentence – greeting (*Hi!*)
- mix of simple, compound and complex sentences

Od	P	S	P		S	P	S	Cs		S	P
⟨ (What)	(have)	(you)	(been doing) ⟩?	⟨	(We)	('re)	(all)	(OK) ⟩	but	⟨ (Andrew)	(has had)
SIMPLE					COMPOUND				conj		

Od
(a cold) ⟩.

P	Oi	P		Od
⟨ (Let)	(us)	(know)	[how you all are doing] ⟩.	
COMPLEX		SCl – NCl		

- omissions and contractions shorten sentences – conversational; more readable

Organisation

- fronted conjunction marks change of direction (*And*)

Cohesion

- pronoun references stand alone with only one proper noun (*Andrew*) – participants familiar and therefore unnamed
- first person pronouns (*I, we, us*) refer to sender and family
- second person pronouns (*you*) – direct address to one known recipient

TEXT 5   News in brief

This kind of writing aims to inform. The focus is on summarising the key details of a particular issue or event. It is aimed at readers who want the facts rather than interpretative comment or personalised stories. The grammatical mood is declarative because the text consists of a sequence of statements.

Phrases

▸ some short phrases (typical of News in Brief): *currently, up* (AdvP), *this year, applications* (NP)
▸ lots of numbers (factual information), usually as modifiers in a noun phrase
▸ dominated by complex noun and prepositional phrases – emotive to engage readers

<pre>
        m   h   q   m   h   q
(even more) pressure on places   With the recession [leaving one in five out of work]
  Adv   det   N   PrepP   prep   NP
</pre>

▸ verb phrases in simple present reflect current situation (*are, mean*)
▸ future time to reflect outcome of current situation (*will miss out on, will be*)

Sentences

▸ comparatively long and contain a lot of information – typical for readership of compact
▸ adverbials provide information: time (*this year, currently*); reason (*With the recession*)
▸ the sentences are complex or compound-complex

<pre>
COMPLEX   S   P   Od   A
‹ (Tens of thousands of students) (will miss out on) (university places) (this year)

        A
[after record numbers apply] ›.
 SCl – ACl
</pre>

<pre>
COMPOUND-COMPLEX   A   A
‹ (With the recession [leaving 1 in 5 out of work]) and (Ø 45,000 people [reapplying
                    SCl – NFCl   conj   SCl – NFCl

                       S   P   A   A
[after missing out last year]]) (applications) (are) (currently) (up) ›.
 SCl – ACl
</pre>

Organisation

▸ short text containing a lot of information
▸ sentence structure is important in helping the reader to extract the information effectively
▸ foregrounded adverbials are emotive – emphasis on recession (*With the recession leaving ... reapplying ...*)
▸ heavy weight at front of sentence drawing attention to reasons for current problems – can be difficult to read
▸ fronted conjunction (*But*) divides already complicated sentence into two sections making it easier to read – avoids compound-complex sentence (which would have had 6 clauses) and focuses attention on university budget cuts

Cohesion

▸ tight structure
▸ lexical sets linked to: university (*students, university places, apply, applications*), statistics (*Tens of thousands, one in five, 45,000, 100,000*), economic problems (*recession, out of work, budget cuts*)
▸ exophoric reference (*this year*) to date printed at top of each page of newspaper
▸ no room for ambiguity in 'News in Brief' report so few pronoun references

TASK 2   Grammatical mood in drama

The following extract is taken from the tragedy *King Lear* by William Shakespeare. In this play, Lear decides to divide his kingdom between his three daughters so that he can enjoy the last years of his life without the responsibilities of his role as king. His favourite daughter, Cordelia, refuses to make a public declaration of love for him and he disinherits her, dividing the kingdom between her sisters, Goneril and Regan. They turn against Lear and their rejection drives him to madness.

Gloucester is loyal to Lear throughout the play. He tries to heal the divisions that have been caused by Lear's ill-advised plan to divide his kingdom. He is, however, guilty of pride in his social status; his self-importance makes him blind to what is really happening around him.

1 Read the extract from Act III Scene vii (lines 27–57) carefully.

At this point in the play, Regan and her husband Cornwall have Gloucester brought before them. After questioning him, Cornwall tears out Gloucester's eyes as a punishment for his loyalty to the king.

The scene is a turning point in the characterisation of Gloucester: his suffering helps him to understand the chaos around him and to feel for others – his physical blindness replaces the metaphorical blindness that has clouded his judgement earlier in the play.

Enter GLOUCESTER, *brought in by two or three servants*

REGAN	Ingrateful fox! 'tis he.
CORNWALL	Bind fast his corky arms.
GLOUCESTER	What mean your graces? Good my friends, consider
	You are my guests; do me no foul play, friends.
CORNWALL	Bind him, I say. [SERVANTS *bind him*
REGAN	Hard, hard. O filthy traitor!
GLOUCESTER	Unmerciful lady as you are, I'm none.
CORNWALL	To this chair bind him. Villain, thou shalt find – [REGAN *plucks his*
	beard
GLOUCESTER	By the kind gods, 'tis most ignobly done
	To pluck me by the beard.
REGAN	So white, and such a traitor!
GLOUCESTER	Naughty lady,
	These hairs which thou dost ravish from my chin
	Will quicken and accuse thee, I am your host;
	With robbers' hands my hospitable favours

	You should not ruffle thus. What will you do?
CORNWALL	Come, sir, what letters had you late from France?
REGAN	Be simple answerer, for we know the truth.
CORNWALL	And what confederacy have you with the traitors
	Late footed in the kingdom?
REGAN	To whose hands have you sent the lunatic King?
	Speak.
GLOUCESTER	I have a letter, guessingly set down,
	Which came from one that's of a neutral heart,
	And not from one opposed.
CORNWALL	Cunning.
REGAN	And false.
CORNWALL	Where hast thou sent the King?
GLOUCESTER	To Dover.
REGAN	Wherefore to Dover? Wast thou not charged at peril –
CORNWALL	Wherefore to Dover? Let him first answer that.
GLOUCESTER	I am tied to the stake, and I must stand the course.
REGAN	Wherefore to Dover, sir?
GLOUCESTER	Because I would not see thy cruel nails
	Pluck out his poor old eyes, nor thy fierce sister
	In his anointed flesh stick boarish fangs …
CORNWALL	See't shalt thou never. Fellows, hold the chair.
	Upon these eyes of thine I'll set my foot.
GLOUCESTER	… Give me some help! O cruel! [CORNWALL *tears one eye out*
	O you gods!

2 Identify the grammatical mood of each sentence.
3 Write a commentary exploring the effects created by the changes of grammatical mood and the way in which these changes influence the audience.

You should use appropriate terminology and linguistic frameworks to explain and evaluate the texts.
   You may like to think about:

• the connotations of the words
• the effect of changes in the grammatical mood
• the use of complete and incomplete adjacency pairs
• the characterisation
• the relationship between characters

COMMENTARY

The extract is dramatic: the action is violent and visually unpleasant for the audience. We become part of a context where order has been replaced by chaos, the rule of law by brute force. The frequent changes in the grammatical mood reflect this violation of the natural order – they are indicative of the disruption that has followed Lear's misjudgement in splitting his kingdom and laying aside the duties of a king while keeping the title and trappings of kingship.

The atmosphere is hostile. There is no cooperation between participants in the dialogue and the language is dominated by words with negative connotations. The number of exclamations reflects the strong feelings underlying the text. Many are vocatives addressed to Gloucester by Regan and Cornwall (*Ingrateful fox!*, *O filthy traitor!*). Gloucester, on the other hand, in a situation where he has no control, addresses the gods (*By the kind gods*; *O you gods!*). The use of exclamatory sentences throughout the extract heightens the tension of the scene. Marked by raised intonation and increased volume on the stage, their delivery intensifies the mood of conflict and the audience's sense of impending disaster.

The grammatical mood also helps Shakespeare to characterise the individual participants. The imperatives emphasise Regan and Cornwall's dominant position. Their repetition of the dynamic verb *Bind* draws attention to the physical threat to Gloucester, while his imperatives are more muted – they represent a request for tolerance and respect (*consider ...*, *do me no foul play*). The imperatives, therefore, clearly divide the essentially good (Gloucester) from the bad (Regan and Cornwall). The authority of the latter and the helplessness of Gloucester remind the audience of the unnatural times that have followed Lear's fateful division of his kingdom.

Shakespeare explicitly draws our attention to the unnatural behaviour of Regan and Cornwall. In the opening of the extract, Gloucester fulfils his role as host, using positive terms of address (*Good my friends, friends*) and reminding Regan and Cornwall that they are his *guests*. His negative imperative (*do me no foul play*) is an attempt to diffuse the tension. Yet they fail to observe the rules of social etiquette (epitomised by Regan's disrespectful pulling of Gloucester's beard) and easily slip into the role of brutal interrogators.

The interrogatives help us to understand the relationship between characters. Initially, Gloucester's questions (*What mean your graces?*, *What will you do?*) demonstrate his confusion – he does not understand Regan and Cornwall's intentions. The fact that the adjacency pairs are incomplete (Gloucester receives no answers to his questions) highlights his position of weakness. This is reinforced by the sequence of questions addressed to Gloucester (*What letters ...?*, *And what confederacy ...?*, *To whose hands ...?*). By leaving him no opportunity to answer, Regan and Cornwall assert their position of power, reminding the audience of Gloucester's vulnerability.

While there are numerous questions, there are few adjacency pairs. The separation of question and answer in the first example (*What letters ...? I have a letter ...*) reflects the mood of conflict. This is reinforced by our awareness that Gloucester focuses on the letter, avoiding the leading questions about his supposed conspiracy (*confederacy*) with *the traitors* and his role in the King's escape. The proximity of question and answer in the next adjacency pair (*Where hast thou sent the King?/To Dover*) suggests that Gloucester's spirit has been broken – he cannot endure the interrogation any longer. Gloucester's image of himself as an animal chained to a stake and baited by dogs symbolises his helplessness in the face of the cruelty that he is about to suffer.

The repetition of the interrogative *Wherefore to Dover?* builds tension, culminating in the violence that follows Gloucester's honest answer (*Because I would not see ...*). This third adjacency pair surprises us. Gloucester's answer is unexpected:

ccepting the inevitability of his position, he defies his interrogators. His emphatic response fails to give Cornwall and Regan the information they want, instead drawing attention to the beast-like qualities of the sisters (*cruel nails, boarish fangs*). As guests of Gloucester, Cornwall and Regan owe a duty of respect to their host and their abuse of his hospitality is represented as unforgivable and unnatural.

The tension created by the dominance of interrogatives and imperatives heightens the atmosphere of the extract: it dramatises the conflict between characters and reinforces the disruption of the natural order. Declarative sentences are often emphatic:

S   P   C
⟨ (I) (am) (your host) ⟩.

or use marked themes to draw attention to key elements.

A   Od   S   P
⟨ (With robbers' hands) (my hospitable favours)/ (You) (should not ruffle) ⟩.

In the example above, the foregrounded adverbial (*With robber's hands*) draws attention to the unnatural behaviour of Cornwall and Regan, while the foregrounded object (*my hospitable favours*) creates an explicit opposition between Gloucester's hospitality and their abuse of it. By placing the phrases at the front of the sentence, Shakespeare brings one of his central themes (natural vs. unnatural) into prominence.

By moving between the grammatical moods, Shakespeare is able to engage his audience with the characters and themes. Alongside the drama of the physical action, the changes help to create the atmosphere of conflict that dominates the play, establish the relative status of the participants, and heighten the tension as the play moves towards its inevitable and tragic conclusion.

TASK 3

1 Choose one of the following writing exercises. When you have completed your text, evaluate the key linguistic features. You may like to use the suggested framework for analysis in Appendix A.

EITHER

Write an instruction text – it could, for instance, tell readers how to make a cake, install a computer programme, or complete a maths problem.

Remember to use an appropriate grammatical mood. Think about the ways in which subordinate clauses can help you to include extra information in a compact way.

OR

Write a script in which you introduce and then interview a celebrity, politican, sportsman or woman, or any other role model. You will need to provide information about their background and achievements and questions you would like to ask.

You need to pay particular attention to the ways in which you formulate your questions. Avoid closed questions and try to make sure that you give your chosen person the opportunity to develop their answers. Think about how you can use different grammatical moods to provide background information, to engage your interviewee and encourage them to talk at length. You could see how effective your script is by using it as the basis for a real interview – either with someone hot-seating as the celebrity, or by choosing someone local.

OR

Produce a leaflet and a script for an advertisement to be shown at the local cinema as part of a government information campaign to influence the behaviour of young people. You could focus on healthy eating, recycling, dealing with emergencies, or issues like drink driving, taking drugs and smoking.

You need to pay particular attention to the ways in which you present information and communicate opinion. The tone needs to balance the formal (hard facts) with the informal (the need to influence young people). Try to vary the grammatical mood in order to engage your readers and to use a range of sentence types, lengths and structures for dramatic effect.

Part V

Discourse

Chapter 10

Discourse

Having considered all the separate linguistic and grammatical units that we use instinctively each day, we now need to look at larger extracts of speech and writing where words, phrases, clauses and sentences interact. As we do this, our very close focus on language and structure will be broadened by a consideration of other key linguistic areas of interest. This chapter can only offer a brief introduction to the complexities of topics like accent and dialect, spelling, etymology and phonology, but it should give you a sense of the possibilities. The aim is to engage you in the process of analysis so that you can begin to see the diverse ways in which we use language to communicate effectively.

After reading this chapter, you should be able:

▶ to recognise and describe variation in language according to the user and the use
▶ to see how text type and context shape lexical and grammatical choices
▶ to understand the role of Standard English as a point of comparison
▶ to appreciate how the study of language structures can help us to become more effective readers and writers

10.1 What is discourse?

In most cases, we study units of spoken or written language that are longer than one sentence – what linguists call DISCOURSE. Whole texts such as a conversation, a text message, a political speech, a newspaper report, a poem are all examples of different kinds of discourse.

Alongside the key constituents of language study (the words, the sentence structure, the cohesion, the sentence organisation and the grammatical mood), we also need to address other important areas:

▶ the background and identity of the speaker or writer
▶ the intended audience
▶ the purpose or function
▶ the situation and circumstances

Considering these areas provides a useful background to linguistic analysis, encouraging us to understand how a text has been shaped.

10.2 Language variation

Language is constantly changing and we need to recognise this. Linguists are interested in describing the ways in which different factors (the period, the place, the context, the participants and the purpose) affect the language we use.

User-related variation

We each tend to have one main USER-RELATED variety – a form of English influenced by our geographical speech community, our ethnicity, cultural background, education, age, gender and social group. This is a form of language that we use instinctively; it comes naturally when we don't consciously think about what we are saying or writing. It helps to define us as individuals and often underpins our personal identity.

Our background governs the sounds, vocabulary and syntax of the language we use, but there are other influences which also contribute to personal language variation. Our state of mind (calm, nervous, panicky, cool-headed), our personality (practical, indecisive, opportunist, retiring) and our emotions (happy, sad, relieved, terrified) can also affect the language we use. Where these qualities may change on a day-to-day basis according to what happens to us, our background has a more deeply engrained effect on the language we use.

Changes to our 'natural' language choice can be conscious or subconscious. We instinctively adapt our language to suit particular situations or occasions. When we move between our different REPERTOIRES (the range of varieties we use to perform different social roles), we call it CODE-SWITCHING. We can chose to move closer to the language variety of those around us (CONVERGENCE) or we may chose to distance ourselves (DIVERGENCE). The more linguistically mobile we are, the more effective we can be in communicating with others.

Such changes are temporary, dependent on the register and the function. Other changes are more permanent – some people make conscious decisions to change their linguistic identity. We can change the vocabulary and grammar we use more easily than our pronunciation. Such decisions may be based on stereotypical attitudes to certain regional accents (pronunciation) and dialects (lexis and grammar), on occupational expectations and experiences, on wishing to belong or to alienate oneself from a particular social or cultural group, or on our educational background.

When we look at a particular text, we need to think about the ways in which it is shaped by the speaker or writer and its intended audience. It can be helpful to think about the following key areas:

- the geographical background
  e.g. the physical location, urban/rural, speech community
- the cultural background
  e.g. historical period, education, occupation, heritage, first/second language
- the social group
  e.g. age, gender, ethnicity, insider/outsider

Alongside our personal repertoire, we also have many USE-RELATED varieties – forms of English influenced by the situation in which discourse takes place, what we are trying to communicate and whom we are addressing. When we study whole texts, we need to be able to make decisions about the way in which language changes according to use.

Everyday we encounter and use many different varieties according to the language situations in which we find ourselves. We may:

- read information and advertising on the back of a cereal packet
- listen to television and radio
- listen to and join in conversations on the train or bus
- read billboards
- speak on the phone
- read and write text messages
- read road signs
- read newspaper reports
- talk about what we've seen and done
- read subject specific text books
- write letters, essays or shopping lists
- hear and use distinctive local language
- hear and tell jokes
- hear and use 'code' words marking insiders and outsiders in school or work

In each case, we instinctively use our linguistic knowledge of language, form and structure to create and understand different kinds of language.

10.3 Register

We call variations in language defined according to their use REGISTERS. In a legal register, a scientific register, a medical register, a poetic register, a colloquial register or a technological register, we adapt language in a particular way according to the intended audience, the situation and the purpose.

To identify and describe distinctive registers, we need to consider three key areas: mode, tenor and field.

1 Mode

When studying a text, we must first make a decision about the channel of communication or MODE. The table overleaf summarises the forms discourse may take.

It is useful to be able to summarise the main features of spoken and written modes and to understand how these two channels interact in both multi-modal discourse and in speech that is written to be read aloud.

Mode	Formal examples	Informal examples
Spoken	interviews lectures sermons	chatting at a party jokes a chance meeting with a friend
Written	reviews essays newspaper reports	mobile phone texts personal emails holiday postcards
Multi-modal (including visual)	films picture books web sites	a cartoon-style note passed around in class a text with emoticons

Speech

Everyday **speech** is spontaneous and transient. It has no permanent form (unless it is recorded) and cannot easily be recovered. The face-to-face context of most spoken discourse means that speech is often interactive and immediate – it is described as a two-way communication because each participant can take part, using non-verbal vocalisations (laughing, sighing, tutting) and body language to underpin meaning. Speech is usually collaborative with participants conforming to the conventions of turn-taking, avoiding interruptions and overlaps whenever possible.

Although informal conversation is normally unplanned, in more formal contexts (interviews and speeches), speakers may research their topic, organise their ideas or even produce a written version to be read aloud. In such cases, speakers consciously adopt some of the features of spoken language in their writing to ensure that they engage their audience.

In spoken language, the vocabulary is often informal – unless the topic is subject specific – and speakers who know each other may use shared lexical items or codes. Speech tends to have a loose grammatical structure with noticeable repetitions, comment clauses (*I know, you see*) to mark shared understanding, and incomplete or rephrased utterances. Pauses, fillers (*um, yea, uhh*), false starts (*I wanted ... the weather's pretty bad today*) and self-corrections (*I was go ... we were going ...*) are distinctive features of this mode. Intonation patterns and pauses mark the end of grammatical units, which are usually made up of multiple co-ordinated clauses rather than subordination. As a social tool, speech allows direct interaction and a speaker can use changes in pace, volume and pitch to underpin the meaning, communicate attitudes and opinions, establish relationships, and draw attention to key items.

The example below is taken from an informal conversation about a holiday in Turkey.

ANNA   Susie ended up playing in a band in the last week
TOM   who did
ANNA   Susie (.) my daughter
TOM   did she
ANNA   bought her a drum down there (2) she was back there every night (.) getting recognised on the streets after the first night

TOM	wow
ANNA	she was on the way there for the second night n some people called out from a restaurant (.) oh are you playing tonight (.) and she thought it was just cos she got the drum under her arm so she said yeah they said same place and she said yup (.) it'll be autographs tomorrow we said
TOM	that's a handsome drum
ANNA	couldn't go anywhere with it then e. e. everybody in the shops and the restaurants and the local people'd come out and either want her to play or they'd want a go on it
TOM	[laugh]
ANNA	turned it upside down and used it as handluggage on the way home

The language is marked by concrete nouns (*band, drum, streets, restaurant*), collo-quialisms (*cos, yeah, yup*), contractions (*couldn't, they'd, people'd*) and exclamations (*wow, oh*). The speaker is telling a story, engaging her listener in the recreation of a personal experience which has taken place in the past. Verb phrases, therefore, tend to be in the simple past (*ended up, bought, was*). The present tense is used where references are made to the present context (*'s*) and a present progressive verb phrase (*are ... playing*) is used in a recreation of direct speech. Exophoric pronoun refer-ences indicate particular physical locations distinct from the context in which the narrative is told (*there*, i.e., Turkey; an unnamed club) and a direct reference to the drum (*that*).

Phrases tend to be short with pre- rather than post-modification.

m	h	m	m	h	m	m	h	m	m	h
a	drum	the	first	night	a	handsome	drum	the	last	week
det	N	det	AdjP	N	det	AdjP	N	det	AdjP	N

The sentences are usually simple, often marked by ellipsis which is typical of speech.

	P	Oi	Od	A
⟨	Ø (bought)	(her)	(a drum)	(down there) ⟩

Loose co-ordination, however, can make the sentences long.

```
   interj   P    S     P        A          S       P                    Od
⟨ (Oh) (are) (you) (playing) (tonight) ⟩ and ⟨ (she) (thought) [Ø it was just [cos she got
                                         conj           SCl – NCl        SCl – ACl

               S    P    interj    S      P      A
the drum under her arm] ] so ⟨ (she) (said) (yeah) ⟩ ⟨ (they) (said) Ø (same place) ⟩
                         conj

      S     P   interj
and ⟨ (she) (said) (yup) ⟩
conj
```

The loosely structured sentence here is compound-complex because of the lack of explicit sentence breaks and the embedding of direct speech (QUOTING CLAUSE *she said* + QUOTED CLAUSE *yeah*) in the current narrative. Punctuation in spoken dis-course is tentatively marked by micro pauses (.) which indicate a break equivalent to a full stop in a written text, but in this extract sentences often run into each other. The repetition of the co-ordinating conjunction *and*, and the frequency of adverbials indicating time (*every night, after the first night*) and place (*from a restaurant, same place, anywhere*) are typical of spoken narrative.

This extract demonstrates many of the features commonly associated with informal conversation. It is spontaneous and interactive: Tom clarifes the identity of Susie the speaker's daughter (*who did*) and affirms his engagement with Anna's narrative using a tag question (*did she*), an interjection (*wow*) and a non-verbal response ([*laugh*]). The interaction is clearly collaborative (the adjacency pair is complete) with Tom providing positive feedback (*that's a handsome drum*) and allowing the dominant speaker to tell her story without interruptions or overlaps. The vocabulary is informal and the grammatical structure loose with noticeable repetitions. Normal non-fluency (*e.e. everybody*), colloquialisms (*she got the drum under her arm*) and ellipsis (omission of subjects) are also typical of informal spoken language.

Writing

Writing is permanent and fixed – it can be re-read and shared with any number of readers. We may write for a personal audience (diary, letter, text) or for a wider impersonal audience (examination paper, job application, letter of complaint). In most cases, feedback is delayed because participants are separated by time and space: an essay can be marked and returned; a letter of complaint can be answered by the recipient. Written language is therefore traditionally described as a one-way communication.

Because of the delay between production (writing) and reception (reading), written texts need to be unambiguous. Developments in electronic English, however, have begun to change the nature of writing as a form of communication. We can receive a reply to emails and texts within a matter of minutes; live messaging services provide a form of spontaneous written conversation that mirrors the immediacy of speech. This means that any misunderstandings can be dealt with immediately.

Writing is often pre-planned and drafted – it therefore tends to be carefully organised and polished. It can be longer and more developed because readers have time to re-read and reflect. Punctuation identifies grammatical boundaries and, in many examples, subordination is more common than co-ordination. Layout (paragraphing, headings) and typographical or graphological features (underlining, capitalisation, changes in font, style or size of print) help to organise the content and draw attention to key ideas.

The example below is taken from the opening of a formal essay.

Tennyson's poems seem often to deal with the internal conflict between melancholy and hope. His characters and personae indeed often appear trapped in a world of their own creation. This essential bleakness can perhaps be explained by Tennyson's own life for there appears to be an autobiographical element in much of his writing. Tennyson's father was a disinherited clergyman who, though cultured, degenerated into alcoholism. The strains of Tennyson's early life perhaps can be seen to manifest themselves in his obsession with inherited depression and mental disorders. As a result his poems embody a sense of alienation and isolation.

s is typical of this kind of written text, the language is formal and abstract reflect-
ng the focus of the content: a discussion of Tennyson's poems. The writer is arguing
 case using adverbs such as *indeed*, and tentatively expressing opinions using
dverbs such as *perhaps* and the modal verb *can*. Abstract nouns (*conflict, melan-
holy, hope, bleakness*) and stative verbs (*seem, appear, appears, was*) are typical of
his kind of text.

Phrases are often long, using both pre- and post-modification to communicate
nportant detail. Co-ordinating conjunctions create compound phrases that add
eight to the argument.

```
    m       m       h       q
    the internal conflict between melancholy and hope
                                    NP
    det     AdjP    N       PrepP
                            prep            NP          conj    NP
```

```
    m       h       q
    his obsession with inherited depression and mental disorder
                            NP
    det     N       PrepP
                    prep            NP          conj        NP
```

Passive verb phrases (*can ... be explained, can be seen*) and non-finite clauses
 the complement site of sentences (*to deal with the internal conflict ..., trapped in
 ...*) add to the formality.

While the sentences are not very long, all but one are complex, using subordi-
ate clauses to add extra information.

```
            S               P       A           P               A
< (This essential bleakness) (can) (perhaps) (be explained) (by Tennyson's own life)
```

```
                                    A
[for there appears [to be an autobiographical element in much of his writing] ] >.
SCl – ACl            SCl – NFCl
```

he only simple sentence provides an emphatic end to the paragraph.

```
        A           S           P           Od
< (As a result) (his poems) (embody) (a sense of alienation and isolation) >.
```

This text is typical of a formal essay and the features of written language are
lear. It has been written for an impersonal, distant audience, where feed-back will
 e delayed. The language and syntax are formal and crafted – indicative of a text
 hat has been drafted and polished. Punctuation marks grammatical boundaries
nd subordination is more common than simple or compound sentences.

Field

 order to comment on the register, we need to identify the FIELD or subject matter
 what a particular text is about. The field is directly linked to a topic or an activity.
 exical choices reflect the content, and recognising groups of related words helps
  establish the focus of a text.

Each of the examples below has a different field and uses language in a distinc-
ve way.

TEXT 1

potatoes
onions
carrots
marg
cheese
eggs

TEXT 2

WORKSHEET 6
DEFAMATION: THE CLAIMANT PERSPECTIVE
Starting point ...
Initially, examination of the law on defamation will begin with the claimant's perspectiv
It will therefore be necessary to consider the following key areas.
1. Jurisdictional issues
2. The value of reputation
3. The definition of defamation.
4. The repetition rule
5. The role of the judge and jury

TEXT 3

It was a town of red brick, or of brick that would have been red if the smoke and ash
had allowed it; but, as matters stood, it was a town of unnatural red and black like th
painted face of a savage. It was a town of machinery and tall chimneys, out of whic
interminable serpents of smoke trailed themselves for ever and ever, and never g
uncoiled. It had a black canal in it, and a river that ran purple with ill-smelling dye, ar
vast piles of building full of windows where there was a rattling and a trembling all da
long, and where the piston of the steam-engine worked monotonously up and dow
like the head of an elephant in a state of melancholy madness.

Hard Times, Chapter 5, Charles Dickens (185

The shopping list has a narrow field of everyday items – the lexical set of foo
Most are plural forms and all are common concrete nouns with no modificatio
(*potatoes, onions, carrots*). The purpose of the text is to inform and its audience
personal. By contrast, the worksheet has a legal field of subject specific wor
(*defamation, claimant, jurisdictional, judge, jury*). There are abstract nouns (*pe*
spective, examination, issues) and general words with a specific meaning (*reput*
tion, repetition, rule). The purpose is to inform and instruct and the intende
audience is impersonal. Where the context of the list is domestic, the context he
is educational.

The language in Text 2 is far more varied. Noun phrases are simple (*DEFAM*
TION), pre-modified (*Starting point, Jurisdictional issues, The repetition rule*) an
post-modified (*The value of reputation*). Verb phrases are marked for future tim
(*will begin, will ... be necessary*) to draw attention to the proposed course of stud
A fronted adverbial (*Initially*) creates a sense of process and a non-finite clause
subject (*to consider the following key areas*) is moved to the end of the sentence aft
a dummy subject (*It*) for clarity.

The field of the narrative is more varied. It uses lexical sets of concrete nouns to describe the urban landscape (*brick, building, chimneys, canal*), pollution (*smoke, ashes*) and mechanisation (*machinery, piston, steam-engine*). Vivid imagery (similes: *the painted face of a savage, the head of an elephant*; metaphor: *interminable serpents of smoke*) adds descriptive detail to the physical representation of the town. Noun phrases are long and contain lots of detail.

```
   m    h      q
   a town ... of brick [that would have been red [if the smoke and ashes had allowed it] ]
                                                NP
   det  N     PrepP
              prep                              NP
                   N      RelCl                      ACl
```

The purpose is creative, but also expressive. The writer uses a lexical set of negative modifiers (*unnatural, ill-smelling, interminable, monotonously*) to communicate his attitude and to develop the mood. Abstract nouns with negative connotations reinforce the negative tone (*madness, melancholy*), while verbal nouns convey a sense of movement (*a rattling, a trembling*). Long compound-complex sentences with multiple embedded clauses and the use of patterning for dramatic effect (tripling: *It was a town ...*; parallelism: *for ever and ever, and never*; *where there was ... and where ...*) contribute to the complexity of the text.

3 Tenor

The TENOR (or **manner**) establishes the social relationship underpinning a text. We have to assess the degree of formality or informality by considering levels of politeness (modal verbs), the relative status of participants and the degree of obligation. The level of formality will dictate the nature of the linguistic and grammatical features.

Informal tenor

Generally speaking, the register tends to be informal where an audience is known. In less formal spoken and written texts (an informal conversation, a personal diary), we may see evidence of non-standard lexis (colloquialisms, slang, dialect words, vocabulary with a private resonance) and grammar (non-agreement of verb and subject, double negatives, regularising of irregular verb forms, elliptical or minor sentences), with fewer examples of subordination.

Formal tenor

Where the audience is unknown, the register is usually formal. In formal discourse (a textbook, a documentary voice-over), we would expect the language and syntax to be more complex, with evidence of subject specific jargon, abstract nouns, post-modified phrases and longer sentences with subordination.

Politeness markers

If we look at the list of sentences below, we can see how the tenor changes according to the lexical and syntactic choices we make.

I wonder if you'd mind sitting down, please?

Would you sit down for me?

You couldn't possibly sit down, could you?

Could you sit down?

Can you sit down? The lesson's about to start.

Why don't you sit down?

Aren't you going to sit down?

Please sit down.

Sit down will you?

Sit down.

Sit!

Each of these sentences require the same action to complete the adjacency pair, but they approach the situation in very different ways and create a different relationship between the speaker and the intended audience. What we see is that the longer the request, the politer the tenor. The exclamatory *Sit!*, the imperative *Sit down* and the use of a tag question on the end of an imperative (*will you?*) are the most direct – they contain no POLITENESS MARKERS. The addition of the interjection *Please*, however, modifies the tone, creating a polite 'request' rather than a direct command.

As the politeness levels increase, the imperative mood is replaced by interrogatives. The use of the question word *Why?* and the negative primary verb *Aren't* encourage cooperation and create a sense of obligation, while modal verbs express the command as a polite request. The modal verbs often take a 'past tense' form (*could, would*) to describe something that is meant to be happening in the present. We describe this usage as 'unreal meaning' – the modal verbs indicate that the event or state is imaginary because it is not yet taking place.

Politeness markers are also seen in the explanation which can accompany a request (*The lesson's about to start.*) and in the indirect question introduced by the verb *to wonder* + *if* (adverbial subordinate clause), which also communicates unreal meaning.

We make decisions about this kind of linguistic choice instinctively. Each reflects a slightly different relationship between the speaker and the intended audience. Where we are familiar with someone, we may not need to adopt the most formal politeness markers; where we speak to people who are strangers or in a position of authority, we will probably choose the more formal options.

Terms of address

Terms of address also affect the level of formality in discourse. In specialised professions, titles are used as a mark of respect:

M'lud	LEGAL REGISTER
The Right Honourable Gentleman	POLITICAL REGISTER
Dr Davis	MEDICAL REGISTER (GP)
Mr Jenkins	MEDICAL REGISTER (CONSULTANT)

We can formally address individuals we do not know well using everyday titles such as *Mr, Mrs, Ms, Miss* and a surname (*Ms Potts*); we can address familiar people informally using their first name (*Carol*) or a nick-name (*Xander*). Considering the effect created by a particular term of address is central to recognising the level of formality. The list below shows how one person may be addressed in a variety of ways according to the relationship that exists between participants.

IMPERSONAL	Mrs Emma Longbourne, 40	NEWSPAPER
	Mrs E. Longbourne	FORMAL LETTER
	Mrs Longbourne	SCHOOL PARENTS' EVENING
	Emma Longbourne	DOCTOR'S SURGERY
	Emma	FAMILY
	Em	CLOSE FRIEND
FAMILIAR	mum	CHILDREN

Relationships between participants

When we look at a particular text, we need to consider the relationship that exists between the speaker or writer, the topic and the audience. An **expert** can create a sense of authority by demonstrating knowledge and understanding of the subject matter; a **non-specialist** can focus on developing a more personal relationship. The kind of language and grammatical structures used depends upon the status and background of the speaker/writer, the focus of the content and the audience.

The table below summarises some examples of the different kinds of relationships that shape discourse.

Discourse	Audience	Writer/speaker	Tenor
TV documentary Compact newspaper	Large Unknown Distant 1-way	Specialist	Formal
Lecture Spoken commentary	Large Unknown Immediate 1-way	Specialist	Formal
Social occasions Reading a picture book at bedtime	Small Known Immediate Interactive	Non-specialist	Informal
Personal letter	Small Known Distant 1-way	Non-specialist	Informal
Phone call to a friend Texting Email	Small Known Distant Interactive	Non-specialist	Informal

Discourse	Audience	Writer/speaker	Tenor
Letter in a local paper asking for information about war-time experiences Job application	Small Unknown Distant 1-way	Specialist	Formal
Teacher in primary school Club meetings	Large Known Immediate Interactive	Specialist	Formal/informal
Family conference via a web cam Business video conference Conference calls	Large Known Distant Interactive	Non-specialist Specialist	Informal Formal
Blogs Web forums	Large Unknown Distant Interactive	Specialist/ Non-specialist	Formal/informal
Meeting new people at work Interview with a bank manager Phoning someone to ask about tutoring	Small Unknown Immediate Interactive	Non-specialist Specialist	Formal/informal Formal

It is important to be aware that in some situations, both formal and informal registers are used: a lecturer addresses an audience on a designated topic (formal register) before opening the floor to general questions (informal register); delegates chatting before the start of a conference (informal register) focus on a subject specific discussion (formal register) once the meeting begins.

Adopting an inappropriate tenor

In most cases, there will be a direct association between the linguistic choices a speaker or writer makes and the mode, field and tenor – the linguistic, syntactic and structural features will match our expectations. Should we adopt an apparently inappropriate level of formality, however, it can affect the mood and there may be a breakdown in communication.

Family or close friends, for instance, may be offended by the use of a very formal tenor (using full names rather than familiar forms). It can make the speaker or writer seem distant and aloof, or suggest a lack of cooperation or a conflict of some kind. A parent chastising a child, for example, may use their first name and surname rather than a familiar contracted form: *Benjamin Lockwood – what have you done now?* Similarly, using an informal tenor in a formal situation (for example, a job interview) can make a speaker or writer seem rude or ignorant of the expected patterns of behaviour. The choice of a markedly informal register (language and content that could be seen as inappropriate) by presenters of a radio show may result in a high level of complaints and questions about the responsibilities of public service broadcasting.

escribing the register of a formal text

Vhen we look at a formal discourse, we need to think about the ways in which it is haped by its use. The extract below (*Oral Answers*, 10 November 2010) is taken rom Hansard, a written record of everything that is said in Parliament.

> **The Deputy Prime Minister**: I can certainly confirm that the right hon. and learned Lady and her party also had plans to make massive cuts in the budget of the Department for Business, Innovation and Skills, which would have affected higher education. Here are a few facts. Every single graduate under our scheme will pay less per month than they do under the scheme that we inherited from Labour. The bottom 25% of earners will pay much less in their contributions to their university education than they do at the moment. Part-time students will pay no up-front fees, and not a single student will pay a penny of up-front fees whatsoever. It is a fair and progressive solution to a very difficult problem.
>
> **Ms Harman**: It looks as though the right hon. Gentleman has been taking lessons from the Prime Minister on how not to answer the question. I asked him about the cut in the teaching grant. The truth is that it is a staggering 80% – 80%. No wonder he is ducking the question. The real reason he is hiking up fees is that he is pulling the plug on public funding, and dumping the cost on to students. Is that not why he is betraying his promise on tuition fees?
>
> **The Deputy Prime Minister**: The graduate tax that the right hon. and learned Lady advocates would be more unfair and would allow higher earners to opt out of the system altogether. We all agree – she agrees – across the House that graduates should make some contribution for the benefit of going to university. The question is, how? We have a progressive plan; she has no plan whatsoever.

he mode here is spoken, but the text has been transcribed. The speakers are both xperts and professionals; their primary intended audience is other politicians experts), but there may also be members of the public in the House of Commons ,allery, unknown readers can access the transcript in print or online, and viewers an see debates on the BBC Parliament channel.

The field is education cuts (*cuts, teaching grant, public funding, budget*) and uniersity fees (*pay, contributions, students, fees, graduate tax*). The political context, owever, also shapes the lexical choices with references to party politics (*her party, ur scheme, inherited from Labour, progressive solution, a very difficult problem, rogressive plan, no plan*) and formal terms of address (*the right hon. and learned ady* – Harriet Harman, the Deputy Leader of the Labour Party; *the right hon. Genleman* – Nick Clegg, the Deputy Leader of the Conservative-Liberal coalition govrnment). While the repetition of *I* reflects the expression and communication of ersonal opinions, ultimately the speakers are representatives of a particular political party.

The tenor is formal. There are no direct politeness markers, but speakers do not nterrupt each other so there are no overlapping turns. The House of Commons is ften adversarial, however, and adjacency pairs are not complete (*... taking lessons .. on how not to answer questions; Is that not ...?*). This suggests that the exchange s not cooperative.

As might be expected, the language is formal and abstract (*truth, promise, solu* *tion, problem, scheme*). Judgemental modifiers reflect party politics: the coalition gov ernment attacks the outgoing Labour government (***massive** cuts*); the Labour Part attacks the coalition government (*a **staggering** 80%*); and the coalition governmer expresses support for its own proposals (***fair** and **progressive** solution*). Perhaps mor unexpected is the colloquial language (*ducking the question, pulling the plug, dumping* which reflects the speaker's challenging tone as she dismisses the coalition goverr ment's proposal. Both speakers use emotive words to stir their audience (Nick Cleg – *massive, unfair*; Harriet Harman – *dumping, betraying*).

The clause sites are all full and the clause elements are often long. The Deput Prime Minister's sentences are always in the declarative mood. They tend to be com plex – perhaps because his oral answers are semi-prepared for Prime Minister Questions which takes place every Wednesday.

> S   P   A   P   Od
> ⟨ (I) (can) (certainly) (confirm) [that the right hon. and learned Lady and her party also
>   SCl – NCl
>
> had plans [to make massive cuts in the budget of the DBIS, [which would have
>   SCl – NFCl   SCl – RelCl
>
> affected higher education]]] ⟩.

Where he does use a simple sentence, the effect is emphatic.

> A   P   S
> ⟨ (Here) (are) (a few facts) ⟩.

The patterning of clauses has a rhetorical effect designed to establish the relativ positions of the coalition government and the opposition.

> S   P   S   P
> ⟨ (We all) (agree) ⟩ – ⟨ (she) (agrees) … ⟩.
>
> S   P   Od   S   P   Od
> ⟨ (We) (have) (a progressive plan) ⟩ ; ⟨ (she) (has) (no plan whatsoever) ⟩.

Ms Harman's sentences, on the other hand, are shorter, possibly because her ton is more confrontational.

> S   P   Oi   P   Od
> ⟨ (I) (asked) (him) (about) (the cut in the teaching grant) ⟩.

The structures still tend to be complex, however, because of the formality of the sit uation.

> S   P   Od
> ⟨ (The real reason [Ø he is hiking up fees]) (is) [that he is pulling the plug on public
>   SCl – NCl   SCl – NCl
>
>   Od
> funding] and [Ø dumping the cost on to students] ⟩.
>   conj   SCl – NCl

She uses an interrogative typical of politicians: the negative form suggests that th truth of her proposition is already taken for granted.

‹ (Is) (that) (not) [why he is betraying his promise on tuition fees] ›?
      neg   SCl – NCl

Describing the register of an informal text

When we look at informal discourse, we also need to think about the ways in which it is shaped by its use. The extract below is taken from a conversation between a grandmother and her grandson.

GRANDMOTHER	OK Harry (.) have you got the things ready =
GRANDSON	= yup (.) what have I g. what now =
GRANDMOTHER	put a bit of oil in the pan (4) stop (.) don't want too much (2) turn the gas on can you remember hów =
GRANDSON	= this óne =
GRANDMOTHER	= well done (5)
GRANDSON	too hígh =
GRANDMOTHER	= no that's fine (.) put those onions you cut in there (2) careful (1) it'll spit as it gets hot =
GRANDSON	= shall I stir thém
GRANDMOTHER	= yes (.) remember onions burn when you're no ‖ looking
GRANDSON	‖ [laughs]
	how long fór =
GRANDMOTHER	= probably about five minutes (2) you'd better add the basil now (3)
GRANDSON	I always think I'll do too much =
GRANDMOTHER	= don't worry (.) it's not critical

The mode here is spoken. The status of the speakers is personal and familiar – although the age and experience of the grandmother gives her a position of authority in this situation. The audience is narrow: it is private and restricted since the two participants speak only for each other. Terms of address are used infrequently because there are only two participants engaged directly in a specific activity. A first name, however, is used as a vocative to attract attention (*Harry*). Although there are no explicit politeness markers, this is a cooperative interaction and there are frequent affirmations (*yup, well done, yes, that's fine, [laughs], don't worry*).

The field relates directly to the activity of cooking with concrete nouns (*oil, pan, onions, basil*), dynamic verbs (*cut, stir, add, turn ... on*) and references to heating (*gas, high, spit, hot, burn*). Other distinctive language use can be seen in the contractions (*don't, that's, it'll, you're, you'd, I'll, it's*) and in other features typical of informal conversation such as prepositions at the end of sentences (*how long for* 'for how long') and false starts (*I g. what now*). Pronoun exophoric references to physical things outside the discourse are also common (***this** one* – the dial on the hob; ***it's** not critical* – the amount of basil).

In informal conversation, we would expect a range of grammatical moods – particularly in one focusing on a specific activity: declarative (*I always think ...*); imperative (*put, stop, turn, remember*) and interrogative (*have you ... , what now, can you remember ..., shall I stir ..., how long ...*). There are simple and complex sentences, but they are usually short.

SIMPLE   S   P   C   COMPLEX   P   Od   A
⟨ (it) ('s) not (critical) ⟩   ⟨ (put) (those onions [Ø you cut]) (in there) ⟩
          neg   SCl – RelCl

COMPLEX   P   Od
⟨ (remember) [Ø onions burn [when you're not looking]] ⟩
          SCl – NCl   SCl – ACl

Sentences are often elliptical with the missing grammatical elements understood from the physical situation.

          C   A   P   Od
⟨ Ø (too high) ⟩   ⟨ (how long) Ø (for) ⟩   ⟨ Ø (don't want) (too much) ⟩

10.4 Text types

We have already seen how we can discuss discourse in terms of the user and the use, enabling us to explore distinctive features of specific varieties according to the identity of the speaker or writer, or the register. Discourse, however, can also be grouped according to its layout, organisation and function.

Layout

The **layout** will often be the first thing that catches our eye and it can help us to make decisions about a text. Typographical features such as capitalisation, underlining, changes in font style and size, images, or the use of lists, bullet points or columns can tell us something about the genre and the linguistic and grammatical feaures we might expect to find. While such features may be typical of a particular text type, writers may also adopt these approaches in a broader context to draw our attention to semantically important elements of a text.

Organisation

At the most basic level, we can group texts according to their **organisation**. A CHRONOLOGICAL text is based on a sequence of events that occur in a logical order. It may use dynamic verbs to describe actions and events, and adverbs (*then*, *next*, *secondly*) to communicate a particular time scale or logical sequence. For example, novels, recipes, instruction manuals are chronological written texts; a cookery programme, a telephone computer helpline and some films are chronological spoken texts. Order is important in these texts: if we rearrange them we can affect the meaning. In some novels and films, the content is purposefully rearranged in a non-chronological order to affect the way in which we receive information – it can change the way we respond to characters and events.

A NON-CHRONOLOGICAL text is structured by a logical development of the content rather than by time. It may use comparison (similarities), contrast (differences) or associations (links) to organise the ideas. For example, magazine advertisements, newspaper editorials, blogs can be non-chronological written texts; television advertisements, debates and informal conversations can be non-chronological spoken texts.

We can rarely be certain about the **intentions** of a particular writer or speaker, but it is possible to gather evidence to help us pinpoint a dominant function and any secondary functions.

Instructive texts (recipes, manuals, subject specific workbooks, practical lessons) aim to tell you how to do something; **informative** texts (newspaper reports, text books, documentaries, essays) aim to give you information; **persuasive** texts (political speeches, advertisements, campaign materials, debates) aim to convince you of something; **creative** texts (poems, comic strips, films, novels) aim to entertain you; **expressive** texts (arguments, blogs, editorials, letters) aim to express feelings, attitudes and opinions; **phatic** texts (greetings, informal conversations) aim to establish social relationships. A formal register is normally linked to impersonal functions (to instruct; to inform); an informal register is often linked to personal functions (to express feelings, attitudes and opinions; to socialise; to be creative).

The function of a text is closely linked to the identity of the speaker or writer, the relationship created with the intended audience, the content, the style and the structure. A written text intended to persuade, for instance, could have either a formal tenor (a coursework essay arguing the case for fair trade) or an informal one (a note left on the fridge door encouraging one student to vote for another in college elections). A spoken text intended to entertain could be formal (delivering an after-dinner speech in the presence of local dignitaries) or informal (telling an anecdote in the pub).

Understanding the typical features of a particular text type – the approach to content, function, language, layout, structure and style – helps us:

‣ to identify a text type
‣ to recognise the ways in which audience, purpose and context affect a text
‣ to recognise when writers and speakers do something unexpected
‣ to evaluate the effectiveness of a text

0.5 Context

Identifying the CONTEXT or background in which discourse takes place is very important since it helps us to recognise the ways in which the wider situation and circumstances affect the linguistic and grammatical choices we make. Public and private spaces, the relative size of an audience, the degree to which the participants are known to each other all affect the kind of discourse produced. The publication of a book by a large publishing house with a potentially international audience, for instance, has a very different context from a message written on a scrap of paper and put in a school lunch-box to remind a child to take medicine at dinnertime.

Situation

When we consider the **situation**, we ask ourselves the questions *when*? and *where*? We need to think about the following key areas:

- the time
  e.g. morning/evening; winter/summer; pre-/post-watershed
- the physical place
  e.g. home, school, office, party, in a book, on television/radio, public/private
- period
  e.g. historical/contemporary; recent/distant
- the occasion
  e.g. family: birthday/meal
  e.g. public: bank holiday/concert
  e.g. cultural: Eid/Diwali/Easter/Halloween/Bonfire Night

By tracing the history of a particular word, we can see how changing the situa tion – the period, for instance – affects linguistic references. The table below record changes in the expressions we have used to describe drunkenness over almost fou centuries.

Word	Meaning	Period
pickled	drunk	mid-17th century
drunk as an emperor		late 18th century
tight		early 19th century
sozzled, under the table		mid-19th century
hit the booze, tanked		late 19th century
plastered, blotto		1910s
squiffy, fried		1920s
hit the sauce, canned, juiced up		1940s
hammered, bombed		1950s
shit-faced, wrecked		1960s
trashed		1970s
rat-arsed		1980s
trolleyed, pissed as a parrot		1990s
lashed, bladdered,wavey, hamstered		21st century

All these expressions are colloquial, and informal language tends to demonstrat more dramatic changes over time than other language forms.

Circumstances

When we consider the **circumstances**, we ask ourselves questions about the wide background of the speaker or writer and the audience. We need to think about the following key areas:

- the age and gender
- the geographical location (accent, dialect)

- cultural background (historical, literary, technological, scientific, religious, political, military, multi-cultural)
- occupational or educational experience (technical jargon, subject specific lexis)
- the group (young people, old people, political, religious, social)

By pinpointing variations in the words used to describe a particular person or thing, we can see how changing the circumstances affects linguistic references. The table below records the expressions different groups use to describe older people.

Younger people	Older people	The media	Parliament
old fogey	golden-ager	older people	older people
coffin-dodger	third-ager	senior citizen	retiree
fossil	pensioner	the elderly	
old bag			
coot			
codger			

The terms of address listed above are categorised loosely, but do reflect the different ways in which language can be used by different groups. Younger people often use terms that are negative in their connotations, while older people use words with positive connotations. In more formal contexts, terms of address tend to be neutral – they are politically correct and avoid making social judgements of any kind. Current discussion suggests that the term 'elderly' is in a transitional phase: it is seen by many groups working with older people as a term implying incompetence and a lack of self-sufficiency. While still seen as acceptable in generic descriptions of an institution ('a home for the elderly'), journalists now consider it inappropriate as a term of address for older people themselves.

Describing the context: formal and informal

The context influences both the production of a text (the linguistic, grammatical, structural and stylistic features) and the way in which its intended audience receives it. The information we collect as we study the context is therefore central to our understanding: it gives the text wider meaning and explains why certain linguistic, grammatical and stylistic choices have been made.

Both texts here are responding to the offer of a job – a specific occasion – and both are addressed to a named person. What makes them so different is the context and the relationship existing between the writer and the recipient.

TEXT 1

6 Brown Lane,
Oxford.

12 March 2012

Mr S Denton,
Swift Insurers,
41-2 Merton Road,
Oxford.

Dear Mr Denton,

Thank you for offering me the position of Assistant Underwriter with Swift Insurers I am pleased to accept the position and look forward to starting employment with your company on 8 April 2012.

As soon as I receive the contract of employment, I will sign and return it as requested. If you require any other information, please do not hesitate to contact me

I believe I will make a positive contribution to Swift insurers and look forward to joining the team.

Yours sincerely,

Catherine Brooke (Ms)

TEXT 2

Hey! Got job. Can't believe it! Waaaaaa! LOL You said it wld be OK. Got letter this am. Wot you doin l8a? Want to go out? Got to celebrate. ☺ Start in month. Excitin or wot
X

The main differences between the formal job acceptance letter and the informal text to a friend are summarised below.

Context

Letter	Text
Response to a specific occasion	Personal response to specific occasion
Formal tone	Informal tone
Impersonal address	Personal address
Traditional formal layout	Distinctive spelling

Register

Letter	Text
Mode: written	Mode: written, but strong sense of spoken voice
Field: occupational, contractual	Field: expression of emotion, social communication
Tenor: intended audience – one named individual (distant relationship), formal SE, politeness markers, formal terms of address	Tenor: intended audience – personal friend (close relationship), informal language use, direct address
Purpose: to inform	Purpose: to socialise; to inform

Lexis

Letter	Text
Abstract rather than concrete language (*position, information, contribution*) No phatic language Lexical set of employment (*position, Assistant Underwriter, team, company*) Formal greetings (*Dear, Yours sincerely*) Proper nouns (*Mr Denton, Swift Insurers, Catherine Brooke*) Politeness markers (*Thank you, am pleased, please*)	Informal greeting (*Hey*) Lots of exclamations to express mood (*Can't believe it!, Waaaaaa!, Excitin or wot!*) Use of emoticon to express emotion Distinctive spelling: abbreviations typical of electronic English (*LOL, wld, Wot, doin, l8a, Excitin*) Limited range

Phrase structure

Letter	Text
Noun phrases are quite varied, but often short Simple: *the position, your company* Pre-modified: m m h a positive contribution det AdjP N Post-modified: m h q the contract of employment det N PrepP – verb phrases are mostly simple, using present tense (*am pleased, receive, require*) – modals indicate future time (*will sign*) and intention (*will make*)	Noun phrases are limited in range Simple (*job, letter*) Determiners omitted No modification: typical of text type, i.e., concise Verb phrases in simple past (*Got, said*) Modal *can* + *neg* to indicate inability to do something (*Can't believe*) Modal to indicate past prediction (*wld be*)

Sentence structure

Letter	Text

Sentence structure is formal with SCls to mark qualifying information
All sentences are complex or compound-complex
 	
    S   P   Od
❬ (I) (believe) [Ø I will make a positive
            SCl – NCl
 	
                    P
contribution to SI] ❭ and ❬ Ø (look forward
            conj
 	
    Od
to) [joining the team] ❭.
   SCl – NFCl
	Sentence structure is elliptical
	Omission of subject (Ø *Start in a month*)
	Omission of primary auxiliaries (Ø *Got job, Wot Ø you doin l8a, Ø Want to go out?*)
	Short simple sentences
	One complex sentence: reported speech
	
	    S P Od
	❬ (You) (said) [Ø it wld be OK] ❭.
	           SCl – NCl

Style

Letter	Text
Impersonal style Practical: getting things done No phatic communication: addressee and writer in formal relationship No familiarity: distant relationship Grammatical mood: all declarative (statement of facts)	Informal style Shared knowledge Restrictive range of lexical and syntactic features Range of grammatical moods: declarative (statement of facts, expression of emotion); interrogative (engagement with addressee – requires response)

In each text, the context shapes the discourse: while both respond to the same occasion, the different audience, purpose and text type affect the tone, language and syntax. The letter has been drafted and polished – the language used is precise and factual with clear references to the present (acceptance) and the future (intended action, contribution to the team). The organisation is clearly defined by the paragraph structure which divides the content into three distinct sections: aceptance; contract; personal contribution. The electronic text, on the other hand, is an example of spontaneous written language – it is short, elliptical (dictated by the size of the screen and possibly by the 'pay/page' billing system) and informal. While facts are included (offer of a job; starting date), the focus is on the writer's emotional response.

Where any reply to the formal letter will be delayed, the recipient of an electronic text can respond immediately, answering the direct questions and making arrangements. In a formal context, judgements are made about the quality and accuracy of the written language. This text, however, is expressive and non-standard spelling and syntax will not be judged by the intended audience. Spelling is often phonetic: it mimics pronunciation, changes or omits vowels, and drops final consonants. Grammatical function words are omitted so that only the semantically important words remain. The informal context means that a distinctive voice emerges, establishing a strong sense of the relationship between writer and reader.

Describing the context: age and purpose

Both texts here have the same basic content, but they have a different context in terms of the age of the writer and speaker, the intended audience and the place of production. The written text is an extract from the Ladybird *Key Words Reading Scheme, Read With Me: Let's Play* (Book 1) by William Murray and Jill Corby, illustrated by Chris Russell. The spoken text is an extract from an informal conversation about the book.

TEXT 1

Here is Kate and here is Sam.

No, no.

TEXT 2

'piano' 'Kate throws the' (2) <u>ball</u> (1) and the dog goes to get it (3) they say (2)
'forte' 'oh no' and the dog digs (.) and he th. he gets the flower out (3) Sam is a
   <u>bad</u> dog cos he done that (.) he dug out the garden to get the ball and the
'accel'/'forte' ↑ pretty ↑ flower (3) and he 'got a flower' (1) Kate says '<u>no</u> <u>no</u>'

The main differences between the reading book and the conversation are summarised below.

Context

Reading book	Conversation
Contemporary, every day experience (modern dress etc) Shared knowledge for writer/illustrator and child reader/adult Typical of narrative (character, setting) Layout (comic strip, illustrations)	Age: six-year-old-girl Family visit Shared knowledge for child/friend of family Location: familiar house Directly related to pictures, characterisation, child's personal experience

Register

Reading book	Conversation
Mode: written/illustrated (multi-modal) Field: everyday, familiar (two children with their dog in the park) Tenor: formal Identity of writer: unknown; expert; impersonal Audience: young readers; unknown; distant; formal BUT engages with readers through development of character/event Purpose: educational (learning to read key words)	Mode: spoken Field: Kate and her dog in the park (ordinary, familiar) Tenor: informal Identity of speaker: known, personal; young Audience: known; immediate; informal Purpose: phatic (establishing a relationship)

Lexis

Reading book	Conversation
Commonplace, restricted range Monosyllabic Repetitive Proper nouns (*Kate, Sam*)	Common-place Mainly monosyllabic, but some disyllabic (*flower, pretty, garden*) Some from reading book (*no no, Kate, Sam*), but also wider range linked to pictures Concrete nouns (*ball, dog, flower, garden*) Pronouns (*it, they, he, that,*) Attributive adjectives (*bad, pretty*) Dynamic verbs (*throws, goes, digs, gets*) Standard use of third person singular (*goes*) and plural (*say*) verb endings Some irregular past tense verb forms used standardly (*dug, got*), others non-standard (past part. *done* for 'did') Co-ordinating (*and*) and subordinating (*cos*) conjunctions

Phrase structure

Reading book	Conversation
Noun phrases are simple and limited in range consisting of just a head word (*Kate, Sam*)	Noun phrases are mostly simple (*the ball, it, a flower*)
	Two modified noun phrases with adjective pre-modifier (*a bad dog, the pretty flower*) Typical of age of speaker and text type (oral narrative)
Simple present tense verb phrases (*is*)	Simple present tense verb phrases, BUT semantically more varied than the reading scheme (*throws, digs, say, gets*)
Simple adverb phrase repeated (*here*)	Simple adverb phrase (*out*)

Sentence structure

Reading book	Conversation
One co-ordinated sentence 　A　　P　　S　　　　A　　P　　S 〈 (Here) (is) (Kate) 〉 and 〈 (here) (is) (Tom) 〉 　　　　　　　　　　conj One minor sentence (*No, no*)	Loosely structured sentences Varied sentence types: SIMPLE 　　　　S　　　P　　interj 〈 (Kate) (says) (no no) 〉 　　quoting clause　　quoted clause COMPOUND 　　　　S　　P　　interj　　　　　　　S 〈 (they) (say) (oh no) 〉 and 〈 (the dog) 　　　　　　　　　　conj 　P　　　　　　　　S　　P　　Od　　A (digs) 〉 and 〈 (he) (gets) (the flower) (out) 〉 　　　　conj COMPLEX 　　　S　　P　　　C　　　　　　A 〈 (Sam) (is) (a bad dog) [cos he done that] 〉 　　　　　　　　　　　　　SCl – ACl COMPOUND-COMPLEX 　　S　　P　　　Od　　　　　　A 〈(he) (dug out) (the garden) [to get the ball and 　　　　　　　　　　　SCl – NFCl　　conj 　　　　　　　　　　　S　　P　　Od Ø the pretty flower]〉 and 〈(he) (got) (a flower)〉 SCl – NFCl　　　　　　conj

Style

Reading book	Conversation
Straightforward Repetitive (reinforcement of key words) Fronted adverbial (*here*) to create exophoric reference to pictures Narrow range of text reflects purpose (learning to recognise words) Pictures provide breadth; opportunity to develop oral narrative	More varied than written text Reflects the difference between the speaker's range as a speaker and as a reader Repetition of *and* typical of young children and oral narrative Pronoun referencing not always clear: need pictures showing two children to understand the exophoric reference (*they*) Prosodic variation underpins oral narrative: begins quietly (unsure); louder volume draws attention to direct speech (familiar from text); word stress (*ball*, *bad*) and raised pitch (↑ *pretty* ↑) draw attention to key words Evidence of normal non-fluency features (*th. he*) and colloquialisms (*cos*)

In each text, the context shapes the discourse: the formality of Text 1 as an educative text is in direct contrast to the informality of Text 2. The reading scheme has been written by an unknown writer who is an expert: the tone is impersonal, the audience distant and unknown, and the function is informative (conveying information which teaches a young child to read). The oral narrative, on the other hand, is produced by a young speaker in a familiar place with a known and immediate audience. The function is creative (a personal account of a shared story). In each case, the context affects the complexity of the lexis and syntax, and the relative formality of the style.

Text 1 has been written to be read aloud. It has been pre-planned and focuses on key words printed in large sans serif font. The written content is restricted by the age and reading experience of the intended audience, but the range is broadened by the accompanying pictures which relate a more complex narrative based on familiar characters and everyday events. As an example of spontaneous spoken discourse, Text 2 demonstrates a linguistic breadth that is quite different to the reading scheme: the six-year-old has more experience in spoken interactions than in engaging with written text. The greater linguistic and syntactic variety is therefore typical.

The location in which each discourse takes place also plays a part in shaping the text. Reading books are published on a large scale and used in a formal context – at school, or at home as part of a learning experience. The spoken text, however, is produced in an informal context where the physical location and the participants are familiar, and the tone is therefore quite different.

10.6 Standard and non-Standard English

To understand and describe the different ways in which language changes, linguists take one particular non-regional dialect of English, STANDARD ENGLISH, as a norm, a point of comparison. We see and hear Standard English everyday – it is a dialect that we can all understand, a variety used in government, the legal system, education and in business. It is what we usually hear on the television and radio because it cuts across regional differences; professional people are more likely to use it because they move around the country and therefore tend to speak in a more standardised way.

Standard English is not, however, the only variety of English. Any form that does not use the same vocabulary or grammar as Standard English is called NON-STANDARD English. This term avoids making value judgements about whether a particular language use is 'right' or 'wrong'. Instead, it allows linguists to describe the ways in which language changes in different situations and from person to person.

Pronunciation may also vary: people from different geographical and social backgrounds often have accents that differ from RECEIVED PRONUNCIATION (RP), a standard non-regional form of pronunciation used by linguists as a norm. Where a particular regional accent tells us something about a speaker's geographical background, RP tells us more about a speaker's social and cultural background. Most RP speakers today use MODIFIED-RP rather than the very formal 'BBC English' of the 1950s. There are many different forms: the speakers use Standard English, but have an accent shaped by their regional and cultural background. This is evidence of the way in which language changes – as regional identity became increasingly important in the 1960s, regional accents began to influence and diversify RP pronunciation.

Using Standard English as a point of comparison

As we have already seen, language is constantly changing, from region to region (geographical variation), from period to period (historical variation), from group to group (social variation) and from person to person (personal variation). We can use our knowledge of Standard English to describe the ways in which language is used in different ways according to the place and the time, and by different people.

Describing geographical variation

Changes in language according to the geographical location result in distinctive regional forms of words, grammar and pronunciation. Variations in pronunciation (accents) constitute a vast and complex area of linguistic study and are not therefore considered in this book, but there are specific linguistic and grammatical features that we can look out for in regional dialects.

Lexis

‣ words that are unique to a particular community

Word	Meaning	Region
claggy	damp/sticky	North-East/East
bairn	child	Newcastle/Scotland
keeking	looking/peeping	Scotland
cwtch	cuddle	Wales
made up	pleased	Liverpool
happen	perhaps/maybe	Pennines: Yorkshire, Lancashire, East Midlands

- colloquial expressions (*like I said*; *big it up*)
- contractions (*init*); abbreviations (*cos*) – also found in informal registers

Nouns

- the omission of plural endings (*I gave him three **pound.***)
- irregular plurals (*childer, housen*)

Adjectives

- double comparatives/superlatives (***more prettier***, ***most fastest***)

Verbs

- standardisation of present tense inflections
  she **like**   (SE *likes*)   we **likes**   (SE *like*)
- regular past tense –*ed* inflection added to irregular verbs
  he **goed**   (SE *went*)   you **taked**   (SE *took*)
- irregular –*ed* participles and past tense forms are simplified (LEVELLING)
  I swam   *I have **swam***   (SE *swum*, –*ed* part)
  I went   *I have **went***   (SE *gone*, –*ed* part)
  *I **done***   *I have done*   (SE *did*, simple past tense)
- archaic -*ing* participle forms (*a-going*)
- *do* used as an auxiliary verb with no meaning attached
  *I **do** go to town regular.*   *We **d'**know him.*
- multiple negatives
  *I **don't** know **nothing**.* (SE *anything*)   *I didn't find **none nowhere**.* (SE *any, anywhere*)
- use of *ain't*
  *You **ain't** going home yet.* (SE *aren't*)   *They **ain't** got the CD yet.* (SE *haven't*)
- use of *aren't* (*I **aren't**.* SE *am not*)
- non-standard negation
  *He's **no** got a dog.* (SE *hasn't*)   *We've **nae** arrived yet.* (SE *not*)
  *I **never** done it.* (SE *did not do* – single occasion)

Adverbs

- omission of the –*ly* inflection   (*We did that **fantastic**.* SE *fantasically*)

Pronouns

- subject pronouns used in the object site when unstressed
  *When I saw **she**, I was amazed.* (SE *her*)
- object pronouns used in the subject site when unstressed
  *He came from London, didn't **him**.* (SE *he*)
- plural forms used for singular references
  *He wanted to see **us**.* (SE *me*)
- weak forms *'ee* (SE *you*), *'er* (SE s/*he*), *'m* (SE *they*)
  *You wouldn't buy that would**'ee**?* (SE *you*)
- reflexive pronoun pattern standardised (poss det + *self/selves*)
  hisself (SE *himself*)   *theirselves* (SE *themselves*)
- archaic possessive pronoun forms
  yourn (SE *yours*)   *hisn* (SE *his*)
- relative pronoun *which* used for human references
  *The girl, **which** lives next door, goes to my school.* (SE *who*)
- demonstrative pronouns and determiners replaced by subject or object pronouns
  ***Them** do look good. **Them** HD televisions are expensive.* (SE *Those*)
- the *wh-* pronoun *what* used as a relative pronoun
  *The football club **what** I go to meets twice a week.* (SE *which/that*)
- archaic pronoun forms (*thou, thee,* SE *you;* ***yon** hill,* SE *that*)

Prepositions

- replacement of prepositions
  *We went **up** Julie's house.* (SE *to*)
  *The journey to town is **along of** 7 miles.* (SE *about*)
- additional prepositions
  *I'm reading how **for to** make it.* (SE *to*)
  *I get **off of** the bus at the next stop.* (SE *off*)
- omission of prepositions (*They looked out Ø the window.* SE *of*)

Conjunctions

- substitution of conjunctions
  *You won't pass exams **without** you do some work.* (SE *until*)

These non-standard features can be seen in social and regional varieties of English. While non-standard lexis is linked to a specific region or group, non-standard grammatical features tend to be similar across geographical and social boundaries. Non-Standard English is often associated with spoken language, which tends to be more informal, but non-standard words and grammatical structures can also be seen in written texts. Diaries and other forms of personal writing (shopping lists, texts, MSN messages, letters) can be marked by non-standard features. Poets and novelists, who use language creatively, may also choose non-standard language in order to develop a sense of character or to create the mood of a particular place or time.

In the example below from the novel *Foxy-T* by Tony White (page 64, Faber & Faber, 2003), the first person narrator uses a form of Black English – a cockney-Carribean-Bangladeshi patois which can be heard on the streets of London and in other urban areas. It represents a social variety of English used by young people to challenge authority and assert a strong sense of shared identity. Using Standard English as a norm, we can describe the ways in which this particular dialect is linguistically distinctive.

> Foxy-T just sat quiet at the table and drank her coffee then had a bit of toast and Nutella when Ruji-Babes fix some. Foxy-T felt a bit like she did last night where she no want him fe look at her. But the smell of him hair gel never fail fe remind her of the thief again and it also remind her a bit of her dream. So that girl just sit there quiet and no say much is it. Ruji-Babes was the one fuss around and aks if anyone want more coffee and that.

We can list the following features:

quiet	adverb used without –*ly* inflection (SE, 'quietly')
fix	simplified tenses: past tense –*ed* inflection omitted (SE, 'fixed')
no want	simplified negative: aux *do* + *not* omitted (SE, 'did not want')
fe	to (SE)
him	object pronoun used instead of a possessive determiner (SE, 'his')
fail	no past tense inflection (SE, 'failed')
remind	no past tense inflection (SE, 'reminded')
that	colloquial use of a demonstrative pronoun referring to someone that both speaker and hearer know about
sit	no past tense irregular verb form (SE, 'sat')
no say	simplified negative (SE, 'did not say')
is it	colloquialism
fuss	–*ing* participle inflection omitted on progressive form (SE, 'fussing')
aks	inversion of consonants (METATHESIS); omission of -*ing* participle inflection (SE, 'asking')
that	colloquialism

In this particular dialect, distinctive features can be seen in the simplification of language patterns. Inflections are dropped on adverbs (–*ly* inflections), past tense verb forms (–*ed* inflections) and –*ing* participles. Irregular past tense verbs are replaced with simple present forms and primary auxiliaries are omitted. The range of pronouns forms in Standard English is reduced and pronunciation can be different.

In choosing this dialect of English, the writer has created a distinctive voice. It enagages the reader by drawing them into a vividly drawn world in which our experience of events is shaped by the language of the narrator. The conversational tone and immediacy of the variety make the reading experience very personal – while we recognise the limitations of the narrator, we trust him and accept his version of events.

Describing social and personal variation

Our social group and our personal identity also shape the kind of language choices we make. Males and females make different lexical choices in conversation; young children developing language skills may use immature pronunciations and simplified grammatical structures; older people may retain examples of usage that is no longer common; people with specialist occupations may use unfamiliar words or familiar words with narrower meanings; someone who is angry or indignant may use language and grammatical structures in ways that are quite different from their normal repertoire.

In the example below, Speaker A (a child of about two and a half) is talking to his mother. As is typical for a child of this age, pronunciation is not yet standard for some of the more complex sounds such as the VOICED DENTAL FRICATIVE /ð/ ('this'), one of the last to be pronounced accurately. Similarly, consonant clusters are often simplified, particularly those containing the voiced POST-ALVEOLAR APPROXIMANT /r/ – this may not be pronounced accurately until the age of four. Non-standard grammar features are also age-related. Children will, typically, go through an accepted sequence of assimilating the grammatical rules of their speech community and will usually be fluent speakers by the age of four or five. Using Standard English as a point of comparison, we can describe the ways in which the language-use in the extract below reflects the age of the speaker.

A   [humming] no (8) no no
B   no no what
A   we naughty boy
B   are they (.) what happens to them when they're naughty
A   in uh new house (1) it's in uh new house
B   mm which is the new house
A   ose ones
B   okay (.) Betty's Club
A   Betty Club
B   are the naughty boys there
A   Betty Club (2) in ose new house (2) fwee naughty boys is come

We can list the following features:

we naughty boy	omission of first person plural verb 'to be' and plural noun inflection (SE, 'we are naughty boys')
uh	immature pronunciation (SE, 'the')
it's	unclear pronoun referencing
ose	immature pronunciation (SE, 'those'); non-agreement of a singular and a plural noun phrase reference (*the new house* → *ose ones*)
Betty Club	omission of possessive inflection (SE, 'Betty's')
ose ... house	omission of plural inflection (SE, 'houses')
fwee	immature pronunciation (SE, 'three')
is	non-agreement of plural subject and singular verb form (SE, 'are')

| come | omission of *–ing* inflection on progressive verb form (SE 'coming') |

In this particular example of child language, the distinctive features can be seen in the simplification of language. Primary auxiliary verbs and inflections (plural *–s*, possessive *–'s*, *–ing* participle) are omitted. Singular and plural lexical items (subject/verb; determiner/noun) do not agree, and pronoun referencing is unclear. Pronunciation is immature: the omission of the voiced dental fricative /ð/ reduces 'the' to the unstressed neutral vowel schwa (/ə/); the voiced BILABIAL APPROXIMANT /w/ replaces the more complex consonant cluster 'thr' (*fwee* for 'three'), which may not be pronounced standardly until about the age of four.

Describing historical variation

Historical language change looks at the different stages a language passes through in its key periods. In order to understand how the English language has changed, we use the following periods: Old English (pre-1100), Middle English (1100–1450), Early Modern English (1450–1700), Modern English (1700–1900s) and Late Modern English (1900–). These divisions are in some senses arbitrary because language change does not take place within neat boundaries. They do, however, help us to see significant periods of change. Once we reach the mid-twentieth century, we become more aware of continuity than change, since the variety of English used seems so very little different from our own.

When we look at the English language in each of the key periods, it is difficult for us to be sure about standard and non-standard usage of the time. We can, however, recognise the differences between formal (published texts) and informal (private texts) usage, and can explore the ways in which English has changed by comparing it with our own standard usage.

The example below was written in 1461, the Early Modern English period. It is a personal letter, but it is written by an employee (Richard Calle) to his employer (John Paston) and therefore adopts a formal tone. The opening greeting is typical of the period: it communicates the respect of the writer for the recipient of the letter. The spelling is perhaps the most immediately noticeable change for a modern reader, but it does not prevent us from understanding the text.

> Right wurshipfull and my mooste reverent mastre, I recomaunde me unto your goode maystreship. Like you to witte that on Childremasse daye there were moche people at Norwich at the shire, be cauce it was noyced in the shire that the Undresheriff had a writte to make a newe aleccion …

We can list the following features:

wurshipfull	worshipful (from OE 'weorthscipe')
mooste	most (from OE 'mæst')
mastre	master (from OE 'mægester', OFr 'maistre', 'magister')
recomaunde	recommend (from L 'commendare')
goode	good (from OE 'gōd', Ger 'gut', ON, 'gōthr')
maystreship	mayorship (from Fr. 'maire', L 'major')
witte	know (from OE '(ge)wit')

Childremasse daye	Innocents' Day, 28 December (from OE 'cildra', of the children; OE 'mæsse', L 'missa'/'mittere', to send away – possibly linked to *ite, missa est*, 'go' at the end of a service i.e. the congregation is dismissed)
moche	much (from ME 'muche', OE 'micel')
be cauce	because (from 'by cause', OE 'bi'; Fr – L 'causa')
noyced	rumoured/reported (from Fr 'noise', quarrel; possibly L 'noxia'/'nocere', hurt)
Undresheriff	undersheriff (from OE 'under', ON 'undir'; OE 'scirgerefa' – 'scir', shire; 'gerefa', reeve)
writte	writ (from OE '(ge)writ', ON 'rit')
newe	new (from OE 'niwe', L 'novus')
aleccion	election (from L 'eligere' – 'e', from 'legere', to choose)

The writer of this letter uses a form of English which reflects the historical period in which he is writing. The grammar does not cause a modern reader any problems since it follows Standard English patterns with which we are familiar. There are some words, however, which are difficult for us to understand because they have since become obsolete (*witte, noyced*). Similarly, the reference to *Childremasse daye*, a festival to commemorate the slaying of the children by Herod, may cause us problems since it is no longer a well-known public holiday.

The spelling of words is significantly different from contemporary English. The final –*e* apparent on many adjectives (*mooste, goode, moche, newe*) and some nouns (*daye, writte*) is a remnant of the system of inflections used in Old English. Some spellings reflect pronunciation (*wurshipfull*), others perhaps reflect a French influence (*mastre*). We can also see the emergence of the conjunction 'because' from its two constituent parts.

The example here gives a snapshot of what English was like in the late fifteenth century. It demonstrates the linguistic influences shaping vocabulary and some of the features of English spelling before the introduction of the printing press in 1476 began the process of standardisation.

10.7 Conclusion

The information in this section shows us how the study of discourse takes us beyond the surface structure of words and grammar to a wider consideration of language at work. We need to understand the key areas that shape language choice and structure, and to recognise the effects that can be created in speech and writing. This will bring us closer to an appreciation of what a particular writer or speaker is trying to communicate and the ways in which she or he aims to do so.

The study of longer, more developed texts requires us to consider the effect different registers, users and uses have on language. We must be sensitive to the ways in which language can vary according to the producer, the purpose, the intended audience and the context. Recognising changes to standard patterns and understanding what lies behind each change helps us to look for the linguistic and syntactic characteristics of a text and to understand how meaning is created.

Chapter 11

Using your knowledge

In this chapter, you have the opportunity to apply the knowledge you have gained about discourse. The close reading activities require you to consider the effects created by the register, by the identity or background of the speaker or writer, by the text type or context. Discussion of the texts also begins to address broader areas of language study, introducing you to etymology (the historical origin of words) phonology (the sound system of a language) and spelling. The writing tasks encourage you to use your understanding of discourse to create your own texts.

11.1 Register

If we can make a connection between form, style and meaning, we are in a better position to appreciate the effectiveness of a text. Analysing the register allows us to understand how the field, tenor and mode of discourse shape the choices a writer or speaker makes. In identifying the focus of the content, the tone, the relationship with the intended audience and the function, we can recognise how a particular spoken or written text aims to affect us as readers or listeners.

TASK 1   Register

1 Read the following texts.

TEXT 1
This text appears on the back of city buses.

No More Filthy Fumes
These low emission buses are helping to reduce pollution
and improve air quality in our city

TEXT 2
This is an extract from a sermon preached on 31 October 2004 in Copleston Road Methodist Church in Cardiff by the minister Andrew Webster. Its focus is Luke Chapter 19, verses 1–10 – the story of Zacchaeus.

'Get down from that tree you wretched sinner, you disgrace, you corrupt and greedy man.' That's what the law required Jesus to say. Only he doesn't play his part, he doesn't follow the script written by the Pharisees and teachers of the law. He breaks the rules to welcome a rule breaker.

'Zacchaeus come down, today I will come to your house' (Luke Chapter 19, verse 5).

In the society of the time there was no greater affirmation of a person than to share table fellowship and this is how Jesus responds to Zacchaeus. Before there is confession there is acceptance, before contrition, affirmation and before repentance – mercy.

2 Make notes on the key features of the register in each case. You will need to think about:

▸ the mode (speech or writing)
▸ the field (the subject matter)
▸ the tenor (the level of formality, the terms of address, the relationship with the audience, the function)

NOTES

TEXT 1

This is an advertisement designed to be seen by bus passengers and other road users. It demonstrates local government commitment to developing environmentally sustainable transport systems.

Mode

▸ written

Field

▸ environmental theme: *emission, pollution, air quality*
▸ alliterative slogan
▸ negative connotations of adjective (*Filthy*) and noun (*Fumes*) undermined by negative *no* in initial position
▸ positive connotations of infinitives *to reduce ... improve*
▸ use of progressive verb phrase (*are helping*) to imply on-going action

Tenor

▸ formal, but engaging directly with wide, unknown audience (***our*** *city*)
▸ noun phrase + compound-complex sentence

```
          S              P              Od                    Od
< (These low emission buses) (are helping) [to reduce pollution] and [Ø improve air
                                             SCl – NFCl              conj  SCl – NFCl

          A
quality] (in our city) >.
```

▸ exophoric reference (*These buses*) creates direct link to specific environment → therefore aims to encourage sense of community responsibility

Function

- inform rather than persuade
- implicitly seeks to encourage people to use service because it is environmentally friendly

TEXT 2

This text encourages the congregation to reflect on abstract ideas that will be relevant to daily life. Beginning with a story from a traditional religious text allows the minister to make his moral lesson more accessible.

Mode

- written to be spoken

Field

- formal polysyllabic language
- proper nouns (*Jesus, Pharisees, Zacchaeus; Luke*)
- emotive vocatives (*you wretched sinner, you disgrace, you corrupt and greedy man*)
- lexical set related to sin (*wretched sinner, corrupt, greedy*)
- abstract nouns related to moral lesson (*fellowship, confession, acceptance, contrition, affirmation, repentance, mercy*)
- exophoric reference to biblical text (*That's*)
- phrases in direct speech (cited from biblical text) tend to be simple (*that tree, your house*) or with some pre-modification (*you corrupt and greedy man*)
- phrases in lesson tend to be complex

   m   h   q
the script [written by the Pharisees and teachers of the law]
det   N   NFCl

   m   m   h   q
no greater affirmation of a person
det AdjP   N   PrepP

- some noun clauses are used in place of phrases (*what the law required Jesus to say, how Jesus responds to Zacchaeus*)

Tenor

- formal tone in formal context
- speaker is in a position of authority, but knows his audience and will have a close relationship with many members of his congregation
- clear structure, i.e., planned and drafted:
  - juxtaposition of direct speech and biblical quotation
  - explanation and application to wider circumstances
- patterning is typical of formal writing/speech → persuasive
- some lexical informality:
  - fronted adverb *Only* – informal replacement for 'But' (change of direction)
  - contractions (*That's, doesn't*)
- direct speech changes pace and engages audience – simple sentence (dramatic)
- quotation from Bible → 2 simple sentences co-ordinated by punctuation rather than conjunction (comma splicing)

- uses contemporary version of religious text rather than earlier text (more accessible)
  - 1917 Hibernian Bible: *Zacchaeus, make haste, and come down; for to day I must abide at thy house*
  - 1971 British and Foreign Bible Society: *'Zacchaeus, make haste and come down; for I must stay at your house today'*
- formality is reflected in sentence structure: seven sentences with 17 clauses
- five sentences complex (*He **breaks** the rules **to welcome** ...*) or compound-complex (*... there **was** ... **than** to **share** ... **and** this **is** ... **how** Jesus **responds** ...*)
- as a spoken text, commas are used to mark pauses where we may have expected co-ordinating conjunctions (*he doesn't play his part, he doesn't follow ...*)
- use of existential sentences (*... there was ..., ... there is ...*)
- text is didactic – aim is to educate intended audience

Function

- function is expressive and instructive

TASK 2   Changing the register

1 Choose either the theme of 'environmental policy' or 'repentance and mercy' and record your personal thoughts on the subject. You may also find it helpful to gather some background information and examples on your chosen topic.

2 Write a formal text (an essay, a report, a documentary voice-over) exploring some key element of your topic.

3 Re-write your text as an informal piece (a conversation, a sensational tabloid report, a blog).

Think carefully about the register and function in each case.

When you have completed your texts, evaluate the key linguistic features. You may like to use the suggested framework for analysis in Appendix A.

TASK 3   Register and public texts

1 Read the texts below carefully.

TEXT 1
This is an extract from a House of Commons Debate recorded in Hansard. Two Conservative politicians are commenting on the disturbance which took place outside Conservative Party headquarters during a public demonstration by students on 10 November 2011.

Public Disorder (NUS Rally) 11 Nov 2010 1.15pm
Michael Fallon (Sevenoaks) (Con): Will the Minister join me in paying tribute to the staff at Conservative headquarters, led by Baroness Warsi, who continued working in a frightening situation yesterday, as did others in surrounding offices? Surely those enjoying higher education are the one group who should be pursuing their point of view by argument and debate, rather than by violence.

Nick Herbert (Arundel and South Downs): I agree with my hon. Friend. Of course it was worrying for the staff at Conservative Campaign Headquarters in Millbank and for other members of the public. My right hon. Friend the Home Secretary spoke to Baroness Warsi during the day about that experience. I also agree with my hon. Friend that this is the place where democratic debate takes place over issues of public policy. No one questions the right of those students to march yesterday and to make their case, and 40,000 of them did so peacefully. There is plenty of opportunity to debate policy, but there is neither a need nor any excuse for a minority to resort to violence.

TEXT 2

This text appeared in a daily compact newspaper.

CREDIT CRISIS SET TO HIT GLOBAL DEMAND

INDUSTRIAL stocks led Wall Street lower yesterday as concerns were raised that the intensifying credit crisis would knock global demand and could impair companies' opportunities to access funds.

The big names sustained significant losses as worse-than-expected manufacturing orders and jobless figures also suggested that household demand was falling off. Industrials also suffered another nosedive, off 7.5 per cent, after data showed the biggest monthly fall in orders in almost two years.

The Dow Jones Industrial Average fell 3.5 per cent to 10,478.92.

2 Write a commentary in which you compare and contrast the register and function of each text.

You should use appropriate terminology and linguistic frameworks to explain and evaluate the texts.

You may like to think about:

- the relationship between the mode, the field and the tenor
- the ways in which the writers/speakers use language to establish a relationship with their intended audience
- how the language choices and style relate to the function

COMMENTARY

Texts 1 (Hansard) and 2 (financial report) both have a formal register. Although the mode of Text 2 is written and Text 1 is spoken and then recorded in a written format, they have many linguistic and stylistic similarities. This is because they both use subject specific language, they both have a formal context, the relationship between the writer/speaker and his material is official, and the relationship with the intended audience is impersonal.

Both texts use formal language. The words are polysyllabic (*intensifying, opportunities, Industrial; minority, democratic, argument*) and there are no informal language features. They use abstract nouns to address complex fields like the ecomony (*crisis, demand, losses*) and politics (*policy, argument, experience*), and have proper nouns establishing specific participants (*Baronness Warsi*) or places (*Wall Street;*

Conservative Campaign Headquarters). Subject specific lexical sets focus on specialist fields: finance (*stocks, credit crisis, funds, losses*) and political democracy (*argument, debate, democratic, policy, make their case*). Both texts relate directly to a specific situation (falling share prices; a student demonstration) and to a general state of affairs (credit crisis; the principles of democracy).

The participants are experts speaking and writing for a specialist audience or an 'interested' general audience. Although the immediate relationship between speakers in Parliament is direct and intimate, the exchange is official and impersonal because of the traditional context, the rules governing participation, mediation by the Speaker and the fact that everything is broadcast. This means that the tenor of each text conforms to our expectations: the relationship established with the intended audience is formal and distant.

The compact report is factual (informative function), using figures (*7.5 per cent, 10,478.92*) and graded modifiers (*lower, biggest*) to assess changes in the economic market, and time references (*yesterday, monthly, almost two years*) to establish a time scale. The Hansard report, however, communicates opinions (expressive function). The two Conservative politicians interact positively, with the questions offering Nick Herbert (the Minister of State for policing and criminal justice) an opportunity to assert the party response to the student demonstration. The fronted adverb *Surely* suggests that the only reasonable answer to the question is 'yes' and his assertion is reinforced by the modals *Will* (politeness marker) and *should* (obligation). The repetition of *agree* establishes a common outlook, which is underpinned by the prepositional phrase *Of course*.

Because most of the language in each text is literal, the use of descriptive language stands out. The emotive pre-modified phrase *a frightening situation* sets the context for the rhetorical opposition of *argument and debate* versus *violence* – the issue lying at the heart of the Minister's question. Similarly, the noun phrase *another nosedive* in the financial report uses a figurative expression describing the rapid downward motion of a plane to give a visual frame of reference to an abstract concept (a falling stock market). Such language use allows the speaker or writer to communicate a specific attitude to the intended audience.

As would be expected in formal speech and writing, the noun phrases tend to be long with a range of pre- and post-modification.

	m		m	h		m	h	q
(worse-[than-expected])		manufacturing	orders		companies'	opportunities	[to access funds]
	AdjP		V*ing*	N		N	N	NFCl
Adj	CompCl							

m	m	h	q
the	one	group	[who should be pursuing their point of view by argument and debate ...]
det	num	N	RelCl

m		q
the	place	[where democratic debate takes place over issues of public policy]
det	N	RelCl

This means that there is often a heavy weight of information – placing a particular demand upon the audience listening to the parliamentary debate live, which is broadcast on BBC Parliament and available online.

Similarly, sentences are long with a heavy weight of subordination to carry the information and comment. The newspaper report has a total of four sentences with 12 clauses. It opens with a compound-complex sentence which introduces the focus of the report (the level of Wall Street stocks) and relates it to the wider issue (the credit crisis).

```
         S            P       O        A        A                      A
< (Industrial stocks) (led) (Wall St) (lower) (yesterday) [as concerns were raised [that the
                                                           SCl – ACl                 SCl – NCl

                                                           A
intensifying credit crisis would knock ...] and [Ø could impair companies' opportunities
                                          conj   SCl – NCl

[to access funds] ] ] >.
SCl – NFCl
```

The only simple sentence concludes the report with a factual statement of the Dow Jones index.

The sentence structure of the spoken exchange in parliament is more varied because the interaction is more complicated. The opening question is complex – there are a total of four subordinate clauses (NFCls *paying tribute ... led by ...*; RelCl *who continued ...*; ACl *as did ...*) in which key information is embedded. This question will probably have been written down before it was spoken; it conforms to the typical structure of parliamentary questions designed to elicit affirmation rather than negation. The response opens with three simple sentences asserting a common viewpoint (*I agree ... it was worrying ... My right hon. Friend the Home Secretary spoke ...*). When the speaker moves beyond affirmation to the wider debate, however, the sentences are complex (*I also **agree** ... that this **is** the place where democratic debate **takes place** ...*) or compound-complex.

```
   S         P                        O
< (No one) (questions) (the right of those students [to march yesterday]) and
                                                    SCl – NFCl                 conj

        O                          S           P       A
(Ø [to make their case]) > and < (40,000 of them) (did so) (peacefully) >.
SCl – NFCl                 conj
```

The style in both extracts is also formal. Terms of address linked to titles (*the Minister, my hon. Friend*) and the use of passive (*were raised*) and modal verb phrases (*should be pursuing, would knock, could impair*) contribute to the tone in each case. The rhetoric of the spoken language, however, is quite different to the factual nature of the written report. The patterning of prepositional phrases (*by argument and debate ... by violence*) and non-finite clauses (*to debate policy ... to resort to violence*) draws attention to the juxtaposition at the heart of the exchange. Balanced phrases (*the staff at Conservative Campaign Headquarters ... other members of the public*), the repetition of key terms (*policy, debate, violence, agree*) and the use of direct contrasts (*There is ... but there is ...*) develop the argument logically, encouraging the intended audience to identify with the points of view expressed.

TASK 4   Register and personal texts

1 Read the two texts below carefully.

TEXT 1

This extract is taken from *Daisy* (Lulu Press, 2007), the autobiography of Hilda Hobart who was born in 1914 in Norfolk. It is the written account of an oral narrative that she told to her niece. This particular episode takes place in 1918.

My father played a part in our Sunday Bath Night. The bath would be filled from the copper and there, in front of the fire, the grime of the week would be soaked and scrubbed away. Passed out of the bath one by one by my mother, my father would wrap us in the towel and rub us dry before passing us on to grandmother who would plait our damp hair so that we had Victorian curls, a crimp or Dodeman curls – Dodeman was the Norfolk name given to snails and I suppose the curls were named after the coil of the shells. We had those curls from wet cloths, twisted into our damp hair. While we bathed, our shoes were lined-up under the big table so that my father could clean the row of them while we slept.

TEXT 2

The extract below is taken from a summary of the vampire novel *Twilight* by Stephanie Meyer. It was written by an 18-year-old, Rachel Thomas, and put on Facebook for a friend who had not read any of the books or seen the first two films, but who was about to see the third film in the sequence.

1. Bella comes to small town – Forks – to live with her dad (has awesome moustache) and meets a beautiful, mysterious family – the Cullens. (Of whom the handsomest of all the handsomes is Edward). And as soon as she sees him she falls in love because she is a shallow little girl and he is pretty!
2. :O They're vampires! Who are incredibly beautiful! Incredibly fast! Incredibly strong! Incredibly clever! Incredibly rich! Incredibly long-lived! Incredibly sparkly in the sunlight! Incredibly nice smelling!
   (Bella isn't disturbed by the vampires hunting humans thing but then it turns out the Cullens kill animals instead. So that's even better.)
3. Edward wants to kill her because of her gooooood tasting blood. Instead, inexplicably, he falls in love with her. They can now no longer live without one another.
4. She hangs about getting to know the loving vampire family:
   Esme = 'mother' vampire
   Carlisle = 'father' vampire and also town doctor
   Emmett, Rosalie, Jasper, Alice, Edward = adopted 'children' (all of whom have INCREDIBLE VAMPIRE POWERS)
   Emmett and Rosalie are married; he is super strong, she super pretty
   Jasper and Alice are married: he can control emotions, she sees the future
   And Edward (unmarried – clearly because no vampire wants to marry him because he's so annoying) can read minds. But not Bella's. But all that goes on in her mind is 'Pretty, sparkly, pretty, sparkly, mmmmmm Edward' so he's not missing much.
5. All Bella thinks about is jumping her vampire lover's bones …

2 Write a commentary in which you compare and contrast the register and function of each text.

You should use appropriate terminology and linguistic frameworks to explain and evaluate the texts.

You may like to think about:

- the relationship between the mode, the field and the tenor
- the ways in which the writers/speakers use language to establish a relationship with their intended audience
- how the language choices and style relate to the function

COMMENTARY

Both texts are personal, dominated by features associated with informality because the written and spoken modes interact: the autobiography is a written version of an oral narrative; the summary uses a spoken voice in a written mode. Both have a personal tone and draw on a field familiar to their immediate audience.

The personal nature of Text 1 can be seen in the recurrence of first person pronouns (*we, I, us*) and possessive determiners (*my, our*), which is typical of autobiography. The field is domestic with a focus on family life: relationships are established through common nouns (*mother, father, grandmother*); the subject matter is developed through references to the family bath night (the nouns *bath, copper, grime*; the dynamic verbs *soaked, scrubbed, wrap, rub, bathed*) and to contemporary hair styles for girls (the nouns *curls, crimp, Dodeman*; the adjectives *Victorian, wet, damp*; the verbs *plait, twisted*).

Two words in particular are distinctive, linking the narrator directly to the period which the account recalls and to a specific geographical location. The first (*copper*) is a reference to the boiler – an example of synecdoche in which the part stands for the whole. The name *copper* refers not only to the material from which the boiler is made, but to the item as a whole. It is an example of a word now obsolete in this particular context. The other (*Dodeman*) is a distinctive name for a snail used in Norfolk – an example of a regional dialect word which links the narrator directly to a specific language community. It is likely to be unfamiliar to English speakers outside the particular geographical area. The 1894 Brewer *Dictionary of Phrase and Fable* cites its usage in a traditional Norfolk rhyme:

Doddiman, doddiman, put out your horn,
Here comes a thief to steal your corn.

The reference in the extract is figurative, taking the idea of a snail's shell to describe the shape of the girls' curls. Other period language can be seen in the references to the portable tin bath used before family homes had bathrooms, and to the *wet cloths* (or rags) used instead of curlers to make curls.

The language in this extract is ordinary because it is describing a familiar family routine: the writer uses concrete nouns and dynamic verbs. Noun phrases tend to be simple or use factual pre- and post-modification.

m	h		m	h	q		m	m	h
the	towel		the	grime	of the week		our	damp	hair
det	N		det	N	PrepP		det	AdjP	N

The function here is creative, describing what happens rather than expressing attitudes – the tone is matter-of-fact and the language used literal. The informal summary, on the other hand, uses language in a very different way because its function is expressive. It aims to communicate personal opinions and attitudes to the intended audience.

Proper nouns immediately establish key names (*Bella, Cullens*) and places (*Forks*) from the popular teen novel that is being summarised, and common nouns establish relationships ('*mother*', '*father*', *adopted* '*children*'). These form the narrative background to the novel along with lexical sets linked to vampires (*sparkly, hunting, kill, blood, POWERS*) and romance (*falls in love, married, wants to marry, unmarried*). Alongside this objective language, the writer uses modifiers to develop character: the positive connotations of adjectives like *clever, rich, fast, strong* are used to characterise the Cullen family; the negative connotations of *shallow* and *annoying* communicate the writer's attitude to the two central characters Bella and Edward. Repetition of the adjectives '*Pretty, sparkly ...*' in Bella's direct thought reinforces this sense of her as superficial. Personal opinion is also communicated through adverbs (*inexplicably, clearly*) and explicit comment (*... he's not missing much*).

The writer's attitude is most apparent, however, in the way in which language is used for comic effect: she aims to satirise the popular novel for her peer group. Repetition of the adverb intensifier *Incredibly ...!* in the minor sentences, the exaggerated use of the modifier *awesome*, the tautology of the superlative phrase *the handsomest of all the handsomes*, the non-standard spelling of *goooood* and the use of the emoticon :O to express simulated shock all create HYPERBOLE – a form of exaggeration used here to create humour. In addition, parenthesis is used for comic asides (*unmarried – clearly because ...*), and the repetitive fragments of Bella's STREAM OF CONSCIOUSNESS (*Pretty, sparkly ...*) are designed to amuse readers because they reflect the supposed triviality of her mind. Where the tone of the autobiography is sincere, the tone of this summary is ironic; the writer does not want her audience to take her language at face value. The repeated use of exclamations and the distinctive lexical choices reflect the writer's attitude to the characters and to the stereotypical romantic plot. The tongue-in-cheek commentary allows the writer to mock the original text good-humouredly .

Although the autobiographical extract was originally spoken, it has adopted the formal register of written language for publication. This means that a formal relationship is created with its intended audience. The personal and familiar tone of its oral origins, however, remains: the focus is on the domestic setting and on family relationships. Even though the terms of address are neutral (*my father, my mother*) with no names or personal vocatives, there is an underlying intimacy.

The relationship created with the intended audience for the summary is more direct. Having been placed on Facebook as a private message for specified friends and circulated via a mailing list, the audience is very clearly defined. This means that the writer and readers already have a good understanding of each other – the language and tone are therefore unlikely to be misinterpreted (for example, the use of the phrase *jumping [someone's] bones*). What is immediately noticeable is the informal tenor which is typical of the genre: although written, it is a form of electronic English which is often marked by colloquialisms (phrasal verbs such as *turns out, hangs about, goes on* and the use of the general noun 'thing' in the pre-modified noun phrase *the vampires hunting thing* ...) and linguistic features more commonly associated with speech (contractions such as *They're, isn't, that's* and free standing relative clauses *Of whom ..., Who are ...*). Other spoken features can be seen in the elliptical style (*... Bella comes to small town ...*) and in the use of initial position conjunctions (*And ..., So ..., But ...*).

The function of each of these texts is to entertain, but they use different techniques to do so. The narrative voice of the autobiography observes and records events in an almost detached way, commenting only once using the tentative stative verb *suppose*. The aim is to engage the reader through a narrative account of a personal experience which will be of interest to family members and to a general readership as a record of life in rural Norfolk in the early twentieth century. The sardonic tone of the informal summary, on the other hand, suggests that communicating attitudes is more important than the objective reporting of narrative detail. Typographical features are used to draw our attention to the different kinds of information that are communicated to the reader: bullet points (sequential ordering of plot information); listing (characters and relationships); capitalisation (comic effect); direct thought (characterisation).

The style corresponds directly to the tone and intended audience. The autobiography is formal using grammatical structures that are standard. A simple sentence opens the extract, leading the reader directly to the focus.

> S   P   Od   A
> ‹ (My father) (played) (a part) (in our Sunday Bath Night) ›.

Compound (*The bath* **would be filled** *... and ... the grime ...* **would be soaked** *and* **scrubbed** *...*) and complex (*We* **had** *... wet cloths,* *twisted* *...;* *While we bathed, our shoes* **were lined-up** *... so that my father* **could clean** *... while we* **slept***.*) sentences frame the main narrative information contained in the long compound-complex sentence at the heart of the extract.

> A   S   P   O   A   P   O   Co
> ‹ [**Passed** out ...] (my father) (**would wrap**) (us) (in the towel) › and ‹ Ø (Ø **rub**) (us) (dry)
> SCl – NFCl   conj

>   A
> [before **passing** us on to grandmother [who **would plait** ... [so that we **had** ...]]] › –
> SCl – ACl   SCl – RelCl   SCl – ACl

> S   P   C   S   P
> ‹ (Dodeman) (**was**) (the Norfolk name [given ...]) › and ‹ (I) (**suppose**)
>   SCl – NFCl   conj

>   Od
> [Ø the curls **were named** ...] ›
> SCl – NCl

As is typical of narrative, the sentences are dominated by adverbials providing information about time (*in our Sunday Bath Night*), place (*in front of the fire*), manner (*from wet cloths*) and reason (*so that my father could clean the row of them*).

The sentence structures in the summary are far more varied and often use structures associated with speech. Many are short and simple (*They're vampires.*) or are grammatical fragments (*Incredibly nice smelling!*). The longer sentences have a loose structure and are mostly compound-complex.

‹ Of [whom the handsomest of all the handsomes **is** Edward.] › And ‹ [as soon as she

SCl – RelCl   conj   SCl – ACl

            S   P   A   A   A
sees him] (she) **(falls)** (in love) [because she **is** a shallow little girl] and [Ø he **is** pretty] ›.

                                     SCl – ACl   conj SCl – ACl

Clauses are often joined by punctuation rather than conjunctions, which means that many sentences consist of sequences of short main clauses. This is typical of the genre and reflects the link to informal spoken language.

            S   P   S   P   O   S   P   O
‹(Jasper and Alice) (are married)›; ‹(he) (can control) (emotions)›, ‹(she) (sees) (the future)›.

Similarly, fronted elliptical relative clauses, fronted conjunctions and the use of listing focus the readers' attention by foregrounding key information in an informal way. These kinds of grammatical features along with the structural lists in which verbs are replaced by a symbol (= replaces the stative verbs 'is' or 'are') ensure that most sentences remain relatively short.

While informing a friend of the background to the new film, the writer of Text 2 is also aiming to entertain the other readers on the circulation list. Her style is therefore appropriately tongue-in-cheek, adopting linguistic and grammatical features associated with electronic English and the language and tone of comic discourse. This makes Text 2 very different from the autobiography in which language is used literally for informative and descriptive purposes.

TASK 5

1 Choose one of the following writing exercises. When you have completed your text, evaluate the key linguistic features. You may like to use the suggested framework for analysis in Appendix A.

EITHER

Tape and transcribe an informal conversation between friends – make sure the participants are happy for you to record their interaction. Make notes on the register, and analyse the sentence structure.

Re-write the informal spoken text as a formal written text – for example as a narrative or a film script.

You need to think carefully about the change in genre and register, and the effect this will have on the content, the layout, the lexis and the grammatical structures.

OR

Choose one of the topics listed below and use it as the focus for a sequence of short pieces of writing which have the same theme but different registers. If you prefer, you may choose your own topic and text types.

FINANCE
- a personal diary entry exploring plans for earning money to buy something you've wanted for a long time

- a newspaper report focusing on the effects of a recession on ordinary people
- a scene from a comic play in which someone asks their bank manager for a business loan to develop an eccentric product commercially
- a blog about managing your money

LOVE

- a poem or song lyrics describing the effects of love
- an extract from an autobiography reflecting on past love
- a twitter feed on the public nature of 'celebrity' love
- a formal speech at a wedding reception about the bride and groom

POLITICS

- an election campaign leaflet persuading householders to support a particular political party
- a worksheet informing students about some key terms and setting them research tasks
- an informal conversation about a current political issue
- an essay about different voting systems

You need to think carefully about the intended audience, the relationship between participants, the purpose, and the lexical and grammatical choices in each case.

OR

Find an example of a subject specific text book and choose an extract from it. Represent the content in a form suitable for a class presentation with accompanying hand-outs.

You need to think carefully about the change in mode and tenor, and the way in which you can make the content appealing to your audience. You may find it useful to create a computer-slide presentation to illustrate the points you make in your talk.

11.2 Text Types

Each text type uses language distinctively according to its function and intended audience. In identifying the focus of the content, the lexical choices, the layout and the organisation, we can begin to understand how meaning is created. Recognising the distinctive features associated with a particular text type is important because it allows us to notice when writers or speakers do something unexpected.

TASK 1   The relationship between text type, language, function and audience

1 Read through the following texts and identify the text type.

TEXT 1

MEASUREMENTS
To fit chest 81 (86:91) cm
Length to shoulder 66 (69:72) cm

MATERIALS
17 (18:19) 50g balls Pure Wool in black
Pair 4mm and 5mm knitting needles
Cable needle
The tension for this design is 21 sts in width and 23 rows to 10cm measured over the
pattern using 5mm needles
PATT PANEL
Worked across 19 sts
1st Row   (RS) K1 tbl, p6, k2, p1, k2, p6, k1 tbl.
2nd Row   P1, k6, p2, k1, p2, k6, p1.
3rd Row   K1 tbl, p6, Cr5, p6, k1 tbl.
4th Row   As Row 2.
5th Row   K1 tbl, p5, Cr3B, k1, Cr3F, p5, k1 tbl.
...

BACK
Remember to check your tension
Using 4mm needles, co 110 (114:118) sts.
1st Row   (RS) K2, [p2, k2] to end.
2nd Row   P2, [k2, p2] to end.
Rep these 2 rows until rib measures 10cm, ending with 1st Row.
Next row Rib 5(7:3), * inc in next st, rib 9 (9:7); rep from * to last 5(7:3) sts, inc in next
st, rib to end. 121 (125:133) sts.
Change to 5mm needles and begin pattern ...

TEXT 2

a once in a life time opportunity (.) I am here in the Techniquest science museum wit-
nessing Venus progress the sun (.) a historic event but too many <u>clouds</u> ↓to see it↓
the sun has ↑cleared↑ but still no Venus (.) more than twenty people here <u>still</u> (2) we (.)
I do not think anyone has seen the transit (10) finally I have seen Venus on the sunspotter which is a telescope which projects the sun onto a piece of paper (3) Venus is at
seven o'clock on the sun starting to move across its surface (.) now I have seen (2)
Venus through the glasses they're so mm ah umm ah they are sō um they are sō um
they are so thick [laughs] that with them on the <u>only</u> thing you can see is the sun
Nine-year-old boy's account of the transit of Venus 8 June 2004

TEXT 3

Bruckner and Britten
FRI
25.11.11   7.00 PM
TICKETS
£6-8

STRAVINSKY   Mass
BRITTEN   Russian Funeral
BRUCKNER   Mass No 2 (E minor)
Conductor   **Hans Königsburg**

Simple and enduring, powerful and
moving, Bruckner's Second Mass is

a nineteenth century masterpiece.
Alongside the dignity of Stravinsky's
Mass and the creativity of Britten, this
will be a concert to lift you from the
autumnal gloom.

TEXT 4

	9.00–9.50	10.00–10.50	11.10–12.00	12.10–1.00	1.10–2.00	2.10–3.00
MON	Integral Equations M/1.03	Further Topics in Probability M/1.03	Integral Equations (even weeks) M/1.03			Linear Spaces and Operators M/1.12
TUES				Regression Analysis Wallace Lecture Theatre	Integral Equations M/1.03	
WED	Further Topics in Probability M/1.03			Linear Spaces and Operators (odd weeks) M/1.12		

TEXT 5

2C. INT. KITCHEN – DAY

In the shadow of a corner cowers a figure, a crude, crumpled human-shaped figurine
made of straw and tinder, reminiscent of a pagan idol. Its head hangs loose from its
shoulders, violently ripped from the torso.

2B. INT. DINING-HALL – DAY

A snail crawls along a cracked and splintered window frame. Has there been movement outside in the grass?

Someone approaches through the weeds. The person approaching is humming to
himself, thus audible to us before he eventually can be spotted through the uncontrolled growth. It's a boy of eleven years, though small and puny even for that age –
KEVIN. He wears an old-fashioned, formal dress reminiscent of a school uniform –
white shirt, grey vest and knee-long trousers. His gaze is turned to the ground as he
obliviously strokes through the weeds around him with a stick ....

2C. contd. KITCHEN – DAY

Kevin enters the room. Almost immediately his gaze falls on the damaged figurine. A
sad, resigned expression flashes over his features. He looks around. In the centre of
the room he sees burnt residues of tin foil, broken glass, a puddle of spilled liquid,
empty beer cans, cigarette butts. He kneels down and starts to collect the litter ...

Carefully, with the tenderness of a nurse, he puts the figurine's head back into position. Then he grabs into his pocket and pulls from it his tools: rusty nails, a piece of chalk and a crumpled bundle of different sorts of string and thread. With the assuredness of someone who has done it many times, he re-connects the head to the body with a few knots.

KEVIN
to the figurine
Silly. You have to be more careful.

2 Drawing on your knowledge of text types and the frameworks of language, compare and contrast the five texts paying particular attention to the genre, the intended audience and the function in each case.

You may like to think about:

- the mode
- the content and tone
- the lexical choice
- the phrase and sentence structure
- the layout and organisation

COMMENTARY

Texts 3 (advertisement) and 2 (spontaneous commentary) both combine the communication of information with a secondary function: Text 3 is persuasive and Text 2 expressive. This combination of functions and the intended audience in each case affects the kind of language used. The tenor is impersonal in the advertisement because it is aimed at a large, unknown audience; the commentary, on the other hand, is personal, addressed to a small, known audience. Both, however, are focusing on what can be seen as a subject specific field (classical music; an astronomical phenomenon) and this inevitably means that the audience will be narrow.

The content is shaped by the text type, the function of the text and the relationship between the writer/speaker and the audience. Because the advertisement is an informative text, factual language providing information about the day, date, time, price and works to be played at the concert are all listed at the start. These are facts that can be checked and are therefore objective. Numbers and proper nouns recur, with bold print to draw attention to the importance of the information. While Text 2 does contain facts (Venus will travel across the surface of the sun; there are more than 20 people; there are lots of clouds), these are secondary to the subjective viewpoint presented in the commentary. This is all about personal experience and an expression of the feelings the occasion evokes in one particular nine-year-old boy.

The language of Text 4 is completely functional: it provides information about times, courses and rooms for each day of the week. Even though the text is intended for a narrow specialist audience, anyone looking at the timetable would recognise the text type and would understand its purpose. The discourse is unambiguous because the facts can be interpreted in only one way. While the first half of Text 3 is also objective, the second half has a different function and therefore adopts a different lexical field, using words that will persuade the reader to buy tickets. As is typical of the text type, the positive connotations of the words shape our response: the abstract nouns (*masterpiece, dignity, creativity*) and the emphatic compound adjective phrases (*Simple and enduring, powerful and moving*) encourage us to view the concert favourably. The positive mood is reinforced by the complex post-modified noun phrase at the end of the text.

> m   h   q
> a concert [to lift you from the autumnal gloom]
> det N   NFCl

The seasonal reference is effective since it sets the negative mood of *autumnal,* symbolic of things coming to an end, and *gloom* against the positive connotations of the dynamic verb *lift.* To understand the symbolism, however, readers need to have a shared experience of autumn as a season of drizzle, mists and dark cold evenings.

Text 2 is more explicitly personal and subjective – unlike text 3, which expresses a specific opinion but creates little sense of a personal voice. Where the tone of the advertisement remains impersonal and detached, the speaker of the spontaneous commentary is directly engaged, expressing feelings as well as recording observations. While this is typical of the genre, the emphasis on the expression of feelings is also directly linked to the age of the speaker and the intended audience (fellow pupils and his teacher). Dramatic premodified noun phrases draw attention to the unique nature of the experience: although the transit happens twice in eight years, there are then gaps of more than a hundred years, so after the 2012 transit, there will not be another one until 2117.

> m   m   h   m   m   h
> a (once in a life time) opportunity   a historic event
> det   AdvP   N   det AdjP   N
>   Adv PrepP

The emphatic present tense and the immediacy of the –*ing* participle in the first grammatically complete sentence also create a sense of drama.

> S   P   A   A   A
> ⟨(I) (am) (here) (in the Techniquest science museum) [**witnessing** Venus progress the sun]⟩.
>   SCl – NFCl

Mirroring the kind of introductions heard on news programmes, the boy creates a sense of time and place in the authoritative tone of a seasoned journalist reporting as events take place around him. The effect is humorous for an adult audience and is reinforced by the juxtaposition of the noun phrases balanced by the contrastive conjunction *but* in the next utterance.

> m   m   h   m   h   q
> a historic event but (too many) clouds [to see it]
> det AdjP   N   conj   AdjP   N   NFCl

Similarly, the overly formal use of *progress* as a transitive verb reminds us that the commentator is a child emulating the role of a presenter. In current usage, 'progress' is an intransitive verb (meaning 'to go forwards', 'to make progress', 'to go on or continue') – its transitive meaning is now obsolete.

Where Text 3 is non-chronological, Text 2 is chronological and this is typical of spontaneous commentaries which recount the development of a particular occasion (for example, the state opening of parliament, a royal wedding, a sports event). The passage of time is marked here with *still, finally, now* (adverbs of time), and with references to Venus in the negative noun phrase *no Venus*, in the present perfective clause which marks a completed event *I have seen Venus* and the simple present tense clause which marks a current event *Venus is at seven o'clock*. In addition, the long timed pause of ten seconds – which is unusual for this text type – represents a period where the boy has nothing to say because he sees nothing change. A more experienced commentator would continue to speak since a ten-second pause may suggest a break-down in transmission in a more formal context.

Like Text 3, the commentary is also informative. It includes facts about the location (the noun phrase *Techniquest science museum*), the number of people present (the comparative noun phrase *more than twenty people*), and a definition of a sunspotter (the relative clause *which is a telescope which projects the sun onto a piece of paper*). The repetition of the first person pronoun *I* and the self-referential laugh, which accompanies the boy's surprise on looking through the glasses, however, is more typical of a subjective rather than an objective text. The voice here is clearly personal and the non-fluency features suggest an inexperienced commentator. The repetition of the incomplete clause *they are so* and the fillers (*mm, ah, umm*) prevent there being a hiatus in the commentary as the boy experiments with the glasses. The laugh accompanies his realisation that their thickness blocks out everything except the light from the sun.

The advertisement is typical of a written mode: it is carefully polished, with thematic initial position complements (*Simple and enduring, powerful and moving*) and adverbials (*Alongside the dignity of Stravinsky's Mass and the creativity of Britten*) to engage the reader. The tightness of the structure can be seen in the demonstrative pronoun *this*: it is both an anaphoric reference backwards to the positive presentation of the concert in the previous sentence and a cataphoric reference forwards to the persuasive final noun phrase. The effect is cyclical, underpinned by the certainty of the emphatic modal verb phrase (*will be*).

The commentary, on the other hand, is spontaneous and informal. It has features typical of a spoken mode: some grammatical units are incomplete with noun phrases functioning as minor sentences (*a once in a lifetime opportunity*); the demonstrative pronoun 'this', the dummy subject 'there' and the verb 'to be' are elided (Ø *a historic event but* Ø *too many clouds to see it*). Self-correction (*we (.) I*), the repetition of the relative pronoun *which*, and the non-fluency features are also typical of spoken language. Although elements of informality or non-fluency can be associated with the text type, professional commentators are remarkably polished in their extended turns. The non-fluency features here are indicative of the speaker's age and lack of experience.

The layout of the advertisement is typical in that it uses typographical features to highlight key points. The names of two of the three composers are highlighted in bold, with the alliteration of **Bruckner** and **Britten** making the heading more eye-catching. Bold capitalised print then focuses on practical information so that readers are immediately aware of the date and the price of tickets. Because the concert is starting half an hour earlier than usual, the time is brought to prominence in a star. The informative section concludes with a list of the composers and works included in the performance. While the music will persuade some people to attend a concert, others may be drawn by a particular conductor. In this advertisement therefore, the conductor's name is in bold to attract attention.

As a written record of the spoken mode, the transcript uses linguistic conventions to try to replicate the nature of speech on the page. They give us a sense of the delivery of the speech as well as its content. Underlined words mark stresses where the speaker draws attention to key words (_clouds_, _still_). Pairs of upward arrows indicate raised pitch as the speaker marks a change in the occasion (↑_cleared_↑) and downward arrows indicate a lowered pitch (↓_to see it_↓) reflecting his sense of anti-climax. Numbers in round brackets show us where pauses are timed because they are more significant than the minimal pauses which often function as an equivalent to sentence punctuation. Square brackets highlight additional vocal effects which give us a sense of the speaker's relationship with his topic. These written conventions are used to help us see the difference between an account of what someone has said (focusing only on the content) and a transcript which also considers how the speech is delivered.

The intended audience of Text 1 (knitting pattern), like that for Texts 2 and 3, is narrow because its field is also subject specific, alienating the general reader with its abbreviations and technical language. The content is restrictive, containing only subject specific references that will be interpreted in the same way by every reader. The function is instructive and its meaning is unambiguous – if followed correctly, the end product will always be the same. Text 5 (film script, from 'Boys Village', written and directed by Till Kleinert), on the other hand, has a creative function – the language is descriptive and the content focuses on using words to communicate a strong visual sense of atmosphere, place and character. The script therefore represents a set of written directions which guide the immediate audience (the director, cameraman, sound crew and so on). Unlike an instructive text, the language of a creative text is open: each reader brings a personal element to the visualisation process and it is the director's role to shape and direct the ultimate sequence of images arising from the written text. When the script becomes a film, the audience is larger and broader, distant and unknown. Since viewers are guided by the director's editing of the material, the appearance of the physical setting and actors, and the addition of music to build the atmosphere, the final film is less open to different interpretations.

The language and tone of Texts 1 and 5 reflect this difference in the relationship between the text and the intended audience. Text 1 is impersonal: it develops no sense of the writer and creates no relationship with the intended audience, aiming only to engage the reader in a sequence of physical actions. It uses the imperative mood throughout. Text 5, however, needs to engage the reader in a creative process – the words need to forge a link between the imagination of the writer/director and the production team with whom he will be working. The voice is distinctive and personal, guiding our eye to key details of the scene and appealing to our senses. All the verb phrases in the main clauses are present tense (_hangs_, _approaches_, _enters_), which is typical of the genre. It helps to create a sense of immediacy, mimicking the panning of a camera over the scene.

Some words linked directly to knitting may be understandable to a general audience (_rib_, _knitting needles_, _Cable needle_, _pattern_), but the abbreviations are often quite unfamiliar and would need to be glossed. While we may be able to deduce some abbreviations (*Patt* – pattern, *rep* – repeat, *sts* – stitches, *inc* – increase), others need clarification. References to specific kinds of stitches (*k* – knit, *p* – purl, *K1 tbl* – knit one stitch through the back of the loop), to specific actions (*Cr3B* – slip 2 stitches purlwise onto the cable needle and leave at the back of the knitting; knit 1 stitch from the left needle; knit 2 stitches from the cable needle; *Cr3F* – slip 1 stitch purlwise onto the cable needle and leave at the front of the knitting; knit 2 stitches from the left needle; knit 1 stitch from the cable needle), and to casting on (*co*) are impenetrable for a non-specialist audience. Text 5 also uses some abbreviations for its specialist audience: **INT** (internal) and **contd** (continued) are references relevant to the production team.

Because the function of Text 1 is unambiguous, the grammatical structures tend to be straightforward. Noun phrases are mostly simple and few determiners are used. The only modification is factual.

m	h		m	h		m	h		m	m	h
4mm needles			cable needle			23 rows			these 2 rows		
num	N		N	N		num	N		det	num	N

The style is elliptical with noun phrases often reduced to a number where the head ('stitches') is understood (*K2* – knit **2 stitches**). Verb phrases are imperative (*K, Rep, inc, rib, Change to, work*), except where they occur as adverbial non-finite (*using 5mm needles, ending with 1st Row*) and finite clauses (*until rib measures ...*). The only declarative sentence gives readers a specific tension guide to ensure that the finished product matches the given measurements.

	S		P		C		A
‹ (The tension for this design)		(is)		(21 sts in width and 23 rows to 10cm)		[measured	
						conj	SCl –NFCl

	A	
over the pattern using 5mm needles] ›.		
SCl – NFCl		

The grammatical structures of Text 5 are very different because it is evocative and emotive, quite distinct from the impersonal tone of an instruction text. It works on two levels: it provides direction for the actor, but it also guides reader response. The three scenes each introduce a key element: the figurine, the boy and the kitchen. The language is therefore descriptive, with long noun phrases and strings of noun phrases using both pre- and post-modification to provide detailed representations of physical appearance.

m	m		m		m		h	q			q
a	crude,	crumpled	(human-shaped)		figurine		[made of straw and tinder],	[Ø reminiscent of...]			
det	AdjP		Ved		N		Ved	N	NFCl		RelCl

m		m		m	h	q	
an		(old-fashioned),		formal	dress	[Ø reminiscent of a school uniform]	
det		AdjP		AdjP	N	RelCl	

m	h	q		m	h	m	h	q		m	m	h
burnt	residues	of tin foil,		broken	glass,	a	puddle	of spilled liquid,		empty	beer	cans,
Ved	N	PrepP		Ved	N	det	N	PrepP		AdjP	N	N

m	h
cigarette	butts
N	N

The attention to detail creates a strong contextual link between the starting point (words on the page) and the end product (a film). It engages the audience and draws them into the created world.

The writer's choice of lexis dictates the kind of mood developed, determining the type of shots taken and influencing audience response. There is a sense of desolation in the descriptions of the broken figurine and the dilapidated environment. The negative connotations of modifiers like *violently, cracked and splintered, damaged, sad, resigned* create a bleak tone, which is reinforced by references to the natural world. The repetition of *weeds* and the noun phrase *the uncontrolled growth* suggest that this place has been abandoned: nature is now free from the order imposed upon it by people. The only suggestions of human activity are indirect: in the *–ed* participle *ripped* and the descriptions of the litter. There is no movement except in the present tense verb phrase *crawls* which describes the snail's insignificant passage across the damaged window frame.

The entrance of the boy, however, changes the mood and draws the audience's attention away from the physical environment. The rhetorical question (*Has there been movement outside in the grass?*), the use of indirect references (the pronoun *Someone*; the general noun *person*) and the fact that the boy is heard before he is seen creates suspense, engaging the audience with the fictional world. Physical description of the boy's appearance (*small, puny*), his clothing (*old-fashioned*) and his mood (*sad, resigned*) create an immediate sense of character. This is developed in the description of his actions: collecting up the litter, mending the figurine. The unexpected use of the dynamic verb *strokes* sets the boy apart from the devastation of the setting. Its connotations of delicacy and tenderness prepare the audience for his interaction with the figurine. The adverb *Carefully* and the prepositional phrases *with the tenderness of a nurse* and *With the assuredness of someone who has done it many times* reinforce the positive mood of the verb.

Although both Texts 1 and 5 are chronological, their structures are quite different. The knitting pattern depends on a sequence of actions which must be carried out in a particular order. There is, therefore, an emphasis on numerical references (the number of stitches for each particular size, the number of stitches to be knitted or purled). The marked themes are short noun or prepositional phrases, drawing attention to the row number (*1st Row ... 2nd Row ... Next row*) or the needles required (*Using 4mm needles*). Adverbials tend to be prepositional phrases (*to end, in next st*) which are repeated.

As a creative text, the structure of the script is far more complex. The fronted adverbial of the opening sentence immediately focuses our attention on a particular part of the room.

A	P	S	S

‹ (In the shadow of a corner) (cowers) (a figure) (a crude, crumpled human-shaped

figurine [made of straw and tinder], [Ø reminiscent of a pagan idol]) ›.
    NFCl   RelCl

The inversion of the subject and verb moves the verb to a stressed position where the negative connotations set the mood, preparing us for the adverb *violently* and the dynamic verb *ripped* in the next sentence. In addition, the delayed double subect creates suspense – we move from the general noun *figure* to the long pre- and post-modified noun phrase which provides the audience with a very visual image. Other fronted adverbials focus on time (*Almost immediately, Then*), place (*In the centre of the room*) and manner (*Carefully*). In each case, the information provided guides the actor or focuses the camera on important details.

Unlike the knitting pattern, the sentences in Text 5 are very varied. Many are simple, but they are not repetitive because of the wide range of lexical choices and phrase structure.

```
        S    P                        C
< (It) ('s) (a boy of 11 years though small and puny for his age) >.
```

```
        S        P        Od
< (Kevin) (enters) (the room) >.
```

```
              S              P        A
< (A sad, resigned expression) (flashes)(over his features) >.
```

The complex sentences are equally varied, using subordinate clauses to provide descriptive detail.

```
        S        P          A                        A
< (His gaze) (is turned) (to the ground) [as he obliviously strokes through the weeds ...] >.
                                    SCl – ACl
```

The style and structure are typical of creative texts, where the writer aims to engage the reader in a fictional reality, using words to develop strong visual images.

Despite having very different styles, the layout in each case uses recognised conventions. Both texts use bold headings as a short cut to indicate the focus of each section and to divide the content into sequential units. Where Text 1 relies on lists of instructions, Text 5 uses conventional prose paragraphs which are typical of formal written English. Other typographical features are linked to the genre. The parenthetical capitalised *KEVIN* individualises the boy who has been described in such detail. By naming him, the writer indicates his importance to the narrative. The centralised capitalised heading marks the movement away from descriptive prose which aims to create a visual image. It prepares us for the direct speech and thus a different kind of characterisation: the boy is now characterised directly through self-presentation rather than through observation. The italicised font gives specific stage directions to the actor.

Each of the texts here adopt frameworks of language that are linked to the intended audience and purpose. Their effectiveness relies on the ability of the writer or speaker to manipulate language and structure to engage the audience, whether the focus is on persuading people to buy something, describing events and responding to them, instructing or entertaining.

TASK 2

1 Choose one of the following writing exercises. When you have completed your text(s), evaluate the key linguistic features using the framework in Appendix A.

EITHER

Take a topical issue and write your own report for broadcast on a particular television or radio progamme, making sure that your report is suitable for the broad cast medium, the type of programme and the time slot you have chosen.

Think carefully about the register, the treatment of the content, the structure, the organisation and the lexical and grammatical choices.

OR

Using your knowledge of spoken language, record a spontaneous commentar (to accompany a sports event, or a special public or private occasion). Transcrib the text. Re-write your 'spoken' text, re-framing the spontaneous commentar as a newspaper report.

Think carefully about the differences between speech and writing, the intended audi ence, the organisation of the content, any additions or omissions, and the kind c lexical and grammatical features associated with the text type.

OR

Find some examples of texts where writers or speakers move between differen text types and registers for comic effect – for example, the 'holy hand grenade scene in the film 'Monty Python and the Holy Grail', or the Second World Wa RAF chav pilots from 'The Armstrong and Miller Show'.
   Write an extract from a script or a novel exploiting the comic possibilitie created by a clash of unexpected registers and text types. Choose a context an characters, then decide on a register that we would not expect them to use.

You need to think about the language and register you would expect your character to use according to their context, and the linguistic features of the register yo intend to use instead. You will need to adapt the lexis, grammatical structures an layout according to the register and text type you choose to use.

11.3 Context

The wider situation (see pages 219–20) and circumstances (pages 220–1) of a tex affect the linguistic and grammatical choices a speaker or writer makes, and th way in which an audience receives it. Asking ourselves questions about when an where a text was produced, and about the background of a speaker or writer help us to identify key contextual features. This kind of information underpins ou understanding of the way meaning is constructed.

TASK 1   Context and text type

1 Read through each group of texts.

TEXT 1   Extract from a spontaneous informal conversation

SPEAKER 1   what about the Turkish holiday?
SPEAKER 2   ah I should get to tell you about the flight back mm which might take
            minute or five [laugh]

SPEAKER 1 oh yes

SPEAKER 2 we were delayed for three hours and when we got on the plane they said the reason it was delayed was because umm before the plane left Bristol (.) they'd were being refuelled (.) that was no problem and the bloke refuelling it (1) drove off without disconnecting it (.) and pulled the side of the plane ‖off

SPEAKER 1 ‖nō

SPEAKER 2 and then they had to [laugh] and then they had to charter a plane to go and get a new panel (2) for the plane (1) fit it (1) and I'm thinking (1) three hours (2) that's not a lot of time to do all that (1) n wondering if they've tested it (1) there was all these knocking noises when we took off (1) terrified me

SPEAKER 1 taking off from where

SPEAKER 2 we were coming back from Turkey with a plane that had the problems coming over in the ‖morning

SPEAKER 1 ‖mmm

SPEAKER 2 we were thinking three hours is a long time to wait but when you think three hours to replace a side of a plane is not a lot ‖really

SPEAKER 1 ‖[laugh] you'd rather

they take a bit more ‖time

SPEAKER 2 ‖yeah

TEXT 2   News report from a tabloid newspaper

ENGINE BLAST PANICS PASSENGERS

A MID-FLIGHT explosion and clouds of debris led to panic yesterday. And a Sky-Go plane had to make an emergency landing.

Passengers saw smoke and flames coming from a blackened engine. Then a worrying hole appeared on the wing. Sandie Rider, 43, from Bristol, said: "It was terrifying. I thought it was the end. People were screaming."

The Sky-Go plane developed prob-lems minutes into the flight. It had to circle for nearly two hours to dump fuel before it could return to the airport. No-one was hurt. But many people were shaken.

The incident has raised questions about the safety of the Sky-Go 376. The airline has grounded its entire fleet while investigators look into the cause. And hard-pressed passengers will once more have to face on-going disruptions.

TEXT 3   Extract from an official airline accident report

SYNOPSIS

On July 17th 1994, Airflight 791 took off from Newtown Airport. After take-off the flight continued on a scenic route up Damston Valley, towards Blacklime Pass (elevation 12,937 feet above mean sea level). Mountains along the flightpath reached between 13,431 feet AMSL and 14,926 feet AMSL. At approximately 1700 GMT, the aircraft crashed into Mount Tregane, 8 miles west of Grangewood Park. The crash site is at an elevation of 11,990 feet AMSL.

Weather conditions during the flight and at the point of collision were reported as fine and clear. No records of turbulence, or up- and downdraft activity were logged and no disturbance was recalled by the surviving co-pilot or passengers.

A total of 100 persons were on board with 75, including the captain and a stewardess, receiving fatal injuries. Five of the surviving passengers were later to die because of injuries received in the crash.

Investigation revealed that the aircraft struck the tops of the trees at an elevation of 11,985 feet AMSL in an area of dense woods. The aircraft continued for a distance of 425 feet from the initial point of contact on a heading of 215° magnetic, on a 4° descending flightpath.

The aircraft was destroyed by the impact and the ensuing fire. Teardown of the engines and investigation of the propeller mechanism proved that the engines were functioning normally at impact.

The aircraft ultimately came to rest on its left side with the vertical stabiliser leaning at an angle of approximately 25°. Many pieces of the main body were ripped off and subsequently found along the tree swath path. The wings were torn away from the attach poles. The empennage was split from the fuselage 2 feet forward of the aft pressure bulkhead. High temperatures entirely reduced the fuselage to molten aluminium, which was found to contain the remains of the burnt carbon fibre longerons and stringers.

2   Make notes on the way in which the context affects the language and style.

You may like to think about:

- the circumstances and situation
- the function and register
- the relationship between the content and the intended audience
- the appropriateness of the lexical and grammatical choices
- any similarities and/or differences between the texts

TEXT 3

The circumstances and situation

	Tabloid report	Informal conversation	Accident report
Circumstances	Professional National Dramatic event Cultural relevance (UK company/ airport) Journalism	Middle-aged participants Familiar Personal experience	Professional Geographical relevance to area where plane crashed Subject specific language Experts
Situation	Daily newspaper	Informal interaction	Official report Restricted circulation

	Public Contemporary Day after event (recent) Account of dramatic event	Home (private) Contemporary Distant (event in past) Humorous retelling of personal experience	Public Contemporary Distant (event in past) Analysis of events, causes/effects

Function and register

	Tabloid report	Informal conversation	Accident report
Main function	Informative	Phatic Informative	Informative
Subordinate function	Expressive	Expressive	
Register: Mode	Written	Spoken	Written
Register: Tenor	Quite formal Large, wide, unknown, distant audience	Informal Small, known, immediate audience	Formal Medium, specialist, unknown, distant audience
Register: Field	Aeroplane explosion Non-specialist	Flight delay Non-specialist	Aeroplane accident Specialist Subject specific

The relationship between content and intended audience

	Tabloid report	Informal conversation	Accident report
Content	Dramatic Emotive General Emphasis on passengers	Narrative Humorous General Emphasis on personal experience	Factual Detailed Specific Emphasis on technical
Audience	Large Wide-ranging Unknown Distant Impersonal relationship	Small Narrow Known Immediate Personal relationship	Medium Narrow Unknown Distant Professional relationship

The lexical choices

Tabloid

▶ **repetition of proper noun** *Sky-Go* to establish direct link between a particular
company and the disaster (sensational)

- **dramatic nouns**: *explosion, panic, emergency, smoke and flames, the end*
- **emotive modifiers and verbs**: *blackened, worrying, terrifying; screaming, shaken*
- **dramatic juxtaposition**: *minutes/nearly two hours*
- **direct speech** maintains tension by giving a voice to one of the passengers directly involved
- **neutral connotations** of *The incident* undermine the drama created in the first three paragaphs
- focus on **what happens next**: *questions, safety, grounded, investigators, cause, on-going disruptions*
- **variety of verbs** performing different functions: past tense verbs provide a narrative of events (*saw, developed*), present perfective verbs describe events begun in the past with present relevance (*has raised, has grounded*), present tense verbs highlight the current course of action (*look into*), and future time references indicate the effect of these actions (*will ... have to*)
- **attitude** towards passengers: *hard-pressed* (i.e., supportive)

Informal conversation

- **topic** related: *flight, delayed, plane, refuelled, refuelling, charter*
- **general words** used in a narrow context: *side, panel*
- **dramatic mood**: *all these knocking noises, terrified me*
- **direct thought** and **progressive aspect** create a sense of immediacy: *and I'm thinking ..., we were thinking ...*
- **time references** creating humour: *a minute or five, three hours* (repeated), *a long time to wait ... not a lot really*
- **informal**: *bloke, n* (and)
- **affirmation** highlighting positive relationship between participants: *[laugh], oh yes, nō, mmm, yeah,*
- **reinforcement** showing that the story has been understood: *you'd rather they take a bit more time*
- **normal non-fluency**: *ah, umm, they'd were being refuelled, they had to ... and then they had to*
- **non-standard**: *there was all these knocking noises*

Accident report

- **subject specific**: *flightpath, turbulence, up- and downdraft activity, fuselage, longerons* (thin metal or carbon fibre strips in the fuselage attached to frames running from front to back of an aircraft), *stringers* (thin metal or carbon fibre strips attached only to the skin of an aircraft), *empennage* (tail section of an aircraft), *pressure bulkhead* (vertical partition dividing an aircraft hull into separate compartments), *vertical stabiliser* (upward-pointing fins which are part of the empennage; also known as vertical tail), *swath path* (band of damage caused by the plane's path through the trees and undergrowth)
- **numerical references**: *elevation 12,937 feet above mean sea level, 13,431 feet AMSL* (height), *1700 GMT* (time), *8 miles west* (location), *100 persons, Five*

(quantity), *a heading of 215° magnetic, a 4° descending flightpath* (direction), *a distance of 425 feet, 2 feet forward* (distance), July 17th 1994 (date)

- **proper nouns**: *Airflight 791, Newtown Airport, Damston Valley, Blacklime Pass, Mount Tregane, Grangewood Park*
- **geographical references**: *a scenic route, Mountains, an area of dense woods*
- **recurring lexis**: *crashed, crash site, the crash*
- **simple past tense** verbs recording events: *took off, continued, crashed*
- **passive** verbs recording findings of the investigation: *was destroyed, were ripped off, were torn away, was split*
- **descriptive words**: *fine, clear* (adjectives defining weather condiitons), *fatal* (causing death), *entirely* (adverb of degree emphasising extent of burning), *molten ... burnt* (modifiers emphasising the extent of the damage to the fuse-lage)
- **dynamic verbs** with negative connotations: *crashed, destroyed, ripped off, torn away, split*

The grammatical choices

Tabloid

- lots of **simple noun phrases** (*smoke, Bristol, many people*)
- **pre-modification** can be factual or descriptive

m	m	h		m	m	h	
A	(mid-flight)	explosion		The	(Sky-Go)	plane	FACTUAL
det	Adj	N	N	det	N	V	N

m	m	h		m		h	
a	blackened	engine		(hard-pressed)		passengers	DESCRIPTIVE
det	Ved	N		Adv	Ved	N	

- **post-modification** is prepositional

	h	q		h	q	
	clouds	of debris		questions	about the safety	of the Sky-Go 376
	N	PrepP		N	PrepP	PrepP

- **sentences** tend to be quite short (approximately nine words per sentence)
- **sentence types**: more simple than complex sentences, with three initial position conjunctions which divide sentences into more easily manageable units

A	S	P	A		S	P	C	SIMPLE
⟨ (Then)	(a worrying hole)	(appeared)	(on the wing) ⟩.		⟨ (No-one)	(was)	(hurt) ⟩.	

S	P	Od		A		COMPLEX
⟨ (The airline)	(has grounded)	(its entire fleet)		[while investigators look into ....] ⟩.		
				SCl – ACl		

	S	P	A	P	Od		COMPLEX
⟨ And	(hard-pressed passengers)	(will)	(once more)	(have to)	[face ....] ⟩.		
conj			mod	verb idiom	NFCl (base form verb)		

Informal conversation

- mostly **simple noun phrases** (*we, the plane, no problem, three hours*)

> **modification** defines specific details

m	m	h		m	m	m	h	
a	new	panel		all	these	knocking	noises	PRE-MODIFICATION
det	AdjP	N		pre-det	det	*Ving*	N	

m	h	q		m	h	q	
the	bloke	[refuelling it]		the	side	of the plane	POST-MODIFICATION
det	N	NFCl		det	N	PrepP	

A mixture of sentence types ranging from four word questions (*what about the Turkish holiday?*) to a rambling loosely co-ordinated 100 word utterance made up of 22 clauses (eight main and 14 subordinate)

MCl S		P			A	MCl	S	P
⟨ (we)		**(were delayed)** ⟩ ...	and	⟨	[when	we got on the plane]	(they)	**(said)**
			conj		SCl – ACl			

INDIRECT SPEECH			Od		
[Ø the reason	[Ø it was delayed]	was	[because	[before the plane left Bristol]	they'd
SCl – NCl	SCl – NCl		SCl – ACl	SCl – ACl	

		MCl		Od	
were being refuelled]	⟨ that **was** no problem ⟩	and	[Ø the bloke	[refuelling it]	
	COMMENT CLAUSE	conj	SCl – ACl	NFCl	

		MCl S		P		S	P
drove off without [disconnecting it]]] ⟩	and ...	⟨ (they)		**(had to)** ⟩	and	⟨ (they)	**(had to)**
SCl – NFCl		conj				conj	

Od		A		Od		MCl S	P		MCl S DIRECT THOUGHT
[charter ...]		[to go and get ...]		[Ø fit ...] ⟩	and	⟨ (I)	**('m thinking)** ⟩	⟨	(three hours)
SCl – NFCl		SCl – NFCl		SCl – NFCl		conj			

S	P		C		MCl		P		Od INDIRECT THOUGHT
(that) ('s) not ...		(a lot of time	[to do ...]) ⟩	⟩ n	⟨ Ø	(Ø **wondering)**	[if they've tested ....] ⟩	
	neg		SCl – NFCl				SCl – NCl	

Accident report

> **noun phrases** are sometimes simple (*the captain, a stewardess, Investigation*) but more often contain pre- and post-modification providing the reader with specific detail

m	h		m	m	h		h	q
the	impact	and	the	ensuing	fire		Five	of the surviving passengers
det	N	conj	det	*Ving*	N		num	PrepP

m	h	q			q
Weather	conditions	[during the flight]	and	at the point of collision	
N	N	NFCl		conj PrepP	

m	h	q		m	h	q
No	records	of turbulence		molten	aluminium,	[which was ...]
det	N	PrepP		AdjP	N	RelCl

> there are lots of listed **adverbials** giving information about time, place

	A		S		P	A		A		A
⟨ (After take-off ...)		(the flight)		(continued)	(on ...)		(towards ...)		(elevation ...) ⟩
	TIME					PLACE	PLACE		PLACE	

> many of the verb phrases are **passive** as is typical of a formal report.
> omission of the 'by+agent' is common – the focus is on the state of the aircraft

$$\langle \text{(Many pieces of the main body) (were ripped off)} \rangle \text{ and } \langle \varnothing \text{ (subsequently) } (\varnothing \text{ found})$$

Labels above: S (Many pieces of the main body), P (were ripped off), A (subsequently), P (found)

(along the tree swath path) ⟩.

A

- other passive sentences use the subject of the active sentence in an emphatic position at the end of the clause

    S   P   A   A

⟨ (The aircraft) (was destroyed) (by the impact) and (∅ the ensuing fire) ⟩.

                                 conj

- since clarity is essential in this genre, the report has many simple and compound sentences

    S   P   S   P   A   COMPOUND

⟨ (No records …) (were logged) ⟩ and ⟨ (no disturbance) (was recalled) (by …) ⟩.

        conj

- complex sentences tend not to be long and are tightly controlled

    S   S   P   Od

⟨ (Teardown …) and (investigation …) (proved) [that the engines were functioning …] ⟩.

        conj   SCl – NCl

Similarities and differences

The intended audience, whether known or unknown, specialist or general, and the context have a direct effect on the content. In the context of a tabloid newspaper, readers expect reports to contain information, but also wish to be entertained by the drama of a story. This is apparent here in the focus on dramatic effects and personal responses to the event. In the context of an informal conversation, the emphasis is on social interaction – information is less important than the creation of a relationship between participants. The content, therefore, is a means to entertain and to create a personal bond: the example here is a narrative account of a personal experience. While both the newspaper report and the conversation aim to entertain their intended audience, the official accident report is concerned only with the analysis and interpretation of data. Because of its formal context, the content focuses exclusively on factual information that can be checked – the geographical details of the plane's flight path and the location of the crash; weather conditions; what happened to passengers and crew; the condition of the plane after the crash. There is no personal response to events and in this extract no interpretation of the facts since the synopsis is focused on establishing what happened rather than why. The report is a legal document which must provide an objective account in neutral, unambiguous language.

Each text has a different purpose and the lexical choices made by the writers or speakers are therefore quite different. The tabloid aims to entertain readers with an exciting narrative, so the language is descriptive and dramatic, with direct speech used to change the pace. The journalist wants to evoke an emotional response in the reader – although there are facts, the emphasis is on recreating the drama of the incident. By focusing exclusively on recording factual details which can be verified, the accident report creates a very different relationship with its intended readers. Rather than recounting a sequence of events for dramatic effect, the aim is to provide an objective evaluation which will lead to an understanding of what caused the crash. The language is therefore dominated by technical subject specific words, numerical references and proper nouns, and the tone is neutral. The only modifiers give additional observational detail (weather conditions, physical damage to the plane, the nature of the wood) which will provide crash investigators with the concrete evidence they need.

What marks the informal conversation as different from these two informative texts is its emphasis on interactive language and its known, very narrow audience. Although the story about the plane dominates the interaction, the phatic language is just as important. Affirmations, questions and reinforcement are central to the development of the conversation and the relationship between the speakers. There is also a difference in the tone since the personal rather than the objective carries most weight here – where the accident report will be read in official, impersonal contexts by experts, the physical context of the conversation is private and familiar. The extended turn presents us with one person's account of a specific experience and its effect on her. Informal language and normal non-fluency features mark this as spontaneous conversation as opposed to the drafted polished written language of the reports.

Grammatical choices also distinguish between the three texts. The number of passive verb phrases and the frequency of adverbials in the accident report are typical of the genre. Simple and compound sentences ensure clarity of expression, and complex sentences are tightly controlled. The informal conversation, on the other hand, is marked by loose and rambling sentence structures which are a distinctive feature of spontaneous conversation. Because the intended audience is immediate, known and small, any confusions can be easily clarified. The accident report, however, needs to be immediately comprehensible to a distant and more wide-ranging audience. There can be no room for misunderstanding. The tabloid report falls somewhere between these two extremes – it has the accuracy and control of a written text, but draws on many of the features of spoken language to engage its audience. Sentences tend to be quite short and fronted initial position conjunctions divide longer sentences into more easily manageable units.

TASK 2   Context, audience and content

1 Read the texts below carefully.

TEXT 1   Extract from a blog

Wednesday, 20 April 2011

Resource Manager: Implementation

Note about the previous post: If you looked at the source code, you may have seen the *Unload* function, implemented as a function returning a Boolean variable. It has now been changed to a *void* function, since I decided the return value was not useful information. These changes have now been applied to that post, and are also reflected below.

Note about this post: There are a lot of long template headers, which unfortunately end up very messy in posts. I will try to think of a way to neaten them up, but until then all I can do is apologise profusely and encourage you to study these headers carefully.

Anyway, I hope you like the post. As usual, let me know your thoughts, opinions and what not. In particular, I'm very keen to hear about errors, typos and so forth. Thanks!

In *Implementation* posts I shall go through the source code for a particular class, explaining as I go. So if you've already seen the code summary post, then you'll have an idea of the functions we have to implement.

Before we get down to specifics of code, we have a few preliminaries. First, we need to protect against multiple inclusions.

```
#pragma once
#ifndef        ENGINE_SYSTEM_RESOURCEMANAGER_HPP
#define        ENGINE_SYSTEM_RESOURCEMANAGER_HPP

#endif
```

TEXT 2   Transcription of a pre-school television programme shown at 6.30am

V/O (song)		every girl and every boy (.) come with us and find a land (.) where magic and mystery (.) take us firmly by the hand =
FROG		= it's time to go to <u>Poppytown</u> =
V/O (song)		= <u>Poppytown</u> (.) Poppytown (.) we're on our way to <u>Poppytown</u> =
ALL		= it's <u>Poppytown</u> =
V/O (song)		= come with us and on our way (.) we'll talk and play (.) we'll laugh and sing (.) on the road to <u>Poppytown</u> (2)
BENJY BEAR		[to tune of 'Grand Old Duke of York'] h. (.) hum <u>hum</u> la la la la la (.) ho hum hum la la la (1) oh the <u>grand</u> old Duke of York =
BOBBLES BUNNY	'forte'	= 'hey' =
BENJY		= he had ten thousand men =
BOBBLES	'forte'	= 'hey' =
BENJY	'accel'	= he marched them up 'to the top of the hill' =
BOBBLES	'forte'	= 'hey' =
BENJY		= and he marched them down again =
BOBBLES		= [laughs] hurray (3)
BENJY		= [waves] hullo everybody (.) were you singing my song =
BOBBLES		= it <u>is</u> a jolly marching song Benjy Bear =
BENJY		= oh thank you Bobbles (.) I'm glad you like it (4)
BOBBLES		[laughs and jumps up and down clapping]
BENJY		I haven't finished singing yet (.) umm (2) what else can my soldiers dó, Bobbles (.) boys and girls =

BOBBLES	'accel'	= oh (.) m (.) errr (.) 'I know I know' (.) have a <u>rest</u> =
BENJY		= have a <u>rest</u> (.) <u>no</u> Bobbles (.) my soldiers aren't going
	'rall'	to have a <u>rest</u> (.) they're going to 'beat their drums' =
BOBBLES		= drúms (.) oh yes (3) <u>drums</u> (.) of course (.) they can
		bang their drums while they march up the hill again
		[laughs] (3)
BENJY		let's all sing together (1) oh the grand old Duke of York
		[marching and beating imaginary drums] (.) let's all
		beat our drums =
BOBBLES		= he had ten thousand men =
BENJY		= they beat their <u>drums</u> =
BOBBLES		= to the top of the <u>hill</u> =
BENJY	'accel'	= and they 'beat them down again'

2 How does the context shape each text?
You may like to think about:

- the situation and circumstances
- the function
- the identity of the writers and their intended audiences
- the content and layout
- the language and grammatical structures

COMMENTARY

These two texts both have a phatic function: they aim to establish a relationship with their intended audience by using direct address and by engaging their readers or viewers in relevant activities. Directly linked to this is the overlaying of spoken and written modes. Text 1 is an example of electronic English, a written form which is marked by its conversational tone and features of spoken language. Text 2 is a transcript of a script written to be read aloud by actors. In this variety, writers consciously imitate spoken interaction, but turn-taking is more organised and there are likely to be fewer examples of non-fluency. Beyond these similarities, however, the two texts are very different because their primary functions, their contexts and their intended audiences are so different.

Text 1 is primarily an informative text, aiming to teach readers how to use a multi-media library for game programming. Its intended audience is specialist – readers will access it via an online search engine which picks up key words, or through advertising on specialist forums and social networking sites. This context makes Text 1 distinctive. It only exists in an electronic form (situation) and the age, gender, geographical location and cultural background of the writer (circumstances) are unknown. The use of technical jargon and subject specific lexis, however, indicates that this is produced by an expert.

In direct contrast, Text 2 is a creative text which aims to engage viewers in a fictional world where named characters interact in a physical environment. Its intended audience is dictated by the time of transmission and the type of programme (situation), and by the pre-school age of the intended audience (circumstances). The identity of the writers is of less importance here than the viewers for whom the programme is written since decisions about content, language and style are all shaped by the context.

The content gives us additional information about the intended audience in each case. Both texts will have an unknown and distant audience, but it will be limited by the focus of the content. Text 1 is subject specific and will appeal to a narrow, specialist audience; Text 2 is age specific and will appeal to a narrow range of pre-school children and their parents or carers. Although viewers can join in with the song and the actions in Text 2, it is essentially a process of one-way communication. Text 1, on the other hand, is a two-way process: the text explicitly encourages feedback from users.

The language of the texts is directly linked to the content and intended audience. Text 1 is dominated by abstract nouns (*variable, value, thoughts, opinions*) and technical terms (*source code, Unload function, multiple inclusions*). While some of the words may be familiar, they are used here with a specialist meaning: *code* is the language used by a programmer which will be transformed by a compiler into machine instructions; a *function* is a set of coded instructions designed to perform a specific task which may produce a result. Even the noun *post* is used with a narrower definition since it refers explicitly to an electronic message on a web log (blog) rather than a system for delivering mail. The pre-modified noun phrase *a Boolean variable* is a subject specific term from the field of maths and logic: it is taken from the name and work of the English mathematician and philosopher George Boole (1815–1864) whose binary algebraic system of true/false values forms the basis for modern computer logic. The form and content of the sample code at the end of the extract is also impenetrable to those who do not know the language.

Another interesting feature of the lexical choice is the juxtaposition of formal and informal language. The conversational linking adverb in the initial position (*Anyway*), the disjunct expressing attitude (*unfortunately*), and the repetition of first person pronouns (*I, we, me*) make this a personal text. Given the subject specific terminology, the formality of some of the expressions (*what not, so forth*) and the use of the traditional distinction between *shall* to express future time and *will* to express intention with the first person, this tone is unexpected. The tension between the formal and the informal tells us something about the purpose of the text. Although it is educative, written by an expert, the site needs to engage and create a relationship with its viewers. There are many other blogs online and the writer needs to convince viewers to choose his rather than another site. Politeness markers (the informal interjection *Thanks!*, the adverb *profusely* qualifying the verb *apologise*, and the tentative verb *hope*) ensure that a cooperative relationship is established, encouraging users to return to the blog.

While the language of Text 1 is specialist, Text 2 is everyday. The content is relevant for a pre-school audience, focusing on a traditional nursery rhyme ('The Grand Old Duke of York') and social interaction. The opening song marks the beginning of the programme and functions as an invitation to take part in the activities that follow. The vocative (*every girl and every boy*) provides an immediate point of contact with the audience. The repetition of the stressed proper noun *Poppytown* then sets the scene, and plural first person pronouns (*we*) and determiners (*our*) create a link between the characters and the audience. Although television is a one way process of communication, programmes for young children encourage partic ipation through their use of imperatives (*take, come*) which develop opportunitie: for interaction.

Words tend to be monosyllabic and none are complicated. Nouns tend to be concrete (*men, hill, drum*) and verbs dynamic (*marched, jumps, beat*). The pattern ing of the lyrics and the repetition of the interjection (*hey*) make it easy for viewer: to join in. The relationship between the two characters is familiar and cooperative Vocatives are used frequently to reinforce names for the viewers (*Benjy Bear, Bob bles*) and to establish a sense of familiarity. There are no interrrupted turns – ever where Benjy Bear rejects Bobbles Bunny's suggestion (*have a rest (.) no Bobbles*) the communication does not break down. Affirmation (*hurray, it is a jolly marching song*) and politeness markers (*oh thank you*) reinforce the positive nature of the interaction. This sense of a known and immediate audience is extended to viewers who are directly addressed (*hello everybody*). The interrogative *were you singing my song*, the polite suggestion *let's all sing together* and the physical actions (*waves marching and beating imaginary drums*) directly engage viewers. Similarly, changes in pace and volume bring the interaction to life and hold viewer attention.

The grammatical structures of each text conform to our expectations. Phrase in Text 1 are wide-ranging with many modified.

m	h	q		m	h	q
a function	[returning Boolean variable]			a way	[to neaten them up]	
	NP				NP	
det	N	NFCl		det	N	NFCl

m	h	q
very keen	[to hear about errors ...]	
	AdjP	
Adv	Adj	NFCl

In Text 2, noun phrases tend to be simple (*them, my soldiers, down*) or with modi fication that will be familiar from the song.

m	m	m	h	q		m	h	q		m	m	h
the	grand	Old	Duke	of York		the	top	of the hill		ten	thousand	men
det	AdjP	AdjP	N	PrepP		det	N	PrepP		num	num	N

There are only two examples of phrases where the post-modification is not a prepo sitional phrase.

m	h	q		h	q
a land	[where magic and mystery take us ...]			glad	[Ø you like it]
	NP				AdjP
det	N	RelCl		Adj	NCl

A similar distinction can be seen in the verb phrases: Text 2 has a more limited range than Text 1. In the pre-school programme, verb phrases in the song and in the conversation are present (*'s, 'm, know*) or modal expressing ability (*can*). There is one present perfective (*haven't finished*) for an action begun in the past and not yet completed, and a future reference (*'re going to*) communicating an action that is imminent. Those in Text 1 are more varied because the discourse has a more formal purpose. Present tense verbs are used for statements of fact (*are, have*), simple past for completed events (*looked*), and perfective for an event in the past that still has relevance (*'ve … seen*). Modal verb phrases indicate possibility (*may have seen*), future time (*shall try*), and intention (*will go through*). The formality of the text can also be seen in the use of the passive voice (*has … been changed, have been applied, are reflected*), which is common in educative texts where the actor (subject) is less important than the outcome (object).

Because of the different audiences, the sentence structure and organisation are very different in each text. Most sentences in Text 2 are simple.

> S   P   C   voc
> ‹ (it) (is) (a jolly marching song) Benjy Bear ›

> S   P   O   A
> ‹ (he) (marched) (them) (up to the top of the hill) ›

There are complex sentences, but none are long. Clause sites tend to be filled with relatively short phrases so the weight of information does not make the sentences difficult to understand.

> S   P   Od   A   COMPLEX
> ‹ (they) (can bang) (their drums) [while they march up the hill again] ›
>   SCl – ACl

The only compound-complex sentence is in the opening lines of the song. Although the object site is filled with a long noun phrase post-modifed by a relative clause, most of the words are monosyllabic and the rhyme (*land/hand*) brings the sentence to an emphatic end. In addition, as part of the titles of the programme, this is not intended to be interactive – it functions instead as a brand marker.

The sentence structures in Text 2 are, as we would expect, very long with frequent use of subordination to carry the weight of information. There is only one simple sentence (*As usual, let me know …*), which is conversational and designed to engage the reader, and one compound sentence (*These changes have … been applied … and … are … also reflected …*). All others are complex or compound-complex. This is typical of a text written by an expert for a specialist audience.

> S   P   Od   A   S   P
> ‹ (I) (will try) [to think of a way [to neaten them up]] › but ‹ (until then) [all Ø I can do] (is)
>   SCl – NFCl   SCl – NFCl   conj   SCl – NCl

>   C   C
> [apologise profusely] and [encourage you [to study these headers carefully]] ›.
> SCl – NFCl   conj SCl – NFCl   SCl – NFCl

In addition, many of the sentences have a marked theme, bringing adverbials to the front of the clause. Some are conversational (*Anyway, As usual*), developing the relationship between writer and reader; others are sequential (*Before we get down to …, First*), establishing the importance of order. This is another significant difference between the texts – the sentences in the transcript are all unmarked making it easier for the young viewers to process the information.

Each text here uses language in a way that is appropriate for its intended audience. It is noticeable that the informative text uses declarative mood since the writer is an expert sharing his subject specific knowledge with readers who wish to learn how to use a multi-media library. The only variation is in the code in a different font which provides directives for the readers to use in their own programming. Because

Text 2 is more directly interactive with its audience, the grammatical mood is more varied with imperatives (*let's sing, let's beat*) and an interrogative (*what else can my soldiers do*) encouraging viewers to join in.

1 Choose one of the following writing exercises. When you have completed your text, evaluate the key linguistic features. You may like to use the suggested framework for analysis in Appendix A.

EITHER

Write a formal written statement of a crime (fictional or real) that you witnessed, including factual details of what happened, the time and place, and the people involved.

Then write an electronic text to a friend recounting the same incident, and record the voicemail you might have left.

You need to think carefully about changes in genre, audience and register, and the effect this will have on the content, the lexis and the grammatical structures.

OR

Write a speech that could be given at a formal, public occasion (for example, a speech by a head boy or girl at the leavers' assembly, the best man's speech at a wedding reception, a speech at a family coming-of-age party).

You need to think carefully about the way in which the circumstances and situation affect the lexis and syntax: the age and gender of the speaker, the intended audience, the cultural background, the occasion and the physical location. You will need to decide on the main and secondary functions of your speech.

OR

Create two characters who know each other well and a physical location in which they can meet.

Write down an informal conversation they might have as though you were creating an individual scene for a play. You need to make their interaction as real as possible by choosing appropriate speech patterns for each character and by showing an awareness of the situation and circumstances.

You need to think carefully about the context, and the way in which it will affect the lexical and grammatical choices each character makes.

11.4 Non-Standard English

We all have different ways of speaking according to our geographical, historical and social background, our personal identity, our audience and the function of our discourse. By recognising any linguistic and grammatical features that are different from the standard, we can begin to explore the ways in which these wider elements shape the language we use.

TASK 1 Geographical variation

1 Read the following extracts carefully.

TEXT 1 *Trainspotting*, 'House Arrest', Irvine Welsh (Minerva, 1993)
This is an extract from a novel using different kinds of English in each chapter according to which narrator is recalling the events. The excerpt below is narrated by a character called Renton who uses a Scots dialect.

Jocky Linton comes ower tae join us. Jocky's pus is shaped like an egg oan its side. He's goat thick black hair flecked wi silver. He wears a blue shirt which is short-sleeved and exposes his tattoos. Oan one airm he's goat 'Jocky & Elaine – True Love Will Never Die' and 'Scotland' wi a Lion Rampart oan the other. Unfortunately, true love did bite the dust and Elaine shot the craw a long time ago. Jocky's now livin wi Margaret whae obviously hates the tattoo, but everytime he goes tae git another one pit ower it, he bottles oot, makin excuses …
– Day-vie. Cah-thy. Loo-kin-gor-jis-the-night-doll. Din-nae-you-be-tur-nin-yer-back … or-ah'll-be-ruh-nin-ah-way-wi-her! … Jocky spat out his syllables Kalashnikov style.

TEXT 2 Informal Conversation
This is an extract from an informal spontaneous conversation between family members. It took place in the Norfolk village of St Faiths in the late 1950s. The transcription here is broad: it does not aim to describe the exact articulation of sounds. Instead it focuses on pronunciations that are significantly different from Standard English, using phonetic symbols to describe the pronunciation (see page xiv) and apostrophes to mark dropped initial and final consonants.

To help you read the transcription more easily, a written version using traditional spelling and punctuation precedes the spoken text.

WRITTEN VERSION
What do you want, girl? — Just called in to see you Nanny. I go back to college tomorrow — Well don't just stand there. Get a cloth and help. Don't know where father is. His sister in the next village what was ill come puffing down this morning and told him all this rigmarole about new houses that they're putting up next to her — Are your feet hurting? — Just my blumen old corns. Here's a ten-bob note for you to spend up London. Don't tell no-one nothing — Oh Nanny thank you. — I dare not tell father I've spare. — Are you sure? — 'Serve you right,' he'd say, 'them chapel shoes don't fit.' He shouldn't be talking to me like that. Here he comes. — Have she just given you ten-bob? Bless her heart. — Are you a-coming in or staying out? — Don't mob me woman. Put a toffee in your mouth. I've been listening to blumen old squit all morning. — I never said nothing. — Well that's a rummun. I could have swore you spoke.

SPOKEN VERSION

| GRANDMA | /wʌdʒuː/ want mawther = |
| GIRL | = just called in to see you Nanny (.) I go back to college tomorrow = |

GRANDMA	= well /dʌn/ /dʒes/ stand there (1) /gɪt/ a dwile an' help (.) /dʌn/ know where father is (2) 'is sister in the nexter village wha' was ill /cʊm/ /əspʌfən/ down this /mɔːnən/ an' told 'im all this rigmarole about new housen tha' they're /əpʊʔən/ up next to /haː/ =
GIRL	= are your feet ‖ hur.
GRANDMA	‖ /dʒes/ me blumen old corns (6) 'ere's a ten-bob note for /jeuː/ to spend up London ‖ /dʌn/ tell no-one /naːθən/ (1)
GIRL	‖ oh Nanny thank you
GRANDMA	I /dʌsn/ tell father I 've ‖ spare /saːv/ /jeuː/ right 'e'd say them
GIRL	‖ are you sure
GRANDMA	chapel shoes /dʌn/ fi' (.) he /ʃʌn/ be /tɔːkən/ to me /lɔɪk/ that (1) 'ere 'e comes =
GRANDFATHER	= /hev/ she just given you ten-bob (.) bless /haː/ ‖ heart
GRANDMA	‖ are /jeuː/ /əcʌmən/ in or /steɪən/ ou' =
GRANDFATHER	= /dʌn/ mob me woman (.) pu' a /tʌfi/ in /jə/ mouth (.) I've /bɪn/ /lɪsənən/ to blumen ol' squit all /mɔːnən/ =
GRANDMA	= I never said /naːθən/ =
GRANDFATHER	= well tha's a rummun (.) I could /ə/ swore /jeuː/ spoke

2 List any examples of non-standard language (dialect words and pronunciations), identifying the standard version in each case.

TEXT 1   Scottish dialect

Dialect words

▸ *pus* — face
▸ *craw* — crow ('shoot the crow' is an expression meaning 'to leave,' especially in a hurry)
▸ *dinnae* — do not
▸ *the-night* — tonight (definite article used with time references instead of 'to' or 'this'

Dropped final consonants

▸ *wi* — with
▸ *livin* — living

Pronunciation

▸ *ower*	rhymes with 'power'	SE over
▸ *pit*		SE put
▸ *oot*		SE out
▸ *git*		SE get
▸ *whae*	rhymes with 'way'; 'h' ASPIRATED	SE who
▸ *tae*	rhymes with 'way'	SE to
▸ *airm*	rhymes with 'bare'	SE arm
▸ *yer*	rhymes with 'bird'	SE your
▸ *oan*		SE on

- *goat* rhymes with 'caught' SE got
- *gor-jis* SE gorgeous
- *ruh-nin* with 'h' aspirated SE running
- *ah* SE I

TEXT 2 Norfolk dialect

Dialect words

- *mawther* young girl
- *dwile* cloth
- *nexter* next
- /əspʌfən/ puffing
- /dʌsn/ daren't
- *mob* scold, nag (possibly from mob – 'to crowd around with vexatious curiosity or attentions')
- *squit* nonsense (slang)
- *rummun* strange one (slang)

Period words

- *ten-bob note* pre-decimal 10 shilling note ('bob' slang for shilling from the late 18th century)
- *rigmarole* confused or incoherent ramblings (from mid 19th century)
- *blumen* euphemism for 'bloody' (colloquial adjective expressing emotion with no real meaning)

Distinctive pronunciation

- /dʌn/ rhymes with 'bun' SE don't
- /dʒes/ rhymes with 'jest' SE just
- /gɪt/ SE get
- /cʊm/ rhymes with 'put' SE come
- /mɔːnən/ 'mornen' SE morning
- /əpʊʔən/ 'apu'en' SE putting
- /haː/ rhymes with 'car' SE her
- /jeuː/ 'ye-oo' SE you
- /naːθən/ 'narthen' SE nothing
- /saːv/ rhymes with 'carve' SE serve
- /ʃʌn/ rhymes with 'shunt' SE shouldn't
- /tɔːkən/ 'talken' SE talking
- /lɔɪk/ rhymes with 'boy' SE like
- /hev/ SE have
- /əcʌmən/ 'acumen' SE coming
- /steɪən/ 'stayen' SE staying
- /tʌfi/ 'tuffey' SE toffee
- /bɪn/ 'bin' SE been
- /jə/ 'yuh' SE your
- /lɪsənən/ 'lisenen' SE listening

Non-standard grammar

- *what* used in place of relative 'who' (*wha' was ill*)
- archaic plural (*housen* for 'houses')
- archaic *–ing* participles (/əspʌfən/ = a-puffing, /əpʊʔtən/ = a-putting)
- multiple negatives ('don't tell no-one nothing', 'never said nothing')
- non-standard past participle simplifying irregular verb 'to swear' (*swore* for 'sworn')

Informal features

- elision of final PLOSIVE 't' before a word beginning with 'd' ('what do' becomes /wʌd/); 'd' becomes a PALATO-ALVEOLAR AFFRICATE /dʒ/ before a PALATAL APPROXIMANT /j/ which is elided ('do you' becomes /dʒuː/)
- final plosives dropped (*don'* = don't, *jus'* = just, *wha'* – what, *fi'* = fit)
- reduction of primary auxiliary 'have' to unstressed vowel /ə/ (/ə/ *swore*)
- dropping of intial position unstressed /h/ (*'im* = him, *'ere* = here, *'e* = he)
- use of preposition *up* instead of 'in' with place (*up London*)
- reduction of suffix *–ing* to /ən/ (/əspʌfən/ = a-puffing, /mɔːnən/ = morning)

3 Compare and contrast the features of non-Standard English in these texts.

You may like to think about:

- the genre and function
- the lexical choice and spelling
- pronunciation
- the grammatical structures
- the ways in which the language is different from Standard English

---

COMMENTARY

Each text here uses a geographical variety – a form of English directly linked to a particular region (Scotland and Norfolk). While this accounts for the main differences between the examples, the genre, purpose and audience also shape the language. Text 1 is taken from a novel; its purpose is to entertain; its intended audience is unknown, general and wide. Text 2 is an example of phatic communication. The transcript records the interaction between three people who know each other well. Although the initial intended audience is very narrow (the participants), recording it brings a wider, specialist readership.

Both texts have a close relationship with spoken language. The first person narration aims to create a sense of the spoken voice and the transcript records an example of a spontaneous interaction between family members. Because of their different genres each text has a different way of recording distinctive pronunciations. Text 1 uses non-standard spelling. While this may look unfamiliar at first, we can still read the text with relative ease because the writer uses the Roman alphabet. We can use our knowledge of Standard English and Received Pronunciation to approximate the regional pronunciation. Text 2, however, as a specialist text, uses phonetic symbols for particular words in order to create an accurate representation of a specific accent and dialect region. Phonetic symbols from the International Phonetic Alphabet (IPA) allow us to indicate exactly how a word is said, but for a general reader it can be a barrier to understanding.

While some readers may recognise the dialect words in Texts 1 and 2 because of their geographical location, other readers will find them impenetrable. Nouns such as *pus* (face), *mawther* (young girl), *dwile* (cloth) and *squit* (nonsense), the adverb *nexter* (next), the verbs *dinnae* (do not), /əspʌfən/ (puffing) and /dʌsn/ (daren't), and the expression *shot the craw* may seem very strange. Equally, while a verb like *mob* in Text 2 may seem familiar, its specific meaning in this context (nag) may not be. Words directly linked to the period – the pre-decimalisation currency (*ten-bob-note*), the informal slang (*rigmarole*), and the euphemism (*blumen*) – will have a wider sphere of reference. These are words linked to people of a particular generation rather than a particular geographical location

As is common in regional accents, the main changes in pronunciation occur in the vowel sounds. Other non-standard features are directly tied to the dialect region. The Scots aspirated 'h' in *whae* and *ruhnin*, and the stretching of a PURE VOWEL or monophthong (**o**n, g**o**t) into a DIPHTHONG (*o*an, *goa*t) can be seen in this extract. The reduction of the suffix –*ing* to /ən/ and the use of a GLOTTAL stop replacing 't' between vowels (/əpʊʔən/ for 'putting') is typical of a Norfolk accent.

There are also, however, some features which are common in spoken language and are found across dialect boundaries. Both texts, for example, contain features that are characteristic of informal speech: dropped final consonants (Text 1 *wi*, *livin*; Text 2 *dʌn'*, *fi'*, *tha's*, *an*); the elision of the unstressed initial position 'h' in Text 2 ('*im*, '*ere*, '*e*); the reduction of vowels (/jə/ for 'your') and unstressed words ('have' → /əv/ → /ə/) to SCHWA (an unstressed neutral vowel); and the running together of words as final and initial consonants are elided (/wʌdʒuː/ for 'what do you').

Dialects are often marked by grammatical forms that now seem archaic. The use of multiple negatives can be seen in the Norfolk dialect ('**don't**' tell **no**-one **nothing**', '**never** said **nothing**'). In Old English, the negative particle *ne* preceded the verb (*ne wæs*, was not) with other negatives used after it for emphasis. This was still seen in Middle English, where *ne* – and later *not* – were reinforced by additional negative words.

... **noon** of us **ne** speke **noght** a word   [Chaucer]

Although multiple negatives are still the norm in many spoken dialects, they began to disappear from standard usage in the sixteenth century (Early Modern English).

A similar process of regularisation can be seen in the plural noun suffix. The –*en* plural inflection (derived from the Old English –*an* plural) existed alongside the –*s* and –*es* suffixes in Middle English up to the fourteenth century – particularly in the Southern dialects. By the Early Modern English period, however, the –*s* and –*es* forms were more common. The older form continued to exist in dialects as can be seen in Text 2 (*housen* for 'houses'), and in a few weak forms that have survived in Standard English ('children', 'oxen').

Verbs are the words most likely to be non-standard in dialects – particularly in the regularisation of irregular verbs. The most irregular verbs in Standard English have three different forms (present and past tense, *–ed* participle), often with a vowel change. In Text 2, a three-form verb is simplified:

> SE *swear* (pres)   *swore* (past)   *sworn* (*–ed* participle)
>
> I could ə **swore**   simple past form used as an *–ed* participle

The *–ing* participle forms with the prefix *a–* (əspʌfən for 'puffing', əpʊʔən for 'putting', əcʌmən for 'coming') are archaic, obsolete now in Standard English, but retained in some dialects. While non-standard lexis tends to be directly associated with a particular geographical region, non-standard grammatical features like these can be found across dialect boundaries.

Both texts aim to represent distinctive forms of spoken language in a written format. The extract from the novel needs to create a strong sense of character, so the writer uses non-standard spelling to draw us in. Similarly, the use of hyphens is a typographical feature which allows the writer to personalise the direct speech. They both divide words (*Day-vie*) and link them into running groups (*Loo-kin-go-jis-the-night-doll*) so that the appearance of the writing on the page tells us something about the way the character speaks. This is reinforced by the metaphor of the Kalashnikov rifle in the third person narrator comment. To appeal to a wide audience, however, the writer must avoid alienating his readers. He therefore retains standard grammatical forms. Text 2 is aiming to do something very different – it is interested in exploring distinctive features of a regional accent and dialect. While the relationship and context are relevant to our understanding of the language used, the primary focus is on the particular variety of English.

TASK 2   Social, personal and cultural variation

1 Read the following texts carefully.

TEXT 1   *Bimbo*, Keith Waterhouse (Hodder and Stoughton, 1990)
This is an extract from a novel in which a Page Three model, Debra Chase, tells the story of her life to counter the 'lies' which have been told about her in the tabloid press.

Now I know what the world is saying: that I, Debra Chase, deliberately hacked off most of Suzie's hair in a jealous rage so as to spoil her chances in the Miss South-east Coast comp. This is a wicked liable. Suzie was still my best friend even though we had become bitter rivals and she had grown what some people called big-headed with success, so knowing how proud she was of her lovely long pink hair I could not of brought myself to do such a thing. ...

No, what happened was a conurbation of not keeping my mind on my work and sheer inexperience. I guess it was daydreaming about the approaching contest and thinking of the look on Suzie's face when she reelised I was an unexpectant contendant that caused me to hack off more of one side of her hair than I should of done.

TEXT 2   Magazine article

This is an extract from a lifestyle supplement in a weekend compact newspaper.

BOOM BOOM! YOU'RE PROPER NANG INNIT. WANNA ROLL WITH THE SAFA DOWN MY YARD?

Do you listen to teenagers and wonder what has happened to the English language? Do you feel as if you've landed on a foreign shore where the locals are strangers from another world?

Teen speak can certainly be bewildering for parents and teachers alike.

And the speed at which it changes can keep the most with-it adult confused.

Influenced by Creole patois and rapper slang, teen speak is a coded language that creates a strong sense of identity for its users while keeping society at bay.

TEXT 3   *Riddley Walker,* Russell Hoban (Picador, 1990)

This is taken from a novel set in a post-nuclear world where civilisation has been devastated. Riddley Walker is the narrator of the novel and his story is an account of life in a society that is only dimly recognisable as our own.

I dont think it makes no differents where you start the telling of a thing. You never know where it begun realy. No moren you know where you begun your oan self. You myt know the place and day and time of day when you ben bearht. You myt even know the place and day and time when you ben got. That dont mean nothing tho. You stil dont know where you begun.

Ive all ready wrote down about my naming day. It wernt no moren 3 days after that my dad got kilt in the digging at Widders Dump and I wer the loan of a name.

2 List any examples of non-standard language and grammar, identifying the standard version in each case.

NOTES

TEXT 1   Idiolect

Colloquial language

▶ *comp*   abbreviation for 'competition'

Spelling linked to pronunciation

▶ *delibrately*   elision of reduced vowel /ə/ which is common in speech, i.e., /dɪˈlɪbrətli/ for / dɪˈlɪbərətli/
▶ *reelised*   realised

Malapropisms (words used mistakenly in place of similar sounding words)

▶ *liable*   'libel'
▶ *conurbation*   'combination'
▶ *unexpectant*   'unexpected'
▶ *contendant*   'contestant' (the replacement of SE 'contendent' with 'contendant' is a common misspelling e.g. 'independant' for SE 'independent')

Non-standard grammar

- *of*   commonly used in spoken language in place of the contracted 've (have) in perfective verb phrases

TEXT 2   Urban youth speak

Colloquial language

- *wanna*   want to
- *with-it*   up-to-date (with current fashions and trends)
- *innit*   general positive expression (from a contraction of the negative tag question 'isn't it?')

Code words

- *Boom boom!*   an expression of approval
- *proper*   very (adverb of degree – intensifier)
- *nang*   cool (adjective)
- *roll*   hang out (verb)
- *safa*   coolest (superlative adjective functioning as a noun phrase, i.e., the coolest people)
- *yard*   one's own house or home (Jamaican)

TEXT 3   Post-disaster society (oral tradition)

Spelling linked to pronunciation

realy	really	
stil	still	omission of unsounded
tho	though	consonants and vowels
myt	might	
wer	were	
oan	own	standardisation (rhymes with 'loan')
moren	more than	LIAISON with linking /r/, elision of /ð/ and reduction of /æ/ to /ə/
kilt, beartht	killed, birthed	replacement of the final voiced plosive /d/ with the VOICELESS /t/

Lexis

got	'conceived'	colloquial
all ready	'already'(Adv)	single word adverb ('previously') replaced by predeterminer (all) + adjective (ready)
differents	'difference'	adjective used with plural noun suffix
naming day		rite of passage directly linked to the community created in the novel
beartht	'(to be) born'	irregular past participle created from noun 'birth'

Omission of punctuation

▸ *dont, wernt*   don't, weren't   omission of apostrophes for contraction

Non-standard grammar

▸ double negatives: *don't think ... no /wernt no*
▸ use of an irregular past participle as a simple past tense: *begun* (began)
▸ use of an irregular simple past form for a past participle: *wrote* (written)
▸ use of third person plural verb forms with first (*I wer*) and third person (*It wernt*) singular pronouns
▸ archaic form of simple past tense of the irregular verb 'to be': *ben* (were)

3 Explore the way in which the social, personal and cultural backgrounds of these texts shape the lexical choice.

COMMENTARY

Text 1 is an example of a personal dialect – an IDIOLECT. The writer has used a written form that is very close to speech and this tells us something about the cultural background of the first person narrator. The style is informal and the trivial content sensationalised, mimicking the tone and approach of a tabloid newspaper. This establishes the main character as a rather empty-headed young woman whose cultural experiences are shaped by her reading of the popular press. There is an underlying irony in the writer's choice of style since Debra Chase seeks to defend her name using the very variety of English that has supposedly been used to misrepresent her.

The colloquial language (*comp*), non-standard spellings linked to pronunciation (*delibrately, reelised*) and the mis-spelling of *contendant* perhaps reflect the educational experience of the main character. These are examples of a cultural variety. The malapropisms, however, represent a more personal non-standard use of language. The confusion between similar sounding words creates humour: the semantic absurdity and the juxtaposition between the seriousness of the tone and the insignificance of the content engage the reader. The comic effect is not cruel since it does not undermine Debra Chase. Instead it creates a very strong sense of an individual voice.

Like Text 1, Text 3 is also a written account shaped by spoken language. The purpose, however, is different since this is a representation of a society in which the oral tradition has replaced writing after some undescribed disaster has taken place. It is a cultural variety, designed to represent a specific community where written language assumes many of the distinctive qualities of speech because there is no longer a written tradition. Contractions are no longer marked with an apostrophe and many words are spelt as they are said – the final silent 'e', for instance, is dropped (*mor* for 'more'). Double consonants are replaced with a single consonant (*realy* for 'really', *stil* for 'still') and complex consonant clusters (*tho* for 'though', *myt* for 'might') are simplified. The spelling of diphthongs is standardised: where English uses the PHONEME /əʊ/ for a range of spellings in words like 'loan', 'bone', 'grown', this text uses just the –*oa* pattern (*oan* for 'own'). Other examples can be linked to the informality of spoken language: words are joined at boundaries by a linking 'r' with consonants elided and vowels reduced (*moren* for 'more than'); and voiced final consonants are replaced by voiceless ones (*kilt* for 'killed', *beartht* for 'birthed'). These linguistic features are used by the author to create a distinctive narrative voice and a vivid sense of the context. Readers have to work harder in order to engage with the fictional world and this makes us read more attentively.

In order to develop this cultural variety, the author of *Riddley Walker* uses words that are directly associated with the world he has created. Ritual celebrations like conception (*got*), birth (*beartht*) and naming (*naming day*) assume a particular importance. While these words are not alien to us, their use in the text helps to establish a distinctive sense of the society in which Riddley Walker is growing up. Similarly, the difference in Standard English between the adjective phrase 'all ready' and the adverb 'already' disappears – in speech these two distinct lexical items can both be represented by /ɔːlredɪ/. The difference between the adjective 'different' and the abstract noun 'difference' also disappears. Such simplifications are associated directly with spoken language . In producing a written account, the first person narrator is attempting to recreate the lost traditions of his society, to produce something less ephemeral than the spoken word. Yet because he is inevitably a product of his society, his written language closely resembles speech

The headline of Text 2 is made up of words that may be alien to some readers. It is an example of language shaped by a social group. Although the grammatical function words are recognisable as Standard English (the pronoun *You*, the preposition *with*, the definite article *the*, and the possessive determiner *my*), the words carrying semantic weight are examples of urban youth speak. This is a form of Late Modern English which creates a strong sense of identity for its users: it is a code language that unites insiders and excludes outsiders. Readers may, therefore, need a gloss to explain the key terms: the adverb intensifier *proper* can be linked to 'very', the adjective *nang* to 'cool', the superlative adjective *safa* to 'coolest', the verb *roll* to 'hang out'. The expression of approval *Boom boom!* has no exact meaning, but can perhaps be seen as equivalent to interjections such as 'hurray'. The general term 'yard', defined in Standard English as 'a piece of enclosed land especially attached to a building or used for a particular purpose', here indicates something more specific (home) – the SE definition has become narrower. Other words used in the headline are typical of informal language in general: the contracted primary verb *'re* (are) and the contracted form *wanna* (want to) where the plosive /t/ is elided at the end and beginning of consecutive words. Such features are closely linked to pronunciation.

The language each extract uses is a distinctive dialect of English, but the grammar is mostly standard. The grammar of the headline, for instance, reflects the informality of speech rather than a distinctive dialect.

P	Od	A

‹ (Wan) (na roll with the safa) (down my yard)? ›
SCl – NFCl

The omission of the primary auxiliary 'do' to form a question ('Do you want to ...') and the contraction of 'want to' (*Wanna*) may make the clause analysis look strange, but these are features typical of informal spoken language. The grammatical forma-ion of the sentence is standard. In Text 3, however there are examples of non-standard grammar: multiple negation (*don't think ... no, wernt no*) and the simplification of irregular verb forms where the *–ed* participle is used as a simple past tense (*you begun*), and the simple past is used for an *–ed* participle (*I've ... wrote*). In addition, the writer uses an archaic form of the verb 'to be' (*ben* for 'are') and non-agreement of subject and verb (*I wer, It wernt*). These non-standard forms help to characterise the first person narrator by creating a distinctive cultural dialect appropriate for a society in which all traditions have been lost.

Each text has a distinctive way of representing an individual or group voice through the variety of English it uses. The headline uses non-Standard English to attract our attention – it aims to make us read on by using a form of English that is fascinating because it is unfamiliar. The narrative extracts use language to create character and to develop a sense of context. While both have links to speech, the personal and cultural varieties are very different because they represent the voices of two distinctive characters who live in quite different physical and linguistic environments.

TASK 3   Historical variation

1 Read the extract below carefully.

TEXT 1   Extract from a sixteenth-century pamphlet
This extract is taken from *The School of Abuse* by Stephen Gosson, a pamphleteer hostile to the popular Elizabethan theatre. Written in 1579, the pamphlet addresses the supposed immorality of the theatre.

In our assemblies at playes in London, you shall see suche heaving and shooving, suche ytching and shouldering to sytte by women; such care for their garments that they be not trode on; such eyes to their lappes that no chippes lighte in them; such pillowes to their backes that they take no hurte; suche masking in their eares; I know not what; suche geving them pippins to passe the time; such playing at foote saunt without cardes; such ticking, such toying, such smiling, such winking, and such manning them home when the sportes are ended, that it is a right comedie to marke their behaviour, to watch their conceates, as the catte for the mouse, and as good as a course at the game it selfe, to dogge them a little, or follow aloofe by the printe of their feete, and so discover by slotte where the deare taketh soyle.

2 List the examples of language and grammar that are unfamiliar.

NOTES

Spelling
▸ *ytching, sytte, soyle*	⟨y⟩ used for ⟨i⟩
▸ *playes, eares, foote, printe*	still evidence of inflected singular and plural nouns
▸ *suche, such*	inconsistent use of inflection for the determiner
▸ *sytte, lappes, catte*	double consonant after a short vowel

- *deare*   'deer'
- *shooving*   'shoving'
- *geving*   'giving'
- *comedie*   <e> added to words with a lightly pronounced <i>
- *conceates*   'conceits', vain pride (from the Old Fr 'concever', Latin 'concipēre); from the fifteenth century, the spelling <ea> was used for words of French origin and the spelling pattern was extended to Old English words in the sixteenth century, e.g *mele → meal*

Period words

- *pippins*   originally the name given to any apple grown from a pip; by the sixteenth century, the term was used to refer to a late-ripening apple with an acid flavour, e.g. the London Pippin (from Fr 'pépin' meaning both 'pip' and 'apple')
- *foot saunte*   a now unfamiliar card game
- *dogge*   to track and watch constantly (from late OE 'docga'; Ger 'dogge')
- *aloofe*   to windward (now obsolete); some way off, apart
- *slotte*   a track, especially a deer's footprints (from Old Fr 'esclot' and Old Norse 'slōth')
- *soyle*   a watery place where a hunted animal takes refuge (from Old Fr 'soil, souil'; Fr 'souille', wallowing-place)

Archaic grammar

- *be not trode*   subjunctive (base form verb 'be' to mark intention); passive voice fully established ('b' + past participle)
- *trode*   irregular past participle (Mod Eng 'trodden')
- *taketh*   archaic 3rd person singular inflection
- *to sytte, to passe, to dogge*   infinitives with the final –*n* adopted from OE dropped
- *shall*   modal system established
- *are ended*   use of primary auxiliary 'be' rather than 'have' for the perfect aspect when the verb is intransitive (no object)
- *I know not ...* negative still used with inversion rather than with the primary auxiliary 'do' (i.e., 'I do not know')

3 Comment on the variety of English used in this extract.

You may like to think about:

- the meaning of words
- unfamiliar and familiar grammatical structures

Text 1 reflects the nature of the English language in the late sixteenth century – it is a form linguists describe as Early Modern English. While we can understand the argument, there are some words which are unfamiliar because language changes over time. We can, for instance, trace the development of the plural noun *pippins* from the French word *pépin* meaning 'pip' and 'apple' to the name of a sixteenth-century apple, and discover that *foot saunt* is a card game. It is more difficult, however, to find any references to *foote saunt* <u>*without*</u> *cardes*. As a twenty-first-century reader, we can only make assumptions.

Some of the unfamiliar words can still be looked up in a dictionary: their meanings are no longer dominant, but we could still use the words in the same way. The verb *dogge*, for instance, is a present tense verb meaning 'to track and watch constantly'; *slotte* is a singular noun describing 'a track, especially a deer's footprint'; *soyle* is a singular noun used to describe 'a watery place where a hunted animal takes refuge'; and *aloofe* is an adverb of place meaning 'some way off'. Each of these words reinforces the writer's opinion that the theatre is a place of immorality – they extend his metaphor of the theatre as a place for men to 'hunt' women, where the 'prey', the vain women who pride themselves on the perfection of their clothes, are the willing victims of the male predators. The writer's references to *sportes* and *comedie* understate the seriousness of his accusations: he wishes to persuade readers that the theatre is an immoral place which corrupts those who attend.

The grammar is distinctive and it reflects the period in which the text was written. The third person singular verb ending *–eth* is now obsolete, having been replaced by the suffix *–s*. By tracing its disappearance, we can see the process of language change at work. In Middle English, *–eth* was the standard ending in the south and southeast of England, the region most influential in the emergence of a standard form. The *–s* form was used in the Northern dialect and only appeared occasionally outside that region in the fifteenth century. By the sixteenth century, however, the *–s* form was increasingly common, existing alongside *–eth*, particularly in writing which seems to reflect colloquial usage. While the 1611 King James Bible retained the old-fashioned suffix used in the early sixteenth-century Tyndale and Coverdale translations on which it was based, the *–s* suffix became the standard form during the seventeenth century. We can still see examples of *–eth* used in poetry at this time because of the need for metrical and syllabic patterning. In the extract we are considering, the *–eth* form may have been adopted to mark the formality of the pamphlet and the serious tone of the writer's attack on the theatre.

Other grammatical features are interesting because they reflect developments in the English language which we now take for granted. Modal verbs (*shall*) and the passive voice (*be not trode*), for instance, emerged in the fourteenth century, but were not fully established until the seventeenth – the text here was written in the late sixteenth century towards the end of this period of development. The subjunctive was used to indicate 'what must or ought to be done' from the fourteenth century and we see this in the reference to the ladies protecting their clothes (*be not trode*). Use of the primary auxiliary 'do' to mark a negative ('I do not know') began to emerge in the sixteenth century, but this

extract adopts the inverted form (*I know not*) which was still common at thi
time. Other non-standard verbs include the irregular past participle *trode* ('trod
den') and the use of the primary auxiliary 'be' rather than 'have' in the perfec
aspect when the verb is intransitive (*are ended*).

In Old English, verb phrases tended to be shorter with inflections marking
changes in tense and voice. As verbs began to be used in strings, however, the lan
guage was able to communicate more subtle variations. By the end of the sixteenth
century, around the time that this text was written, grammar was beginning to
resemble the standard forms we use today. Where we see examples of non-stan
dard usage, it is because we are identifying the survival of forms that are now obso
lete.

TASK 4 Non-Standard English

1 Choose one of the following writing tasks. When you have completed your text
evaluate the key linguistic features. You may like to use the suggested framework
for analysis in Appendix A.

EITHER

Create a character and write the opening of a first person narrative in which we
learn about the narrator through the non-standard language she or he uses as
well as the content of what he or she says. Your lexical and grammatical choices
should tell the reader about the identity of your character.

Think carefully about the personal, social and cultural context so that you can make
informed decisions about the kind of language and grammar to use. You need to
have a clear idea about the setting, so think about the situation (the time, physical
place, period and occasion) and the circumstances (age/gender, geographical loca
tion, cultural background, occupational and educational experience, group alle
giances).

OR

Write a newspaper article about a distinctive form of twenty-first-century English
with a headline that aims to attract attention by its use of a non-standard dialect

You may find it useful to do some research so that your article can explain the key
linguistic features, the context and the reason this particular dialect of English is
so important to its users. In composing your headline, think about the lexical and
grammatical features that best represent the dialect you are writing about and aim
to create something dramatic that will stand out.

OR

Script a conversation between a speaker of Standard English and a speaker who
uses a regional dialect. Aim to bring out the linguistic identity of each participant
through the lexical and grammatical choices you make.

Think carefully about the characteristics of informal speech and the linguistic con
text of the non-standard speaker.

Re-write your conversation to show evidence of convergence – the interaction is cooperative and the participants adapt their language choices to reduce the linguistic differences between them.

Re-write the text again to show evidence of divergence – the interaction is uncooperative and the participants choose to draw attention to their linguistic differences.

Explain the changes you have made in each case and the effects you have created.

Chapter **12**

What next?

The interesting thing about language is that it is around us all the time – we can never say we know it all, or that we've finished learning. This book has set out to give you a framework, a starting point from which you can explore the infinite ways in which we encounter language on a day-to-day basis. From here, you can begin to broaden your linguistic horizons, finding out more about phonology, etymology, language variation and text types.

Keep a language scrap book so that you can collect interesting examples of language in action. You could look out for emotive or sensational news reporting, an extract from a novel that is particularly effective at drawing you into the fictional world, a political speech that is obviously using linguistic and grammatical patterning to shape the way you see the world, an advertisement with clever word play, a confrontational interview, Christmas cracker jokes that make you groan, dialect words, comic ambiguities, a ruthless film review, a 'viral' tweet. The possibilities are endless. Your collection can be a work in progress that helps you to sharpen your analytical skills. Leave plenty of room to make notes and develop a framework of analysis that works for you. Keep practising and the terminology will quickly become part of your natural repertoire.

And read about language. It does not matter what level you are, there is material available that is just right for you. All kinds of books and articles are written on the subject – use libraries and the internet to find things that interest you, and expand your background understanding. A sound knowledge of language concepts helps in the study of text analysis because it alerts us to the wider reasons for the linguistic and grammatical choices speakers and writers make. Appreciating the bigger picture will give you a clear sense of why the small details are important: grammar is a means to an end – it helps you to recognise the ways in which meaning is constructed.

While grammar itself may be regarded as unexciting and monotonous, a set of rules and definitions to be learnt by rote, I hope that seeing it in action has convinced you of its wider relevance. This isn't an example of book-learning that once conquered can be safely put away on the top shelf and forgotten – linguistic knowledge and understanding are practical skills that get better with practice. So, having finished reading and experimenting with the tasks, be open to the spoken and written language around you; actively engage with what you read and write, hear and say. Understanding the effects created by lexical and grammatical choices can change your relationship with language forever.

Part VI

Appendices

Suggested framework for analysis

While each text you consider will have different linguistic and syntactic features, you can use a general framework to help you identify key features. The most important thing to remember is that this is only a guide – you do not need to work systematically through every category, but must learn to be discriminating. Comment on the examples that will help you to support your argument.

The guide is divided into sections relating to the language areas used in the book as a whole. It uses key questions to help you analyse and evaluate the personal writing you do in each 'Using your knowledge' chapter, or to organise your approach to any text you need to read closely.

The first headings give you a general starting point for any task, but you will not necessarily be able to use all the other headings straight away because they are directly linked to specific chapters in the book. When you have completed the two chapters on words, for instance, it will make sense to concentrate on the questions listed under the 'Words' heading; when you have also worked through the chapters on phrases, you will be able to focus on the questions listed under 'Words' and 'Phrases'.

Remember this guide is meant to support you in your study of grammar, so you need to find a method of using it that works for you. The most important thing is to make sure that you are exploring **how** the lexical and grammatical choices **create meaning** – 'feature spotting' is not an effective way to analyse text.

Questions to ask yourself

Audience

- Age? size? known or unknown? distant or immediate? expert or non-expert?

Purpose

- Instructive? informative? persuasive? creative? expressive? phatic?

Content

- Subject specific or everyday? personal or impersonal? topical, recent past or distant past? factual or fictitious?

Text type

> Advertisement? brochure? commentary? description? electronic English? essay leaflet? letter? narrative? newspaper? poem? report? script? speech? sponta neous conversation? travel guide? etc.
> Is there anything interesting about the **organisation** or the **layout**?

Words

> Are there any particular **word classes** that dominate the text? – concrete o abstract nouns? count or non-count nouns? pronouns? modal verbs? stative o dynamic verbs? tensed verbs? questions or negatives? adjective or adverb mod ifiers? conjunctions?
> Is there anything significant about the **position** of the words?
> Are the **connotations** of the words significant?
> How do the writer's or speaker's choices relate to the meaning? – text type purpose? content? intended audience?

Phrases

> What kind of **noun phrases** are used? – pre- and post-modification?
> What kind of **verb phrases** are used? – time scale? aspect? voice? modality?
> What kind of **adjective and adverb phrases** are used? – pre- and post-modifi cation? position?
> How do the writer's or speaker's choices relate to the meaning? – text type? pur pose? content? intended audience?

Clauses

> What **type** of clauses are used? – main? subordinate? a mixture?
> How are the clauses **structured**? – subject? predicator? object(s) complement(s)? adverbial(s)? vocative(s)? interjection(s)?
> Are the subordinate clauses **embedded** or **standing alone**? – structure? posi tion? function?
> Is there any **grammatical ambiguity**? – accidental? for comic effect? dramati effect?
> How do the writer's or speaker's choices relate to the meaning? – text type? pur pose? content? intended audience?

Sentences

> What **type** of sentences are used? – simple? compound? complex? compound complex? minor?
> How are the sentences **linked**? – lexical patterning? substitution? ellipsis? link ing adverbs and conjunctions?
> How are the sentences **organised**? – marked themes? end focus? dummy sub jects?

- Are the **grammatical moods** distinctive? – declarative? interrogative? imperative? exclamatory? subjunctive? movements between the different moods?
- How do the writer's or speaker's choices relate to the meaning? – text type? purpose? content? intended audience?

Discourse

- How has the text been shaped by its **speaker or writer**? – geographical background? cultural background? social group?
- What is distinctive about the **register**? – mode? field? tenor?
- What is distinctive about the **context**? – situation? circumstances?
- Is there anything **distinctive** about the kind of language used? – standard or non-standard? spelling? geographical variation? social and personal variation? historical variation?
- How do the writer's or speaker's choices relate to the meaning? – text type? purpose? content? intended audience?

Glossary

This glossary contains a brief definition of key words you may find useful in your study of language. The key term is in **bold** with examples printed in *italics*.

abstract noun   Nouns that refer to a concept or thing that has no physical qualities (*fear, experience*).

accelerando   A term used to describe speech that is getting faster (**accel**).

accent   A set of distinctive pronunciations that mark regional or social identity.

active voice   A grammatical structure in which the subject is the actor of a sentence.

actor   The person or thing responsible for the action of the verb (***The boy*** *threw a stone.*).

adjective   An open class word that defines attributes of a noun (*the **extravagant** party*) and that can also express contrasts of degree (*Although **slower** than the others, he is **most accurate***).

adjective phrase   A phrase which has an adjective as its head word.

adjunct   An adverb or adverbial that relates directly to the meaning of the verb, giving details of time, manner and place.

adverb   An open class word that describes the action of a verb (*The child slept **soundly***); that can act as an intensifier (***really** quiet*); and that can function as a sentence connector (***Perhaps** we should leave now*).

adverb phrase   A phrase which has an adverb as its head word.

adverbial   An optional element of a clause which gives us information about time, manner and place.

affricate   Sounds made by a complete closure of the air passage followed by a slow release of air (***church, jam***).

agent   A linguistic form describing who or what is responsible for the action of a verb (***The girls** ate their pizza; the pizza was eaten by **the girls***).

agreement   A grammatical relationship between words in which the choice of one element determines the form of another (*The dog **barks**; they talked amongst **themselves***).

ambiguity   Any language use where there are multiple possible meanings.

anaphoric   A form of referencing in which a noun phrase points backwards to something mentioned earlier in a text (***The garden** was in full bloom. **It** was ablaze with colour.*).

archaism   A word or phrase no longer in current use, but not yet obsolete.

article   A term used to distinguish between definite (*the*) and indefinite (*a/an*) references to nouns.

aspect   The time scale of a verb, which may be complete (*has fallen*) or in progress (*is falling*). There are two forms: **progressive** and **perfective**.

aspirated   Audible breath accompanying a sound.

asyndetic   The linking of linguistic units without a conjunction (*The area was surrounded as policemen, security guards, office workers, protestors, local people poured into the street*).

attributive   Adjective phrases or other modifiers that precede the head noun in a noun phrase (*The shiny polished table*).

auxiliary verb   A verb that precedes the lexical verb in a verb phrase (*I do work hard; She can visit; the clouds were gathering*).

base form   The minimal form of a word to which endings can be added.

bilabial approximant   A sound produced by closing the lips and moving the tongue from one position to another (*why*).

cardinal number   The basic form of a number (*one, two*).

cataphoric   A form of referencing in which a noun phrase points forwards to something mentioned later in a text (*They sat waiting, five friends drawn together by the past*).

chronological   Arranged in order of time from the earliest to the latest.

clause   A group of words, usually with a finite verb, which is structurally larger than a phrase. Clauses may be described as **independent** (main) or **dependent** (subordinate).

cleft sentence   A sentence that has been rearranged using the dummy subject *it* + *be*.

closed class words   Grammatical **function** words like prepositions, determiners and conjunctions.

closed question   A question which can be answered with yes or no (*Is it raining today? Does the train on Platform 2 go to London?*).

code-switching   A movement between different varieties of language depending on who the participants are, the purpose and the context: for instance, moving between a regional and a standard dialect, or between a first and second language.

cohesion   Links and connections which unite the elements of a sentence or text.

collective noun   A noun that refers to a group of people, animals or things, but which can take both singular and plural forms (*flock, government*).

collocation   Two or more words that frequently occur together as part of a set phrase.

command   An utterance intended to get other people to do something.

comment clause   A commonly occurring clause that adds a remark to another clause in parenthesis (*It was raining, you see, and I didn't want to get wet.*)

common noun   A noun that refers to a general group of objects or concepts (*star, book, idea*).

comparative   A form of adjectives and adverbs used for comparison with the inflection *–er* or the adverb *more* (*faster, more compassionate*).

comparative clause   A subordinate clause expressing comparison using the subordinating conjunctions *as* and *than*.

complement   A clause element that adds extra information about the subject or object of the clause after a copular verb (*The weather grew stormier by the hour*).

complex sentence   A sentence made up of one main and one or more subordinate clauses.

compound-complex sentence A sentence made up of both co-ordination and sub-ordination.

compound sentence A sentence made up of at least two main clauses joined together by a co-ordinating conjunction.

concord The agreement of a verb and its subject in terms of person and number.

concrete noun A noun that refers to physical things like people, objects, places or substances.

conditional clause A subordinate clause which normally begins with *if* and expresses a condition.

conjunct A sentence adverb with a linking function (*however, otherwise*).

conjunction A closed class word whose function is to join together two parts of a sentence.

connotations The associations attached to a word in addition to its dictionary meaning.

consonant cluster A series of consonants which have no intervening vowel (*sprout, chlorine*).

context The background situation and circumstances in which spoken and written language take place.

contraction A shortened form of a word joined to a preceding word (*won't, they're*).

convergence A process in which people adjust their accents and dialects so that they reduce the difference between them.

co-ordinating conjunction A word that joins elements of equal rank (*and, but, or*).

co-ordination The linking of lexical items which have the same grammatical status (*soft and blue; up and down; laughed and cried*).

copular A linking verb used to connect clause elements (*The child **seemed** miserable*).

count noun A noun that refers to things that can be counted and has a plural form (*dog, dogs*).

crescendo A term used to describe speech that is getting louder (**cres**).

declarative A grammatical mood used to express a statement (*The road is very wet.*).

degree The comparison of adjectives and adverbs: comparative (*clearer, more ridiculous*) and superlative (*clearest, most ridiculous*).

deictic, deixis The use of words or expressions that rely on the context to convey meaning (*this, those, over there*).

demonstrative Determiners or pronouns that distinguish one item from another similar one (*this/that, these/those*).

denotation The dictionary definition of a word.

dental fricative A sound produced by a partial blockage of the airstream resulting in friction as the air is forced through a small gap between the teeth (***the**, voiced; **the**atre* unvoiced).

dependent clause A clause which cannot stand alone. Also called a **subordinate** clause.

descriptive An approach to language study based on observation of language in use focusing on appropriateness and acceptability rather than on concepts of 'right' and 'wrong'.

determiner A closed class word which specifies the number and definiteness of a noun (*the, a, some*).

dialect A language variety marked by distinctive grammar and vocabulary, which is used by a group of speakers with common regional or social backgrounds.

diminuendo A term used to describe speech that is getting quieter (**dim**).

diphthong A vowel in which there is a sound change (*rain, time, ear, home*).

direct object A clause element directly affected by the action of the verb (*The horse kicked **the boy***).

direct speech The actual words spoken by a person which are recorded in a written form enclosed in quotation marks often with an accompanying **quoting clause** (*'You are really late today,' she said*).

discourse Any unit of spoken or written language that is longer than a sentence.

disjunct A sentence adverb giving the speaker or writer a chance to comment on the content or style of a sentence as a whole (***Fortunately** we didn't miss the bus*).

divergence A process in which people adjust their accents and dialects so that they increase the difference between them.

double negative A structure in which more than one negative is used in one verb phrase (*We **didn't** do **nothing***).

dummy subject *It* or *there* in the subject site of the sentence, which do not carry any meaning.

dynamic A verb that expresses an action rather than a state and that can be used in the progressive aspect (*sprint, are sprinting*).

–ed participle A non-finite verb form marked by an *–ed* inflection for regular verbs. Also called a **past** participle.

elision The omission of sounds in speech.

ellipsis The omission of part of a sentence which can be understood from the context.

embedded clause A subordinate clause which functions as a post-modifier in one of the clause sites in a sentence and is dependent on the head of the phrase in which it occurs.

end focus The positioning of a clause element at the end of a sentence, drawing attention to important new information.

etymology The study of the origins and history of words.

exclamatory sentence A sentence marked by an exclamation mark which expresses emotion.

exclamative A sentence beginning with *what* or *how* which expresses the speaker's feelings (*How cool is that!*).

existential *there* A sentence in which *there* functions as a dummy subject followed by a delayed subject after the verb *to be* (***There** is a **good restaurant** opposite the cinema*).

exophoric A form of referencing in which a lexical item points directly to the wider linguistic context (***That** man is tall*).

extraposition The moving of a subordinate clause from its normal position in the sentence to a new position following the dummy subject *it*.

field An area of meaning (for example, *law*) which is characterised by common lexical items (*judge, jury, defendant, prosecution*).

finite Verb phrases marked for tense, person and number (*the girl shouts, they shout, she shouted*).

first person A direct reference to the speaker or writer (*I*), or to a group of people including the speaker or writer (*we*).

focus The arrangement of clause elements so that attention is focused on a particular linguistic item which is of most importance (***suddenly** it all seemed clear; it was **the dog** that alerted them*).

foregrounding   A change in the sequence of clause elements in order to draw attention to a particular linguistic item.

form   The word class and structure of a word.

forte   A term used to describe loud speech.

fricative   Sounds made by releasing air through a small passage making a hissing noise (*vanish, father*).

fronting   The movement of a clause element other than the subject to the beginning of a sentence.

function   The role of words and phrases within a clause (*subject, predicator, adverbial*).

function word   Grammatical words like conjunctions, prepositions and determiners which express grammatical relationships.

glottal stop   A sound produced when air stopped completely by tightly closed vocal cords is released .

gradable   An adjective or adverb that can be compared (*faster, fastest*) or intensified (*so fast*).

grammar   The set of rules underlying a language which enable speakers and writers to construct well-formed sentences.

grammatical theme   The first major grammatical constituent in a sentence (***The man** was exhausted. **Shouting triumphantly**, he finally crossed the finishing line.*).

grammatical word   A word that belongs to a closed class (also called **function** words).

head word   The main element in a phrase.

homonyms   Words with the same sound and perhaps spelling, but different meanings and origins (*left* – past tense of 'leave'; *left*– opposite of 'right').

homophones   Words that are pronounced the same, but that have different spellings and meanings (*flour, flower*).

hyperbole   Exaggeration used to heighten feeling and intensity, or for comic effect.

hyponyms   Words where the meaning of one form is included in the meaning of another (*flower* – *rose, poppy, carnation*). The inclusive term (*flower*) is called the **superordinate**.

idiolect   An individual's own distinctive way of speaking.

idiom   An expression that cannot be literally translated from the meaning of the individual words (*He gets up my nose* → *He annoys me*).

imperative   A grammatical mood expressing a directive (command, warning, pleading, inviting); there is usually no subject and the verb is in the base form.

indefinite pronoun   A pronoun which defines quantites.

independent clause   A clause where the verb phrase is finite and which makes sense by itself.

indirect object   An animate being that receives the action of a verb and which can be repositioned at the end of a sentence after the preposition *to* (*We gave **our grandmother** a present. We gave a present **to our grandmother***).

indirect speech   The words of a speaker reported in the form of a subordinate clause introduced by *that* (*They said that the weather would be fine today.*).

infinitive   A non-finite verb which is in the base form with the particle *to* (*to work*).

inflection   The ending added to a word to show a particular grammatical relationship (*–ing, –ed, 's*).

–*ing* participle   A non-finite verb form marked by an *–ing* inflection. Also called a **present** participle.

initial position The grammatical site at the front of the sentence (***Suddenly***, *the door opened*).

intensifier An adverb that adds emphasis as a pre-modifier to an adverb or an adjective (***so*** *cold,* ***very*** *unfortunate,* ***really*** *slowly*).

interjection A word expressing emotion that is grammatically separate from other clause elements (*Yuk!, Shhh!*).

interrogative A grammatical mood expressing a question in which the subject and verb are inverted.

intonation The quality or tone of voice in spoken language.

intransitive A verb (or preposition) that does not take a direct object.

inversion Reversing the order of clause elements (*they have screamed; have they screamed?*).

irregular Language forms that do not conform to standard patterns.

levelling The loss of distinctive features in regional accents and dialects as a result of contact with other language forms.

lexical set A group of words related in meaning.

lexical verb The head word in a verb phrase which conveys an action, state or process.

lexical word Any word belonging to an open class.

lexis The vocabulary of a language. Also called **lexicon**.

liaison A process that changes the pronunciation of words at boundary points.

linking *r* The introduction of a sound between two syllables to make pronunciation easier (the linking 'r' in *here and now*).

main clause A clause that is independent and makes sense on its own.

marked theme The movement of a clause element other than the grammatical subject to the beginning of a sentence (***Increasingly unsure what to do next***, *she looked out of the window*).

metathesis The rearrangement of sounds or letters in a word (*prehaps* for *perhaps*).

minor sentence A sentence or utterance that lacks one or more of the clause elements and that often occurs as an unchanging formulaic structure. (*Taxi!, no way!*).

modal An auxiliary verb that marks contrasts in attitude such as obligation, possibility and prediction (*must, can, will*).

mode The medium of a text, normally speech or writing.

modification The use of one linguistic item to specify the nature of another (*The* ***speckled*** *ducks quacked* ***persistently***.).

modified-RP A regionally neutral accent that has been adapted by the addition of some regional or personal characteristics.

monosyllabic Having one syllable.

mood The form of a verb phrase in a main clause that dictates whether the sentence is declarative (statement), imperative (command) or interrogative (question).

multi-word verb A lexical verb common in informal speech that consists of a verb and one or two particles (*knock over*).

negation The use of negative forms to convey disagreement or contradiction (*not, never, nothing*).

non-chronological Arranged according to the development of ideas (similarity, difference, association) rather than time.

non-count noun A noun that refers to things that cannot be counted and usually has no plural form (*courage, electricity*).

non-finite   Verb forms that are not marked for tense, person or number such as *–ing/–ed* participles and infinitives.

non-restrictive clause   A relative clause giving additional information (often in parenthesis) which is not necessary to identify the noun it refers to (*The man, who has long hair, is thin*).

non-standard   Any variety that differs from the standard form of a language used as a norm.

normal non-fluency features   Hesitations, repetitions and false-starts which are common in informal conversation.

noun   An open class word with a naming **function** which can usually be marked with plural and possessive inflections.

noun phrase   A phrase which usually has a noun as its head word and that can **function** as a subject or object in a clause.

number   A grammatical classification marking singular and plural.

object   The element of a clause which follows the verb and which is affected by it.

object complement   A complement which gives more information about the object of a clause.

open class words   A group of lexical words (nouns, adjectives, verbs and adverbs) to which new words can be added.

open question   A question which requires specific additional information in the answer (*Which colour suits me best? How long will I have to wait?*)

ordinal number   Numbers that indicate the order of a sequence (*first, second*).

palatal approximant   A sound made by putting the tongue against the middle of the palate and moving it downwards (*light, yet*).

palato-alveolar affricate   Sounds made by placing the tongue at the front of the mouth near the alveolar ridge, briefly blocking the airstream and then releasing it causing some friction (*church, judge*).

parallelism   The patterning of linguistic items to create a sense of balance and logic.

parenthesis   The use of brackets, commas or dashes in written language to mark out optional information in a sentence.

participle   The non-finite form of verbs which can occur after an auxiliary verb (*were **flying***), before the head in a noun phrase (*the **tangled** kite*), or as the first word in a non-finite clause (***Running** for the train*).

particle   A grammatical **function** word which never changes its form – for instance, an adverb (*cleared **up***) or preposition (*believe **in***) in a multi-word verb

passive voice   A grammatical structure using *to be + –ed* participle in which the subject and object can change places in order to alter the focus of a sentence (***The book** was returned eventually **by the student***).

past perfective   A grammatical structure using the past tense of *have + –ed* participle to describe an action completed before a specific time (*She **had already finished** the book*).

past progressive   A grammatical structure using the past tense of *be + –ing* participle to describe an on-going activity that was not complete before a specific time (*We **were laughing** hysterically*).

past tense   A verb phrase marked with an *–ed* on regular verbs to indicate an action that took place at an earlier time.

perfective aspect   A grammatical structure in which the verb *to have* is followed by an *–ed* participle (*The dog **has barked** all day*).

person A grammatical term used to describe the number and kind of participants involved in a situation.

personal pronouns Subject pronouns (*I, you, he, she, it, we, they*) replace a noun phrase in the subject site and object pronouns (*me, you, him, her, it, us, them*) replace a noun in the object site of a sentence.

phatic Language used to create social contact.

phoneme The smallest distinctive sound unit in a language.

phrasal verb A verb and any related adverb particle.

phrase A group of words that has a head word and may have other dependent words. It can fill one of the clause sites in a sentence.

piano A term used to describe speech that is quiet.

plosive Consonants made by a complete closure of the air passage followed by a sudden release of air (*pig, bad, dangerous*).

plural A grammatical expression signalling 'more than one' (*trees*).

politeness marker A linguistic element used to indicate respect which is grammatically separate from other clause elements (*please*).

polysyllabic Having more than one syllable.

possessive A word (*mine, his*) or inflection (*Mark's, the boys'*) marking possession.

post-alveolar approximant A sound produced by placing the tip of the tongue curled backwards towards the top of the mouth, near the alveolar ridge (*race*).

post-modification Lexical items that follow the head word in a phrase and are directly related to it (*The book which is out of print*).

predicative Adjective phrases or other modifiers that follow a copular verb (*The sky grew dark*).

predicator The verb phrase in a clause (and any lexical items directly related to it).

pre-modification Lexical items that precede the head word in a phrase and are directly related to it (*The solitary butterfly; so quickly*).

preposition A closed class word, like *in, on, of*, that expresses a relationship between two lexical items

prepositional phrase A grammatical structure made up of a preposition and a noun phrase (*in the forest*).

present perfective A grammatical structure describing a past action with present relevance in which the present tense of the verb *to have* is followed by an *–ed* participle (*It has rained continually all day*).

present progressive A grammatical structure describing an ongoing activity that is not yet complete using the present tense of *be* + *–ing* participle (*You are looking great*).

present tense A verb phrase where the verb is in the base form or is marked with an *–s* on third person singular to indicate an action that is currently taking place or a habitual action (*He visits on Tuesdays*).

primary verb A verb that can function as a lexical or an auxiliary verb (*be, have, do*).

progressive aspect A grammatical structure in which the verb *to be* is followed by an *–ing* participle (*Something strange is happening*).

pronoun A closed class word that can replace a noun phrase.

proper noun A noun naming a distinctive person, place or other unique reference which is marked with a capital letter in written language.

pun Word play which uses different meanings of a word, or two words with similar forms and different meanings, for comic effect.

pure vowel A vowel made up of only one sound (*hen, dig, pat*).

qualifier   A phrase or clause that post-modifies a head word (*the dog **sniffing the lamp-post**; afraid **of the dark***).

question   A sentence or utterance that requests information or some other kind of response.

quoted clause   A clause containing the actual words spoken in direct speech and usually marked by speech marks in written language (*'**What are you doing?**', shouted the headmaster.*)

quoting clause   A clause accompanying direct speech that tells us who has said something (*'It's cold today,' **whispered the boy.***).

rallentendo   A term used to describe speech that is getting slower (**rall**).

Received Pronunciation   An accent which has a high social prestige and is not connected to a particular geographical region (**RP**).

reflexive pronoun   A grammatical **function** word ending in *–self* or *–selves* in which the subject and object are directly related (*I cut myself*)

register   A variety of language defined according to use which can be decribed in terms of **mode, tenor** and **field**.

regular   A term used to denote linguistic forms that conform to the rules of a language.

relative clause   A subordinate clause beginning with a relative pronoun which post-modifies a noun (*the tree **which** is covered in apples*).

relative pronoun   A grammatical **function** word which marks the beginning of a relative clause post-modifying a noun (*The fireworks **which** were illuminating the sky*).

repertoire   An individual speaker's range of spoken and written forms.

repetition   A device which emphasises an idea through the recurrence of individual words, phrases or clauses.

restrictive relative clause   A relative clause that helps us to identify the noun by restricting the range of reference (*The man **who has long hair** is thin*).

rhetoric   The use of dramatic or persuasive words and structures in spoken and written language to manipulate the response of the intended audience.

rhetorical question   A question used for dramatic effect that does not require an answer.

rule   A principle of language structure which prescriptivists use to dictate 'correct' and 'incorrect' usage.

schwa   An unstressed vowel sound which often occurs at the end of words or as a vowel in unstressed syllables (*teacher*).

second person   A reference to a person or persons being addressed by a speaker or writer (*you*).

semantic field   Content linked by the occurrence of words with associated meanings.

semantics   The study of the meaning of language.

sentence   A grammatical structure made up of one or more clauses. In written language, the beginning is signalled by a capital letter and the end by a full stop.

simple sentence   A sentence made up of one main clause.

split infinitive   The separation of the particle *to* from the base form of a verb (*to seriously **panic***).

standard   The form of a language considered to be the norm and used as the medium of education, government and the law. Varieties which differ from this are said to be **non-standard**.

Standard English   A non-regional dialect of English which is seen by many as a prestige form.

stative verb   A verb that expresses states of being or processes in which there is no obvious action (*know, believe*).

stream of consciousness   A form of first person narrative that aims to portray the thoughts and feelings of a character directly, often using loosely connected and punctuated grammatical structures to reflect the spontaneity and associative nature of mental processes without the intervention of a narrator.

subject   A noun phrase or a noun clause which is usually the actor in a sentence.

subject complement   A complement which gives more information about the subject of a clause. (*The child looked exhausted*).

subject-specific lexis   Words relating to a specific field or topic.

subjunctive   A grammatical mood which expresses something hypothetical or tentative. It is no longer used widely, but occurs in formulaic expressions and following *If* structures (*If I were to come . . .*).

subordinate clause   A clause that cannot stand alone as a complete grammatical sentence, but needs another clause to complete its meaning. Also known as a **dependent** clause.

subordinating conjunction   A conjunction used to introduce a subordinate clause (*until, although*).

subordination   The linking of lexical items which do not have the same grammatical status, where the subordinate clause is dependent on a main clause (*Because it was late, there were no buses running*).

substitution   The replacement of one lexical item with another (*the computer → it*).

suffix   An ending that can be added to the end of a word.

superlative   A form of adjectives and adverbs used for comparison with the inflection *−est* or the adverb *most* (*fastest, most compassionate*).

superordinates   Inclusive general words (*flower*) which can be replaced with more specific words (*daisy, buttercup, rose*).

syntax   The study of the grammatical relationships between words in a sentence.

tag question   An interrogative structure attached to the end of a sentence which expects a reply (*That's expensive, isn't it?*).

tenor   The formality or informality of the relationship between a writer or speaker and the intended audience.

tense   A change in the structure of a verb to signal changes in time scale.

thematic adverbials   Adverbials that have been moved to the front position in a sentence for dramatic effect (*Over the bridge, past the church, down the hill, the country lane stretched away from them into the distance*).

third person   A reference to other things (*it*) and people (*she, he, they*).

transitive   Verbs (and prepositions) that have to be followed by an object.

turn-taking   The organisation of speakers' contributions in a conversation, which may be equal, or may be dominated by one of the participants.

typography   The study of features of the printed page.

use-related   Spoken or written English influenced by the subject matter, the purpose, the intended audience and the context.

user-related   Spoken or written English influenced by the geographical location, ethnicity, cultural background, age, gender and social group of the speaker or writer.

variety   Language use which has distinctive features because of its context, intended audience and purpose.

verb An open word class that expresses states, actions and processes and which can be marked for tense, aspect, voice and mood.

verbless clause A clause that contains no verb (*Although happy . . .*).

verb phrase A single lexical verb or a group of verbs consisting of up to four auxiliaries and a lexical verb.

vocative The word(s) used to refer to people when talking to them.

voice The form of a verb phrase which can alter the relationship between a subject and object without changing the meaning of a sentence. There are two forms: **active** (*The bird ate a snail*) and **passive** (*The snail was eaten by the bird*).

voiced Sounds made when the vocal cords are drawn together and the air from the lungs has to push them apart, creating a vibration (*violent, month*).

voiceless A sound made when the vocal cords are spread apart so that the air can pass between them without obstruction (*fish, shoe*).

wh- questions Questions introduced by *wh-* words (***What** do you want?*).

word The smallest grammatical unit that can stand alone. Words are divided into two groups: lexical (open class) and functional (closed class).

word class Groups of words such as nouns, adjectives, and prepositions with characteristic features.

word order The arrangement of words in a sentence.

yes/no questions Questions marked by the inversion of the subject and the first verb which expect 'yes' or 'no' for an answer.

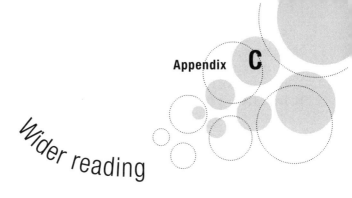

Wider reading

Grammar books

J. Aitchison (2010), *Aitchison's Linguistics: Teach Yourself* (Teach Yourself, Hodder Headline)

K. Ballard (2001, 2nd edition 2007), *The Frameworks of English: Introducing Language Structures* (Palgrave Macmillan)

N. Burton-Roberts (1986, 3rd edition 2011), *Analysing Sentences: An Introduction to English Syntax* (Pearson Longman)

D. Crystal (1980, 6th edition 2008), *A Dictionary of Linguistics and Phonetics* (Wiley-Blackwell)

D. Crystal (1988, 3rd edition 2004), *Rediscover Grammar* (Longman)

G. Finch (1998, 2nd revised edition 2003), *How to Study Linguistics: A Guide to Understanding Language* (Palgrave Study Guides, Palgrave Macmillan)

D. Freeborn (1987, 2nd edition 1995), *A Course Book in English Grammar* (Palgrave Macmillan)

S. Greenbaum and G. Nelson (2002, 3rd edition 2009), *An Introduction to English Grammar* (Longman)

G. Leech, S. Conrad, B. Cruickshank and R. Ivanic (1989, 2nd edition 2001), *An A–Z of English Grammar and Usage* (Pearson Longman)

G. Leech, M. Deuchar and R. Hoogenraad (1982, 2nd revised edition 2005), *English Grammar for Today: A New Introduction* (Palgrave Macmillan)

S. Russell (1993, 3rd revised edition 2001), *Grammar, Structure and Style: A Practical Guide to Advanced Level English* (Oxford)

General books

N. F. Blake and J. Moorhead (1993), *Introduction to English Language* (Palgrave Macmillan)

B. Bryson (2009), *Mother Tongue: The Story of the English Language* (Penguin)

D. Crystal (1987, 3rd edition 2010), *The Cambridge Encyclopedia of Language* (Cambridge University Press)

D. Crystal (1995, 2nd edition 2003), *The Cambridge Encyclopedia of the English Language* (Cambridge University Press)

D. Crystal (2nd revised edition 2002), *The English Language: A Guided Tour of the Language* (Penguin)

M. Montgomery (1986, 3rd revised edition, 2008), *An Introduction to Language and Society* (Routledge)

L. Truss (2003), *Eats Shoots and Leaves* (Fourth Estate, 2009)

L. Truss (2005), *Talk to the Hand* (Fourth Estate, 2009)

Index

Major page references are printed in bold type. Sample texts are printed in italics.